Tokyo Life, New York Dreams

Tokyo Life, New York Dreams

Urban Japanese Visions of America, 1890–1924

Mitziko Sawada

UNIVERSITY OF CALIFORNIA PRESS

Berkeley / Los Angeles / London

University of California Press
Berkeley and Los Angeles, California

University of California Press, Ltd.
London, England

© 1996 by
The Regents of the University of California

Library of Congress Cataloging-in-Publication Data

Sawada, Mitziko, 1928–
    Tokyo life, New York dreams : urban Japanese visions of America,
  1890–1924 / Mitziko Sawada.
      p. cm.
    Includes bibliographical references and index.
    ISBN 0-520-07379-7
    1. Japanese American men—New York (State)—New York—History. 2. Japanese Americans—New York (State)—New York—History. 3. New York (N.Y.)—Emigration and immigration—History. 4. Tokyo (Japan)—Emigration and immigration—History. 5. Immigrants—New York (State)—New York—History. I. Title.
F128.9.J3S29 1996
974.7'1004956—dc20   96-19699

9 8 7 6 5 4 3 2 1

Dedicated to the Memory of

*Sawada Katsumi (née Ishibashi) (1904–1989)
and Sawada Bunji (1896–1950)*

*Hi-imin in San Francisco, Berkeley,
Seattle, and New York, 1922–1942*

Contents

LIST OF TABLES — ix

LIST OF MAPS AND ILLUSTRATIONS — xi

ACKNOWLEDGMENTS — xiii

NOTE ON TRANSLITERATION — xv

GLOSSARY — xvii

1. Introduction — 1

2. The Japanese Immigrant in New York City — 13

3. Culprits and Gentlemen: The Legitimation of Class Differences in Meiji Emigration Policy, 1891–1908 — 41

4. Changing City, Changing Lives — 57

5. The Road to Success — 87

6. "Go East, Young Man!" — 116

CONTENTS

7.
Maidens of Japan, Women of the West: Japanese
Male Perceptions — 145

8.
Conclusion — 174

APPENDIX 1: STATISTICAL CONCLUSIONS
CONCERNING THE PROFILE OF THE
JAPANESE IN NEW YORK — 183

APPENDIX 2: TABLES — 187

NOTES — 195

SOURCES CONSULTED — 245

INDEX — 263

Tables

1. Honseki of 553 Japanese Citizens Registered at the New York Consulate General, 1909–1921 — 187
2. Honseki of 1,956 Japanese Citizens Issued Certificates of Residency by the New York Consulate General, 1912–1924 — 188
3. Birthplaces of 2,992 Japanese Male Residents of New York, 1920 — 188
4. Passports Issued for Travel to United States, Tokyo Honseki Residents, 1902–1914, 1916 — 189
5. Japanese Population in New York City, 1890–1924 — 190
6. Age of Travelers to United States, Tokyo Honseki Residents, 1907–1916 — 191
7. Age of 2,992 Japanese Male Residents of New York, 1920 — 191
8. Japanese Immigrants to United States, 1891–1924 — 192
9. Points of Entry into North America of 2,992 Japanese Male Residents of New York City, 1920 — 193

Illustrations

Maps

1. Japanese Prefectures   15
2. Tokyo, 1894   64
3. The Fifteen Wards of Tokyo   65

Figures

1. "Japanese Village, Luna Park," Coney Island, 1903   31
2. "Japanese Rolling Board," Coney Island, 1904   33
3. Illustration from *Amerika*, 1907   96
4–7. Illustrations from *Seiyōmusume katagi*, 1897   106–109
8. Cover to *Tobei no hiketsu*, 1906   130
9. Two pages of English conversation from *Tobei no hiketsu*   131
10–11. Advertisements in *Tobei no hiketsu*, 1906   132–133
12. Cover to *Amerika monogatari*, 1908   168

Acknowledgments

As a student who began her doctoral program past middle age, when most people are planning for retirement in another sixteen years or so, I could not have proceeded with the assurance that I did without the help of many individuals and institutions on both sides of the Pacific Ocean.

David Reimers, Marilyn Young, Sumiya Mikio, Nishikawa Shunsaku, Nakagawa Keiichirō, Kamei Shunsuke, Ōkubo Takaki, the late Maeda Ai, Sugimoto Teruko, Ōhashi Kazuhiro, Earl Kinmonth, the late Albert Romasco, Mary Nolan, Margaret Hunt, Sharon Sievers, Glenn Omatsu, and Russell Leong gave indispensable assistance in the early years of the project, introducing me to unfamiliar territory, reading, and offering intellectual guidance and support. Yukiko Hanawa and an unknown reader gave me important advice when I first submitted the manuscript to University of California Press. In the later stages Miriam Silverberg was most generous. She offered inspiring insights, comments, and precious time, as did Paulla Ebron, e. frances White, Samuel Fromartz, and Valerie Matsumoto, who read portions of the manuscript. I am truly indebted to them. Patricia Vidil, historian, companion, and partner, pored over the whole work before final submission to the press. Her consistent support, when I felt unable to devote the hours necessary to complete my work, was decisive in preserving my sanity. My family and extended family in New York and Tokyo sustained my efforts with optimism and trust, helping me achieve much more than I believed I could. I regret that my brother, Kenichi, did not survive to see the final product.

ACKNOWLEDGMENTS

The digging up of materials would have been impossible without the patience and generosity of Sōma Tamiko, who was then in the Social and Political Section, National Diet Library; Inouye Yūichi of the Diplomatic Record Center, Foreign Ministry of Japan; Hori Kunio, Tōkyōto Kōbunshokan; Kitane Yutaka, Meiji Shimbunzasshi Bunko, University of Tokyo; Nagahama Satsuo, Sankō Toshokan; Yuji Ichioka, Asian American Studies Center, UCLA; and Yasuo Sakata, Japanese American Research Project, UCLA. The library personnel at Keio University, Tokyo Woman's Christian University, and the Research Library, New York Public Library also gave indispensable aid. In addition, New Yorkers Haru Kishi, the late George Gentoku Shimamoto, Mitsuye Ōhori Katagiri, Yeiichi Kelly Kuwayama, John Manbeck of the Kingsborough Historical Society, and Lisa Garrison provided me with or directed me to rare and precious primary sources. Countless others—some of whom I barely know—gave me clues that steered me to vital people and places. Their interest and assistance were invaluable.

Financial support from the New York University history department, a Fulbright-Hays Fellowship, UCLA's Japanese-American Studies Post-Doctoral Fellowship at the Asian American Studies Center, and a Sasakawa Faculty Research Grant from the UCLA-Japan Exchange Program helped me through the years.

Sheila Levine of the University of California Press was unfailing in her patience and confidence in me. My original manuscript rested for many years in her files. I also owe thanks to Monica McCormick, Scott Norton, Larry Borowsky, and Rebecca Bauer for their assistance in the final stages of publication. Kate Blackmur provided her cartographic skills to the century-old map of Tokyo, and Karen Graubard inserted the final manuscript changes in the bibliography and notes.

Note on Transliteration

Japanese names are shown with the surname first, followed by the given name, as is the practice in Japan. However, for individuals who were or are permanent U.S. residents or citizens of the United States, the given name precedes the surname.

Japanese writers who are known by their pen names are referred to in the text by their given names. For example, Ozaki Kōyō and Shimazaki Tōson are referred to as Kōyō and Tōson. Japanese terms that appear frequently and are integral to the text, such as *seikō, ken, imin,* and *hi-imin,* are italicized and translated only once when they appear initially.

Macrons for Japanese terms are used throughout the text, except for those in which common usage has eliminated them, such as Tokyo, Kobe, or Kyoto.

In the bibliography, Japanese surnames and given names of authors whose works are in Japanese are not separated by a comma. Surnames and given names of authors with Japanese names whose works are in English are separated by commas.

Glossary

abirete.	ability; merit and intelligence.
Amerika tamashii.	spirit of America.
chūryūkaikyū.	middle class.
fu.	urban prefecture.
hi-imin.	non-migrant; designation given to merchants, students, professionals who were not laboring immigrants.
honseki.	registered family domicile.
imin.	migrant; designation given to skilled and unskilled laboring immigrants.
issei.	first generation.
ken.	prefecture.
kindai.	modern; modernity.
kinken chochiku.	thrift and savings.
koseki.	household registry.
kosekihō.	household registry law.
ku.	ward.
nintai.	perseverance.
renai.	love.
risshin shusse.	advancement and achievement.
ryōsai kenbo.	good wife, exemplary mother.
seikō.	success.
sekkyokuteki.	positive; active.
shimpo.	progress.
Shitamachi.	low district of Tokyo.
tobei.	crossing to America.
tobei netsu.	crossing-to-America fever.
wayō.	Japanese-Western.
Yamanote.	high district of Tokyo.

CHAPTER 1

Introduction

> *After about five minutes, the lines of the boat were loosened. As we sailed off, the dresses of the women on the dock became blurs in the distance and resembled flowers in a garden. The sight of the glorious Hudson, majestically flowing into the sea, unfolded before our very eyes. The tall buildings of New York City loomed high in the center against the brilliant summer sky. On the city's right, across the Hudson, soot and smoke hung over the cities of New Jersey. On its left, hosts of vessels which had gathered from the ports of the world, sailed freely back and forth under the Brooklyn Bridge. And beyond that, Brooklyn. The Statue of Liberty, with a halberd [sic] up high in one hand, stood over the water far beyond the harbor, commanding a view of this fearsome, awesome, and peaceful battlefield.*
>
> —Nagai Kafū, *Amerika monogatari*
> (Stories from America)

Nagai Kafū, the Meiji writer, wrote this short but vivid paragraph when he came to New York City at the turn of the century. To Kafū, the panorama of New York harbor, its breadth and its busyness, connoted a battlefield in which freedom—the freedom to move and engage in commerce—was a vital factor. In this battlefield people competed with each other intensely but with gentility and politeness. In his short stories based on his years in the United States, Kafū also wrote of freedom of another sort: a personal life unfettered by the restrictive and rigid social demands made on one by family, relatives, teachers, and other elders as in Japan. *Amerika* and, most of all, New

York were symbols of youth and dynamism that signified these freedoms. Yet they also instilled fear and awe—a tension that resulted from the expectations of a new life and the anxieties of not knowing exactly how it would unfold.

The American scholarship on Japanese immigration to the United States in the late nineteenth and early twentieth centuries largely focuses on the migration of Japanese to the Pacific states.[1] Most of the earlier works utilized American English-language sources. Yuji Ichioka broke that practice in his pioneering efforts, relying on Japanese-language sources, many of them based on immigrant writings, and adding a vital dimension to the historiography.[2] Nevertheless, American knowledge about Japanese immigrants is broad and assumptive, contributing to a general and homogenized view of Japanese immigrants as peasants from four poor agricultural prefectures in southwestern Japan, uneducated, unmarried, and male. The assumption that all Japanese immigrants shared these characteristics is based largely on evidence of the early years of migration, when laborers were imported from Hiroshima-, Wakayama-, Yamaguchi-, and Fukuoka-*ken* (prefecture) to work in Hawaii and California. There is little room left for the exceptions, who represent an integral part of any group of people and who, in the New York and East Coast cases (as well as, I suspect, on the Pacific Coast), constitute a stark contrast to the all-encompassing view.[3]

Other than sociologist T. Scott Miyakawa's essay and the book by Haru Reischauer, which in part is about her maternal grandparents, who settled in New York, nothing has been written in English about the Japanese on the East Coast.[4] When I began this work I thought a research project on the Japanese who chose to settle in New York City was feasible. However, I soon realized that vital primary sources were insufficient and inadequate for a satisfactory study and that I should think of another subject. A Fulbright-Hays Fellowship altered this quandary, giving me the opportunity to delve into national and private archives and libraries in Japan. As a result, my focus in this study has shifted significantly. My original intent was to analyze the story of Japanese immigrants to New York—their origins and background, journey and initial settlement, work, immigrant organizations and businesses, residential patterns, and social and family relationships. However, I have paid far greater attention to the preimmigrant period and examined the mentality of the urban educated Japanese male—his world, and his cultural understanding of that world and the world beyond the Pacific Ocean. He is cast as a prototype of the Japanese who decided to travel and live in New York City.

Another part of the decision to explore the preimmigrant mind-set stemmed from my own experience as a person whose background is Japanese. It began with an observation I had about myself during the early part of my research period in Tokyo. I was born in the United States but attended high school in Japan, so I knew the language and, of course, "looked like them." Until I began my research I had never lived in Japan as an adult. I spent my first two months in a harassed state, attempting to behave according to what I perceived as Japanese conventions and norms. The experience was dismal and exhausting, and my behavior was artificial. As I learned gradually (and happily), the people with whom I associated did not have the expectation that I should conduct myself according to Japanese ways.[5] My posture, walk, gestures, way of speaking and facial expressions demonstrated that I was not of the same culture. Thus, my hosts excused my numerous faux pas with the phrase "*Amerikajin dakara*" (because you are an American), which in some instances could have indicated a sense of disdain or superiority but in most cases was a sign of acceptance and acknowledgment, not simply a polite gesture. This experience helped to inform the approach I subsequently took in addressing the process by which people attempt to familiarize and adjust to new situations in alien surroundings. It has to do with understanding and utilizing the components of cultural knowledge to fit oneself into specific circumstances. However, one discovers that the components constitute only a segment of a culture, incomplete and superficial in some cases, that fails to bridge the gap one strives so assiduously to close.

In the course of my work in Japan, I learned that the Japanese in New York differed qualitatively in class and geographic makeup from those on the West Coast. This information helped further to validate the task I had set for myself. The only resemblance between the two populations was that both comprised single males. Urban or urban-oriented, educated, aspiring to the middle class, and older, the New York Japanese came to the United States as individuals, not in groups, and chose to settle in a city 8,000 miles from their homeland, a place without an active Japanese immigrant community or an established immigrant route from Japan. They bypassed the many manipulators and brokers of labor who played significant roles in the larger migration to Hawaii and the Pacific states. Large-scale importation of Japanese labor as induced by the industrial needs of California or Hawaii was not the norm in New York. Employment opportunities were diverse and often insecure, and the immigrants lived and worked in scattered areas of the city. Additionally, since the 1890s both the American and Japanese governments had placed obstacles in the way of Japanese migration to the United States. All in all, it is remarkable that these individuals made their way to New York at all.

In the past two decades, historians have authoritatively retold the story of the immigrant experience, referring to the rich foreign-language sources of the emigrant country to study the immigrants *before* they came to the United States. *The Polish Peasant in America*, written in 1918 by sociologists William I. Thomas and Florian Znaniecki, is the classic of the genre, in which the preimmigrant period is presented as a major and crucial part of the immigrant experience.[6] Since then, Jon Gjerde has drawn upon this approach to reconstruct cultural-economic change and adaptation among middle-class agricultural Norwegian settlers in the Midwest.[7] Other cases in point are the important studies by Virginia Yans-McLaughlin, Josef Barton, and Dino Cinel.[8] These significant works have transformed the scholarship of U.S. immigration, placing it in a capitalistic world framework, heeding the preimmigration and postimmigration political and socioeconomic environments, focusing on subjective as well as official and published accounts, and, most significant, analyzing the material in relation to historical realities, cultural mores, social values, and political ideologies. They have shown that homogenization was neither the typical experience nor the wish of the immigrant. Each immigrant group, we find, had a unique history. Each underwent complex processes of cultural maintenance and change. No population went through inevitable, automatic, and total transformation. These points may seem obvious, but a sweeping consensus interpretation in the past portrayed immigrants as eventually assimilating into an already existent American society. This view has become part of our folk culture. As each new wave of immigrants hits the United States, especially when harsh economic circumstances prevail, this interpretation is glorified, as in recent times with the emphasis on the Asian "model minority."

In clarifying the new approach, Virginia Yans-McLaughlin appropriately stated that it frees scholars from the formerly "ineptly bound field" and addressed three areas: "the international ecology of migration; a questioning of the classical assimilation model, which proposes a linear progression of immigrant culture toward a dominant American national character; and, through references to other national experiences in Asia and Latin America, a denial of American exceptionalism."[9]

Sucheng Chan skillfully placed Asian Americans in this framework, paying particular attention to preimmigrant regions. She wrote: "Only by looking at the emigration end of the story will we fully understand the motivation of emigrants, and until we know what impelled millions of people to undertake often risky transoceanic voyages, it will be difficult for us to place the emigrants/immigrants themselves at the center of our research."[10]

I believe that only in this context can we attempt to reconstruct the cultural milieu of values, behaviors, and attitudes of an immigrant group. Here, then, I focus considerable attention on the preimmigrant sociocultural environment of young, educated, urban Japanese males, addressing their expectations and the motives behind the emigration of some. I place them in a rapidly expanding urban Japan, using Tokyo as the prime locus of study. I analyze the messages these youths received and attempt to link them with their hopes and aspirations and to reconstruct their subjective vision of life in the United States.

Necessarily, this vision was tied in closely with what these youths had been taught formally and informally, what they had gained as developing individuals in a developing country. It would seem that such a group should have been highly valued in a fast-changing and industrializing country such as Meiji Japan.[11] The nation had been actively participating in the Western world of capitalism for only three decades at the turn of the century. It was deeply committed to attaining a primary political and economic position in East Asia, a goal dictated by historical pressures to industrialize and to counter Western encroachments on Asia. Japan was dedicated to grooming its youth to become responsible citizens of this new Meiji world—a few to pilot its endeavors. A middle class was fast emerging, and the social structure was being altered to accommodate a new elite whose wealth and position did not depend on birth. Rather, education and entry into the world of commerce, business, or the government bureaucracy determined one's future status. The supposed benefits of this world, however, were distant and elusive for the vast majority. Most encountered rigid barriers to advancement, which were only exacerbated by the nation's ambitious political and economic programs. They had little hope of gaining entry to one of the few prestigious colleges and universities, so promising positions in government and business remained out of their reach. At the same time, the erratic economic world kept them from obtaining or sustaining stability by other means. Many individuals, trained in the new primary and secondary educational system and cherishing aspirations to gain important roles in the emerging modern world, confronted the lack of viable avenues to a stable and secure future.

The experiences and knowledge these individuals acquired in Japan combined to formulate a view of the world—a view of Japan and of the United States and the West. Their view of Japan was, in fact, fairly realistic; their expectations of American society, by contrast, were profoundly unrealistic, created from anticipatory dreams and fantasies—what anthropologist John Caughey terms "an imaginary social world."[12] Caughey bases his discussion on observations of the late-twentieth-century United States. Cultural knowledge, a conceptual system of beliefs, rules, and values, is the crucial factor in his analysis. This system of learned cultural knowledge describes and defines a person's perspective in experiencing and understanding the world—not only the actual social world but also the imaginary social world, one constructed by introspection, dreams, daydreams, streams of consciousness, and the like.[13] People construct the imaginary social world in part through "anticipation," the conjuring up of future settings and recalling of "social scenes from books, magazines and newspapers."[14]

Likewise, in *Transforming the Past*, an analysis of kinship change among Japanese Americans, anthropologist Sylvia Yanagisako argued that cultural knowledge is based on "a system of symbols and meanings in the context of a social history of kinship relations."[15] She pointed out "a grave error of most studies of ethnic families in America," which associate family traditions with a static past. Bearing in mind Yanagisako's approach, I look upon "tradition" in Meiji Japan as dynamic and changing. In fact, it could not persist as in the past. Symbols and words ascribed to "traditional" ways of acting and interacting evolved, were reformed or "recast," as Miriam Silverberg suggested in her work on 1920s Japan, and became the basis for a continually altering sociopolitical environment.[16]

Thus, in this work I will attempt to recreate a historical imaginary social world of the early-twentieth-century urban Japanese male and place it in the context of a social, political, and economic universe in which views of the world were being transformed. The Meiji-Taisho media informed this imaginary social world in crucial ways. Indeed, the media were rich with works that introduced the United States to the Japanese during the three decades beginning with the Sino-Japanese War (1894–1895). Nagai Kafū, for instance, displayed a keen understanding and perception in his fictional accounts, written during his almost four years in the United States (October 1903–July 1907). These were based on his experiences in various parts of the country, particularly New York City. Other men (and they were, in the main, men) also had spent years of rigorous work and study in the United

States, traveling extensively and frequently. They were students, journalists, merchants, writers, critics, ministers, lawyers, social activists, business and government officials, and, at the very least, tourists. Their works were not official or approved by the government. Rather, they reflected the preoccupations of private citizens.

Falling into a variety of genres (including short stories, subjective histories, or practical travel guides), both nonfiction and fiction, their works range from impressionistic to pragmatic. But whatever the form, these writings are a crucial source for understanding the messages Meiji Japanese readers received about the United States and *Amerika tamashii* (the spirit of America). They provide a unique view of what some Japanese encountered, experienced, and felt about the United States in the late nineteenth and early twentieth centuries and what motivated them to travel across an ocean and a continent to reach their destination.[17]

This literature, produced in late Meiji and early Taisho Japan and now housed in Tokyo's private and public libraries, includes a wide variety of works that, happily, have survived earthquake and war. The material is uneven in quality, but it covers an intriguing variety of subjects: details on travel, including practical advice on passport laws and procedures; depictions of America as the land of money and women; advice on jobs; descriptions of schools and how to enter them; dissections of the American character; and observations on the women's suffrage movement, family life, race and prejudice, freedom and opportunity. These works were widely read, for once an author had touched U.S. soil, he could pass for an expert. One book, published in 1921, had six printings within the same number of months.[18] Another work, by a writer who spent two years in the United States in the 1910s, had thirteen printings in twelve years.[19] A practicum by a Christian socialist advocate of emigration to the United States, first published around 1901, was reprinted fourteen times within five years.[20] Such material provided a formula for modern youth aspiring to the new Japanese individualism or looking to emigrate to the United States. Evaluations of the United States ran the gamut from exaggerated praise to denunciation. Understandably, adoration was more prevalent in the period up to World War I, when many patriotic Japanese sought a world position for their country comparable to that of the United States. These writers had a common goal: to help formulate a new identity and to explicate how Japanese individuals could achieve ends similar to those attained by successful Americans. They wrote to prepare young people for education, careers, or both in Japan—or for potentially more rewarding, but more difficult, lives in the United States.

The publications on the United States constituted only one of the varieties of reading matter that nourished an increasingly literate population.[21] They took their place alongside a vast literature intended to inspire the Japanese people to a greater commitment to national unity and order. Formal pronouncements, school textbooks, teachers' materials, and other works issued from state institutions were the official sources for disseminating such ideas. However, the government was not the sole producer of these ideological tracts. Notable public and private figures, intellectuals, journalists, and writers lent a hand to the effort.[22] Like the material on the United States, their works were published in newspapers, in popular magazines, or as books, often carrying the imprint of Hakubunkan, the most influential publishing house of the time.[23] Novels in particular appeared in great profusion. These form an important part of my discussion, for I believe fiction is integral to our understanding the process by which people sought to accept, question, challenge, refuse, and assimilate ideas in Meiji Japan, which was undergoing extensive change nationally and internationally. James Fujii's approach to analyzing fiction as crucial to the discourse on cultural understanding provides an important basis for and confirmation of its use as a significant historical primary source.[24] According to Fujii, the prose narrative (*shōsetsu*) in modern Japan showed "the signs of . . . belonging to the currents of flux and change wrought by industrialization and urbanization" and functioned as "the site of many competing voices inscribed with particular interests and desires."[25] The "many competing voices" included those of the ideologues who were "all around," as Carol Gluck pointed out, "plying different interpretive trades in different social places" with a common goal: the creation of stability and national loyalty, fundamentally through the use of "ideological representations, . . . as if to obliterate the meaning of economic contradictions."[26] The writings on national unity and those on the United States converged to create a complex tapestry of attitudes and concepts that interwove public and individualistic concerns. Together, I will argue, they played a significant role in constructing a new ideology of personal achievement set within the context of a capitalist world.

My investigation addresses two major areas, both concerned with would-be emigrants' images and visions about the United States. First, I explore their points of contact with the outside world, including places of work or schooling, associations and organizations, and other, less structured public places where a person was one of many and acted as such. Success in this sphere depended, in part, upon one's understanding of how Americans achieved success. A person's worth was measured not only by the obvious factors of education and occupation but also by demeanor, attitudes, and behavior, qualities that were formed by cultural knowledge about how to function successfully in an American world. What was the necessary "spirit" for independent action, and how was it acquired? What were the perceptions of the American valuation of work and its connection to upward mobility? What were the lessons to be learned from the experienced advocates of *tobei* (crossing to America)? In reading about these aspects of life, the would-be emigrants constructed a picture of a world into which they wished to enter with assurance and optimism.

Closely related to a person's achievements in the public sphere was one's life in the private sphere, the second area of concern. An individual's role (or desired role) in the public sphere determined the flexibility and freedom he or she enjoyed in the private sphere. I explore in particular men's social relationships with women. How were those relationships in the United States defined and perceived by Japanese? How different were they from Japanese practices? And what were their effects on love, courtship, romance, marriage, and gender relations, both in the United States and Japan? What was published about American women and their relationships with Japanese men?

Chapter 2 begins with a brief summary of the makeup of the New York Japanese, a unique group that differed from the archetypal Japanese immigrant population. A description of their work experiences and relationships with women in New York City follows. In the main they had come to the city with understandings and qualities that should have prepared them for easy adaptation into American urban life and rapid acceptance by the inhabitants. Nevertheless, New York proved to be an alien place that bred confusion and contradictions. For the majority, expectations and experiences were in direct opposition to each other. The discussion here sets the stage for an examination of the preimmigrant culture and the motivations and expectations of the educated urban individuals who chose to leave the developing industrial and military homeland. For many, the New York experience signified an ironic end to their imaginary world, which bore little relation to the real world. Their lives in the United States can be described as no less harsh than those they left behind in Japan.

Chapter 3 examines the evolution and establishment of the concept of *hi-imin* (nonmigrant) and the political strategies behind differentiating it from *imin* (migrant). This is important in understanding the Japanese government's domestic policy of responding to the United States and favoring the hi-imin emigrant over the imin in representing the country abroad. Drawing from Japanese laws, regulations, and Foreign Ministry instructions promulgated in the heat of the immigration controversy between the United States and Japan (1891–1908), I argue that Japan's actions concerning emigration to the continental United States represented more than mere acquiescence to U.S. demands. It signified a keen sense of independence and timing—and, of course, the wish to convey a positive self-image to the West. The hi-imin classification was Japan's way of restricting laborers from emigrating to the United States and resulted in the legitimation of a de facto discrimination based on social class in its issuance of passports to the United States.

Chapter 4 utilizes Tokyo as the model of the urban environment from which the Japanese came. Within Japan, intense migration to Tokyo was taking place. In this city, the port of entry into the newly established modern educational system and subsequently into the world of work, one learned whether one could join the elite sector of society or be left to coexist with the ordinary and commonplace. The rigors of a capital-scarce society and the nation's concentration on larger financial ventures created frequent dislocations in the economy, which affected the young Meiji individual's smooth transition into adulthood.

Into this unsettling situation came a variety of popular reading matter—books, magazines, novels—that purported to introduce ambitious Japanese youth to the spirit of enterprise. Thus, Chapter 5 will focus on material from popular Meiji culture regarding the notion of success. I explore self-help youth magazines, tobei publications, and best-selling serialized novels that appeared in major newspapers. All of these types of works helped formulate the attitudinal and behavioral stance of the modern Meiji individual. The examples present a Japanese notion of success in the United States, a discourse on the secrets that propelled Americans to success. How did this literature contribute to young people's view of the world and social values? What were the contradictions, if any, between the socially approved conceptions of ethical behavior and these products of popular culture? By exploring this environment, we can better understand why the New York Japanese decided to pursue life in a distant and different culture. We can also begin to speculate on the complexity of the decision to emigrate, going beyond the purely economic motives of earning a living.

In Chapter 6 I analyze *tobei netsu* (crossing-to-America fever) and the advocacy of tobei by educated, pro-American, and liberal Japanese. Their works suggest a group of people doubtful of the efficacy of studying, working, and living in the preimmigrant world as opposed to the immigrant world. Notions of the United States as the land of freedom and opportunity constitute a significant part of this group's point of view. These ideas take on a particular significance for us because cultural knowledge of the United States was shaped by ethical standards of the Meiji ideologues. Filtered through this lens, the United States's development into a wealthy, productive state was seen as the result of its particular cultural and moral precepts. The pragmatic and less abstract experiences of Japanese daily life provided another element in the value and attitudinal system of the tobei advocates.

Chapter 7 addresses gender relationships as perceived and practiced by Japanese men. The codification of the family system during the Meiji period resulted in a de jure recognition and legitimation of male superiority. However, it also created tensions and insecurities among men stemming from their expected roles as authority figures. Their relationships with women suffered from these tensions and frequently led to empty marriages or to divorce. I argue that the notion of egalitarian relationships with women in the United States, though not the central motivating force for emigration, contributed to the belief that personal life in the United States was less confining and arbitrary than in Japan.

The story of the women also needs to be told. Those who came to the East Coast were, in the main, wives of men already here. Some came to attend college in the United States.[27] Many had education. Many had urban awareness. Like men, they were inundated with the state ideology concerning family and the inferior political and social role of women. How did this affect their thinking, their lives, their aspirations, their experiences in the United States? What were *their* dreams? What were the experiences of housewives as compared to working women? What happened to the students? Did they end up in spinsterhood? I touch on some of these issues, but, needless to say, this important subject cannot be treated as an appendage or merely as a chapter. It merits a separate and comprehensive study. Another book is in order.

Armed with attitudes and behavior taught in Japan intended to familiarize a person with the social manifestations of Western modernity, the urban Japanese male came to urban America with a set of values not substantially different from those espoused in the United States. Both nations, engaged in a fiercely competitive capitalist arena, formulated and reformulated ideologies to aid in the creation of public unity, order, and responsibility. However, differences between the two societies rendered the New York Japanese individual's cultural knowledge of the United States ineffective, particularly in a country marked by strong currents of racism and nativism. His choice of a "better life" was based on a careful accumulation of knowledge, an understanding gained by culling, sifting, and digesting information gathered and propagated by others about a heterogeneous group of people—information colored by the preconceptions, selective observations, and ideological goals of the writers. This viewpoint was irrelevant in the socioeconomic environment of a progressive America, a painful awakening that overturned his dreams of change. The complexities of shaping an identity in a less than welcoming United States were as intense and severe as the shaping of an identity in a tumultuous and transforming Japan.

Thus, my purpose is to present the world of the United States as it might have been constructed by literate Japanese youth in Japan before they left for American soil. It is about images and visions, an attempt to recreate the Japanese construction of a homogeneous, mysterious and exotic American Other.

CHAPTER 2

The Japanese Immigrant in New York City

In order to set the stage for this and subsequent chapters, I will briefly summarize the substantial differences between the New York Japanese and the Japanese on the West Coast. This profile, based on the majority of Japanese who registered at the Japanese Consular Office in New York during the 1910s and early 1920s, is crucial to our understanding some aspects of the preimmigrant's dreams about the United States. A thorough statistical analysis, including documentary figures, is found in the appendices and tables.

The Japanese migration to New York began in the 1890s and steadily increased through the first two decades of the twentieth century until it was abruptly halted by the U.S. government in 1924. Figures ranged from fewer than 1,000 emigrants before 1898 to more than 4,600 in 1920 (see Appendix 2, Table 5). Some arrived in New York after a sojourn in the West, often having worked their way across the country. Others sailed around Cape Horn or through the Panama Canal, traversed two oceans, and landed on the eastern shores of the United States in New York, Philadelphia, Baltimore, or Boston. Still others came via Cuba, British Columbia, or Mexico (see Appendix 2, Table 9).

About one-tenth of the New York Japanese came from the city of Tokyo or Tokyo-*fu* (urban prefecture) (see Appendix 2, Tables 1, 2, 3). Almost 20 percent had urban origins, coming from the five major cities of Tokyo, Yokohama, Osaka, Kobe, or Kyoto. The rest were from the smaller cities and rural areas of the forty-six *ken* (rural prefectures) and *fu* throughout Japan (see Map 1).[1] However, these figures alone are misleading, for between 1891 and 1920 government statistics indicated that 33 to 48 percent of the Tokyo population had *honseki* (registered family domiciles) in other ken. We can only assume, therefore, that the official figures underestimated the number of New York Japanese who came from Tokyo, for these figures did not account for individuals who were de facto, but unregistered, residents of Tokyo.

Socially, the New York Japanese were of the newly forming middle class or close to it. Almost three-quarters held hi-imin passports as opposed to imin passports.[2] Hi-imin were generally students, merchants, businessmen, and professionals and were required to have a middle school education or its equivalent. Imin, by contrast, were largely skilled or unskilled laborers, whom the Japanese government discouraged from emigrating to the United States. National leaders were responding to the barrage of verbal contempt Americans heaped upon Japanese labor immigrants, as well as the U.S. government's requests that Japan limit the emigration of laborers. Furthermore, they were anxious that the Japanese who came to the United States should represent their country in a way befitting citizens of a rising nation-state. In contrast to the New York Japanese, the majority of the Japanese on the West Coast were listed as imin.[3]

Males outnumbered females in New York as on the West Coast. When the Japanese government banned the emigration of picture brides in 1921, the number of passports issued to women bound for the United States as a whole decreased by 31.2 percent. However, in New York the number of women increased. In 1919 females constituted less than 8 percent of the New York Japanese population; in 1922, almost 25 percent. The majority of these women were wives of men residing in New York. This suggests that the Japanese government issued passports exclusively to wives of hi-imin and discriminated against imin wives of Japanese males on the West Coast.

In 1920 three-quarters of the Japanese males in New York ranged in age from twenty-one to forty, the majority being older than thirty. Less than 6 percent were twenty or younger. Half of the females were between the ages of twenty-one and thirty, leading us to conclude that they were probably young wives. This is in sharp contrast to the profile of Japanese immigrants in the United States as a whole, of whom three-quarters were younger than twenty-five when they entered the country.

On average, the Japanese who came to New York had received more education than those on the West Coast. Often they had been educated

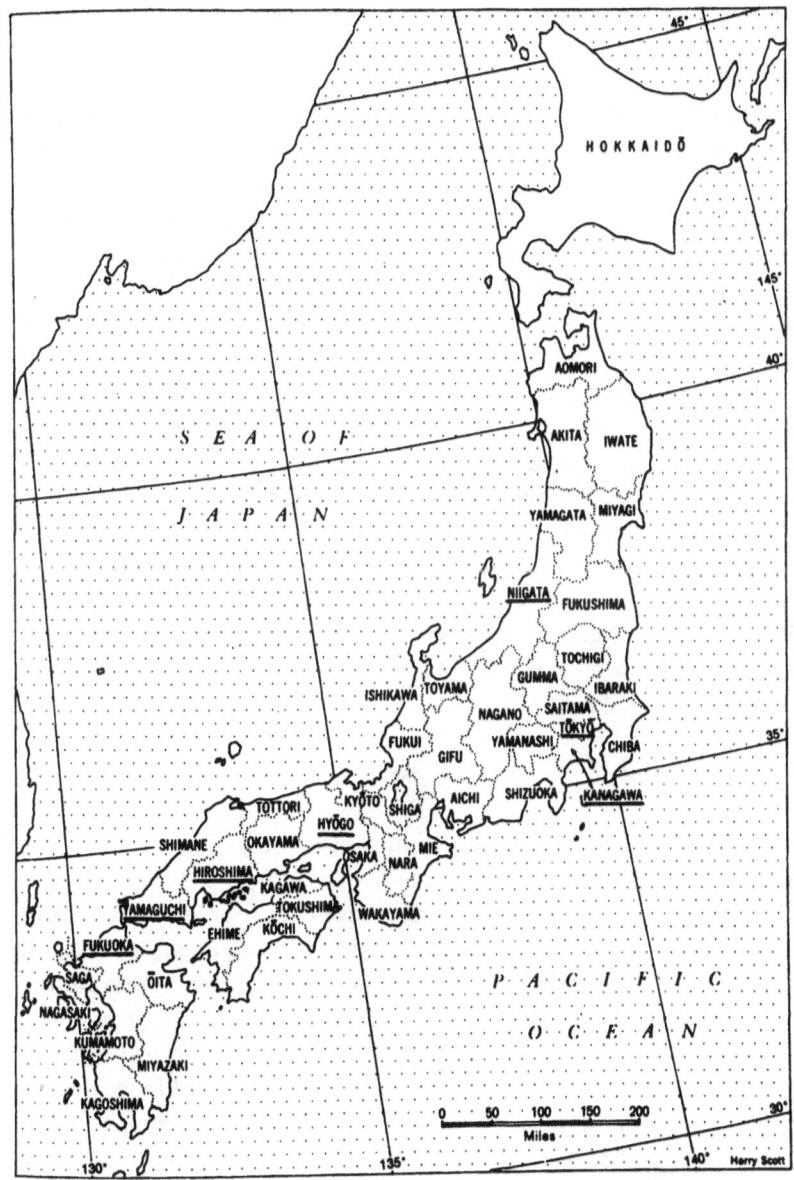

Map 1. Japanese prefectures. The underlined prefectures provided the greatest number of Japanese in New York City (based on Appendix 2, Tables 1, 2, and 3). Map adapted from Mikiso Hane, *Modern Japan: A Historical Survey* (Boulder, CO: Westview Press, 1986), p. 91.

in Tokyo or one of the other four large cities, where the major high schools, vocational schools, and public and private colleges and universities were located. The predominantly hi-imin and urban orientation of the New York Japanese suggests that, unlike the Japanese on the West Coast, they were primarily aspirants to the middle class (if not members already). They probably had more options in Japan as salaried or white-collar workers than those who settled in the West. But, like their counterparts on the West Coast, they did not want to remain in Japan at that time of their lives.

Japanese students and businessmen made up the largest group of arrivals in New York. Because people of that category, plus a few government officials (2.5 percent), constituted the majority of the population, the accepted notion is that they were not in the category of "immigrants"; rather, they were temporary residents, most of whom eventually returned to Japan. However, one cannot assume that they acquired an education or profited in business and returned to Japan. The evidence suggests that a large percentage did not maintain the status of student or businessman. Rather, they settled in the United States and toiled as unskilled workers.

• • •

When people decide to leave a familiar environment for an alien one, the unknown aspects of their future lives assume a quality of unreality and idealization. Negative stories they may have heard become forgotten or are disregarded, if temporarily. Fear plays an important part, of course, but when a person takes the first physical step of leaving old surroundings, it reflects a conviction that somehow the new will provide a better life. The Japanese who made the decision to go to the United States had the confidence that their quality of life would improve. For those who made the decision to go to New York City, especially those possessing a little capital and education, the possibilities seemed unlimited.

Reports from Japanese who had traveled to New York did not chronicle the endless violence and humiliation that Japanese on the West Coast experienced. The pioneering *issei* (first-generation) newspaperman and historian of the Japanese in New York, Shōzō Mizutani, wrote that prior to the Sino-Japanese War, New Yorkers failed to distinguish between Japanese and Chinese and hounded "our compatriots who strolled in Central Park screaming 'Chinamen!' and threw stones at them."[4] However, he continued, Japan's victory in 1895 brought a "closer relationship" between the two countries and "drastically transformed New Yorkers' views and feelings about Japan and the Japanese."

He described the following decade as a time of intense "perseverance and determination" for Japan, which sought to show the world that it possessed the capability and capacity to become a first-rate power. The Japanese consulate, which had occupied boardinghouses in Manhattan on West 9th, West 23rd, and near West 57th Streets, established its first formal consular residence in 1902 in an apartment on Central Park West.[5] After Japan's unprecedented victory over "formidable Russia" in 1905, the United States increasingly expressed "extraordinary friendship for Japan," and the people of the Atlantic Coast received Japanese nationals "with warmth and cordiality." New Yorkers, in particular, allowed the Japanese "to profit and enjoy recognition." Mizutani also noted that the Japanese goods exhibited at the 1904 St. Louis World's Fair elicited such praise and admiration that after the close of the exposition, the leftover goods were brought to the East to be sold.[6] Additionally, New Yorkers proved their friendliness during the May 1907 visit of Gen. Kuroki Tamemoto Tamesada, a hero of the Russo-Japanese War (1904–1905). The visit was recorded in exaggerated detail in Mizutani's history and hyperbolized in the magazine *Amerika*: "Kuroki fever in New York has risen beyond the boiling point! . . . New Yorkers respect his fighting spirit!"[7] The *New York Times* gave him front-page coverage and faithfully reported his every movement and his impressions of New York City, West Point, horse racing, and American women.[8]

Tobei publications expanded on the attractions of New York, which they portrayed as the ideal city for Japanese. A thirty-two-chapter geography of the city, illustrated with transportation maps and drawings, gave sketchy descriptions of buildings, banks, water and gas lines, land value and ownership, leases and contacts, J. P. Morgan, and housing.[9] Magazines and books covered topics ranging from a tailoring school to student life, employment, operating a restaurant, and the New York clothing trade (subtitled "The Success of the Jewish Immigrant").[10] These works never presented New York as a teeming, populated, dirty, busy city. There were no descriptions of small, crowded operations producing goods by independent and specialized processes, nor of the monopolization of jobs by particular ethnic groups depending upon the industry and the nationality of the entrepreneur or the foreman. Neither did these publications point out social and cultural distinctions between the foreign- and native-born, the Anglo-Saxons and the southeastern Europeans, or the Jews and the gentiles, nor within ethnic or religious groups themselves.[11] One enthusiastic article characterized New York City as "an oddly international town" where people of many races lived "without conflict" and "became assimilated in an orderly way."[12]

Shōzō Mizutani began editing the newspaper *Nyūyōku shimpō* in 1916. Little is known about him except that when he took over, the paper enjoyed a dramatic increase in circulation and soon changed from a weekly to semiweekly.[13] One could assume that, given Mizutani's position as a newspaperman, resident of New York City, and trustee of the Japanese Association of New York, his history, *Nyūyōku nihonjin hattenshi*, would provide valuable information about the New York issei. The details regarding population, geographic origin, age, and occupation are useful and important. Unfortunately, however, there is little that could help us construct an in-depth portrait of the hi-imin: the attitudinal lives of the majority of the New York Japanese, their perceptions about the United States before they left Japan, and the degree to which their expectations, dreams, and fantasies were realized.

Mizutani's history gives a one-sided picture of New York and the New York Japanese. The project was supported by and reflected the thinking of the Japanese Association of New York, a group of influential individuals. Japanese firms, banks, and merchants gave additional financial assistance. An office was provided by Dr. Jōkichi Takamine, a successful and active leader of the Japanese community.[14] Count Ōkuma Shigenobu—twice prime minister, an advocate of empire, a supporter of Japanese-American trade and Japanese emigration to the United States, and a friend of the Mitsubishi combine—contributed the foreword. He praised New York as the center of American culture and finance, a place where Japanese could help create "a model society in North America" dedicated to education, technology, and trade.[15] The book's supporters and those who gave Mizutani source material and corrected the manuscript (he listed eighty-nine names in the introduction) occupied important positions in the New York Japanese business community.

Consequently, the promotion of Japanese trade and business in the United States was a major theme of the book—over one-third of its nearly 900 pages. It also included a brief historical description of Japanese-U.S. relations: the first Japanese governmental mission in 1860, when Japan was still under Tokugawa reign; American views of

Japan, including those of Commodore Perry and Townsend Harris; American opinions concerning the Sino- and Russo-Japanese Wars; a short ten-page "survey" of the Japanese exclusion "problem"; and biographical sketches of three noteworthy New York residents, including Takamine.[16] The permanent Japanese residents of New York, the majority of the community, and their occupations and institutions were given a scant 150 pages, or one-sixth of Mizutani's history.

Without question, Japanese on the East Coast did not encounter the virulent and continuous acts of hostility directed at Japanese in California, Oregon, and Washington. In those states yellow-peril xenophobia gave rise to the formation of the Asiatic Exclusion League, the San Francisco school controversy in 1906, alien land laws, racial incidents from Washington to Wyoming, and an exclusionary and fearful atmosphere for Japanese.[17] A writer in a New York Japanese immigrant newspaper, the *Japanese-American Commercial Weekly,* praised New York City in comparison to San Francisco: "San Francisco elicits hatred as when a samurai enters an *eta* [outcast] village.... The prejudices of the people of San Francisco ... should burn and disintegrate like the houses in the recent earthquake.... New York is a mature and discreet adult compared to San Francisco which is a demon brat."[18] Another article, in *Tobei shimpō,* described Seattle as being preferable to San Francisco but noted that New York welcomed Japanese "even more."[19] As Mizutani pointed out, New York's great geographic distance from Japan kept away the "swarms of Asians" that immigrated to the West, a blessing for those who chose to end up in New York.[20]

However, despite their insignificant numbers and the fact that the majority held hi-imin passports, the New York Japanese did not encounter the golden opportunities they expected as literate and educated people. Though they worked as menial laborers, saved some money, and learned English as suggested by the tobei publications, the world of socially valued work rejected them callously. In 1921, the year Mizutani published his history, 75 percent of the New York issei were engaged in domestic labor, a slight improvement over the 90 percent figure prior to World War I.[21] Given that increased U.S.-Japanese trade attracted larger numbers of Japanese business and bankers to New York, the actual number of domestic workers probably remained unchanged.[22]

The story of Toyohiko Campbell Takami (1875–1945) illustrates how one early immigrant overcame his beginning as a domestic worker.[23] Takami achieved success as a medical doctor with a private practice near Fort Greene Park, Brooklyn, and as chief of the

Department of Dermatology at Cumberland Hospital. His affluence eventually enabled him to own a summer home in Cold Springs Harbor, Long Island. With Jōkichi Takamine, Takami figured prominently in the formation and leadership of Japanese immigrant institutions in New York.[24] Born in Kumamoto-ken, he began classical Chinese studies at six and was sent to a traditional boarding school at age twelve. His father planned for his son to become a Shinto priest. However, Takami's own aspirations differed. He secretly attended a mission school because the "daily routine of Chinese literature, exercise and discipline began to wear on my nerves, and besides, I did not want to become a Shinto priest."[25] He was introduced to the English language, became intrigued by the story of Niishima Jō, the Christian educator who stowed away to the United States on a whaling ship in 1864, and decided that his future lay in getting away from home and crossing the ocean, as Niishima did, to the United States.

During a vacation period, he set out on foot for Osaka, a journey that took him two months. Fifteen years old at the time, he planned to enlist the aid of a cousin and train to become a seaman. His cousin agreed and arranged for him to become a live-in domestic worker for a captain's family and to attend navigation school. However, Takami grew impatient and decided to look for a job on a ship. He hired on as a mess boy on a vessel that traveled between ports on the Japan Inland Sea. Finally, in March 1891, one year after leaving home, he landed a position as a captain's boy on an English steamship. "I bought the English National Readers and a Japanese-English dictionary . . . and started on a new adventure into the outside world."[26] The ship traveled to Shanghai, Hong Kong, and Singapore, traversed the Indian Ocean, the Red Sea, and the Suez Canal to Port Said, continued to Constantinople, touched Odessa in Russia, and arrived in Southampton, England, two months later. The captain and his wife hired him as their household worker until the ship sailed for New York, intending eventually to send him to navigation school when the ship docked. However, Takami wrote: "While I was very appreciative of their kind consideration for me, I had no intention of becoming a seafaring man. I had finally reached America and I intended to stay, at all costs, to get an American education as Joseph Hardy Neesima [niishima] had done before me."[27]

When he was allowed to go ashore in New York in October 1891, he "wrote a short note of appreciation" to the captain and his wife and left the ship. He headed for a boardinghouse for Japanese seamen near the Brooklyn Navy Yard. "After a month of despair," he finally landed a job as a mess boy on an old navy ship. The chief steward and chief cook were both Japanese. The chief cook was "well-educated in Japan and had come to America to go to college," but like many of his compatriots he was unable to acquire enough funds to fulfill his desires. Befriended by him, Takami eventually became assistant cook and then, when his friend returned to Japan, chief cook. During this time Takami assiduously studied English and the Bible at a "Chinese Sunday School" on Fulton Street under the guidance of a retired college teacher, Nancy E. Campbell. Campbell took a special interest in him, and their close relationship resulted in his conversion to Christianity. Following her suggestion, he resigned from the Navy Yard position and moved to her home to enter high school. His educational career began in September 1893, when he left New York to attend Cushing Academy in Massachusetts.

Takami's life had taken a fortuitous turn at this time. Thanks to Campbell's interest and support in him, his ability to take advantage of her help, and his determination to fulfill her expectations, he attended exclusive Eastern schools and entered the medical profession.[28] During his summer vacations he worked as supply man and cook for the Department of Welfare's hospitals for underprivileged children and as a steward on furniture merchant John Sloane's yacht. However, these summer jobs, even though they were in the category of domestic labor, cannot be considered in the same vein as his earlier ones, for his wages went for books and clothing, not for everyday living expenses. He received tuition scholarships throughout his school and college years, and Campbell treated him as her own son.[29]

Takami's early work experience at the Navy Yard, however, was typical. A large number of Japanese men became domestic workers in New York City. In 1890–1891, over half of the 600 Japanese issei in the New York area lived and worked in Brooklyn. The Navy Yard was a sprawling center located east of the Brooklyn Bridge in Wallabout Bay, where the East River naturally widened. It housed work sections for specialized workers: blacksmiths, machinists, painters, plumbers, coopers, joiners, riggers, and others associated with shipbuilding. Their job was to repair and resupply U.S. Navy ships. The Navy Yard faced Park Avenue and Navy Street, and its workers populated the narrow streets close by on York, Prospect, Sands, Concord, and Gold.[30] The Japanese congregated in this area not to blend in with the crowd of semiskilled and unskilled laborers but to take on particular domestic jobs as kitchen workers, stewards, mess boys, or cooks in the Yard or on the battleships.[31] Significantly, the Navy Yard was the one and only place in New York to which they could go knowing that other Japanese would be working there. Other than at the Yard and in Japanese-run businesses, they found work in scattered and isolated places.

Of the remaining 300 issei who lived in Manhattan, approximately 50 were government officials, business representatives, or small business owners. The rest worked as domestic workers.[32] Like Takami, many early Japanese immigrants had sailed to New York as cabin boys or galley helpers on American ships, one of the first groups comprising thirty-two individuals hired during the U.S. fleet's Asian tour in 1881. Some came on commercial carriers and jumped ship in New York harbor. Their illegal entry excluded them from any official count, Japanese or American.

Toward the end of the decade, a number of Japanese workers in the U.S. Navy began to be released from service. They looked for work, seeking out the few Japanese "Brooklynites"—including boardinghouse and restaurant owners—who lived on Sands or Gold Streets.[33] One Tokujirō Iwase, a native of Chiba-ken (near Tokyo), served the Navy from 1884 for more than twenty years and recommended more than 100 of his fellow Japanese as workers. He was released with a pension in 1907, the year the Navy enforced a regulation prohibiting the hiring of non-U.S. citizens.[34] At that time, the Brooklyn Japanese began to disperse, and the gradual exodus of people and organizations to Manhattan started. Although in cases such as Takami's domestic labor was a temporary condition, for the majority of Japanese in New York it became a way of life. Other avenues of employment were not open to them. The same situation held on the West Coast, where Japanese who did not work as agricultural laborers often became household workers or "school boys," young men who worked while going to school or saved to attend school at a future time.[35]

One anonymous individual, in strong contrast to Takami, suffered through the more typical Japanese experience. Relegated to domestic work, he went from job to job, experienced isolation and bitterness, and was unable to realize his original goal.[36] This young man, like others, dreamed about the United States, read about the "land of freedom and civilization," and decided that to be "honored and favored by capitalists in Japan" he had to acquire "new knowledge in America." After being investigated by the Japanese government and experiencing "a great deal of difficulty and delay," he was issued a student passport and finally embarked from Yokohama for Victoria, British Columbia.

His account, written (remarkably) in English, articulated the fear, anger, disappointment, loneliness, and feelings of servility that were common among "the army of domestic servants." He served as a house boy, launderer, cabin boy, kitchen helper, dishwasher, butler, and waiter in boardinghouses, homes, mansions, and yachts; traveling from Victoria to Tacoma and Portland and finally across the continent to New York City. Each time he carried the hope that moving to a different and larger city would lessen his disillusionment with the United States, a feeling that surfaced as soon as he touched Tacoma, a city with "muddy streets and the dirty wharf." His first domestic job was "uncomfortable and mortifying," full of "subduing . . . vanity and overcoming from the humiliation and swallowing down all the complaints, weariness and discouragement." Succeeding jobs brought the same indignities. Employers as well as fellow housekeepers and cooks could be intolerant and unreasonable. He recalled: "Sonorous voice from the cook of my slowness in peeling potatoes often vibrated into my tympanum."[37] However, he also discovered as time progressed that some employers were easier to work for than others—one woman even "arranged . . . not to have any company and very often . . . dined out" during his examination periods. The young servant "adored her as much as Henry Esmond did to Lady Castlemond."[38]

He finished high school with the intention of attaining a college degree, but with each successive job his desire grew fainter and less feasible. In addition, his studies in college differed substantially from those in high school:

Some say Japanese are studying while they are working in the kitchen, but it is all nonsense. . . . How often you are disturbed while you have to read at least three hours succession quietly. . . . [O]nce I attended lecture after I have done a rush work in the kitchen. It was so tired felt as though all the blood in the body rushing up to the brain and partly sleepy. My hands would not work. . . . [M]y head so dull could not order to my hand what professor's lecture was.[39]

The difficulties of working for a degree while earning a living at the same time effectively nullified his original rationale for coming to the United States.

Time, he observed, had a way of dulling the initial feelings of humiliation. Domestic work required "no honor, no responsibility, no sense of duty, but the pliancy of servitude" and served to deaden any sense of independence. "I have commenced to manifest the interest of my avocation as a professor of Dust and Ashes," he wrote: "Years' husbanding of domestic work, handicapped and over-interfered by mistress, their [the servants'] mental agilities are reduced to the lamentable degree. Yet, matured by these undesirable experience, most of them are quite unconscious of this outcome, as little by little submissive and depending habit so securely rooted within their mind."[40]

Indeed, live-in work, which was more prevalent than day work for these men, prevented them from having control over their own living and working conditions and decreased the likelihood of their moving to more rewarding, self-motivated occupations. For such people, domestic service was a "prison." Social relationships with people outside of the workplace, which might lead to alternative avenues of employment, were difficult to initiate and maintain. Often an employer's fair treatment solidified the employee's loyalty to the extent that any semblance of independence irretrievably dissipated. The emotional attachment of a servant to the woman of the house in particular, as well as her concern about his health and ability to work, served to complicate the "unconscious servile habit of action." Sometimes his relationship to her developed into "adoration," as in the case of the anonymous young man and his "Lady Castlemond." In the servant's eyes, the employer's family gradually became his family, and a vision of any free and independent life faded.

The Japanese domestic workers elicited varied reactions from their better-established countrymen. In one tobei publication, the author of an essay on New York employment opportunities praised the desirable qualities of the Japanese in New York, "a majority of whom were domestics."[41] Contrary to the young man who wrote about disillusionment with housework, this author considered isolation positive because it gave workers time to read and study. "Japanese help" had the reputation of being clean, neat, sober, earnest, strict, and industrious, qualities that encouraged clubs and families to hire them. The work of a cook, butler, or houseworker was presented as uncomplicated. Furthermore, wages were attractive. Even without being fluent in English or having considerable work experience, Japanese servants could get higher wages than white servants.

The best way to save money was to work as a cook ("if you don't mind the grease"). "Plain" cooks easily averaged $40 to $50 a month. "Fancy" cooks could earn $75 or more. Noted the tobei essayist: "Western cooking is easy even for the novice.... Japanese cooking is tedious and difficult since each dish has to be flavored in the pot. Westerners always boil their food and take it to the table as is.... [E]ach person uses salt, pepper, or something else such as a sauce, as desired."[42] As a cook one was fed and housed and did not have to purchase special clothing such as that required of a butler. Also, many Japanese took on accounting responsibilities in the kitchen, a duty that could have lucrative advantages. No other type of domestic work—housework, butler, valet, and general housework for couples—offered the benefits of a cook's job for saving money.

Butlers were generally in charge of the dining room and "could be looked upon as one notch above waiters," although duties and status varied according to the family. However, the ability to speak English was a prerequisite, as butlers usually had to answer the front door and the telephone. Many people coveted a butler's position because it was "clean," but the monthly wages, between $50 and $55, made saving money difficult. The butler had to spend more money on personal appearance. Nevertheless, the most rewarding aspect of this work was that by "heeding each action, each move, each word, each phrase," at the dining room table, one could absorb much about American manners and personal relationships between spouses, parents and children, siblings, and friends.[43] General housework was the least desirable occupation and included "making beds, washing windows and bathrooms." "Anybody off the boat" could do it. It paid anywhere from $15 to $35 a month, a wide range.[44]

Significantly, the essay ended with an unanswered question—"What do Americans think of dishwashers whose native country won a war against Russia?"—implying that Japanese should be respected and deserved better jobs than domestic work. In the same vein, Mizutani pointed out that domestic work was clearly demeaning and should never be considered more than a temporary form of employment. It attracted only certain groups among the European immigrants—"the Irish and the Latins, first, and then the Russians and Italians, but rarely the English or French.... [T]raditionally, household work is labor with close ties to slavery. Even labor unions do not consider it legitimate. Therefore, it is not ideal for our countrymen."[45]

However, he conceded that for the majority of young Japanese in New York, "differences in race," inability to travel around the city, and ignorance of the English language prevented their working in factories or for transportation companies. He failed to mention that certain semiskilled or unskilled jobs were given exclusively to members of specific ethnic groups depending upon the industry, the entrepreneur, or the foreman, and that laws gave preference to native-born citizens over aliens in certain public work. He complained that some Japanese with less than an elementary education were "like nomads," going from job to job without meaning in their lives. Their "peculiar characteristics" of "servility, idleness, and narrow-mindedness" hindered self-growth and thus the ability to change occupations. Others decided to come for a fixed number of years, intending to save money and then return to Japan. Of these, "nine out of ten" gave up their will to persevere and succumbed to drink or gambling. The "self-sacrificing" worked "as hibernating dragons in a pond" to save for an education or to set themselves up in business.

Citing an Imperial University graduate who achieved economic security in the United States, Mizutani stated his belief that educated people with the strength to surmount hardship were able to rise "above water level" within several years. However, others who completed high school in the United States while working as domestics could not secure a financially stable life. They lacked the skill to seek positions in U.S. firms or failed to enter into the small immigrant businesses, which could accommodate only two or three employees at most. Most Japanese firms, except for "one or two exceptions," recruited their staff in Japan, so Japanese immigrants in the United States were "shut out." Mizutani thus painted a dismal and pessimistic picture for the majority of domestic workers, including those who were educated and harbored aspirations and appropriate determination.

Leaders of the community attempted to alleviate the situation by establishing a special employment section in the Japanese Association during World War I; but, significantly, even though it was a time when employment levels were high, they lacked placement opportunities for Japanese and failed to devise an "appropriate" plan.[46] Regardless of their good intentions, they were unable to solve the situation. Their establishment of arbitrary standards regarding necessary and desirable character traits undermined the effort, as did their belief that the majority of domestic laborers lacked the wherewithal to lift themselves out of the kitchen. The harsh reality was that once an immigrant was forced to succumb to that work, change and success became elusive.

One other type of criticism of domestic workers appeared in the *Japanese-American Commercial Weekly*.[47] Japanese men in the United States were blamed as having "many faults similar to the faults of women." The author, an "anonymous woman," listed the desirable qualities in men—frankness, sociability, generosity, a forgiving nature, respectability, and reliability—qualities she found lacking in Japanese men in the United States. An editorial comment following her piece explained that because many Japanese were domestic workers and supervised by women, they became "low and weak-willed," uninterested in acquiring the "strengths and merits of Americans." Instead, they were satisfied only with the superficial aspects of American life. Yuji Ichioka quoted reformer Ozaki Yukio as writing in 1888 that male domestic laborers developed "a maid-servant's servility" and that they were "a blot on Japan's national image."[48]

Toyohiko Campbell Takami also reflected these prejudices. When he returned to school in the fall after working during the summers, he noted that many of his white friends had spent summers abroad or at their vacation homes "in Maine or other places." "I am sure," he confided, "that I did not tell them I had spent my summer in the kitchen of the Floating Hospital."[49] This leader among New York Japanese implied that even operating a business related to domestic work was second-rate and undesirable. He wrote about an old friend from his Navy Yard days who prospered running a Japanese laundry in Brooklyn: "I asked him how on earth he ever got into such a business. He said that he had obtained a job in a Chinese laundry and learned all about the laundry business in a month. Now, he could do the work better than a Chinese laundryman.... I was very grateful that I did not come to America to be a laundryman."[50]

The stigma cast upon domestic labor and laborers by Japanese community leaders was confusing for a number of reasons. First, Japanese workers could not seek employment in the diverse small manufacturing industries that dominated the New York City economy. These provided job opportunities for the many immigrants from Europe even though they, too, spoke no English.[51] Japanese immigrants had no access to employment in the key productive sectors of the city's economy, such as the garment industry, building trades, or printing, or the many smaller, home-based industries, such as flower or candy making, shoemaking, or tobacco. Rather, the types of employment that were open to them or to which they congregated kept them isolated from the majority of the city's immigrants. They were not even on the periphery of the key industries. Their compatriots who ran specialized small businesses hired them, but these operations required only periodic help and paid little. Other immigrant businesses would *yobiyoseru* (call over) relatives or friends from their home area in Japan. Japanese firms and banks preferred to hire employees in Japan.

Second, being told that domestic service could lead to success and then having to suffer its condemnations and humiliations served, at best, to legitimate disdain for the work and the workers and, at worst, to foster self-distrust and destroy confidence. The prophecy that domestic work robbed one of "manliness" was not difficult to realize. Such employment could serve to instill "unmanly" manhood, a stereotype sometimes used by compatriots as well as Westerners to describe Asian men. Also, it played on Japanese perceptions of gender and class, putting the Japanese domestic worker in New York in a state of perpetual subordination and inferiority.

Domestic workers constituted a substantial majority of the Japanese population in 1921, when Mizutani wrote his history. He estimated that approximately 500 of the little more than 4,500 Japanese in New York represented the government or Japanese firms or banks or owned small independent businesses.[52] The latter were scattered from the Navy Yard vicinity in Brooklyn to Cherry, Madison, East 19th, East 33rd, and West 123rd Streets in Manhattan. These businesses—import-export houses, wholesalers, boardinghouses, restaurants, grocery and general stores, tailor shops, photographers, and newspapers—catered in the main to the small Japanese population.

One of the more successful stores was Katagiri and Company, which still operates on East 59th Street in Manhattan. Katagiri also owned a vegetable and poultry farm on Long Island to supply his store and Japanese ships.[53] There were at least five Japanese tailors in New York, two of whom attended the Mitchell Sewing School, well known to tobei individuals because one of its graduates regularly advertised his "high-class" Tokyo tailoring establishment in *Amerika*. Judging from the addresses of the Japanese tailors in New York (Amsterdam Avenue; inside the McAlpin Hotel on Broadway and 34th Street; West 40th Street; and in the New York Times Building on Broadway and 42nd Street), they probably catered to white Americans as well as Japanese.[54]

The first Japanese-language newspaper was published in Brooklyn by a Japanese student in 1897. The publication was short-lived; Mizutani stated that a majority of Japanese could keep abreast of current news through regular English-language New York newspapers and magazines, so the vernacular newspapers could only "fill a minor news deficiency."[55] The *Japanese-American Commercial Weekly* (*Nichibei shūhō*, later, *Nichibei jihō*) began publishing in 1900, moved to St. Louis temporarily in 1904 during the international exposition, returned to New York, and was taken over by Takami and some friends in 1916. *Nyūyōku shimpō*, established in 1911, "competed on a par" with the *Japanese-*

American Commercial Weekly. Mizutani became its editor in 1916 and, beginning in 1917, published the paper semiweekly. Both papers ceased publication in 1941 with the outbreak of World War II. One of the problems of publishing a Japanese-language newspaper in the early years was the unavailability of type. In 1904 one newspaper, *Nyūyōku jihō,* arranged to print in Japanese using Chinese type, but the experiment failed. Both the *Commercial Weekly* and the *Shimpō* imported type from Japan.[56]

The three Japanese churches in New York began as Christian boardinghouses in Brooklyn and Manhattan. The first, the Sands Street Mission, near the Brooklyn Navy Yard, was begun in 1894 by Kinya Okajima, a former California railroad construction worker and evangelist. Okajima walked across the United States to New York, was befriended by Takami, met Nancy Campbell, and began teaching at her "Chinese Sunday school." However, friction between the Chinese and Japanese "boys" led him to seek other avenues for proselytizing, and thus he established the first Japanese mission in New York on the upper floor of a seamstress's house. Two years later, aided by Campbell, the Central Methodist Church, and a Baptist minister, Okajima moved to larger quarters on Concord Street, and in 1910 he formally established the Japanese Methodist Mi-i Church at the Grace Methodist Church on West 104th Street in Manhattan.[57]

Yoshisuke and Barbara Hirose married in 1898, opened a Christian boardinghouse on Prospect Street, moved to East 54th Street the following year, and moved again in 1901 to East 57th Street. Their mission was designated the Japanese Christian Institute in 1913. The institute, under the leadership of Sōjirō Shimizu in 1914, grew rapidly and became the largest Japanese Christian church in New York.[58] At about the same time (1908), Ernest Atsushi Ōhori started a Christian boardinghouse with funds from the Reformed Church in America, established the Japanese Christian Association the following year, then moved to West 123rd Street, providing dormitories (one for women), a library, and meeting rooms. He retired in 1916.[59]

Boardinghouses that did not operate under Christian auspices and catered to Japanese workers in New York City often provided both lodging and food. Senzō Kuwayama opened a restaurant and boardinghouse on West 58th Street in 1914 for men, mainly domestic workers.[60] It housed forty to fifty roomers during the busiest months and half that number in the summer, when the workers headed for resort areas in the mountains and at the seashore.

Boardinghouses served other functions besides providing food and lodging. At one time, Kuwayama tells us, part of his premises was used as a hat factory by an immigrant who was unable to find suitable work.[61] But its most important subsidiary function, as with many other Japanese boardinghouses, was to provide the physical space in which the men could enjoy leisure activity: "cards, dice throwing—in other words, gambling—which was an important source of comfort for them." Kuwayama rated success in gambling as a sign of "having guts," a necessary ingredient for achieving success. Unlike Mizutani, who complained that nine-tenths of the domestic "nomads" were inferior and worthless, Kuwayama saw *all* immigrants as courageous: "America seems like a place where the ambitious, the aggressive, the strong, and the competitive come together. It is a meeting place for people of many races and nations who have the strength to develop away from each of their old circumstances.... To survive in New York one needs extraordinary guts."[62]

Criticizing the attitudes of Japanese community leaders toward their less fortunate countrymen, Kuwayama also described the leisure activity of employees of Japanese banks, businesses, and trading firms. Most came to the United States without families and could join the exclusive Nippon Club, a privilege not enjoyed by most immigrants. However, the Nippon Club, like the boardinghouses, provided the space and atmosphere in which a person could relax and enjoy cards or plan for golf tournaments, which Kuwayama considered forms of gambling: "Under these circumstances, one begins to doubt the community leaders' calls for moral reform and social discipline. Gambling at the boarding houses is raided by the police and the unlucky domestic workers are considered criminals. Gambling at the Nippon Club is named a sport, recreation, pastime, or game for white-collar workers and looked upon as a natural form of entertainment. One can easily conclude that there is little difference between the two."[63]

This observation by Kuwayama illustrates the class distinctions between residents of the boardinghouses and their Nippon Club counterparts. The immigrant working-class population was defined as separate and unequal by the Japanese community and business leaders, as shown not only by Mizutani but also by Takami and writers in the Japanese immigrant press. Kuwayama, like Takami, began as a domestic worker but rose to open and operate the Miyako Restaurant, the only successful Japanese restaurant in New York City that catered to both a Japanese and white clientele before World War II.[64] Like Takami, he also was

Fig. 1. "Japanese Village, Luna Park," Coney Island. Photo: Wemlinger (1903). From Brooklyn Public Library.

sympathetic to the plight of the Japanese domestic workers. The difference was that Takami led and worked through organizations established "so that no Japanese person would die a pauper's death or need to fear illness or adversity."[65] His low estimation of any work even slightly connected to domestic labor has been cited. Kuwayama, however, barely mentions community institutions in his autobiography. Neither does he minimize the worth of domestic work. Rather, he philosophically points out what he considered to be the contradictions between the leisure activities of the middle class and those of the working class. Kuwayama and Mizutani at either extreme, and Takami somewhat between them, articulated varying moralistic attitudes toward their notions of "immigrant behavior." These attitudes, also part of the thinking held by ideologues in Japan, were instrumental in the Japanese government's decision to differentiate between immigrants and nonimmigrants, as we shall see in the following chapter.

One of the more unusual and successful businesses in which issei engaged was the operation of amusement concessions at Coney Island (see Figure 1). Mizutani wrote that this practice originated when an enterprising man started a "Japanese tea garden" in 1896 in Atlantic City, New Jersey.[66] Hoping to attract more vacationers, he remodeled part of his concession and set up two tables for a rolling ball game.[67] The alterations succeeded beyond his expectations, and "swarms of customers" came, bringing "unforeseen profit." Because this business did not require a great deal of capital, Mizutani noted, it attracted a number of issei, including "more than ten" in "the summer pleasure area" of Coney Island, Brooklyn. Others also opened concessions at Rockaway Beach, Brooklyn; Atlantic City, Asbury Park, Newark, and Cape May, New Jersey; and Philadelphia. The business was so successful that some Chinese entrepreneurs "passed themselves off as Japanese" and went into the business.[68]

Mizutani described Coney Island as a spot where "most New Yorkers who were lower than middle class customarily spent their leisure time." From spring through early winter, "tens of thousands of dollars" were spent on games, theater, swimming, eating, and drinking, providing "work and profit" for the Japanese.[69]

Nagai Kafū's short story "Akebono" (Daybreak), originally printed in *Amerika monogatari*, recounts one night in the lives of Japanese workers at a Coney Island concession.[70] Kafū calls the amusement area a place "exemplifying the coarsest scene of seething humanity which probably cannot be found anywhere else in the world." His vivid description combines the glittery ugliness and beauty of the place:

Using electricity and water, there is every conceivable huge, showy device which astounds the masses of people—so many different kinds that one cannot keep track of them. Some exhibits give a little knowledge about history or geography. There are also suspicious-looking dance halls; obscene vaudeville houses; spectacular fireworks displays. And on a clear night, when one goes across New York Bay on a river steamboat, the impressive illumination of the electric lights are like daybreak lighting up the night sky and the far-off high and low buildings across the water look like a panorama of a sea god's palace.[71]

In the midst of this raucous fantasy world, "Japanese Rolling Ball" had the reputation of being "one of the most popular of all the games" (see Figure 2). However, its primary attraction was that one could "examine" a Japanese person, "a still unusual phenomenon"; winning the game and getting one of the prizes that crowded the rolling ball stalls was of secondary importance.[72]

Kafū noted that the owners were generally men over forty who had left Japan after suffering hardship. In the United States, too, they had

Fig. 2. "Japanese Rolling Board" from "Glimpses of Coney Island." Photo: Blanchard (1904). From Kingsborough Historical Society.

luckless lives, went through "every experience," and reached the conclusion that "the world would get on some way"—that human beings did not die easily "even if they were forced to scratch at the earth."

Their faces have taken on the look of survival, of a boss, a brave warrior, a roughneck. And the people under them—the ones hired to count the rolled balls and to give customers their prizes—have yet to complete their life course in the world of failure. They are the unemployed who would be happy becoming the assistant boss or the young men who came to America recklessly thinking that they could work and study at the same time.

I was one of those workers and thought that it did not matter what I did. My only goal was to save money to go to Europe.[73]

According to Kafū, it was a world where hi-imin and imin worked side by side. Their class positions did not determine their working conditions or wages.

The workers' wages at the stall where Kafū worked were twelve dollars a week, less than at other stalls, which paid fifteen or sixteen dollars.

The owner bragged that his workers did not have to spend one penny for living expenses: "I give you three meals and besides, you can sleep in the store." Sleeping in the store meant that one was given a cot in the back of the concession, an airless receptacle enclosing the intense heat of the summer afternoons. Kafū described one older man who at three in the morning, the end of the working day, took out a blanket, spread it on the wooden counter, and lay down. One of the younger men, who looked like a student, sarcastically remarked:

"Sleeping on that counter again? You'll dream well tonight."
"Who wants to sleep in the back? It's a nest for bed bugs. You should learn how to sleep on a board, too."[74]

The conditions in Kafū's fictional account of the Japanese in Coney Island in 1906 are not far removed from those recalled by Haru Kishi, whose husband helped run a Coney Island concession in the 1920s.[75] Haru came to New York City as a young bride of eighteen. She came, she says, "to cook three meals a day" and clean for the workers who lived together above the concession in a wooden house. Ruefully, she remembers, "That was my honeymoon." Her life in the United States was not at all what she expected and totally different from her life in Japan.

Born in Tokyo in 1904 to a middle-class family, she remembers her childhood as being "carefree and happy." She attended a girls' high school, learned some English, and was influenced by a teacher's stories about how Japanese "should go abroad and see other people and other countries.... Sometimes he would close his lesson book and caution the class not to stay in small, crowded Japan, and I was captivated.... If it weren't for him, I might never have come to America." When talks began about marriage to Eikichi Kishi, "a businessman in New York," she expressed interest; not only had he been a longtime resident of the United States, but she thought he "looks nice," though he was more than twenty years her senior.[76] Her cousin, a Mitsubishi employee who was on a trip to Japan with Kishi, introduced them. "My parents were worried about my coming all the way to New York, but they found out that Kishi was a serious man and respected his parents. Our marriage was decided very quickly."

They met early in December 1921, Haru applied and got her passport the same month; their marriage took place on December 27, and on January 6, 1922, they embarked on a ship for Seattle. They crossed the continent by railroad.

We arrived in New York and I came to the summer concession, or rather, I was dragged into it. I was shocked and disgusted to learn that this was "the business."

I knew nothing about cooking. I never cooked in my life. There was a coal stove which I had to learn to use, a two-gas-burner hot plate, a wooden bathtub in the kitchen, and I had to cook for all those people. At first I just put the meat on the burners. Nobody told me what I was supposed to do. I was the only woman among fifteen men, sometimes more.

Work started around noon and continued until two o'clock in the morning: "My husband would bring the money upstairs and put it on the table to count. We had a mountain of money every night—I've never seen so much at once."

Haru's husband, Eikichi, "of good family," had come to New York in 1910 at the age of twenty-seven, planning to become a student. Unable to save enough money for school, he worked at various jobs and then became an assistant to the manager of one of the largest Japanese amusement concessions. It was during this time that Haru arrived in New York. She recalled: "Kishi was a scholarly type who hated manual labor and business. But he had to run the Coney Island 'skiball' game in the summer and work for a Japanese merchant in the winter. He was too poor to go back to start life again in Japan." He and Haru worked at Coney Island for three or four years, then ran a concession at Rockaway Beach and operated a small gift shop on Dyckman Street in Washington Heights, Manhattan, during the winter months. When the lease expired at the shop, business had reached a low. The early days of the Depression had set in, and the Kishis moved to Bayonne, New Jersey, to work at a year-round concession. But this also failed to prosper, not only because of the nation's economic slump: "During a presidential election year, I've forgotten which one, the police had to show how good they were and a big clean-up campaign took place. They closed the gambling joints and stuck their noses into everybody's business including the legitimate ones. All the Japanese 'bust up.' Our business wasn't affected, but since the other stores left, we also had to leave." The Kishis moved back to Manhattan, but their debts mounted; they could not pay the rent, were evicted, and had to move again, this time to a one-room apartment behind a laundry.

During those years Haru bore four of their five children. The first was born in January 1924, two years after she arrived in New York. Not knowing much English, she courageously entered a hospital, taking a dictionary, paper, and pencil to communicate with the doctors and nurses. "I really don't know how I did it. It was very hard. I didn't know anything about childbirth. I was in the hospital for ten days. Kishi came to see me just twice. He said that the doctors were taking care of me. He didn't even tell my friends about the baby, so they didn't come either. I guess that's the way Japanese men are."[77]

Kishi got a job in Manhattan as a general domestic worker. Because it was day work ("he was away from six [in the morning] to nine [at night]"), he had only one afternoon off every two weeks. One year they began a lampshade store ("I don't know where Kishi got the money"), renting space from a fellow Japanese. "But when the business started to make profit, the rent went up, and someone else took over the store. It was taken from under us. So he had to go back to 'family work.' "

Their life changed somewhat after the youngest child entered school. They operated a small lampshade store; Haru made the merchandise by hand. The store was closed by the FBI in January 1942 after the outbreak of World War II, but customers continued to place orders, and Haru worked at home. Although most of their life in pre–World War II New York took place after the period of our concern, the constant moves, changes in jobs, financial insecurity, unemployment, and worry of their lives typified the experiences of earlier Japanese immigrants.[78]

Haru Kishi was one woman among fifteen men when she first arrived at Coney Island, not unusual among the Japanese in New York, where the average ratio was one woman to ten men. Her husband, fortunately, had been able to return to Japan to find a wife, an opportunity not readily available to the majority of issei men. An interviewee in the *New York Nichibei* in 1985 observed that the Japanese men in California could work hard, buy property, and marry a picture bride. They even had children and grandchildren. "But New York was a business town. Not only was buying property impossible, but getting a decent apartment was hard. You couldn't marry, either."[79]

The dream of meeting American women, socializing with them, perhaps even marrying one, remained a dream for most Japanese men. There were only eighty-two cross-racial marriages registered at the Japanese consulate between 1909 and 1921, a majority of the total during 1920 and 1921.[80] The Japanese male population of New York City, according to the official Japanese statistics, was more than 3,000 in 1920. Assuming that not all registered their marriages and that some unions were common-law (including, possibly, many interracial relationships), one could speculate that the percentage of married males in

New York was greater than the official figure of 2.5 percent. Nevertheless, that figure is far short of the national average of married Japanese males, which was about 30 percent in 1920.[81]

The story of Kinichi Iwamoto provides another example of how marriage was handled. Raised and educated in Nagoya, he came to the United States to continue his medical training.[82] Inspired by his father, who had lived in San Francisco for seven years and worked in a tobacco factory, and by an article in his high school bulletin, Iwamoto decided to come to the United States. After graduating from medical school in Nagoya, he secured a good job in a prefectural government office but wanted "to live independently in America, a good place where people could work and save money to go to school." Arriving in 1920, he worked in Tacoma at a sawmill for about six months, saving "a considerable amount of money." Iwamoto crossed the continent by rail to New York City and attended Columbia University for two years, working part-time in a research laboratory. He received his M.D. in 1923 and began his practice in 1924 on West 70th Street. Regarding marriage, he observed that Japan's ban on picture brides in 1921 made it impossible for the issei in New York to marry. He remained single until 1930, when he was thirty-five.

"I remember only about three Japanese women who were of the right age, but they had peculiarities and I was uninterested," he recalls. He socialized with an Irish woman for "two or three years," but "every time a female patient telephoned," she became "insanely jealous." Eventually he met and married a nurse of German extraction who worked at the hospital with which he was associated. They had two children and lived together until her death in 1961.

None of the surviving accounts regarding marriage—Takami's romantic story of meeting and marrying a Japanese woman studying at Mount Holyoke College;[83] Jōkichi Takamine's marriage to a southern woman; the Christian minister Ōhori's returning from a visit to Japan with "a sweet young Japanese wife to help in his labor for souls";[84] Kishi's and Iwamoto's experiences—can be considered typical. Marriage procedures in the United States were not natural nor as free as men envisioned, and bringing a wife from Japan was expensive and cumbersome. I have not come across instances of picture-bride marriages in New York City, though some may have taken place. Those with some status in the Japanese community probably experienced less difficulty than the majority of men, who remained single. However, seeking and finding a mate did not come with ease for any Japanese man in New York; even those mentioned were already in their thirties when they married.[85] Kishi was forty.

We can only surmise about the majority regarding their relationships with women. Nagai Kafū's *Amerika monogatari* includes "Chainataun no ki" (An account of Chinatown), a graphic narrative of Chinatown's back-alley tenement slum area, "a showplace of the worst depravity, disease, and death."[86] The inhabitants had fallen so low that "it was impossible for them to sink any lower." In this environment Kafū came across prostitutes who catered to Chinese and Japanese customers. In a run-down building occupied by Chinese:

Unexpectedly I came across a door on which a ribbon with a bow was attached, like a sign. The door opened halfway, revealing a thickly powdered American woman who peeked out as soon as she heard footsteps in the hallway. She called out to us using Chinese and Japanese words she had picked up.
    ... These women congregated here intending only to satisfy the animal desires of the Chinese—and of a certain class of Japanese, too.[87]

In the magazine *Amerika*, Katagiri Kuryō also wrote about Chinatown.[88] He toured the city one evening with "a good-looking lively young man," Uemura, who was to leave the following day for a new job. Uemura took it upon himself to escort Katagiri, newly arrived and naïve, around the city and to celebrate his departure. They stopped at bars along the way, each stop fostering greater camaraderie between the two men. Eventually they boarded the el. The writer did not know where they were headed, but his good mood thwarted any feeling of unease or ignorance. The train carried only a few people—a group of chattering painted women, "six or seven lower-class workers who are chewing tobacco," and four or five couples "sweet-talking among themselves."

... Occasionally Uemura looks over the women without saying a word, but finally he says:
    "Hallo, girl."
    "Hallo," one of them answers.
    "How's business?" he asks, and crosses the car to sit next to the women.
    I cannot hear what they are saying because the train is so noisy, but when he comes back to his seat he laughs loudly, "A-ha, ha, ha, ha!"
    "Uemura! You're making a fool of yourself. You're disgracing Japanese! You're embarrassing me in public. . . . "
    "A-ha, ha, ha, ha! Sorry! Sorry! . . . a green fellow like you doesn't recognize the animals you see over there. Those women are whores. They're going to work now. . . . [T]o them we're like gods."

They got off the el and came to an ugly and unruly bar in Chinatown.[89] A "dark-skinned Japanese" customer was speaking in "sloppy English" to a woman. Eventually Uemura arranged for Katagiri to be entertained by one of the prostitutes in the place. Katagiri, angry and insulted, fled. He ended his piece with the declaration: "I never met Uemura again. Promising young men like him get tainted by the freedom in America and surrender to reckless self-indulgence. Unconsciously they sink into the abyss of vice and sin."

The moralistic and superior tone of this piece implies that not everyone was equipped to take advantage of the freedom offered in the United States. Such liberty was detrimental to an upstanding character; it "tainted" some hi-imin types and led them to seek entertainment and pleasure in places where "dark-skinned Japanese" frequented.[90] Kafū, fascinated by the slums of New York City, nevertheless expressed contempt for the "certain class of Japanese" who associated with people catering to Chinese. Racism, patriotism, and class biases are evident in the works of Kafū and writers like him. However, the accounts are conspicuous for their descriptions of how individual men solved their inability to form relationships with women of whatever nationality. I am not suggesting that Japanese men would not have sought prostitutes had they been able to freely associate with women in the United States. However, I suspect that many did so because they, like the women they sought, were ostracized from the mainstream of work and social relationships.

Objectively, the Japanese in New York as a group had qualities that could foster easy acceptance. They were not numerous. A segregated Japanese neighborhood never formed. A large number were educated, and some knew English. The Japanese government, adhering to the agreement with the United States, tried to control their movement and activity. Advice in the vernacular newspapers emphasized the need to live up to the image of a "civilized" population.

The literate and educated people who left Japan for New York thought life in the United States would not be difficult. They had absorbed some knowledge about the United States before departing: the careful lessons the tobei writers taught; articles in the self-help publications; the popular novels that mentioned the United States, its people, the West, and Western ways; and, of course, hearsay and stories heard from relatives, friends, and returnees. The immigrants combined information from all these sources to create a vision of the United States. Not all Japanese had the same vision, but their perceptions were generally positive. However, despite their backgrounds and the cultural knowledge about the United States that they gathered in Japan, the majority of the Japanese who came to New York were unable to live up to the expectations and dreams they carried with them. Their work lives and personal relationships took unexpected turns. Without extraordinary perseverance, good luck, and the foresight to take advantage of situations and opportunities as Takami had, they faced lifelong bachelorhood, unskilled or semiskilled domestic labor, and an income that at best barely supported the comfortable, independent middle-class standard of living they hoped for.

Though the immigrant world presented obstacles, life in the preimmigrant world also had failed to fulfill the promises of a bright future for many of the educated and ambitious. Myriad changes in Meiji Japan created anguish, frustration, and disappointment among the youth: divergent understandings within families, at school, in the workplace, and in social situations; political upheavals, complicated by increasing bureaucracy that intruded upon everything from textbooks to passports and private political thought; and an overbearing state ideology that engendered patriotism, new class biases, sexism, and feelings of superiority over all Asians. These transformations spurred some to leave the country. Two significant forces helped shape an attitudinal basis for the decision to emigrate. One was the legitimation by the Japanese state of the essentially homogenized middle-class standards established for its population. In the government's emigration policy, these standards were exemplified by passport categories that explicitly differentiated between desirable and undesirable citizens as representatives of the country abroad. (The next chapter traces the evolution of the concept of hi-imin and its establishment as a passport designation.) The other force, the Meiji Japanese urban world, helped solidify the hi-imin image as an ideal toward which the citizenry should strive. Chapter 4 will focus on Tokyo as the example of the Meiji city, the hub of education, media, and government and a growing commercial sector. These two forces provided the framework in which visions of the United States became etched in the minds of those who were propelled to uproot their lives and move to another country. It is not far-fetched to surmise that those who reached New York carried cultural baggage loaded with these particular notions of their preimmigrant world.

CHAPTER 3

Culprits and Gentlemen
The Legitimation of Class Differences in Meiji Emigration Policy, 1891–1908

In April 1891 two ships, the *Remus* and *Pemptos,* arrived on the Pacific shores of the United States carrying, respectively, fifty-three and twenty-two "low class and densely ignorant" Japanese men and women. The Japanese consulate in San Francisco, alarmed at the adverse publicity and embarrassed by accusations that the Japanese were not adhering to the congressional contract labor laws of 1885, sent two offensive clippings from U.S. newspapers to the Foreign Ministry in Tokyo and exhorted the government to act quickly and decisively to limit emigration to the United States.[1] The U.S. government had strengthened contract labor laws in March 1891 by authorizing special Treasury Department agents to patrol coastal cities and turn back the onslaught of what the U.S. press called "dirty Japanese."[2] The American legal advisor to the Japanese legation in Washington warned that the *Remus* and *Pemptos* had brought a different class of Japanese to the United States "in comparatively large numbers . . . induced to leave Japan by hope of improving their condition . . . not from open port . . . but from remote parts of the interior."[3] He demanded that immediate action be taken against persons who "lure Japanese away under false promises" and that the punishment should be "prompt and severe."

A year later the San Francisco consulate, still besieged by "loud . . . adverse comments" in the U.S. press and not getting satisfactory results from the Tokyo government, sent a telegram begging that strict restrictions be placed on the number of laborers emigrating to the United States.[4] The government sent copies of the consulate's communication to the governor of each ken and fu and dispatched special confidential letters to the governors of Hiroshima-, Wakayama-, and Kumamoto-ken, the three southwestern ken supplying the most emigrants.[5] The correspondence called upon the vigorous enforcement of emigration restrictions. Year after year, reports, instructions, and requests for advice made their way back and forth across the Pacific, together with clippings from U.S. newspapers condemning the "slave trade," "prostitution," and "contract laborers" as well as consular reports on anti-Japanese harangues by U.S. labor leaders, "Oriental" exclusion advocates, and their fellow travelers.

Scholars of Japanese-U.S. relations at the turn of the century have concentrated on the anti-Japanese climate in California, American racism, Theodore Roosevelt's role as a maker of foreign policy, and the details of the U.S.-Japanese diplomatic correspondence of 1907–1908 leading to the Gentlemen's Agreement.[6] In explaining Japan's role, these scholars devoted more attention to governmental leadership and the development of foreign policy than to the domestic measures that augmented foreign policy—measures that belie the widespread assumption that the United States "victimized" Japan. In the context of foreign relations, Japan indeed could be considered the victim, but in the context of its political, military, and industrial aspirations, its actions concerning emigration to the continental United States also signified a keen sense of independence and timing, a wish to convey a positive self-image to the West. Its emigration policy represented more than mere acquiescence to U.S. demands.

From 1891 to 1924, the period of Japanese immigration to the United States prior to World War II, the correspondence among agencies of the Japanese Foreign Ministry and local governments as well as with U.S. federal, state, and city governments continued to express the tone established in the early 1890s. The Japanese were earnest and conciliatory with the Americans, insistent, querulous, and arbitrary with each other; the Americans were complaining but tolerant and paternal toward the Japanese. The Japanese government acted in response to U.S. actions. The focus of both governments' attention was the meager number of Japanese nationals who disembarked in the port cities or made their way to the western United States. Indeed, whereas close to 30 million people came from Europe between the Civil War and 1924, the Japanese immigrant population at its height constituted a mere 0.1 percent of the U.S. population.[7]

In analyzing Japanese immigration it is important to bear in mind the world roles of the United States and Japan, particularly in East

Asia—always in the background, always behind the official pronouncements and statements on immigration. Japanese immigration to the United States was unique during this period in that the relationship between the two countries, ranging from amity to anxiety, played a major part in defining exactly who was an immigrant. The Gentlemen's Agreement of 1907–1908 and the National Origins Act of 1924—the former a promise by Japan to restrict emigration, the latter an exclusion by the U.S. government—were culminations of the immigration controversy. They not only explicitly dictated government actions toward Japanese immigrants but also implicitly illustrated the power relationship between the two countries. Immigration was merely an issue, a tool used by both the United States and Japan to clarify their stands in the world and with each other until its termination in 1924. Although the countries' hierarchical relationship to each other remained the same, their positions with respect to the rest of the world went through qualitative change.

In 1891, when the *Remus* and *Pemptos* arrived, the United States and Japan were still young nations in the world of modern imperialistic belligerence, keenly cognizant of areas outside of their borders. The United States had manifested its destiny in the Caribbean and the Pacific and made secure its territory in North America; Japan prepared for an embroilment on the Asian continent in as early as 1873, when the Satsuma fanatics sought to invade Korea (the same year the government established conscription), and attacked Taiwan in 1874. As industrializing countries, both sought to forge empires, take advantage of advancements in technology, establish markets for their goods, secure raw materials for their factories, offer credit to their friends, and assert power over the weak. By the time World War I broke out, both countries had already experienced victories and acquired new territories and were on the threshold of assuming new roles in relation to the established powers, which were to emerge from the war debilitated and in debt.[8] These developments defined the parameters of foreign policy relations between the two nations as exemplified by the stance each took in the famous immigration controversy at the turn of the century.

Seeking to participate as an equal in the Western capitalist world, between 1891 and 1909 Japan took measures to regulate emigration to the continental United States, whether directly or via Hawaii, Canada, or Mexico. The government determined that only people worthy of representing a growing, imperial East Asian nation be approved for travel to the United States. They should not be "low class" or "densely ignorant." Japan eventually settled on a policy in 1908 that officially separated Japanese travelers into two specific passport categories: hi-imin (nonmigrant) and imin (migrant).[9] The manner in which the nation devised the hi-imin/imin policy sheds light on a neglected yet highly significant dimension of U.S.-Japanese relations.

Hi-imin was a new term designating a person who neither was a laborer nor intended to engage in labor once in the United States. The label served to differentiate students, professionals, merchants, clerks—people with ostensibly respectable class background, education, and status—from imin, the laborers. Although theoretically hi-imin did not intend to settle permanently in the United States, there were hi-imin who became permanent settlers and therefore could be considered emigrants. The literal translation of the terms into English creates confusion as to the specificity of the categories, for they were not cut and dried and gave rise to some ambiguities. The attempts by the Japanese government to issue passports only to hi-imin proved unworkable in the long run, for human ingenuity and error overrode any rules and regulations. In addition, there was no guarantee that hi-imin who were not employed by a Japanese firm or the government or enrolled in an American educational institution would engage only in nonlaboring occupations, become students, or remain temporarily in the United States. Prejudice in the United States, anxiety, and discouragement effectively diminished their original intentions and status.

The concept of hi-imin began evolving in the last decade of the nineteenth century, when Japanese laborers first entered the United States. It can be traced to the Chinese, who utilized it beginning in 1882, when the United States passed its first exclusion act against Chinese laborers.[10] Thereafter the U.S. government allowed entry only to Chinese whom the Chinese government certified as "other than laborers." The Japanese government, acutely aware that the United States could subject its citizens to the same treatment, worked to initiate its own restrictive action and avoid being subject to the exclusionary actions of a foreign power. Convinced and satisfied that its military, industrial, and political capacities surpassed China's, Japan made it known to U.S. officials that individuals who received passports to go to the United States were not of the "lowly Chinese" type—they were citizens of a rising competitor nation.[11] Furthermore, from the Japanese government's standpoint, the wave of emigration to the United States never assumed the major economic and political importance of the imperialist push into East Asia.[12] Japan's main object in its relationship with the United States was to maintain friendliness while carrying out that push.

In order to live up to its new world role and to guarantee that its citizens properly represented it as a modern nation, the Japanese government issued a series of laws to regulate the emigration of individuals to the United States. Publications for emigrants to the United States consistently stressed that only solid and honest individuals who believed in "family," who could call their wives and children to join them and thereby help foster good Japanese-U.S. relations, should be encouraged to go.[13] They should not exhibit the behavior of the earlier, "animal-like" emigrants to the United States, who "picked their teeth, picked their noses, scratched their heads, and undressed in public."[14] These were the habits of the "lazy" residents from the provinces, who "work one day and take off three, work three days and take off a week."[15] Emigrants must be prepared to behave in a "Western" manner and strive to "fit into American society."

We must seek to avoid clashes with customs. By striving to assimilate with white people social relationships can be moderated. If our compatriots desire individual success, they must forget that they are Japanese.... [I]f not, we will be treated as the Hawaiian Japanese immigrant and have to endure the shame of being called "Jap" from morning to night.[16]

The government's first statutory step regarding emigrants was the *Imin hogokisoku* (Emigrant protection ordinance) of 1894, a measure that, with minor changes, became the *Imin hogohō* (Emigrant protection law) of 1896.[17] Earlier, all travel had been subject to the *Kaigai ryokenkisoku* (Overseas passport ordinance) of 1878, which vested authority over passport applications in the Foreign Ministry and in government officials at the separately administered open-treaty ports.[18] A year after enactment of the Imin hogohō, a revised overseas passport ordinance transferred that responsibility to the ken and fu administrators, who were directed to review the travel requests of "those who go abroad (other than to China and Korea) for the purpose of labor."[19] The language in the Imin hogohō regulated the actions of emigrant agents, or *imin toriatsukainin*, who were defined as all "individuals and businesses who engaged in the recruiting of and securing passage for laborers to go abroad." U.S. immigration reports complained that the imin toriatsukainin had sent laborers as "steerage passengers" to the United States.[20] In addition, they had operated loosely and in some cases fraudulently by providing passports and promises of employment in the United States to Japanese agricultural laborers, convincing many "to sell everything they had in the world to pay their passage across the Pacific."[21]

The new law required agents to have a license from the local ken or fu administrative office, which also had to approve all agreements with imin. An agent had to deposit 10,000 yen to guard against nonfulfillment of the agreement or to provide return passage or financial aid in the United States if needed.[22] Agents' fees were not to exceed amounts established by the government, and they were prohibited from receiving gifts of money or goods. The local administrators were responsible for limiting the activities and number of emigrant agents and companies as well as preventing abuses of the law.

Though issued for the purpose of "emigrant protection" and not specifically forbidding laborers from emigrating, the law established financial requirements for those wishing to go abroad. The requirements frequently went unobserved, however. Ironically, it was the detailed nature of the law that made infractions possible.[23] In fact, an emigration publication of 1902 advised would-be imin that passport practices differed in the forty-three ken and three fu, prompting some ingenious individuals to move to another area or to change their honseki to ken where their applications would be approved more readily.[24] Others achieved the same goal by entering into marriages of convenience with people already holding required passports, changing names, forging documents, stealing, or acquiring travel papers from relatives, friends, acquaintances, or middlemen who provided them for a fee. It is significant that the number of emigration companies increased considerably following the promulgation of the Imin hogohō.[25] Innkeepers, sailors, captains of ships, outfitters, ticket agents, labor recruiters, and a wide array of imin toriatsukainin were ready to accept handouts in exchange for passage (or, in many cases, empty promises), even though the law specifically forbade bribes. Unsuspecting victims would be swindled into paying exorbitant sums for passports or passage, traveling to Kobe or Yokohama to wait in boardinghouses they could ill afford for boats that never came. Horror stories abounded of scalpers and cheats accumulating money from imin. The sums that could be gained through such infractions tended to make trivial the most punitive article in the Imin hogohō.

The current of imin and profits flowed back and forth across the Pacific.[26] In early 1900 the foreign minister apprised his officers in the Commerce Section that the Northern Railway Company and the Oriental Trading Company had negotiated an agreement to import 2,500 Japanese laborers into the United States.[27] Transmigration from Hawaii to the U.S. mainland, denounced and partially cut off by the

United States in 1907, provided another source of imin, and others came via British Columbia and Mexico.[28] Another group of emigrants, loosely called *jiyū-imin* (free emigrants) to differentiate them from imin under contract, also journeyed to America, sometimes with the help of the emigration companies but more often by accumulating financial means independently.[29] With newly scheduled routes to Seattle and San Francisco, the Nippon Yūsen Kaisha (NYK) and the Tōyō Kisen Kaisha became formidable competitors of the U.S.-owned Pacific Mail Steamship Line, Occidental and Oriental Steamship Company, and Northern Pacific Steamship Company. NYK made an auspicious start by monopolizing (ironically, with Japanese government sanction) emigrant transportation rights to Hawaii and became the leading trans-Pacific passenger line.[30] Third-class fare to San Francisco, which was $46 in 1895, dropped to $25 in 1903 and increased only slightly to $30 in 1906.[31] Everywhere along the way, from the towns and villages the imin left to the farms and work camps in the United States, intermediaries of every conceivable variety made a few dollars, some a few hundred dollars or more.[32] The number of passports issued for travel to the mainland United States steadily increased, from 1,764 in 1896 to 10,562 in 1900. Laborers constituted 62 percent of the total in 1896 and 84 percent in 1900.[33] Thus, while officialdom attempted to curb the emigrant trade, economic factors spurred it to expand.

Alarmed that the "right kind of people" were not going to the United States, the Japanese government ordered on August 2, 1900, that "a total ban on the travel of all imin to North America and Canada be enforced temporarily."[34] Periodically it communicated with ken and fu officials to reiterate the ban and directed its consuls in the United States and Canada to "exercise strict control" over individuals who "emigrated with the intent of engaging in labor" or who assumed "designations other than laborers."[35] In order to frustrate imin attempts to move to ken where passport applications could be approved more easily, the government limited the issuance of travel permissions to persons who had lived in a particular ken or fu for more than six months. As a consequence, the emigration figures for laborers to the United States shrank considerably. In 1901 the government issued only 1,986 passports, less than 19 percent of the 10,562 it had issued in 1900.[36] During the next half-decade laborers received only 6 to 7 percent of all passports issued to Japanese individuals destined for the United States. Then a reversal set in, with the ratio of laborers rising dramatically to 20 percent in 1905 and steadily climbing until 1908.[37] The government realized that unless it explicitly defined who qualified for the category of "other than laborers," imin would continue to obtain passports for travel to the United States.

In July 1904 Foreign Affairs Vice Minister Chinda Sutemi sent a confidential communication to the governor of Hokkaidō, the chief of the Tokyo metropolitan police, and the ken and fu governors.[38] Citing the August 1900 ban on the travel of laborers, he criticized its "unintentional effect" on "authentic merchants, students, and other useful nonlaborers," which impeded "the promotion of overseas trade." In order for merchants and students to have flexibility, the government would have to establish and strictly control criteria for travel. According to Chinda, there were four categories of legitimate nonlaborers, or *hirōdōsha:* those engaged in commerce; students; individuals wishing to go to the United States to study its commerce, industry, and agriculture; and those with "special authorization" from the government. All travelers had to have sufficient funds, at least eleven years of education or appropriate technical training, employment prospects as clerks or technicians in commercial houses, and fluency in English.[39] Wives and minor children of imin already in the United States were included among those allowed to emigrate.

Although the definitions seemed explicit enough, they were still subject to interpretation. Japan needed a degree of flexibility so it could send people abroad to acquire skills, technical information, and business know-how and to gain experience in negotiating, selling, buying, and living in the West. Numerous inspection teams, including representatives from a variety of governmental bureaus, trade associations, business firms, manufacturing concerns, scientific groups, educational institutions, dairy farm associations, and transportation agencies, journeyed across the Pacific to learn firsthand the basis of U.S. wealth and prestige. Knowledge acquired through foreign travel would help prepare Japanese nationals to assume the positions of the many highly paid foreign technicians in Japan. As a result, laborers continued to acquire passports to the United States simply by stating that their objectives for travel were business or education. In November 1905 Chinda circulated another memorandum regarding student applicants and warned that officials were being too lax;[40] they must verify that applicants attesting to having ample educational funds used those funds, "without question, for the pursuit of knowledge." However, Chinda emphasized that all bona fide students be given every "convenience and accommodation" in keeping with the concept of unrestricted travel for "civilized" individuals and scholars.

Chinda's memos revealed the government's dilemma. It had no objection to the restriction of imin emigration. The problem was how to devise a foolproof method of differentiating between imin and hi-imin. Who would be responsible for implementing the policy—Japan or a foreign government? In the case of the latter, Japanese leaders were determined not to undergo the humiliation of the Chinese, who had to abide by "incredibly elastic" U.S.-defined barriers.[41] Pride and necessity dictated that the decision and action rest with Japan, not the United States. The Americans were aware of this, for as early as 1892 a U.S. diplomat to Japan told his superiors that the Japanese feared exclusion laws and would "seek to keep their laborers from going where they [were] not welcome."[42] In 1899 the commissioner of immigration in San Francisco wrote approvingly of the Japanese government's intention to investigate the character of the emigrants because they were "an index of the nation at home."[43]

Another significant factor in Japan's thinking was strategic. Given the political drama unfolding in East Asia, it was important that good relations be maintained with the United States. The Russo-Japanese War cost significantly more than the Sino-Japanese War, and the nation was faced with increasing military expenses, territorial acquisitions to develop, and a worrisome balance-of-payment problem. Foreign borrowing was considerable and used primarily to buy materials and equipment for industry and armaments.[44] Japan needed time and was in no position to defy the United States. It therefore sought to restrict imin emigration.

In February 1907 Japan took the initiative to remove "the feeling of irritation" and advised U.S. officials that it desired to enter into "some arrangement on the subject."[45] It was clear that the government's main concern was to curb imin emigration. In November U.S. Ambassador Thomas J. O'Brien proposed that all Japanese in the United States be required to register at the nearest Japanese consular office within one year of their arrival or be deported.[46] Reflecting the "precise attitude" of the secretary of state, the communication directed the Japanese government to keep tabs on its citizens in the United States and to ensure that they did not engage in labor.

A month later the Japanese government responded, calling the U.S. proposal impractical and unfair.[47] Excluding Hawaii, Foreign Minister Hayashi Tadasu pointed out, there were more than 100,000 Japanese scattered in consular districts covering "several hundred miles" in the United States, and the consular offices had little knowledge of their whereabouts. A large number of them surely would fail to register on time. Legal and peaceful residents, he protested, must not be subjected to "indignity and humiliation" and an "intolerable amount of injustice" comparable to the "rigorous measures of personal examination and vexatious identification as on the occasion of entry." He characterized the ineffectiveness of the Japanese ban on laborers as "partial," suggesting that it was "not so complete a failure" as the U.S. ambassador claimed. Mistakes, which were "natural and inevitable," were attributable to "inexperience . . . not to wilful dereliction of duty."

This situation had to be remedied, of course, but Hayashi denied that American laborers on the Pacific Coast had suffered because of unfair Japanese competition. In fact, Americans received wages "nowhere higher than there." Hayashi pointed out that even when the Japanese immigration figures were at their highest, the U.S. figures were overblown, surpassing those of Japan, which included laborers going in the "guise of merchants or students." In fact, he said, the annual number of Japanese immigrants "never, at its greatest flood, equalled . . . the number of immigrants who frequently enter in one day at the port of New York." As for anti-Japanese attacks by U.S. citizens, Hayashi stated: "The domestic control and restriction of emigrants are purely administrative functions, and confer no power upon the Japanese government to agree in advance that the evasion of such control and restriction at home, or in violation of similar laws or registration abroad, shall deprive the culprit of the protection guaranteed to him by treaty." Hayashi was not about to ignore any U.S. infringement of the international agreement. It was the responsibility of the U.S. government to give fair and equal treatment to "culprits."

Hayashi's oversolicitous regard for Japanese subjects in the United States served notice that Japan was a newly emergent and independent power in East Asia. The tone of the communication was not apologetic but straightforward, asserting that Japan sought a solution to the problem of imin emigration and that U.S. suggestions of Japan's failure were exaggerated. However, Hayashi also took care to express the nation's willingness to listen to U.S. demands, a position that skillfully juggled two contradictory stances. It was both assertive and acquiescent. More important, his use of the word "culprits" to indicate imin indicated that the Japanese government shared the U.S. prejudice against laborers as less than equal members of society and had no qualms about unequivocally eliminating their travel. Viewed in this light, Hayashi's altruistic defense of his citizens becomes an empty gesture. The imin issue was merely a tool used in achieving broader foreign policy goals.

Reinforcing such a view was the Japanese government's internal correspondence, which, in comparison to its correspondence with the United States, displayed a notable lack of regard for imin. Reports, correspondence, orders, memoranda—all insisted that labor emigrants be barred from leaving for the United States. Japanese representatives in the United States pleaded with the Foreign Ministry to stop the flow, and the Foreign Office issued to its consular officials numerous orders that were strikingly similar in content. The officials were "not to grant passports" and "not to recognize valid passports" and should "detail an official to the Mexican-U.S. border." However, no measure was comprehensive enough, and imin continued to make their way to the United States.

On February 18, 1908, one year after Hayashi's initial letter stating that Japan wished to come to "some arrangement" on the subject of imin, Hayashi acceded to the U.S. demand for registration of Japanese citizens, although here again his tone was conciliatory but authoritative, cooperative but somewhat conditional.

[T]he Imperial Government . . . are averse to adding to the obligations already incumbent on such Japanese subjects another obligation, which might under easily supposable circumstances work unmerited hardship. At the same time they fully realize the value of frank and harmonious cooperation . . . [and] will establish a system of registration as soon as practicable. . . . [W]hile no effort will be spared to make the registration as complete as possible, the Imperial Government will not consider that the absence of registration constitutes a reason for the forfeiture of residential rights.[48]

He agreed to the United States's demands for registration of Japanese citizens because it seemed "one of the most effective means of preventing fraud" and "the strongest safeguard of the rights" of merchants or students who were forced to resort to labor "through some unanticipated misfortune." Hayashi's decision reflected Japan's desire to avoid rupturing the "traditional friendship" between the two nations. A year earlier the Berlin press had forecast an international crisis between Japan and the United States, and in 1907 talk of war had begun to circulate freely in U.S. newspapers. Sources of the rumors were placed variously in Germany, France, and the White House.[49] In mid-1907 the White House had announced the forthcoming cruise of the U.S. Pacific fleet in Asian waters. Japanese reactions were many, but pragmatic considerations limited the government's options. Japan was not in a position to confront the United States militarily, and in March 1908 it extended an invitation to the fleet as a gesture of friendship.[50]

In this atmosphere, the registration system was formally established by law in May 1909, a little over a year after Hayashi's initial agreement to the U.S. proposal.[51] Theoretically, the Japanese government now had the means to oversee and make an official accounting of its citizens in the United States. New arrivals had to register at the Japanese consulate within seven days. A passport, or *koseki* (household registry), and one or more witnesses were needed to verify identification. Registration entitled individuals to a certificate of residency. Those failing to register could be denied a certificate, though the consequences of not having one were not specified. Citizens already resident had to register by September of the following year.

Before the system was established, the Japanese government calculated the number of emigrants to the United States from the number of passports issued. Persons not leaving Japan within six months after being issued a passport had to return it.[52] Once abroad, each citizen had to reregister with the consular office every ten years, although available evidence does not indicate that this was done with regularity. The system was most effective in recording those who left and later returned to Japan. It did not provide a rigorous means of accounting for citizens in the United States.[53]

As Hayashi had predicted in his memorandum, the registration system proved difficult to implement. The government sent detailed instructions to its consulates in the United States and Canada regarding the system's execution: recording information on cards for each individual; filing according to honseki; color-coding for males and females; writing names in Japanese and Roman characters; providing space for changes of address.[54] The consulates wrote the Foreign Ministry requesting advice on various significant questions as well as matters of bureaucratic detail: "What happens to those who are away or busy and cannot register?"; "Aren't Japanese nationals being denied nationality if a certificate is not issued to nonregistrants?"; "Please authorize the consular office to purchase additional filing cabinets." The New York consul complained that Japanese citizens could not be located and that Japanese steamship companies should be asked to provide information on ticket sales. The San Francisco consul sent a clipping from a local Japanese-language newspaper criticizing the process, noting that the only people registering were those desiring to travel again and those of draft age who could avoid conscription in Japan by going abroad and registering annually.[55] The article also denounced the Japanese Association of America (which was organized in part to aid the government in the registration drive), claiming that one emigrant was denied a certificate unless he paid a fee to the association.[56] Because the regulations stipulated that an organization "designated by the Consulate" could serve as a witness for registrants, membership in the association became an unstated prerequisite for any applicant. Nonmembers had to be sponsored by two association-appointed witnesses. From the available evidence it is impossible to determine the success of the registration process or the percentage of registered individuals, but doubtless it was a thankless task for officials and a bothersome one for citizens.

After almost eighteen years, the Japanese government brought the imin issue to a resolution, or so it thought, with a final set of instructions to local administrative offices regarding the issuance of passports.[57] In November 1908, nine months after Hayashi informed the United States that Japan was instituting the registration system, the term *hi-imin* was introduced for the first time to define explicitly people other than imin. This category was to end the many "divergences" and misinterpretations of earlier years by "more strictly supervis[ing] travel to the United States and Canada." With the imin and hi-imin designations, the Japanese government differentiated "culprits" from "gentlemen"—those whom it considered laborers, both skilled and unskilled, "who have less opportunity for cultivation," from those of the "educated classes," who theoretically did not intend to settle permanently in the United States.

The imin/hi-imin concept had been articulated by U.S. Ambassador O'Brien three months before, at a gala dinner held by the Japan Society in New York in August 1908. He spoke briefly about the immigration controversy: "[I]t becomes a serious question to determine where the line between laborer and the gentleman must be drawn."[58] The critical issue was the "line." Earlier in the year O'Brien had apprised Hayashi of the U.S. definitions of skilled and unskilled laborers, listing a number of "essentially physical" and "less physical" or "neither manual nor mechanical" occupations.[59] Hayashi had replied to O'Brien that the Japanese government found nothing "inapplicable" in these definitions.[60] However, in the instructions of November 1908 to local administrators, the government did not define imin by occupation. Rather, it identified specific groups of people whose passport applications should be rejected: imin who returned to Japan and stayed longer than six months; women suspected of intending to commit "illegal acts such as prostitution"; women married to imin and registered in the koseki less than six months; children older than seventeen; and adopted female children who were legally part of the imin's family and less than five years old. Adopted male children who were considered legitimate family heirs were not mentioned. Thus, even though the categories of imin and hi-imin were established, their definitions did not specify occupations and were so vague as to allow for misinterpretation, misunderstanding, or error.

A lengthy section of the instructions on imin covered what the Americans had claimed was a much abused category: "settled agriculturalist," a person who operated "under the ownership or leasehold of a joint investment enterprise and thus had considerable financial means."[61] Much to the embarrassment of the Japanese government, farm laborers had been hired by "settled agriculturalists" and brought from Japan. The November 1908 instructions directed local Japanese authorities to investigate the financial condition and personal histories of those identified as "settled agriculturalists" and enforce the "strictest and most minute restrictions." Significantly, with the new instructions the Japanese government subjected its emigrant passport applicants to the same "indignity and humiliation" for which they had criticized the United States earlier.

This investigative technique also became the approved method in determining the legality of hi-imin passport applications. On the assumption that persons "other than imin" were numerous, diverse, and "impossible to specify by law," local officials were to submit reports to the Foreign Ministry on an applicant's background, conduct, and financial standing. Administrators were warned to use the "utmost vigilance" and "common sense," empowering them with sweeping authority to elicit information in judging a passport applicant's truthfulness. By delving into an individual's life and motives, the government determined whether an applicant could be considered hi-imin.

The general rule was that, to qualify as hi-imin, applicants had to have proof of adequate financial means and at least a middle school education or similar training. In the case of students, it was imperative that the authorities differentiate between "truthful and fraudulent" applicants. They should ignore the misconception that only children of upper-class families studied abroad, for less well-to-do students often duped government officials into believing that they were "gentlemen." Students preferring a U.S. education over a European one had to present convincing arguments for their choice, for not only was the former costlier than the latter, but educational standards were "higher" and the facilities "more comprehensive" in Europe than in the United States. Furthermore, the cost of living in the United States exceeded the cost of living in England, France, or Germany.

Merchants and individuals wishing to engage in commerce had to have "direct connections" with a business concern in their area of destination, have a thriving trade, prove their practical business background, and possess capital. To bring employees from Japan, the branch office abroad had to verify its "clear and unequivocal" need to hire, and employees had to possess "considerable business experience" and education. Persons who desired to go on inspection tours of industry, agriculture, or finance needed to have "extensive educational backgrounds" or provide proof of outstanding experience in their field. Entrepreneurs had to have reliable financial backing. Those with only a middle school or similar education could not be expected "even remotely" to carry out the responsibilities relating to mature businesses and therefore were to be rejected.

Under these instructions local administrators held substantial discretionary power to gather information on an applicant's finances, education, experience, and conduct. The result was that the competence, tact, and opinion of an individual government administrator determined whether one was granted a passport or not. Officials' decisions could be based on nothing more than inference, hearsay, or reputation. Most significant, the instructions sanctioned the separating of travelers into two categories and the assignment of labels that followed emigrants to the United States. This system legitimized class differences emerging in capitalist Japan. According to the Japanese constitution of 1889, society consisted of commoners and nobility, but the government's definition of the imin/hi-imin categories implied that there were more desirable and less desirable commoners. All laborers, whether skilled or unskilled, were imin and thus denigrated. Students, merchants, and professionals were hi-imin, people whose superior class background permitted their traveling to the United States. However, regarding their settling permanently in the United States, hi-imin found themselves in a precarious and ambiguous position.[62] On legal Japanese records they were hi-imin, but in the United States they were simply "Orientals"; their hi-imin status did not give them immunity from racist affronts or discrimination. In fact, to Americans the distinction between imin and hi-imin was nonexistent.

The imin/hi-imin system devised by Japan during the years from

1891 to 1909 did not arise in a vacuum. Born of the imin controversy, nurtured by political trends in Japan and the United States, and mirroring the class image of modern capitalist society, it reflected the Japanese government's desire to assert its pride, independence, and integrity, to counteract U.S. actions that diminished its status in the world of power politics, and to maintain control over its citizens. Nevertheless, Japan's system of passport designations turned out to be only a stopgap measure. Japanese officials were erratic at best in categorizing citizens. The standards and definitions seemed unambiguous but in practice were impossible to apply consistently. There were always gray areas. Despite the Japanese government's efforts, beginning with the Imin hogohō in 1896, the temporary restriction of imin emigration to the United States in 1900, Chinda's memos of 1904 and 1905, Hayashi's agreeing to establish a registration system in February 1908, and the Japanese government's instructions to local governors in November 1908, it was clear that the banning of laborers could be achieved only by banning *all* Japanese immigrants. The only way a part of the people could be excluded was by excluding all. The United States took that most extreme of actions in 1924, removing from Japan the responsibility for keeping "undesirable" citizens from emigrating.

CHAPTER 4

Changing City, Changing Lives

In June 1901 the city of Tokyo passed an ordinance forbidding citizens to venture outside of their homes without footwear.[1] The stated intent was to improve public hygiene, but it seems more likely that, in keeping with the crucial political, economic, and military goals set by the architects of Meiji Japan, the concern was for the appearance of *kindai Nippon* (modern Japan).[2] This concern was the social complement to the nation's geopolitical objectives, which, once achieved, would guarantee it a position of equality with the industrial capitalist countries. This ordinance reflected the many others that, from the early Meiji period on, prescribed proper action for members of a unified, homogeneous, orderly, and above all urbane society. Limitations were placed on behaviors such as mixed-gender bathing or nakedness, which up to that time had not been considered unusual or unnatural.[3] Lifestyles were being altered, not only because of Japan's push to become a wealthy capitalist power but also because the government made specific demands that people assume different roles now than in the past. The process was no more convulsive than changes wrought in other times or places, but it was difficult nevertheless. Countless aspects of Japanese citizens' daily material and affective lives—their ways of acting, thinking, experiencing, evaluating, responding, and relating with each other—were being transformed.

One of the changes that occurred in Tokyo was the construction of an urban mentality. Born of an indigenous Tokugawa city culture, it converged with the outlook of the many who came to Tokyo from the provinces. More important, it was colored by the drive to create kindai Nippon. Japan was not an exception to the rule that great shifts of population take place during periods of industrialization; statistics show that the non-native-born population of Tokyo hovered between one-third and one-half of the total between 1891 and 1920.[4] From 1898 to 1907 between 40,000 and 60,000 people migrated to Tokyo annually, twice as many as the number of migrants to Osaka.[5] In 1908, 60 percent of Tokyo's population and 65 percent of its labor force was non-native.[6] In addition to the classic rural-to-urban migration of the agricultural poor, young and ambitious individuals flocked to the city seeking entry into middle schools, colleges, and universities, the government bureaucracy, businesses, and the publishing and literary worlds.[7] They were not the elite but those aspiring to the *chūryūkaikyū* (middle class), a designation coined shortly before the Sino-Japanese War. Their response to social change in Meiji Japan was to move to the city with the expectation that life would improve, a crucial factor in the shaping of the new mentality of the Tokyo citizen. Large-scale relocation took place in the opposite direction, too, as city people moved to the provinces as teachers, administrators, and the like. They constituted part of the national unification effort by the state to educate and homogenize, an important facet of the shifts of population taking place throughout the country. For these people, coming *from* Tokyo conferred special status and privileges; the appellation *Tōkyōjin*—native of Tokyo—became increasingly common after the Sino-Japanese War. In the early Meiji years this designation was not consciously class-defined, although implicitly it had to do with class, for it called attention to a new breed of people who strove to adjust and conform to changing economic and social conditions. The fact that they came from the capital city, not "the country," signified their circumstances rather than their class aspirations.

The concept of the city as a distinctive and influential place was not new, but its role as the birthplace of a national culture to be disseminated to the rest of the nation was. The pioneering folk anthropologist Yanagita Kunio, writing in 1929, observed that in the past the emblems of knowledge—books and education—originated in the capital city, Kyoto, and could be appreciated only by the confident and ambitious who, "with book bags on their backs," traveled to the city to acquire learning.[8] Kyoto was "precious," the one city in the whole country until foreign trade and commerce spurred the growth of other cities.[9]

The literate were the agents of Kyoto culture, which was to be unconsciously absorbed or consciously imitated. However, the city did not have an exclusive and "inseparable relationship" with learning and the arts, for the roots of these endeavors reverted to the ancient rural past, long before cities became part of the landscape: "They go back to ancient times when each one of our ancestors resided among the rice fields. These themes were piled into flower baskets from remote places to end up decorating the homes of aristocrats."[10] In this process, two currents developed—"folk" and "aristocratic." The former became vilified as "vulgar," whereas the latter was esteemed as "refined" and flourished as the sole representation of the culture of the city. Yanagita lamented the arbitrary subordination of folk culture and dedicated his whole life to discovering, exploring, and revitalizing Japanese folk traditions. In *Toshi to nōson* he assessed contemporary politicians as "unequivocally shallow" in matters concerning culture and criticized their establishment of Tokyo as the rallying point for education, writing, and all other forms of the arts merely because that city was the locus of governmental power.

The transformation Yanagita wrote about is a point of departure in defining the Tokyojin. The urban/rural dichotomy still prevailed, but in kindai Japan culture was to derive from the city; it was no longer "folk."[11] The urban shoved its way into the rural, and the provinces became the recipient of Tokyo's influence, far more pervasive because the national mentality originated as state policy in Tokyo. That process, in turn, gave existence and meaning to the Tokyojin, a species qualitatively different from citizens of other cities and areas in Japan. They possessed a strong geographic alliance, a sense of superiority, an attitude of tolerance or disdain toward those from less well-endowed localities, and an acute awareness that they were natives of the political, economic, and ideological center of the nation. The modern Tokyojin, however, was not a descendant of the *Edokko* (native of Edo) of the previous period, nor an elegant and polished product reborn from the old Edo culture, a factor that made it easier in some ways to assume modern qualities.[12] The use of the word *Tokyo* divorced the Tokyojin from their pre-Meiji counterparts.[13] The old Tokugawa regime had been overthrown by forces from the provinces, and the Meiji government was in the hands of outsiders.[14] Likewise, the old Tokugawa nobility was replaced by another, curious and even willing to take on some ways of "the barbarians." Edo signified a past that had run its course and a culture that had diminished. Tokyo signified the present and the future—Meiji, not Tokugawa. By early Taisho the meaning of Tokyojin had established itself firmly in the minds of the Japanese people.

The geographic mind-set of the Tokyojin is described vividly in *Botchan,* a satirical 1906 novel by Natsume Sōseki (1867–1916) about a young man from Tokyo who goes to teach in a distant provincial school.[15] As a Tokyojin, he reacts with scorn, based on preconceived notions about the area and its people. His initial impressions are as follows:

> As the boat came to a stop with a deep blast of its siren, a barge pulled away from the shore and made towards us. The lighterman was completely naked except for a red loincloth. What a barbaric place! Though, of course, nobody could have worn a kimono in that heat. . . . The place was a fishing village and looked about the size of the Ōmori area in Tokyo. What a fool they'd taken me for to bring me here! No one could stand a place like this. . . .
>
> When we arrived I was also the first to jump ashore and, grabbing a snotty-nosed kid who was standing there, I asked him where the middle school was. He looked blank and said he didn't know. Dimwitted clod! How could anybody not know where the school was in a pint-sized place like this?[16]

The superiority and arrogance of this young Tokyojin was not unusual. During the middle Meiji and Taisho years, various features that defined kindai Japan came to be concentrated in Tokyo. In addition to being chosen as the seat of government in 1868, the city became the central location of banks and houses of finance, many business establishments, prestigious universities, the book-publishing world, the chemical, paper, and machinery industries, and almost every other major field of social and economic endeavor. Osaka retained a key position in the national economy as a commercial city with a sizable textile industry, but it lost its status as the chief financial center to Tokyo in the early Meiji period.[17] The big fire of 1872, dubbed "the blossom of Tokyo," engulfed the heart of the city and destroyed old feudal structures, government buildings, and official residences.[18] It prompted the requirement that new construction in the center of Tokyo be of bricks or stone. Under the supervision of a British engineer, a brick-paved road, one of the first of its kind and later the major shopping street in the Ginza area, was completed in 1877.[19] Army headquarters, the police office, and a community of European-style government buildings appeared one by one in the large, razed space near the Imperial Palace. The construction of "Mitsubishi Londontown," a bastion for the business and financial combine, began in 1892 and lasted until 1905.[20] This area, known today as Marunouchi, was adjacent to the Imperial Palace and the site of the soon-to-be established Tokyo Central Station, the transportation hub of the nation.

As Edo, Tokyo had been the home of the Tokugawa shogun government, but its choice as the new capital placed it in direct contrast to the old capital of Kyoto. It was designed not to have the latter's detached, aristocratic, and aesthetic quality, which was important only in the execution of official and formal pronouncements and rituals. Tokyo was to assume a far more prominent place as the showplace of the nation, nurturing a political and economic existence appropriate to a modern capital city. A formal Tokyo metropolitan government was set up, enabling the city to operate as an autonomous unit and subordinating any semblance of self-government.[21] This was the same as other political units in Japan, but Tokyo's position as the capital gave it an exclusive and unique identity that no city—Osaka, Nagoya, or Kyoto—could claim.[22]

One of Tokyo's legacies was the relationship of people to space. The city was by far the most crowded in the country. A population of more than a million in the 1890s doubled to more than 2 million by 1920 and, if suburban expansion is taken into consideration, tripled to over 3 million.[23] The center of mercantile Edo, home to the merchants, craftspeople, and laborers who catered to the aristocrats and their followers in the Tokugawa period, was squeezed onto the two banks of the Sumida River, which ran from north to south in the eastern part of the city. It still remained crowded in the Meiji period, even as the population expanded and the metropolitan border stretched toward the suburban south, west, and north. The density of this section, Shitamachi (low district), was never alleviated.[24] In 1903 two-thirds of Tokyo's total population and close to three-quarters of the dwellings were in Shitamachi. In 1920, 60 percent of Tokyo's people lived there.[25]

Parts of Shitamachi remained the marketplace of the city, but its identity was transformed by new ways of conducting commerce and utilizing capital. The demise of the Tokugawa economy, the opening up of the country to foreign trade, and the subsequent outflow of gold and silver proved a fatal blow to the powerful merchants and wholesalers who had reaped profits by manipulating money and credit. Two large establishments dating back to the Edo period were able to survive the traumatic changes of the early Meiji period by actively supporting and financing undertakings for the new government.[26] Some lesser merchants lived on their reputations for awhile, but as it became clear that the clientele was changing, their operations changed, too. The first department store made its appearance in 1886, to be followed by Mitsukoshi, formerly the two-century old Mitsui textile outlet, Echigoya.[27] These stores adapted to mercantile transformations and catered to increasing numbers of urban customers by stocking a variety of consumer items, including kimono and an assortment of Western merchandise—clothing, hats, and leather goods. They displayed them in show windows and glass cases, utilized a variety of advertisement methods, and offered entertainment in the stores, thereby cultivating a consumer consciousness that recast material whims as "firm decisions"—a pressing need to buy.[28] This was a far cry from the personal, formal, and less ostentatious practice of bringing goods from a storehouse and presenting them to a customer, a form of selling that depended upon the individual merchant's perspicacity and sociability. Eventually the shopping district adjoined the financial, business, and government districts of the city, which had entrenched themselves next to the Imperial Palace.[29] In many ways, much of Shitamachi retained the character of old Edo. Rows of merchant houses, elegant restaurants, and houses of pleasure that had catered to the Tokugawa elite now were patronized by high-level government officials and businessmen.[30] These houses gained reputations and profits by clinging to old ways of commerce and leisure and a strong sense of identification with Edo.

The eastern part of Shitamachi became the industrial area, emitting odors, noise, and dirt that had been unfamiliar two decades before. People congregated to work and live or, if work was unavailable, to loaf. By mid-Meiji, the largest slums in Tokyo festered there.[31] Epidemics of cholera, typhoid fever, smallpox, and dysentery occurred with greater frequency beginning in the 1890s, consequences of overcrowding, poor sanitation, and urban industrialization. Tokyo's death rate from pulmonary tuberculosis, also called "worker's cough" or "worker's lung," became the highest in the country.[32] Disease, deterioration, and impoverishment were the by-products of industrial Shitamachi, which had been a bustling center in pre-Meiji Edo.

In 1890 Tokyo had only six factories with more than 300 workers, the largest being a printing factory with over 2,000 employees, four times larger than any other in the city. The majority of manufacturing plants in Tokyo, as in the rest of the country, were largely unmechanized, employed less than five workers, and produced domestic consumer items and textile goods for export. They retained prefactory organization methods, utilized local transportation and consumer services, and were not competitive with modern industry.[33] Labor relations remained like those in traditional merchant houses, with *oyakata* (master; literally, parent substitute)—labor bosses, foremen, or small shopowners—wielding control over apprentices and operatives in such areas as the distribution of work, work function, job protection, and housing, often for a percentage of their wages.[34] In 1897 the number of textile and machine shops increased markedly. Although economic growth was slowed temporarily by slumps at the turn of the century and immediately prior to World War I, Tokyo's importance in the production of machinery, machine tools, textiles, and a large variety of consumer items and its position in the printing trade were assured by the end of the Meiji era in 1912. World War I stimulated the growth of heavy industrial facilities, in which the factory system and modern wage labor began to take greater hold. These plants came to be concentrated in the Keihin region between Tokyo and the port of Yokohama, two cities connected by rail as early as 1872.[35] However, small-scale factories remained in Shitamachi.[36] Being a resource- and capital-poor country and wary of foreign investment, Japan had to combine a few key, large-scale industries capitalized by the government and a larger number of more modest, small-scale enterprises financed by private investors.[37]

Government capital was invested in finance, defense, transportation, and education, the foundations of an expanding imperial state. The nation's first major modern military assault on its Asian neighbor provided a shot in the arm. Aided by an improved banking system, continuing textile exports, sustained heavy taxation, and prudent borrowing of foreign capital, expenditures in military and colonial enterprises rose significantly.[38] By this time the government was shifting industrial and financial control to large business cliques that consistently directed their energies toward the building of national power. Nevertheless, economic development was skewed; even though Japan produced the largest battleships in the world in 1910, it was not until the 1930s that the nation achieved self-sufficiency in textile machinery or in the machine tool industry.[39]

The boundaries of the fifteen *ku* (wards) of Tokyo are said to have been based on topographical considerations (see Maps 2 and 3). Following the north-to-south ku boundaries that cut through the center of the city, we see a demarcation between Shitamachi and Yamanote (hill district), the eastern and western parts of Tokyo.[40] Shitamachi, as

Map 2. "Complete Map of Tokyo, Japan." By Arai Kisaburō (1894). 48×70 cm. From National Diet Library, Tokyo.

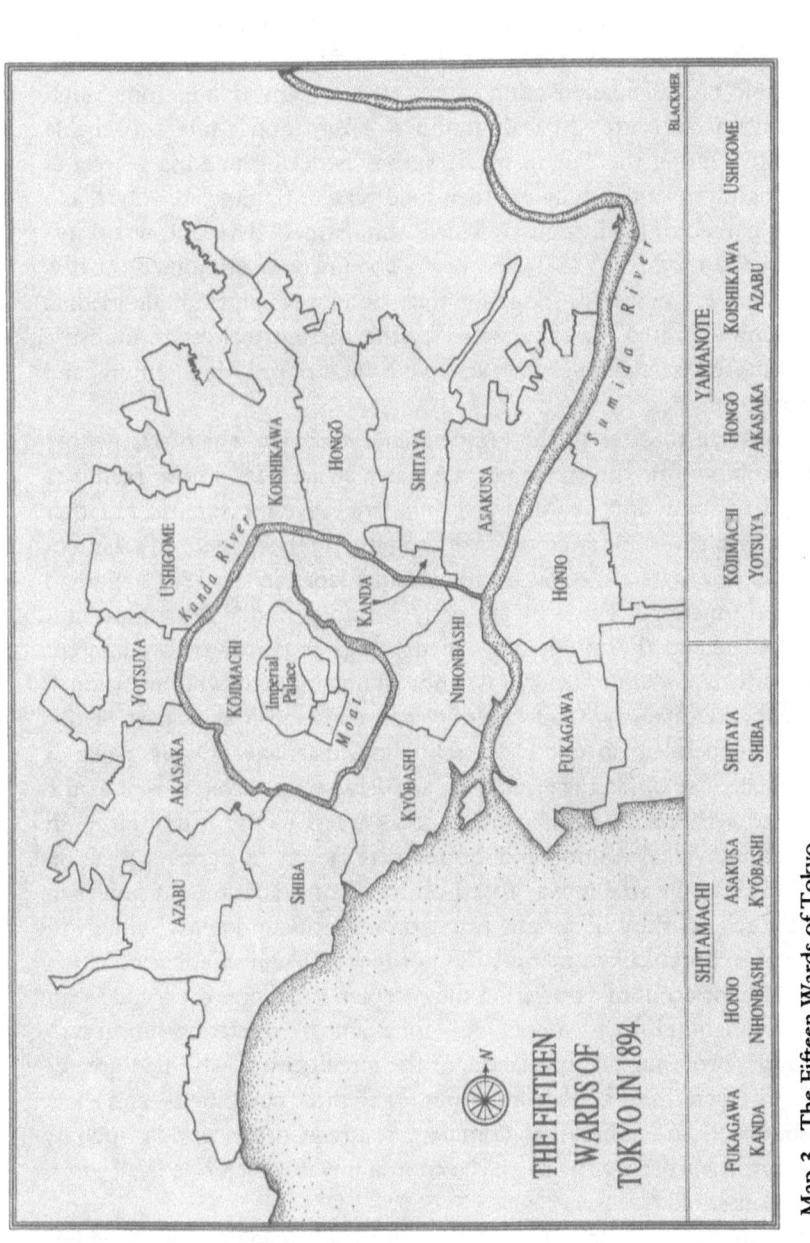

Map 3. The Fifteen Wards of Tokyo.

its name implied, was low and flat, the exact opposite of Yamanote, which before the 1890s boasted 800 hills, ridges, and valleys. The formidable task of maneuvering rickshaws and carts uphill from Shitamachi was an acute physical reminder of Yamanote's unapproachable quality. During the Tokugawa days, the district included large estates belonging to feudal lords and their followers, untrammeled woods, and large parcels of land, some of which were farmed. The land was transformed in the Meiji and Taisho years, when new wealth joined the old, farms slowly vanished, shopping areas developed, and middle-income housing appeared, hastily erected by the nascent real estate industry. Yamanote no longer was the exclusive habitat of pre-Meiji samurai and daimyo families.

It began to cater to the growing chūryūkaikyū, which was neither the nobility nor the laboring class but a social class whose members acquired status and wealth based on quantitative measurements rather than by birth or inheritance. Like the term *Tokyojin, chūryūkaikyū* began to designate a specific group in kindai Japan in the 1890s and had gained functional usage by the early Taisho period.[41] It is important to understand the multiplicity of meanings as perceived by different individuals, for chūryūkaikyū was not an uncontested, unidimensional, essentialist category. One's identity and consciousness as part of this group depended on one's job, schooling, marriage, friends, place of domicile, use of language, accent, and leisure activities, as well as the myriad activities of daily living, such as access to the marketplace, in which individual volition and desires were factors. A person's position in this class invariably was based on levels or gradations of power in social relationships in specific places or at specific moments. The gaining of a chūryūkaikyū identity did not mean the automatic acquisition of social or economic power; in the complex social order it could mean subordination in certain contexts—for example, in relationship to employers, professionals, specialists, or the intelligentsia, who had greater wealth, specialized knowledge, clout, or all three combined—and a less subjugated and sometimes dominant status in other worlds, such as among one's peers at work, in the community in which one lived, or in the household.

To many, however, living in Yamanote as a Tokyojin symbolized being part of the chūryūkaikyū. One-family homes were built in Yamanote and its adjacent suburban sections to attract the bureaucrats, military personnel, employees of business firms, journalists, and teachers—people who earned salaries, not wages, who were mobile, educated, achieving, and cognizant of contemporary and past social relationships and status. Mid-Meiji terminology such as *chūryūno jūka* (middle-class dwellings) and *chūryūmuki jūka* (dwellings suitable for the middle class) or, in late Meiji, *chūryū jūtaku* (middle-class residences) began to appear and became part of the standard vocabulary. These homes took on a private character different from that possessed by the majority of homes, which served as places of both work and rest.[42] To live in one's own house, regardless of how tiny, with a gate, a wall or fence, and small front yard was not a widespread goal at first, but as the middle-class population increased, it became something to pursue.[43] The urgency extended into living styles, for homes began to take on aspects of Western architecture. Magazines utilized the term *wayō* (Japanese-Western) to connote a new way of life, not a mere imitation of the West but a "recod[ing of] Western institutions and practices for indigenous Japanese consumption."[44] One architectural journal of 1898 instructed its male readers to: "furnish a large ten-mat room with a table and chair, keep a coal stove going in the winter, and upon returning home from the office, remove your suit jacket and don a maroon smoking jacket. Read a book as you grip a large British-style pipe between your teeth."[45]

On the surface this advice seemed to advocate an imitation of the West, but it cannot be interpreted so simply. Its symbolic meaning conveyed aspects of Japanese authority and authoritarianism, which state and private ideologues used in the complex process of redefining Japanese culture and constructing a national ideology. Authority was assumed in this short passage by its inclusion in a magazine specializing in architecture. Acknowledging that brick and stone structures were beyond middle-class incomes, the publication reminded its readers of the skill of historically trained Japanese craftsmen. They could construct wooden structures that integrated a wayō sensibility and style. A Japanese class-oriented material culture was thus legitimated and given authority. Authoritarianism was conveyed in the detailed (and seductive) description of how to effect a wayō *and* kindai way of life. Western accoutrements replaced Japanese things in a Japanese setting for afterwork leisure: a stove, not a hibachi (charcoal brazier); a pipe rather than a *kiseru* (Japanese-style pipe); a maroon smoking jacket in preference to a kimono. The article did not mention the price of the products or their availability. The implication was that anything less was not kindai enough; readers were left to figure out how to acquire such items. Similar to the 1901 ordinance that prescribed wearing footwear in public, these ideas cultivated the use of the products of technology to mold new attitudes, practices, and behavior, to recast Japanese culture. In this context, Yamanote connoted a way of life directly opposite that of Shitamachi, with its pockets of slums.

In the northern Yamanote wards—Hongō, Koishikawa, and Kanda—less affluent but intellectual and artistic families established their residences alongside the institutions of higher learning. Small areas of poverty existed, but they were not typical. By 1925 Yamanote was home to the rich, the fashionable, the intelligent, the cultured, and the modern. Establishing a residence there meant that one was middle class. Its two southwestern ku, Azabu and Akasaka, became the residential areas for foreign diplomats and business representatives.[46]

However, it is a mistake to assume that the boundaries of Shitamachi and Yamanote were unchanging or that their functions were exclusive of each other. The topography of Tokyo changed as hills were shaved, land was reclaimed, and buildings, rails, and roads were built. Both sections included areas that were not typical. Rigid categorizations such as "middle class" for Yamanote or "laboring class" for Shitamachi are oversimplistic. It goes without saying that each section contained parts more characteristic of the other. In fact, two of the largest slums in Tokyo were in Yotsuya- and Azabu-ku, lightly populated wards right in the middle of western Yamanote.[47] Additionally, some merchants in Shitamachi amassed greater wealth than any Yamanote salary earner could save in a lifetime. However, in assessing the Tokyo origins of the Japanese in New York, it is useful to distinguish between these parts of Tokyo in a general way, bearing in mind that the designations reflected the people's perceptions about the different sections of the city: desirable or less desirable, rich or poor, Tokyo or Edo, cultured or common. All of these characteristics were stereotypical and extreme, but each contained some reality. Yamanote and Shitamachi, considered (respectively) aristocratic and plebeian by Tokugawa society, had become, in the view of many, bourgeois and proletarian (respectively) by the Taisho period.[48]

The multidimensional characters of both Shitamachi and Yamanote are important in examining the addresses of the sixty-eight Tokyo honseki residents who registered at the Japanese Consulate General in New York between 1909 and 1921 (see Appendix 2, Table 1).[49] They were about evenly divided between Shitamachi and Yamanote: thirty from Shitamachi, twenty-nine from Yamanote, and another nine from residential sections in the suburban west and southwest. Thirteen had addresses in the two most exclusive Yamanote wards, Azabu and Akasaka. Three were from large slum areas in Honjo-, Fukagawa-, and Nihonbashi-ku in Shitamachi, and another was from a Yamanote slum pocket in Hongō-ku. Most of the Shitamachi residents came from densely populated sections but were outside of the *most* heavily populated areas.

The addresses did not favor a particular ward in Tokyo or a particular district in a ward; they represented a cross-section of Tokyo. This scattered pattern of Tokyo addresses, combined with the diverse geographic origins of the New York Japanese from the forty-five other urban and rural prefectures, indicates that a tight network of migration was not operating. Except for the four in the slums, more than half of the addresses were in the residential areas of the less crowded Yamanote, the suburbs, and the merchant sections of Shitamachi. The density of Shitamachi was such that small factories and home industries existed side by side with merchant/business residences. Therefore, it cannot be assumed that the four emigrants with addresses in the slum section were poor.

These findings, combined with the statistical evidence that the preponderance (more than half) of the Tokyo hi-imin were students and merchants, suggest that the Japanese in New York were strongly aware of what it meant to be a Tokyojin, possessor of the new urban mentality, the kindai Japanese. The politics of emigration were such that each citizen approved for travel to the United States as a nonmigrant had an unstated mission as an unofficial representative of Japan. Who possessed the capabilities essential for this responsibility other than members of the chūryūkaikyū, whose importance and size grew with the development of the modern capitalistic system? People of this class served an integral and necessary occupational, social, and ideological function in Japanese society and were crucial to the nation's success in the expanding twentieth-century world. The Tokyojin served as the chūryūkaikyū's prototypes.

What, then, motivated ambitious kindai Tokyojin to leave Japan and cross an ocean and another continent to end up in bustling New York, USA? One can easily assume that given their backgrounds, training, and aspirations, they could serve their nation and government well and, as the 1890 Imperial Rescript on Education prescribed, "advance the public good and promote common interests." They were the occupiers of new workplaces, the recipients of standardized education, the agents and shapers of Meiji middle-class culture. Were their talents and skills not precious enough to represent the values and "fundamental goodness" of the country and to be of service to Meiji Japan?

In 1890 the Meiji period was in its twenty-third year. Members of the generation born during the throes of the changeover from Tokugawa to Meiji were adults. National decisions and developments had taken place during their youth and altered their lives to the extent that their parents' experiences were no longer relevant. Their backgrounds, whether rural or urban, were becoming increasingly homogeneous. Major cultural alterations had taken place during their lifetimes: compulsory education and standards of ethics; national conscription; the emphasis on loyalty to the state, not only on the part of recruits but also by the populace in keeping the military armed, fed, and clothed; the effort to convince the people that the nation was only as great as their patriotic fervor was genuine; and the notion that the country was one big imperial family, which, among other things, was an attempt to compensate for the erosion of the family- and kin-based economic system. Shifts in their lives, attitudes, and behavior occurred as the result of overt acts by the nation-state, including the merging of more than 170,000 villages into approximately 12,000 political units.[50] Yanagita regretted this measure, which not only dealt a final blow to an already weakened local community leadership but also abolished communal lands, one of the more positive aspects of preindustrial Japan. He also observed that the disempowering of the communal economic structure, the use of standardized language in schools, and the bureaucracy virtually guaranteed the gradual extinction of dialects and local usage of words.[51] These changes, combined with world events and national growth, created an environment in which relationships to the sources of power, wealth, and prestige and the bases of political power were altered.

In addition, the Meiji adult lived in a society no longer separated into rigidly defined feudal status categories. At the end of the Tokugawa period, class barriers had already begun to disintegrate. In the fourth year of Meiji (1871), the registry laws abolished the clan system and divided the population into nobility and commoners, the former including imperial household members and the highest echelon of the Tokugawa. A special designation for samurai families was allowed briefly, but this fell into disuse because it bestowed no legal authority or privilege, though it carried the weight of the memory of superiority.[52] In 1890 only 1 percent of the population was entitled by property and tax qualifications to vote.[53] On the surface it would seem that political decisions favored the formation of an increasingly vast group of commoners who represented the majority of the populace, but egalitarianism was not the basis of the newly structured Japanese society. Another, more loosely structured social system developed, but it retained hierarchical features. The constraints of society emanated from the real political world and the fluctuating economy, which was increasingly centralized and under the control of large financial cliques.

It was in this historical framework that the chūryūkaikyū emerged. Their cultural attitudes evolved from those of the initial bureaucrats in Tokyo and the provinces, people of education, experience, and expertise. Many early bureaucrats were from the former samurai class—not from the minority who were instrumental in the overthrow of the Tokugawa and who later became the leaders in industry and politics but from the majority representing all grades of samurai, including those who sold family names to wealthy merchants and modest retainers who were clerks and teachers in feudal domains or on the staffs of their lords' estates in Edo.[54] In the changeover to Meiji, the government redirected their talents into bureaucratic occupations and thereby dissipated any energy that could be used to upset the fragile social order.[55]

As the government work force expanded into newly established bureaus, departments, agencies, and offices, the samurai-educated functionaries who had permeated national and local governments were replaced by recruits from a commoner populace. Indeed, between 1886 and 1920 the number of bureaucrats in Japan increased by almost 670 percent.[56] The civil service was composed of two divisions, each stratified into hierarchical groupings. The lower division grew to comprise more than 95 percent of all civil servants in 1913, an indication that the bureaucracy was in the main a vast group of office workers. Nevertheless, becoming part of the government work force remained a most difficult and prestigious accomplishment. Beginning in 1887 an applicant had to pass stringent written and oral examinations controlled by a committee made up almost entirely of professors in the Faculty of Law, Tokyo Imperial University.[57] As would be expected, the most promising positions were meted out to its law graduates. Kyoto Imperial University also funneled students into the government, but on a lesser scale.[58]

Graduates of private or specialized colleges filled the gap left by the imperial university elites, but they were destined not for positions that led to the "top"—that is, the national government level—but rather for the less prestigious local and provincial office jobs. Furthermore, not even a college diploma and a passing grade on the civil service examinations guaranteed an applicant a position. Appointments were made from a list of qualified applicants who had been helped along by influential connections, letters of recommendation, and gifts of persuasion to appropriate people.[59] A middle school diploma qualified one to enter as a lower-level clerk, but this position offered almost nothing in the way of promotions.[60] The obvious outcome of the examinations was that the Tokyo government exercised strict control over hiring for the central and provincial bureaucracies, and the preeminence of government jobs was inviolable. More important, the examinations were instituted in 1887, one year after the establishment of a comprehensive national education system, and thus the system and the use of "standardized" knowledge gained credence and authority.[61]

The avenues of employment that opened up when one had acquired appropriate educational skills were considerable in the early Meiji years. Ironically, however, beginning with the period when national compulsory education was instituted, those avenues gradually declined in number to the extent that unless one had graduated from a particular institution, entry into positions of promise in the bureaucracy, companies, and banks was impossible. The examination was not the only hurdle. Imperial university graduates could expect better jobs and higher starting salaries than graduates of private and specialized colleges, professional schools, and technical and vocational schools.[62] By 1917 more than 50 percent of the Tokyo and Kyoto Imperial University graduates were entering corporations. At the Sumitomo Bank, new employees were placed in one of four categories depending upon their alma mater and field of study. Salaries differed according to category.[63] Graduates of Keio University and the government-sponsored Tokyo Higher Commercial College (the present-day Hitotsubashi University), institutions given university status in 1903, also were guaranteed jobs and quick promotions: they attained managerial positions within ten years and became executives in twenty, "rivaling the situation of government employees."[64] The road to the highest levels of educational advancement was determined as early as middle school (seventh to eleventh year of education), when achievers in the system were tracked to take the examinations for a three-year higher school in preparation for the three- or four-year imperial university course.[65] Although the higher schools were originally set up by the Ministry of Education to "carry out the education necessary for those who wish to go into business as well as those who wish to enter a higher level school," in reality they became stepping stones for entry into an imperial university. This process became formalized in 1894 with the setting up of the higher schools as separate and distinct institutional components of the educational structure.[66] As was to be expected, acceptance into the higher schools became increasingly difficult: admission rates narrowed from 67 percent of the applicants in 1895 to 34 percent in 1901 and 20 percent in 1908.[67] Exacerbating the situation was the fact that a growing number of the applicants had failed the three-day entrance examination in earlier years. Therefore, as the number of middle school graduates increased, the possibility for entering higher school decreased.[68] Admission to an imperial university (Tokyo and Kyoto until 1907) was out of the question without a diploma from a higher school of repute. The First Higher School of Tokyo was on the top of the list, followed by the Third Higher School of Osaka. Those who failed the higher school examinations entered one of the many lesser professional or specialized schools that catered to middle-class students. These institutions offered a wide array of courses in the arts and sciences, and some even accepted applicants who lacked a middle school diploma. Some students attended these schools while waiting for another chance to take the examinations for higher school. Others sought credentials that might help them to obtain employment in a firm with some promise. The fortunate few could go abroad to the United States or Europe to overcome their disappointments and difficulties. Graduates of the lesser schools joined the thousands who entered the work force annually, going from job to job, waiting to see which would promise a secure future, and perhaps ending up in one of the many risk-ridden small business firms, far short of the ideal position: government employment.

Seventy-five percent of the businesses operating in 1905 were capitalized at less than 50,000 yen, hardly able to pay a college graduate's salary.[69] The worst scenario for a new graduate, of course, was that jobs might be completely unavailable. In 1891 a youth magazine lamented that more than half of the private college graduates in politics and economics were unemployed.[70] Prospects improved slightly during the Sino-Japanese and Russo-Japanese War booms, but the continued scarcity of capital and its concentration in larger financial institutions made economic depression familiar to the Japanese people. Wide variations in rice output, fluctuating prices, surpluses in cotton textiles, unsteady interest rates, bank failures, irregular trade with China after the Sino-Japanese War, and an intermittently stagnant stock market were clear signs that shifts in the economy occurred frequently and created unstable employment conditions. There were financial panics in 1890, 1897–1898, and 1900–1903, a postwar recession in 1907–1908, a panic in 1914 after the outbreak of World War I, rice riots in 1918, and another panic in 1920–1923.[71]

The kind and level of education people received transcended the simple school-to-job trail.[72] Those who completed middle school became part of the growing middle class aspiring to work in nonlaboring jobs. Such jobs increased in number, but not necessarily in prestige, as the number of capitalist functions and needs grew. Most middle school graduates did not become professionals or employees in the large companies, occupations that were almost as elite as those of the civil servants slated for high government positions. Nevertheless, having gone beyond the compulsory educational level, they cherished a set of attitudes that stemmed from the highly materialistic goals they (or their parents) set for themselves in kindai Japan. Young people's attitudes toward hierarchy and authority began to be defined by extremely individualistic responses to the changes occurring in their world of work. The value that had been placed upon perseverance, loyalty, and consistency meant that higher offices could be achieved only after years of hard and uncomplaining work, regardless of the prestige or respectability of one's alma mater. However, when perseverance and loyalty were combined with skillful manipulation, self-serving routes to the top could be shortened.

The dual nature of career advancement is an important aspect of the novel *Ukigumo* (Floating clouds) by Futabatei Shimei (1864–1909). It was first published in two sections in 1887 and 1888, and its third section appeared in 1889 as a serial in a Tokyo magazine.[73] The story centers around two young men (one of them based on the author), the divergent ways in which they pursue their careers as government workers, and their responses to social approval or disapproval of their actions. Bunzō, the hero, moves to Tokyo after the death of his father to live with his uncle, a samurai turned teahouse owner. He attends classes in a neighborhood school for awhile; then, upon hearing about scholarships offered by a normal school (equivalent to university preparatory school), he takes the examinations and is accepted. Despite graduating with high grades, Bunzō spends an "arduous" six months without work. Finally, through the assistance of a friend, he enters the government bureaucracy. He is among the last group of employees hired prior to the institution of the civil service examination system. Although the novel was published before the period of our concern, Bunzō's observations portray the not-unusual quality of bureaucratic office situations:

> On the first day he was given a document to check and when he was settled at his desk he surveyed the room. Around him were men engaged in all kinds of work: copyists with their heads tilted importantly to one side; checkers who studied the work before them like monkeys searching for fleas; accountants turning over the pages of their books with a busy air, their brushes between their teeth.
>
> Just opposite Bunzō was a man of about fifty with a deeply furrowed brow who flipped the beads of an abacus without pausing, rapidly blinking his eyes. Suddenly he held his hands still, and, fingering the beads, said ". . . Six by five is seventy-two—no—six by five . . . ," as if the welfare of the entire world depended on this calculation. . . .[74]

Bunzō's position eventually becomes permanent. He settles into two years of monotony, wasting "the learning he acquired with such sacrifice," and develops "a false sense of security," thinking he is "safer than he proved to be."[75] He is jarred out of his complacency when he is dismissed abruptly in an office reorganization, not because of unsatisfactory work but because his manner is not appropriately submissive.

By contrast, his coworker, Noboru, advances, for he has successfully manipulated his situation. His superior is a man who feels "the greatest contempt for the old feudalistic hierarchy" and "loudly voice[s] criticism of the arrogant ways of his fellow bureaucrats"; if anything in the office displeases him, he displays his anger without hesitation.[76] Most of the workers do not know how to please him.

> Only Noboru knew. He copied the gentleman's speech and gestures and even assumed the way he cleared his throat and his manner of sneezing. The imitation was almost perfect. . . . When the older man spoke to him, Noboru rushed over to his desk and listened respectfully, his head cocked knowingly to one side. After he had finished speaking, the young man would smile broadly and reply most humbly. . . . He was neither distant nor too friendly. Everything was done in accordance with the chief's wishes; he was never contradicted. Moreover—and this is the most important point—Noboru took note of the mistakes made by other division heads as a device for praising the man.
>
> Once the chief's wife expressed a desire to have a Pekinese for a pet. No sooner said than done. Before a day passed, Noboru had got hold of one and presented it for her inspection. The chief looked at the dog and remarked that it seemed to him to have a rather strange face. Noboru agreed that it indeed had a strange face. The chief's wife suggested that it was considered desirable for a Pekinese to have a ratlike face. Noboru said that

to be sure it was thought to be better if a Pekinese had such a ratlike face, just as the lady had said, and he had complacently patted the dog's head.[77]

The vivid portrayal of the boredom of work strikes a familiar chord, as does the description of an ambitious employee catering to his superior. However, most significant are the two characters' divergent responses toward hierarchical relationships in the bureaucracy. Bunzō is not rebellious, but neither is he obsequious. Noboru, by contrast, is blatantly obsequious, hoping to advance up the career ladder. The others, the majority, behave passively, doomed to remain in positions not far above where they started. However, obsequiousness might help one gain *risshin shusse* ("advancement and achievement," an oft-heard term among educated youth after the Sino-Japanese War), depending on the circumstances and the skill of the worker in assessing his superior.[78] Obsequiousness was a natural outcome of risshin shusse and its counterpart, *nintai* (perseverance), two moral precepts to which youth striving for success had to conform. However, for people who failed to trudge along and finally reach the pot of gold at the end of the rainbow, these two precepts worked in contradiction to each other.[79] If one were persevering and patient, a whole lifetime might go by without the attainment of rewards, which the ambitious did not wish to be postponed until old age. However, *perseverance* could be interpreted in ways other than it had been in the harsh preindustrial past, when it was a necessity of life. For the truly ambitious, it could be combined with notions that contributed toward risshin shusse, a talent with which Noboru was particularly endowed. Flattery and manipulation were the tools he used, nothing new in the range of human behavior.

The goals of capitalist society gave a new dimension to certain moral precepts, for people's work experiences were no longer related to their daily lives as in a precapitalist society. The common person in the Tokugawa world was not weighed down with the luxury of private ambition. The interrelatedness of work and life, the importance of cooperation, and the moral precepts that regulated behavior were spelled out clearly, although it would be inaccurate to assume that they remained static during the more than 200 years of Tokugawa rule.[80] By contrast, the organizations and enterprises in which the commoners of the Meiji period increasingly worked had little or nothing to do with their immediate lives; tasks were abstract, and the goods produced were disjointed parts, from which the whole was assembled in various stages and places. The end product was consumed far away from the place of production.

The daily work in which Bunzō, Noboru, and the accountants and clerks engaged had no relevance to their lives, dreams, or aspirations. It consisted of tasks prescribed outside of their realm of control, and it affected people with whom they had no contact. It reeked of boredom.[81] What gave their lives some meaning, more to Noboru than to others, was the quest for risshin shusse—an aim that, if achieved, could bring privileges and material benefits—ownership of a chūryū jūtaku and other trappings of middle-class consumer culture.

The aims and structure of the Meiji bureaucracy changed with the gradual replacement of the original samurai personnel, but compared to the business world it was relatively stable. This fact, combined with its elite role in Meiji society, makes it a crucial indicator of middle-class sensibilities in this period. Government personnel were prototypical middle-class Meiji individuals anxious for a secure and comfortable life. Their importance was enhanced by the prestige of public responsibility. The status and privilege of officialdom engendered not only hierarchical relationships within the bureaucracy, as we have seen, but also an authoritarian attitude toward the public, a posture that evoked memories of early samurai officials. Samurai authoritarianism in the past gave credence to the authoritarian behavior of Meiji bureaucrats. Their interpretations, assumptions, and pronouncements were sacrosanct and to be accepted as such by the commoner regardless of the weakness of the argument or the irrationality of the purpose. In fact, bureaucrats were not encouraged to think of their work as being for the public good. Their authority was directly connected with imperial authority and explicitly conveyed in the oft-repeated phrase "*kanson minpi*," which translates as "respect for officials, contempt for people." Even the lowest bureaucrat was superior to any ordinary citizen.[82]

An apt illustration of the superiority and scorn felt by government employees appears in Natsume Sōseki's *Botchan*, based on the author's own experiences as a teacher in a rural school.[83] Although outside the realm of bureaucratic officials and clerks, teachers indisputably were authority figures, hired to impart learning in the national public school system as directed by the Tokyo government. The Ministry of Education controlled textbooks, curricula, sizes of classes, types of schools, and teacher education and qualifications. Instructors used standardized texts, had standardized teaching guides, and taught standardized speech based on elite Yamanote Tokyo speech. Graduates of urban colleges often served as teachers in unfamiliar rural districts.

A nonachieving student in a three-year college in Tokyo, Botchan graduates, "strangely enough," and lands a job teaching in a middle school on the island of Shikoku in the Inland Sea, far from Tokyo. The job is unglamorous and thankless for a Tokyojin. Botchan describes his first day of teaching as follows:

> I took some chalk and left the staff room for the second class, feeling as though I were marching into enemy territory. When I reached the room, I found that the boys in this class were all bigger than those in the previous one. Since I have the typically light, compact build of a Tokyoite, I didn't feel that I exuded any sense of authority, even standing on the dais. . . . But I thought that if I once showed any weakness to these oafs, I would never be able to regain control, so I began the lesson in a good loud voice and rolled my r's a bit as we do in Tokyo, to give some body to what I was saying. . . .
> . . . the pupils just sat there and gaped at me in a befuddled way.
> . . . I started using the rough, punchy language of downtown Tokyo, which is my specialty. At this, the boy right in the middle of the front row, who looked the strongest in the class, suddenly jumped to his feet and said, "Sir!" . . .
> "You're speaking too fast. I can't understand what you say. . . ."
> " . . . If I'm speaking too quickly, I'll slow down, but I'm from Tokyo and I can't speak your dialect, so if you don't understand my accent, you'll just have to wait till you get used to it."[84]

Botchan's arrogance and intolerance are relentless. Nowhere is it more evident than in his deliberate use of the rapid Shitamachi dialect of the merchants, completely alien to his students, who are accustomed to the leisurely dialect used in Shikoku.[85] Even though the novel is about Botchan's increasing defiance of bureaucracy and authority, he remains totally unforgiving of his students and their provincial ways, as in a march to a rally celebrating victory in the Sino-Japanese War:

> When they weren't singing war songs or yelling, they were chattering among themselves. You'd think that it would have been possible to walk without chattering, but all Japanese are born into the world mouth first, and no amount of scolding would stop the boys. Plain chattering wouldn't have been too bad, but this vulgar crew were saying insulting things about teachers. . . .
> In the same way that a merchant will bow and scrape and continue to cheat you, the general run of pupils will apologize without the least idea of giving up mischief. On reflection, it seems the world is composed entirely of people like those boys. . . . [T]hey think you're a fool and too naive if you take their apology seriously. . . . The only way to make someone really apologize is to beat him until he truly regrets what he's done.[86]

Botchan's status as a teacher and his Tokyo origins entitle him to be abusive and punitive without restraint. His word is to be obeyed without opposition, his actions unquestioned. The story is a satire about the values placed on false and meaningless attributes, for in reality Botchan and the other members of the faculty are poorly suited to assume authority or merit respect. However, because he is a teacher from Tokyo, Botchan is accorded both.

This blind respect of authority, ridiculed by Sōseki, was an aspect of kindai society that cannot be understood simply as an extension of pre-Meiji attitudes toward authority. Its significance was not the same. Although oppressive economic and political controls were harsh facts of Tokugawa Japan, in community- and family-related economic units authority was a meaningful concept. In Meiji society it lost that socioeconomic dimension and took on another one based on the political concept of the nation-state as exemplified by imperial authority. The concept was personal and impersonal at the same time. The emperor was the authority figure of the nation, the father, as it were, to whom the people were to be respectful, loyal, and obedient. Measures of national importance—such as the Imperial Rescript on Education of 1890, a document that prescribed ethical principles rather than educational policy—were promulgated in the name of the emperor. The chain of authority descended from the emperor to more proximate figures—fathers, husbands, teachers, employers, older brothers—all male, of course. Therefore, the ideological notion of authority included a distinct personal aspect from which it was difficult to escape.[87] The specific timing of Japan's emergence as a modern state, the social and economic contradictions faced by the populace, the need for order and unity, and the development of strong military and imperial structures all were key factors requiring that authority be absolute and inviolable.

However, modern society was encumbered with various new institutions—political, military, legal, and educational—that tended to make relationships "less personal and more instrumental." Individuals developed "a capacity for engaging in impersonal relationships, for dealing with others solely by virtue of specific roles which they fulfilled rather than as whole persons."[88] One was identified by one's role, although the assumption cannot be made that it was binding or unchanging. A person's role could be authoritarian under one set of circumstances and subservient under another; people were "actively involved in the process of making meaning out of their historical moment."[89] Nevertheless, subordinates were expected to accept the authority of those in authority roles. Consequently, Botchan's students consider him the unimpeachable authority, and he looks at the students as faceless "oafs," receptacles into which he crams information. In this respect, the attitudes and behavior of subordinates—the students in relation to Botchan, and Botchan in relation to the officials of the school—are significant. Although authority remained inviolate, challenges were part of the Meiji political and social drama.[90]

Significantly, the power of authority was evident in every aspect of a person's life, from the all-inclusive family, education, and work worlds to the political arena, in which laws and regulations limited political protest and opposition. Civil and military police were visible parts of the landscape, there to enforce numerous regulations and statutes controlling almost every aspect of citizens' lives—lodgings, advertisements, restaurants, public morals, pawn shops, prostitution, gambling, mixed baths, nakedness, used-clothing dealers, brokers, waitresses, speculators. This was particularly so in Tokyo, where the military and metropolitan police forces worked in close cooperation.[91] One of the major responsibilities of the police, beginning in 1889, was to perform household sanitation inspections for public health reasons and to ensure social control by, among other things, verifying nameplates on front entrances and checking to see that all boarders and roomers were registered according to the law. By 1908 the police were authorized to conduct spot inspections and investigations with impunity.[92] A contemporary saying went: "The difference between a Tokyo cop and the chestnut burr? Nothing. Boiled or roasted, they don't get soft."[93] Clearly, Japanese were not unaware of the restrictions on their lives.

The barriers to setting oneself up in business were as conspicuous as those involved in attaining a position leading to high-level bureaucratic employment. The fits and starts experienced by the generation that confronted the problems of small business were natural themes for a number of Meiji writers. One such work was the autobiographical *Ie* (Household) by Shimazaki Tōson (1872–1943).[94] Published as a newspaper novel in 1910–1911, it takes place during 1898–1910 and touches on many aspects of life of Meiji Japan, including economic and workplace realities, migration to Tokyo, the use and place of provincial dialects, the status of women, and education. In each of these areas, the shifting meanings of authority and contestation take on a significance that helps us understand change in a changing society. All of these are woven into the story, giving us some flavor of one middle-class household's situation. In the following excerpt, Tōson writes about his brother's premature and unexpected ascendancy to head of the household:

> Minoru's father, Tadahiro, had been . . . the patriarch of a village and an influential landlord. He was a man who spent his entire life in anguish. After brooding for some time over the condition of Japan, he abandoned his home to devote himself to patriotic activities. Thereafter, Minoru was obliged to take over as head of the family at the age of seventeen. The young and dutiful son became a victim of circumstances.[95]

After his father's death, Minoru remains in his father's house and is elected to local governmental office. All the people of the area respect him highly. However, hoping to improve his fortunes by entering into business, he decides to move to Tokyo. There he meets with a series of failures. Each scheme ends in disaster, and he goes deeply into debt. He finally is sent to prison for conducting illegal transactions and never recovers from the negative effects of his imprisonment, which is repeated later on in the novel.

Upon his release, Minoru tries to set up another business, producing a carriage that operates on the same principle as a rickshaw. A family friend from the same province, "called 'Boss' by his employees, . . . a wholesaler in a commercial district in Tokyo," invests an exceptionally large amount of money as capital and supervises the business from behind the scenes.[96] However, Minoru is able neither to recover his losses nor to get the business off the ground. He attempts a fourth venture; another failure. No one in the family is exempt from the consequences of his financial disasters.

> Oshun [Minoru's daughter] then talked about what had happened at home. The day she returned from school, a public auction was being held at home. Those items of furniture necessary for everyday living were bought by an acquaintance, who arranged to return them to the family. Bailiff, pawnbroker, secondhand shop—words connoting the miseries of life—fell from Oshun's lips.[97]

Minoru continues to experience bankruptcies, always repeating the same mistakes and falling deeper into debt each time. He sells valuable art objects and even the clothing that has been homespun "with such care and patience" by his mother. His creditors seize everything, and the family once more is forced to move to cheaper quarters. To compound the misfortunes, Minoru is sent to prison again. These repeated setbacks force his two younger brothers (particularly the Tōson character) to take over the moral and financial responsibility of the household.

Upon Minoru's release from prison the second time, the two brothers decide that he should leave Japan. The story of Minoru mirrors that of Tōson's eldest brother, who left Japan for Taiwan.[98]

Although the household occupies a respected role in the community, its status does not adequately protect the family from the obstacles and difficulties of life, many of them inherent in adjusting to the new society. No one in the family is spared. Various tragedies—the death of children, sicknesses, mental retardation, invalidism, and insanity due to venereal disease—are compounded by frequent moves, frequent loss of money, the squandering of capital, and above all the endless search for a secure way to make a living. Not even Tōson's fictional nephew, son of his eldest sister, is immune, despite his youth:

> Shōta seemed depressed. He came to Tokyo before Sankichi [Tōson] and rented a small house in Honjo to live with Toyose, but they soon moved out. He sent his wife home and tried to make business contacts on his own. His temperament did not let him take an easy walk. With minimal resources, he traveled as far as Hokkaidō and Sakhalin, only to return empty-handed. Coming home from Kolsakov, he was stricken by a serious illness and had to stay at an Aomori inn until he recovered. All his schemes were attempted without much capital. Once he planned a sale of Iwaki coal; another time he started lessons in conversational Chinese, intending to go to South China. He still had not found any promising work and was at the end of his patience.
>
> His eagerness for business success was spurred by the fact that all his uncles were now gathered in Tokyo. . . . Shōta was impatient to establish a house in Tokyo, too, and this desire was uppermost in his mind.[99]

Shōta eventually moves to Tokyo, but his life continues to be studded with business failures. Thinking that Nagoya might offer better opportunities than Tokyo, he moves again, becomes a "second-rate stockbroker," contracts tuberculosis, and dies at the age of thirty-five.[100]

The tense world of small businesses overwhelms the Shimazakis and causes their final deterioration as a family unit governed by the prescribed hierarchy of authority. Minoru sees his life disintegrate and is incapable of earning a living. Likewise, the other male members, except for Sankichi (Tōson), cannot achieve even a semblance of stability. Sankichi is saddled with the support of the "weaker members" of the family and unwillingly doles out his meager earnings as a provincial teacher and later on as a struggling writer. He also draws on his wife's dowry and takes on loans.

Small business constituted a persistent and important component in Japan's industrial and capitalist development, but many who envisioned themselves as "independent entrepreneurs" encountered unsparing instability and uncertainty. The heterogeneous mixture of small businesses that made up this world included retail, wholesale, construction, local transportation, amusement, food, professional services, and small-scale manufacturing of consumer items such as ceramics, household goods, and clothing.[101] This sector was slow in adapting to modern industrial methods of production and concentrated on native industries, taking advantage of an abundant and cheap labor supply.[102] It was dependent upon and subordinate to the large-scale industries for capital, materials, jobs, orders, and markets. Small businesses ran the gamut from operating independently of large enterprises to subcontracting to participating in a putting-out system, but the operations were private. They gathered capital privately, and therefore profit or loss was a matter of private responsibility. All the decisions regarding what to produce, where to produce it, where to get capital, how many workers to hire, how much to produce, and where to sell it were left to individual entrepreneurs, but such decisions were subject to "large capital or large industries, or indirectly [influenced] by them through the mechanism of the whole national economy."[103]

Many enterprises were family-run, but the number of members they could support depended upon the scale of the business and the number of sons in the family. Expansion was modest, and technological innovations were few, for risks increased as enterprises expanded—risks not only in terms of failure but also in terms of borrowing capital, an area in which the government offered little help.[104] Capital was considerably costlier for small businesses than for large concerns and generally unavailable from banks. Thus, businessmen frequently turned to friends and local pawnbrokers, moneylenders, and wholesale merchants who charged exorbitant interest rates.[105] Competition was cutthroat among small businesses, particularly in finding new markets and sources of raw materials. Bankruptcies were frequent, businesses often changed to new products, labor turnover was high, and the little available capital was inefficiently used, preventing the hiring of better-educated people at higher pay. The fluctuations they experienced partly reflected the ups and downs of the economy, but even during normal economic times their situation failed to stabilize markedly.[106] Of course, a few small businesses grew to become lucrative enterprises, managed by sharp-minded individuals who chose fortuitous moments to follow "the path to wealth."[107] However, they were the minority; the vast majority of businesses remained small and unpretentious.[108]

Of all the different types of enterprises in Meiji Japan, the small business remained tied most closely to pre-Meiji practices, not only in terms of production methods but also in the relationship between employers and employees. As long as a business remained viable, this traditional approach was feasible. Authority and loyalty were strong factors in this relationship. The employer would take responsibility for and personal interest in the employee and his family; in turn, the employee would work far beyond what was required in the more modern industries and, if business were slack, would not press for prompt payment of wages.[109] However, if a business became untenable or, as in Minoru's case, did not get off the ground, these practices were meaningless.

During Minoru's attempt to perfect a multipassenger rickshaw, with time and money fast running out, the wife of his most trusted longtime employee comes to him:

She walked in, and Minoru saw by the look on her face that something was on her mind. After some hesitation she began. "Of course, it's not for me to question you; it's your business and you are all experienced men. But I wonder when we're going to see some results? I have nothing but my husband's words and I can't feel secure any more."

Minoru coughed several times before he said, "You mean about the vehicle? We have a good engineer working on it. There's nothing to worry about."

"I know. My husband keeps saying he's sorry to worry you about money.... The truth is, he's so pressed for money, he tells stories to his mother when she comes up from the country, he cries, and he puts on all kinds of acts to get money out of her."

"I've told your husband, if you need money, it's in the bank."

"Thank you very much. I feel better hearing you say so, but somehow ... unless we can see some light ... not knowing how long it's going to be before the business starts producing...." Her eyes were still unsure. "If my husband finds out that I came to talk to you, he'll explode. But you know, we women are not like men. We worry a lot about small things."

Not wanting to offend Minoru she did not pursue the subject further.[110]

What is most striking about this passage is that it gives us a picture of an authority figure being confronted not by an unhappy male subordinate but by his wife. The Meiji ideological hierarchy positioned women on the bottom, as formalized in the 1898 Civil Code. This held true in all groups—from the most poverty-stricken to the wealthiest households, small to large economic enterprises, factories, workers' organizations, school faculties, and all formal and informal gender-mixed social gatherings. Japanese male perceptions of women in Japan and the West will be discussed later (see Chapter 7), but the passage above gives us some idea of the complexities inherent in Japanese gender roles. The wife does not directly challenge Minoru's role as the authority figure—in fact, she steers the conversation so as not to antagonize him while taking precautions to not jeopardize her relationship to her husband. Nevertheless, her confrontation of Minoru is conscious and deliberate. This unexpected and oppositional stance taken by a woman presents us with another dimension of how authority was contested in the turbulent Meiji world. However, she does not demand that Minoru pay her or her husband. Dore's observation that traditional relationships were "wholly inimical to hard economic bargaining" seems to hold here.[111]

Minoru's oblique behavior probably was not uncommon and reflected adjustments to shifts in the Meiji socioeconomic environment. He displays some sense of concern in order to minimize or postpone conflict but does not offer or act to alleviate dissatisfaction. On the contrary, through inaction, he makes the employee responsible for seeking out solutions to her money problems. Though he preserves the outward trappings of authority, in practice he is ambivalent and ineffectual. In the end, Minoru cannot sustain his role as the authority figure in the business, and the employees disperse, a common occurrence in the highly fluid occupational structure of Meiji Japan.

The overriding result of Japan's industrial and capitalist development during the crucial years of 1890 to 1924 was that the nation was catapulted into a competitive and assertive world position within a short time. The process rode roughshod over a large number of people, providing neither real opportunities nor guidance. The era was full of contradictions for most, not least for aspiring, literate, urban, middle-class individuals. In many instances, as in the case of the Shimazaki household, the pre-Meiji notions of authority and the new ways of life contradicted each other. Smooth social change was impossible. The obstacles to obtaining certain occupations heightened their value and, in turn, made it clear where a person stood in relationship to society. In addition, the passage of time tended to make authority seem more vague and uncertain, and people were faced with trying to determine its exact nature while adhering tenaciously to the values of obedience, loyalty, and faith.

In this world, then, it was crucial for youth to find a route to success. The paths to this destination became a significant topic of popular literature. Members of the intelligentsia and the economic and political worlds—journalists, bureaucrats, political and liberal reformists, businessmen, entrepreneurs, and travelers—helped pave the way for laboring class and chūryūkaikyū alike. In a world fraught with conflict and disappointment, it was imperative to achieve harmony and consensus by firing the burning desire for success—money, wealth, and standing—and by enlightening youth about the obstacles that stood in their way. In essence, the writings for youth purported to show how to grab opportunities and utilize ambition, foresight, and acumen to their fullest advantage. The golden world of kindai Nippon was within the reach of those willing and able to persevere, uplift themselves, and take on responsibility as national leaders in Asia's leading nation.

CHAPTER 5

The Road to Success

Be honest, faithful, industrious, save your money.
Be industrious; be earnest; be truthful; and don't take a drink during business hours.
Work to the interest of the man who employs you....
Select an occupation, stick to it, don't touch liquor, tobacco, or cards; keep away from fast women....
Stick to your business; don't get discouraged; seize your opportunities.
Be honest, hard working, and accurate.

The secrets of success as enunciated by a number of "great men" in the United States were displayed prominently in the July 1, 1904, issue of the magazine *Seikō* (Success).[1] The great men included "the shoe manufacturer, Douglas," "the medical doctor, Atkinson," and "the library director, Jones." These names were not easily recognizable by the average American, but what average Japanese knew that? Drawing their lessons from the sayings and lives of men who had achieved success on a grand scale in the United States—the Andrew Carnegies, John D. Rockefellers, Theodore Roosevelts—the self-help and success journals of Meiji Japan taught their readers about the inventiveness, industriousness, and dedication of the movers of American capitalism. Some British and a few French and German models dotted the pages of *Seikō*, and following Japan's victories in the military arena, particularly after the Russo-Japanese War, Japanese examples began to appear, articulating lessons prescribed by leaders in government, business, the professions, and the arts. However, the American examples were by far the most numerous.

The articles about the United States, in particular the ones that told of Japanese perceptions about American success, give us some understanding about the vision held by educated urban youth who desired to go to the United States. Achieving success did not only mean that one possessed the virtues of hard work, perseverance, frugality, dedication, and so on, which the "great Americans" displayed and which belonged to the Japanese work ethic as well. It also meant that one had learned and was cognizant of special attributes that were basic to the Americans' accomplishments. If understood correctly, they could launch Japanese youth on their own road to success.

What special attributes were deemed important? What justifications were offered for devoting one's life to money-making and gaining material wealth? To us, almost a century later, writings concerning these issues seem extremely naïve and idealistic. However, it is clear that they were written with great seriousness, whether they were half-page commentaries on attitudes toward success or long dramatic fables charting the course of a young man's ascent up the mountain of success, complete with swamps, deep forests, turbulent rivers, and boulders to symbolize the setbacks he experienced en route. The discussions tended to belittle what were considered pre-Meiji Japanese qualities, explicitly or implicitly, and could easily have led some readers to assume that anything "backward or regressive" must be Japanese.

In the aforementioned issue of *Seikō*, the short, one-sentence principles were printed in two columns: one in English, the other in Japanese in the imperative form conforming to the English originals. What is striking about these lists, of course, is that they included the English, a message as important as the principles themselves. This bears consideration, for it goes beyond the obvious emphasis of learning English as one of the prerequisites to the road to success.

Undoubtedly, individual Japanese needed foreign language skills to conduct trade with Westerners or to acquire technical knowledge. Knowing a foreign language was necessary for a kindai individual's self-esteem. But why English? Why not the other European languages? Voices extolling continental European languages and cultures, after all, were not silent. However, the stress on English as the preferred foreign language and the United States and Great Britain as the preferred cultures/nations was an important acknowledgment of the historical and political developments of the time. Both countries exemplified industrial growth and progress. Britain was the major imperial power of the nineteenth century. The United States followed closely behind and then secured an almost equivalent position in the first decade of the twentieth century. Moreover, the newer country had the advantage of an expansive land mass and vast resources, material qualities important in shaping what some contemporary Japanese writers described as the typically American traits of invention, talent, enterprise, adventure, and even romance.

The emphasis placed on the learning of English paralleled the increased use of English-language phrases and words in Japanese, a development that occurred in conjunction with the establishment of Yamanote speech as the official form for kindai Japanese. Dutch, Portuguese, and bits of Spanish had filtered into the Japanese language during the Tokugawa era, but in early Meiji, newly introduced products of everyday use—clothing, furniture, toilet articles, housewares, food—heralded the growing "Japanizing" of English words.[2] New technology and the reshaping of material culture resulted in words such as *ūski*, *samichi*, and *torampu*, early Japanese counterparts of "whiskey," "sandwich," and "playing cards" (probably taken from "trump"). The still-used *baketsu* (bucket), *matchi* (matches), and *tonneru* (tunnel) developed somewhat later. Compound Chinese characters were devised to express some of the new material products—*kisha* (train), *yōfuku* (Western clothing), *denpō* (telegraph)—but in the main English words, with a sprinkling of German and French, were absorbed to form new Japanese words.[3] As time passed some meanings went through subtle but definable alterations. *Haikara*, first used in 1898, was taken from "high collar." Originally a term of contempt to designate "snobs who returned from abroad," within a short time it took on a new meaning—"stylish" or "chic"—which it retains to this day.[4] These were not translations. They were foreign words with distinct Japanese inflections and sounds that eventually merged into the Japanese language and became accepted virtually without reference to their foreign origins.

The introduction, increased usage, and final inclusion of these terms form a basis for analyzing kindai and its relationship to the absorption of "Americanness" on the road to success. Japan was not a stranger to the cataclysmic results of European colonization and empire, in which non-European histories, regions, and countries became abruptly segmented, fragmented, and stigmatized. In fact, in the early Meiji period the adoption of English as the national language was briefly contemplated.[5] However, Japan was not going to succumb to passivity nor accept an inferior position in that kind of colonial world. The country had an overwhelming sense of the dominant Western Other and single-mindedly sought membership in that coveted realm of dominance. In order to effect this, a unique and cosmopolitan construction of the Japanese identity had to be shaped—not a mirror image of the West but an assertive and self-conscious "Japaneseness" as the basis of kindai language, lifestyles, attitudes, and behavior. Care had to be taken so the West would not accuse the nation of mere imitation, although Japan never succeeded totally in escaping that charge. Ultimately, the Japanese wanted the Western capitalist world to acknowledge their endeavors as legitimate, acceptable, and appropriate.

The entry of new Japanese words with English roots into the vernacular was an important step in the shaping of the new Japanese identity. This occurred in conjunction with the emergence of a new socioeconomic class, the molding of the Tokyojin, and with state decisions regarding emigration laws, passport regulations, education, military service, and civil behavior. For our purposes, one of the most relevant areas of the complex process of shaping this new identity was what Japanese knew (or thought they knew) about the United States. The image of the United States that was created in conjunction with the self-definition of the kindai Japanese is crucial in analyzing the decision of some chūryūkaikyū Tokyojin to leave Japan for the United States.

In 1900 youth who had entered public schools when the compulsory education system became solidified were twenty years old and faced major decisions about their adult lives. More students were finishing middle school, particularly in the cities.[6] The people with whom we are dealing were not the average or typical Japanese youth of the period; those who finally made their way to New York City constituted a small minority. However, they were among the many young people who congregated in the cities, specifically Tokyo, hoping to take advantage of specialized technical and educational facilities or to work in nonlaboring jobs commensurate with their educational achievements. Armed with their hopes and ideals, they looked for ways to be the exceptions, to overcome the tides of the times and embark on the practical road to success.

The Tokyo publishing world provided an array of reading matter for these individuals. Self-advancement publications, books, and articles on a variety of subjects appeared for a variety of youth: students of English, business, science, and legal studies; girls and boys; young kindai women and men; consumers; housewives; the literati. Many were published by a single publishing house, Hakubunkan, which dominated the publishing world to such an extent that the period from the mid-1890s to the early 1920s was called the *Hakubunkan jidai* (Hakubunkan period).[7] Beginning with the publication in 1871 of the Japanese translation of Samuel Smiles's *Self-Help*, a book that emphasized individual responsibility in the development of the work ethic, such messages appeared in a wide array of youth magazines.[8] The more popular publications had circulations ranging from 12,000 to about 16,000, and one even had a circulation of more than 500,000.[9] Initially they catered to children from ten to fifteen years of age, but by the turn of the century the audience included young adults, indicative of the growing number of graduates of the Meiji school system.[10] By that time the self-advancement publications had evolved to focus primarily on the notion of *seikō*. They not only impressed upon young minds the importance of the work ethic but also contained teachings on good manners, speech, and tasteful dress; educational and occupational opportunities; leisure activity; and ways to establish such enterprises as a tailor's shop, a pawnshop, or a usury business. What useful advice readers gained from this potpourri is questionable, but a young man of Meiji Japan learned that to be worthy one must possess diligence, assume wholesome and pragmatic attitudes toward making money, and display acceptable cosmopolitan behavior. *Seikō* had a double meaning. It connoted not only the final goal, which was the achievement of success, but also tenacious adherence to effective and utilitarian action in the pursuit of that goal.

The term began to be utilized widely during the years between the Sino- and Russo-Japanese Wars, a period of economic downturn. Discussions on *seikō* began to appear in magazines, including two major ones: *Taiyō*, published by Hakubunkan, and *Chūō kōron*, which remains a popular journal for the intelligentsia. In 1902 a leading labor leader commented that there was "not a single place where the word 'success' is not to be seen."[11] The post–Russo-Japanese War years in particular saw such a tremendous jump in the publication of popular success literature that one well-known member of the Meiji intelligentsia remarked that the readers' "eyes are like saucers."[12] The magazine *Seikō* commenced publication in 1902, and its circulation rose to 15,000 within three years.[13]

The writers of *Seikō* included a diverse group of intellectuals, businessmen, and journalists with backgrounds ranging from conservative to socialist to Christian, differentiating it from other youth magazines.[14] In less than 100 pages, each issue of *Seikō* touched on a wide variety of subject matter—ambition, literary pieces, biographies, moral training (consistently the largest section), confidence, philosophy of success, family, business, overseas activity, editorials, and English. The magazine was divided into sections, and the articles were concise, generally running a maximum of four or five pages. Its readership, judging from the emphasis on urban education and jobs and from readers' letters, consisted of Tokyo youth or rural youth who went to Tokyo to become students.[15] *Seikō* echoed and reechoed the message that young people should first move to a city, preferably Tokyo, to prepare for adulthood.

Each issue included a three- to six-page section entitled "*Kisha to dokusha*" (reporter and reader) in which questions and answers were presented on a variety of topics, including travel abroad, schools and entrance examinations, jobs, health, medicine, parents, work-study, self-study, and counseling. The requests show that the majority of readers sought to enter some college or military, vocational, or technical school. Some wished to travel to the United States. Noticeably few aspired to government higher schools or imperial universities; in three randomly chosen 1909 issues of *Seikō*, only one question out of seventy-nine was about entering a government higher school. *Seikō* was less than encouraging about students' chances of obtaining an elite education and emphasized the difficulties of being accepted into the First or Third Higher Schools, a prerequisite for enrollment in an imperial university. It advised readers to try for the "most prestigious" private schools—Waseda, Tokyo College of Accounting, and Keio—and the government-sponsored Tokyo Higher Commercial College, even though the educational facilities of these schools were "somewhat imperfect" and "somewhat inadequate" and there was no guarantee that graduates could expect promising occupations.[16]

In addition to *Seikō*, there were a number of magazines, books, and pamphlets specifically devoted to tobei.[17] More specific in their goals, these writings were aimed at young people who were convinced that their prospects for achievement lay on the opposite shore of the Pacific Ocean. *Tobei shimpō* (News on crossing to America), a monthly that began publishing in 1907, boasted sales in eighty bookstores in Tokyo the following year.[18] Socialist Katayama Sen's introductory books about the United States were said to have sold to more than 100,000 readers.[19] *Tobei zasshi* (Crossing to America magazine) and its successor, *Amerika*, organs of Katayama's tobei organization, devoted their pages to matters concerning the United States. It is significant that popular journals such as *Seikō*, which were published for a general audience, nevertheless attached primary importance to American examples in their interpretations of the success ethic. All of these publications taught, entertained, and stimulated young adults who were, or desired to become, part of the rapidly forming chūryūkaikyū.

Hidden amid the array of articles reciting formulas for self-advancement and success, most of which repeated the "secrets of great Americans," lurked an important concept reminiscent of the individualistic and private ambitions depicted by Futabatei Shimei in *Ukigumo*. Although the many publications did not encourage baldly selfish behavior such as that displayed by Noboru, who disregarded coworkers and curried favor with superiors, they did stress that individual action was the key to success. The Japanese terms *kojin* and *kojinteki*—respectively, the noun and adjective forms of *individual*—were not used to express the specific behavior, but their essence was conveyed in the adjective *sekkyokuteki* (positive, active), such as in *sekkyokuteki kōdo* (positive action).[20]

In a 1904 article in *Seikō*, "*Gendai to sekkyokuteki hōshin*" (A sekkyokuteki policy for the present), the head of Keio University contrasted Western motivation with Japanese motivation by placing them at opposite extremes: positive and negative, active and passive.[21] He wrote that the Tokugawa seclusion policy, "a still prevalent condition," exemplified the Japanese outlook: "Ah, like a frog who remains in a pond and the river god who glorifies only the river, the Japanese is unaware of the great waters beyond." The article encouraged youth to leave Japan, "a place with too many people and meager wages." They should venture abroad, where profitable businesses prevail to aid in the "expansion of national power." The author cited Korea as an example. Japanese youth had matured in a country "already open to the world and dedicated to the policies of progress and development" and thus had benefited from an education "based on the learning of the whole world." They also had learned foreign languages "as preparation for going abroad." Why then, didn't they leave? The answer, wrote the author, lay in the "denial of the other"; the spirit of seclusion as inherited from the Tokugawa past prevented Japanese from recognizing or acknowledging anything outside of "the self." This spirit was inward-looking. It engendered a self filled with "retrogression and conservatism." It bestowed an aimless asceticism. The article persuaded educated Japanese to emigrate, particularly to areas that would enhance national power. It was a call to youth to venture beyond the confines of the islands of Japan and take advantage of the vast learning they had gained as citizens in new kindai Japan.

The writer proceeded to analyze *kinken chochiku* (thrift and savings), a phrase he correlated with the "denial of the other." He stated that although kinken chochiku was usually looked upon as a matter of principle, it also affected people's lives on an important day-to-day economic level. Neither principle nor economics was evil or harmful. However, when kinken chochiku became the basis for deprivation, loss, or misfortune, it was destructive, defiled by negativism. Kinken chochiku had spawned weakness and wretchedness in the way people lived, the author contended. Houses were built on foundations that loosened "with the slightest wind." The people ate "pickles and greens," their diet only a "little more refined than the diet of a monkey." The Japanese didn't eat nearly as well as the average person in the United States or Europe. Rather, they subsisted on "diets of poverty,"

... eating food without nutrition and then working one's body to excess; ... eating rice with barley and some greens twice a day when one could eat them thrice; eating two bowls when one could eat three.... This is the kinken chochiku which is so ardently proclaimed and religiously followed! This is the result of negativism. Why aren't we able to attain a superior standard of living equal to that in the U.S. and Europe? Why don't we strive to have a superior life which is equal to an American or European's?[22]

Japanese people had been poisoned by kinken chochiku. It fostered negative and passive behavior. Sekkyokuteki motives, by contrast, came from the need to expand—in business ("don't settle for ten thousand yen") and through travel, to promote foreign intercourse and to develop national power outside of Japan. The author urged Japanese to move to the outside, away from themselves.

Clearly, the article promoted the imperial aims of the nation. To realize these goals, people had to foster a "go forward" attitude, one expressed by the term *shimpo* (progress). Another author illuminated the inferiority of East Asians "who know only to preserve their capital and know not to march forward and accumulate.... [A] great culture in Asia is in the making. To be sekkyokuteki, people of the East must lift the banner of shimpo not only in matters of the military, but also in business, literature, and all other endeavors."[23] The timing of these articles was significant, for when these issues of *Seikō* were published, the fate of Korea was being determined by Japan and Russia in a conflict that had entered its fourth month. Patriotism during this war was graphically evident on the covers of *Seikō*, for the five semimonthly issues from April 1 to June 1, 1904, featured admirals, generals, commanders, and lieutenants who achieved battle fame in the Russo-

Japanese War. The models of the West were not forsaken, however; during the rest of the year the faces of Andrew Carnegie, Thomas Edison, and Democratic Party presidential hopeful Alton B. Parker adorned the covers, sharing the limelight with Hegel, Landsdowne, and Ibsen. What these individuals held in common concerning specific sekkyokuteki motives is not clear.

These explicit trumpet calls to go outside the self and to exploit the Other conformed to the national aims of imperialism and expansion, but another, more complex and perplexing attitude was evident. This included a perception of the Other not only as inferior but also as exploitable, as a means of fulfilling one's own selfish needs. It was a view that encouraged eating three bowls of rice instead of two. It repudiated the sacrifice of the body and therefore repudiated the sacrifice of the spirit. Taking action only as needs arose or as a defensive measure was considered an expression of negativism; thus, kinken chochiku could not be tolerated in a new sekkyokuteki society. The reader was left with a confusing set of messages: positivism and the Other; negativism and the self. Going out, going beyond oneself, was seen as the essence of profit and achievement. Concentrating on the self hindered acquisition, denied the Other, and caused weakness. One must focus on the self, not be frugal, satisfy one's own needs, and raise one's standard of living. In this context, the self and self-recognition became the essence of accumulation and profit. The important strategy to succeed, then, was that one had to balance the Other and the self. Probably without great concern for the logic (or illogic) in the arguments, readers took what they could from articles such as these. The clearest message was that the principles of thrift and savings could not remain as guidelines for the new Japanese world.

The question that remained unanswered was how a sekkyokuteki attitude was to be achieved. How was one to acquire it in Japan, which had little in common with resource-rich countries like the United States? What was the secret?

The magazine *Amerika*, which made liberal and superficial use of value-laden words such as "progress," "struggle," and "responsibility," touted the accomplishments of men such as Hearst, Bryan, and Rockefeller, as well as successful Japanese already settled in the United States (see Figure 3). However, some articles did more than merely recount the lives of men of achievement. A lead article, "*Beikokujin wa naniyueni kigyōshin ni tomeruka*" (Why are Americans endowed with the spirit of enterprise?), written by an anonymous "Henry," preached the

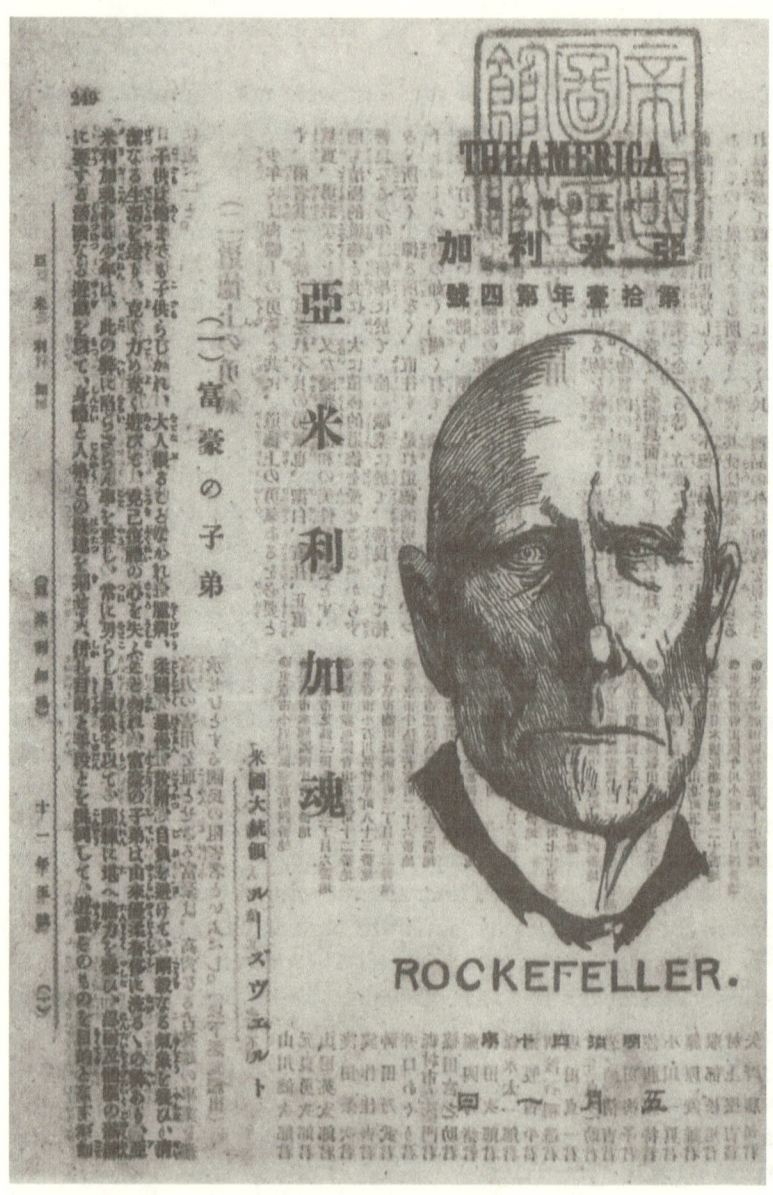

Fig. 3. Illustration for lead article, " 'The Spirit of America,' by American President Roosevelt," *Amerika* 10:4 (1 May 1907).

behavior and attitudes necessary to gain success.[24] The article urged readers to brave risks, be ready to compete, and willingly adapt to changing circumstances: "Although we see many successful Japanese in America, their achievements are equivalent to but one strand of hair from amongst a multitude of cows, for no one can compare to the fierce competitive struggles of the people of America."

Henry dismissed as misleading the explanations given for the fierce American competitive spirit, such as self-centeredness ("a trait which ignores all but the pursuit of the dollar") or entrepreneurial effort based on "high and noble" values. He believed the fundamentals of the American spirit could be understood only by analyzing American education and the social environment. Henry focused on American families, in particular the characteristics of child-raising. During his return to Japan from New York, he was struck by the "extreme liveliness" of the American children on board the passenger steamer. Most did not suffer from seasickness, and their conduct and conversation were totally different from that of Japanese children. For example, a girl of four or five who was on deck

> hung over the railing of the ship looking as if she might fall into the sea. Startled, I ran to her, intending to catch her, but just at that moment, her mother appeared, and I concluded that all would be safe. However, to my amazement, her mother seemed quite self-possessed, patted her child on the head and asked, "Are you playing nicely?" Then, totally ignoring any danger to the child, the mother walked away. I thought to myself: "American mothers are bold and daring!" . . . One would think that the appropriate response would be to run and stop the child. Some American mothers might do just that, but it is customary in that country to expect that children look after themselves.[25]

Henry admitted that this kind of practice might result in "injurious consequences" at times, but he noted that Americans interpreted such experiences in a positive light. In Japan children were always admonished to be well-behaved and obedient, so much so that when they reached maturity they lacked independence. Wet nurses cared for them during infancy, and maids accompanied them to school. Freedom was unknown to them. They were incapable of making independent decisions upon reaching the stage of life when it was necessary to do so.

In the United States, by contrast, the educational approach helped children gain self-confidence. One child, not more than eight or nine, could have been traveling by himself, "for I never saw his parents." He walked up and down the ship's deck, "erect, looking composed, and nonchalant, with both hands in his pocket like an adult." To Henry's wonder and admiration, the child was a linguistic genius. "He knew English, of course, and spoke French and Spanish with the greatest of ease." He could travel by himself throughout Europe without any difficulty. "There are those who may think that these children are special cases and that they are accustomed to traveling around the world. That is not true. There are many such children in the United States."

Henry stated that both girls and boys were taught to be self-sufficient at an early age, although he did not mention girls' upbringing beyond this brief reference. American children packed their own luggage, ordered their own food at restaurants ("not like Japanese children, who would eat what is placed before them only after getting approval from their mothers"), and were not upset or saddened if their parents took extended trips to foreign countries. They gained independence by taking responsibility and learning from their parents' examples, not by reproof and correction: "Already at the young age of ten, American children are adroit conversationalists concerning their plans for their business future.... At sixteen or seventeen they work out ways to be independent of their fathers.... At twenty-two or three they would be considered a disgrace if they remained dependent and gnawed on their father's leg."[26]

Even the wealthiest American fathers regarded labor as "sacred" and encouraged their sons to begin their independent lives by "earning bread from the sweat of labor." Every son was expected to hold his own job. Some foreigners looked upon American fathers as selfish, but the fostering of children's independence was the "essence of American education." Rich children were not coddled or spoiled, Henry wrote. There were a few exceptions, but these were the results of improper parental upbringing and an attitude that considered labor "ignoble."

Henry did not refer to the affluence of the American families in the article. His Japanese examples were limited to middle-class or well-to-do families. The article left readers with the impression that these were the norms: All American children, regardless of social class, grew up in an environment that stressed self-sufficiency from an early age and in their maturity were rewarded with affluence. By contrast, Japanese children grew up in a protective environment not conducive to self-sufficiency and economic independence. They lacked the adventurous spirit necessary to succeed in business, and few attained the success that came so easily to Americans.

The results of child-rearing in the United States provided important evidence of what was possible when young minds were properly influenced and illustrated the generation-to-generation connection that Henry characterized as the basis of the American spirit of enterprise. However, to Japanese readers unendowed with this paternal benefit, this description of child-rearing only served to emphasize the cultural differences that eased and promoted the American youth's entry into economic adulthood. Where were the examples that could serve as more practical guides for the eager Japanese aspirant to success? How was one to act with independence, be outgoing, learn foreign languages, travel, and expand if one was unfortunate enough to have been born and raised in Japan?

Abe Isō, a Christian socialist, minister, Anglophile, and professor at Waseda, attempted to offer an easy-to-follow description of the behavioral and attitudinal Japanese world that could nurture a sekkyokuteki outlook.[27] Entitled "*Nihonjinwa naniyue fukenzen naru gorakuni fukeruka?*" (Why do Japanese indulge in unwholesome leisure activity?), the article began with the assertion that the tone and temper of a people can be ascertained from their various recreations.

The Americans and British like outdoor sports in particular. The Germans enjoy music and theater as well as beer-drinking. They also enjoy sports, but compared to the Americans and British, the variety is limited. The main German sports activities are ice skating and dueling. The French also enjoy music and theater, but do not engage in any active sports. The Spanish seem to have festivals throughout the year and are forever merrymaking. The major activities of the Chinese are smoking opium and gambling.

The hierarchy of peoples is unmistakable. Anglo-Saxons were without question the most superior, Chinese, the least so. The world-shaking advancements of the Americans and British were reflected in their zeal for outdoor sports. The Americans had their baseball, the English, their cricket—games that were valued as national pastimes. As soon as they settled in a foreign place, Abe noted, their first order of business was to set up an athletic field. The author seemed to approve of a colonial power's showing off its national game to a colonized people as an example of cultural superiority. His observation foreshadowed future Japanese subjugation policies in which, as colonizer, it promoted its culture as advanced, vigorous, confident, and successful.

In addition to their national sports, the Americans and British enjoyed boating, lawn tennis, football, and soccer. Weather permitting, they were always prepared to engage in some sport outside. During the winter months leisure activities took place indoors, and the interest in music and drama was as intense as the enthusiasm for outdoor sports. This well-rounded, healthy, and wholesome attitude toward recreation was the basis of Anglo-Saxon prominence in the world and the development of "bodies of steel and nerves of iron.... It is said that an English woman considers a government cabinet minister to be the ideal mate. If not a cabinet minister, then a crew member of a sculling team from Oxford or Cambridge—a clear indication that the whole nation is interested in sports and does not censor it as coarse or unrefined." The lesson was that even as an adult, a person should continue participating in sports.

Western recreations were a far cry from the "feminine, inactive, and retiring" leisure activities of the Japanese. Abe grumbled about the "indecisive and makeshift nature" of Japanese pastimes that stemmed from the national fondness for storytelling songs and dramas—so "absurdly lengthy" that they required "thirty minutes to an hour for one piece." Japanese music and the game of *go*, all of which took place indoors, were unenergetic and unhealthy and reflected the "slow and tedious nature of our citizenry." The only active sport was *sumō*, a spectator sport in which most people did not participate. Abe listed three reasons for the insignificance of outdoor sports in Japanese life. First, historical social class roles required only the samurai to subject themselves to harsh physical discipline (in order to excel in the martial arts). Second, "the aristocratic society regarded any physical labor with contempt.... [P]hysical activity other than the martial arts was the function of people of lower rank." Finally, the impossibility of moving about freely in Japanese dress or in Japanese houses effectively discouraged energetic activity. Settling down on the *tatami* was incompatible with physical movement; in sharp contrast, chairs and tables in Western houses did not hinder movement. Abe pointed out that the Japanese tendency toward inactivity was apparent even among emigrants to the U.S. West Coast. They clung to the practices of the past, a weakness that "subjects them to numerous temptations, many which we in Japan cannot imagine." Restaurants and brothels existed wherever Japanese congregated, as well as gambling parlors run by Chinese, who contrived "to extract the blood of our compatriots." These regressive attitudes toward physical fitness were indicative of people saddled with unhealthy leisure habits. An altered outlook was necessary. Appropriately, sex as a physical activity was unmentioned and ignored.

Despite Abe's socialist thinking and sympathies for a classless society, he and other writer-teachers inundated Meiji youth with examples of affluent and well-rounded Americans who traveled widely, knew foreign languages, attended the theater, appreciated music, and engaged in exclusive sports such as tennis. Incredibly, the writers failed to mention that only an elite minority of American youth could enjoy this lifestyle, and they disregarded the fact that it was inaccessible to the majority of Japanese youth. Nevertheless, their writings communicated a sense of the potential for change. They prodded youth to learn about and absorb the tenacity, acumen, and physical determination of "great Americans," qualities that were the necessary stepping stones to success. The ridicule of non-Anglo-Saxon groups, including the Japanese themselves, seems to indicate a comprehensive acceptance of Anglo-Saxon values and a conviction that imitation could rescue the Japanese from sinking to the level of the Chinese or southern Europeans.

However, this interpretation overlooks an important element: the presentation of differences between the groups as behavioral—the necessary escape valve: The Japanese could alter their behavior to conform to the needs of a kindai nation-state. Although the undesirable qualities of passivity, inactivity, and disdain for physical exertion were "Japanese," they were defined as remnants of the pre-Meiji era, when a rigid class structure dominated society. The writers insisted that these behavioral qualities were inappropriate and should be discarded by the new Meiji society. However, social class and lifestyles enjoyed by affluent people in kindai Japan were not to be discarded—in fact, they were to be pursued. Abe's acclamation of Anglo-Saxon sports; the Keio University administrator's disparagement of kinken chochiku; and Henry's appreciation of the well-traveled linguistic child genius all pointed to the ideal of material success held by people striving to assume a new chūryūkaikyū identity.

However, with respect to severe unemployment, the prevailing advice contradicted the familiar exhortations to obtain a college education and pursue a bourgeois lifestyle. Articles on unemployment emphasized that not everyone had the capacity or the talent to attain success in middle-class terms. In a *Seikō* article, a faculty member of Keio University questioned the value of higher education for all.[28] His reasoning was based on the fact that Japan had not yet progressed to the point where labor was esteemed. Manual work still carried the unfortunate "vestige of the feudal era." No one wanted to become a laborer. Everyone desired a higher education, but jobs did not exist for all graduates, and therefore unemployment ensued. The author argued that some people were unfit for education and "a role in the upper class"; he believed institutions of higher learning should weed out people better suited to "using their hands." The writer did not demean labor; in fact, he promoted the sanctity of labor. But his intention was not to make the laborer's status equal with that of educated middle-class individuals. He wanted to make it more palatable.

In the same vein, Baron Dan Takuma, engineer, executive of the Mitsui Company, and master of corporate entrepreneurship, counseled the readers of *Seikō* regarding the shortage of jobs.[29] He said Mitsui offered one job for every twenty to thirty applicants each year, a terrifying prospect for youth who persevered in school beyond the compulsory requirement of six years. "There are some who say they would work without pay and beg for employment," Baron Dan wrote. "I cannot condone such an immoral condition. . . . It can result in countless abuses, a danger for any industrialist of substance." He acknowledged that college graduates anguished over the employment situation but suggested that the worth of a diploma was overrated. Two decades of education tended to make students and their parents look upon a diploma as "a kind of talisman." When a youth was "thrust onto the violent waves and winds of the great ocean of life, the thousands of volumes of knowledge locked in the deepest corners of his heart" were of little consequence.

Looking back at his years at "a school called the Institute of Technology in Boston, Massachusetts," Baron Dan recounted the story of a brilliant student in his class, "a refined and honest young American." Three or four months before he was to graduate, this young man unexpectedly announced his withdrawal from college. He had received a job offer from a major cotton trading company in New Orleans and had to leave immediately. A diploma meant nothing to this particular firm; it was merely a piece of paper certifying that a person had completed his education. "It had nothing to do with merit or the company's confidence in that person." His friend advanced steadily and achieved a prominent position in the firm. The author went on: "I do not mean to imply that diplomas have no value and should be ignored. However, I consider that knowledge of life itself is paramount. . . . [A] diploma does not guarantee that a person has acquired that knowledge. The final worth of a person is determined by his 'ability.' "[30]

Ability was the most important element in Baron Dan's formula for success, even overriding education. He used the Chinese compound characters read as *sainō* in Japanese as the translation for *ability* but incorporated a new reading, *a-bi-re-te*, combining Western and Japanese notions of merit and intelligence. This linguistic alteration creatively combined a new word with a familiar compound to produce an interpretation in keeping with the institutional and cultural changes that took place in Japan.

The timing of the article in relation to world politics was particularly significant. It was published in the post-Russo-Japanese War period, when Japan acquired southern Sakhalin, became the dominant imperial power in Manchuria and Korea, and was a growing presence in a weak and fragmented China. In 1910 it annexed Korea. These step-by-step encroachments onto the Asian continent established Japan as a military power in competition with the Western imperial nations. Economically, the state-subsidized large-scale industries of banking, shipping, and heavy industry had achieved a stable footing, aided by the tremendous jump in military expenditures during the Sino-Japanese and Russo-Japanese Wars. Large private corporate enterprises increasingly became the overseers of capital formation and financing for industrial purposes.[31] The textile industry had grown to the extent that Japanese cotton, which was targeted mainly at domestic consumers at first, began to spread to foreign markets, particularly China, as factory production began to take over hand production at the turn of the century. Japan's exports of raw silk, produced as the key supplementary domestic industry by peasants, superseded those of China and the European countries between 1909 and 1913.[32]

Nevertheless, the economy was subject to irregularities in production levels, interest rates, stock market indexes, consumption levels, and employment rates. Cyclical troughs and peaks became endemic to the economic development process. The massive primary expenditures on war, military-related and strategic industries, and colonial administration seriously compromised any benefits economic growth may have brought to society. As E. H. Norman suggested, according to John Dower, "the 'success' of the Meiji state was, almost inevitably, the tragedy of the Japanese people."[33] A large segment of the population had to accept the economic uncertainties, be part of the forces of production (temporarily at times), and willingly sacrifice for an expanding, wealthy, and strong Japan. The ideas that not everyone should expect to advance beyond a compulsory education and that some people should be willing to assume responsibilities beneath their training and/or expectations were prerequisites if the nation-state was to maintain its dominance over the populace, prevent conflict and disorder, and gain the coveted position of power in the world.[34]

Notwithstanding the uncertain and straitened circumstances facing the Japanese people, popular articles failed to explore the deeper socioeconomic causes of the distress and anguish experienced by Meiji youth. They presented circuitous arguments that valued labor and, in doing so, justified the lack of jobs for the educated. By rejecting the Tokugawa aristocracy and pointing to the structural defects of that class society, the articles seemed to place the common person in the Meiji period in a position of esteem, perhaps even equality with the privileged and well-to-do. Nevertheless, such articles held labor in contempt. They did not criticize the growth of a newly formed, educated, salaried chūryūkaikyū whose members faced limited prospects for success. The gist of the articles was that people had to extricate themselves from the past and overcome unemployment, job shortages, "the diet of poverty," business failures, and low standards of living by skillfully blending self-sufficiency, activism, and ability. The true sekkyokuteki spirit would thereby ensue. The onus of unfavorable social conditions was placed squarely on the shoulders of people who "misunderstood" the essence of kindai attitudes and behavior; *they* were guilty of blocking Japan's progress.

The articles were confusing and bewildering, for in reality one could never be employed in a firm such as Mitsui without higher education. Furthermore, the repetitious parade of abstractions failed to clarify a worldview helpful in obtaining the fruits of the kindai world. Rather, they emphasized conformity, patience, and obedience: Citizens should wait for a place in the sun by adhering to society's rules and should not question the disruptive social and economic forces that made their lives less than stable. However, because these platitudes were reinforced by personal observations from respected and successful kindai Japanese leaders, it was difficult for the young and inexperienced to refute the logic. Didacticism and repetition served to authenticate this point of view.

In conjunction with the many teachings on the creation of a new Japanese sekkyokuteki spirit of endeavor, dedication, and success, writings on the accumulation of money also appeared in seikō magazines as well as in popular fiction. Money had to be made morally acceptable, for in the not-distant past those who handled it, the merchants, were relegated to the lowest stratum of society. During the course of the Tokugawa period, the merchants' importance in the country's economy grew; they became the moneylenders, transactors of domestic trade, landowners, and purchasers of samurai family names. But the stigma attached to mercenary matters as unclean and uncouth persisted.[35] With Japan's entry into the world of capitalism, ideas and actions concerning money—acquiring it, using it, making it pay, and touching it—had to be made acceptable and desirable. The profit motive was no longer a vice, nor was conduct for profit dishonorable.

Justifications for the practice of making money peppered the pages of *Seikō*. Articles suggesting the fusion of the past and present conveyed approval of profits as long as the profit seeker understood the "true Bushidō."[36] Honor and integrity were Bushidō's important elements and should be the basis of moneymaking. Thus the elite pre-Meiji disdain for commercial transactions was replaced by the kindai view, which acknowledged their necessity. "Don't belittle material things," urged *Seikō*, for "man cannot live without bread. . . . Bread and the spirit have to be valued like the two wings of a bird."[37] Without such a dual appreciation, one could not transform one's fortunes without embarrassment and "accumulate ten thousand yen from one hundred yen in eleven years."[38] The possibility of engaging in diverse and divergent trades, running the gamut from operating a pawnshop to making and selling cosmetics, became feasible; as long as moneymaking occurred with the correct awareness and spirit, all avenues were open.

Two particularly interesting novels appeared in the *Yomiuri shimbun* in serialized form. Both projected themes about the value of money and the attitudes necessary in dealing with it. The daily *Yomiuri*, first published in 1874, was aimed at a wide reading public, in contrast to the more political newspapers. It had been the best-selling newspaper until the mid-1880s. When increased governmental pressure caused political newspapers to fail, new newspapers geared more toward entertainment began to proliferate, spurred by technological advances in the printing press and the growth of advertising.[39] Cartoons, novels, serials, interviews, and "unabashed commercialism" were decisive elements in keeping newspapers afloat.[40] In this competitive environment the *Yomiuri*, which had a circulation of 15,000 to 20,000 in the mid-1880s, lost its number-one status, and moved aggressively to regain its former popularity. In 1886 it altered its policy to place greater emphasis on serialized novels: circulation rose instantly.[41] Together with the *Osaka Asahi, Tokyo Asahi*, and *Mainichi* (which in 1906 was renamed the *Tokyo Mainichi*), the *Yomiuri* held a major position as an important mass-circulation daily and source of information and entertainment.[42]

A variety of novels appeared one after another, including translations of Western fiction (Edgar Allen Poe's *The Black Cat*, in 1887, was

Fig. 4. Illustration from the newspaper novel *Seiyōmusume katagi*, *Yomiuri shimbun* (1897). Toshinori clutches forty pounds of cash given to him by Mario to repay gambling debts. Note the blending of Japanese and Western aesthetics.

one).[43] Some issues featured two novels, one of which always ran on the first page. A contemporary editor claimed: "Lengthy novels are the way to suck in readers." Novels were the "artillery" of newspaper sales policy.[44] The *Yomiuri* won fame as the primary literary arts newspaper for the masses and helped writing get established as a legitimate profession in Japan.[45]

For a month and a half in 1897, the *Yomiuri* ran the inappropriately entitled novel *Seiyōmusume katagi* (Characteristics of Western maidens) by Yanagawa Shunyō (1877–1918), a lesser Meiji writer who won acclaim as a newspaper novelist (see Figures 4–7).[46] This melodrama was

Fig. 5. Illustration from *Seiyōmusume katagi*. Toshinori learns that he is the legitimate heir to his mother's estate.

essentially about the acquisition of money and status. However, it is as interesting for its transformation of Western forms into the Japanese literary genre as for its elucidation of how to amass wealth. Like many of the earlier newspaper novels freely adapted from Poe, Dumas, Disraeli, and other popular writers of the West, the story was reconstructed and made to fit the Japanese mode.[47] Shunyō converted some names of persons and places into Japanese. Others took on sounds that were somewhat close to the original. Thus, "Peter Smith" became *Sumisu Pita*; "Marion" changed to *Mario*; "David" to *Tamito*; "Theresa" to *Terusa*; "Sophia" to *Soyako*. The names became Japanese names, and by assigning Chinese characters to all of them, Shunyō made them more familiar to readers. As he stated in the first installment:

This is a real story which I heard from a friend.... The characters are not typical Japanese men and women, but entirely different and difficult to understand.... [T]he events would not occur in Japan. The society, customs, and situations are unfamiliar. So are the feelings. However, if you,

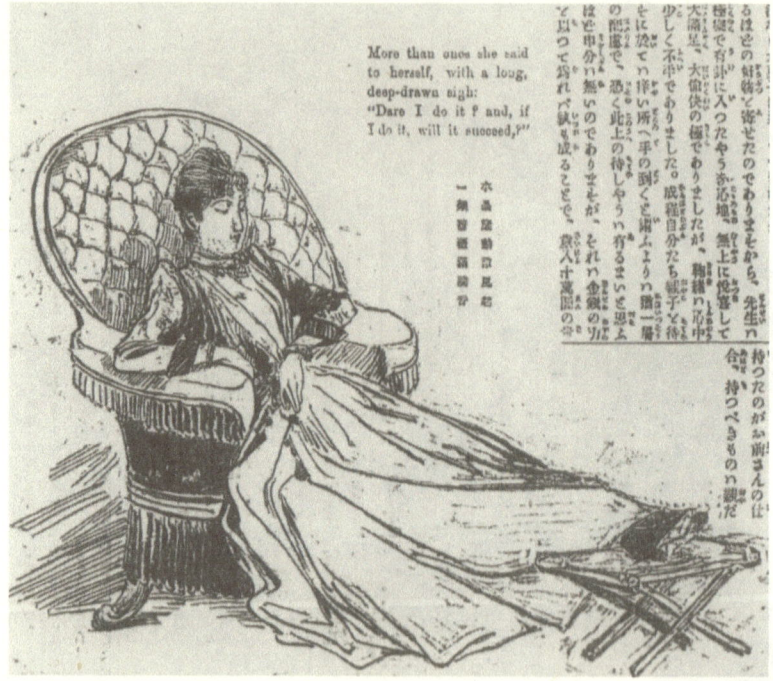

Fig. 6. Illustration from *Seiyōmusume katagi*. Mario calculates ways to lure the wealthy Toshinori.

my readers, were to appreciate the smell of butter in this story, it could provide one moment of amusement.[48]

And amusement it provides, for the novel is extravagant in its portrayal of nobility and refinement, gambling and attempted suicide, love and innocence, and, most of all, wealth and happiness. It offered a Japanese rendition of the West to ordinary newspaper readers. The illustrations depict non-Japanese characters and surroundings with Victorian styles of clothing and housing interiors. The figures bear a mixture of Western and Eastern facial characteristics, not unusual in Meiji illustrations, although to a Westerner they are not recognizably Western. The illustrations are, in fact, Japanese constructions. To the Japanese of the time, though, they contained qualities that were unquestionably Western and "un-Japanese," and thus the gap between the alien and the familiar was narrowed for readers.

Fig. 7. Illustration from *Seiyōmusume katagi*. Toshinori and Mario spend their "unrestricted and incalculable wealth" in Paris.

The story centers around the hero, Toshinori, and two young women: Mario, who seeks "a wealthy, refined, promising husband," and Soyako, whom the hero sees in a field in an early installment, "making his heart pound." Coincidences abound, usually bringing about favorable resolutions. Toshinori, Dr. Sumisu's ward, who is "treated a trifle better than as a gatekeeper," discovers through a newspaper ad that his mother was of noble and wealthy birth and that the estate is looking for her heirs. Despite his having lived under simple and humble circumstances as a youth, his "naturally aristocratic" demeanor, his remarkable resemblance to his ancestors, and the fact that he does not "smell of the soil" confirms that he is the rightful heir. He is given responsibility over matters of the estate, substantially increases its holdings, and brings fame and honor to his family name.

Mario, Dr. Sumisu's daughter, learns about his aristocratic birth and blackmails him into marrying her. At one time she rescued the hero from gambling losses accumulated in a night of misguided self-indulgence; now she threatens to divulge his evening of debauchery if he refuses. "Europeans are not awkward about speaking up," comments author Shunyō, "not like Japanese." Toshinori agrees to the marriage, not only because of Mario's threat but also because he is an honorable young man and feels a great debt to her as well as to her father.

Then, at a social event before his marriage to Mario, Toshinori meets the young woman he saw in the field, Soyako, and learns that she is the daughter of a count. He spends a pleasurable evening with her and declares his love, but his honor and his guilt about the secret gambling debt prevent him from pursuing her. However, after six installments of an unhappy married life, Mario conveniently commits suicide, and Toshinori is free to wed Soyako. Love triumphs; the hero is rich; and the reader has been entertained for forty-eight days by a romantic melodrama. Dogged perseverance is not the only method for gaining wealth; the pursuit of appropriately useful connections, some of which could result in unexpected turns of fate, may be equally fruitful. Manipulation is not recognized or mentioned. Rather, Toshinori's naïveté and virginity, his nobility and honesty, are the keys. The reader concludes the series with the fantasy that love and money can be attained and that there is no contradiction between wealth and happiness. The admonition that the "events would not occur in Japan" seems irrelevant.

By contrast, *Konjikiyasha* (The golden demon) deals with the unprincipled lust for monetary gain, its destructive effects on human relationships, and the difficulty of liberating oneself from that abyss.[49] The idea was taken from an American novel (Bertha M. Clay's *The White Lily*), a means used frequently by Japanese writers to multiply their creative output and stay in print.[50] Written by Shunyō's teacher, Ozaki Kōyō (1867–1903), it was the most popular newspaper novel of the turn of the century, running from 1897 to 1902, with some lapses because of Kōyō's ill health. Kōyō, who was known already for a number of works (the first published in 1885) and commanded respect in the Tokyo literary world, was employed by the *Yomiuri* in 1890 and quickly became a favorite writer as well as a mentor to many known Meiji novelists.[51] Up to the time *Konjikiyasha* appeared, newspaper novels were peopled by characters who sometimes took on the voice of the author and spouted morals, comments, and critiques (as in Shunyō's piece). One chief editor of a leading newspaper wrote that the purpose was to offset and "plant ideals in" the "ignorant" minds of the female readers:

[T]hey only look for stories which would stimulate their psyches in an emotional way. They indulge in insignificant feelings of joy, anger, pathos, and pleasure . . . and prefer life to unfold as in the changing patterns of a kaleidoscope. . . . [U]nless a story fills their hearts with an acute pessimism, they are uninterested. If any lofty ideal is presented, our female readers assault us saying they do not understand it.[52]

This severe criticism of a significant segment of the newspaper-novel readership, however, was not to have crucial or lasting influence upon the Meiji novel. In fact, *Konjikiyasha* falls squarely into the genre at which this criticism was directed. It does not teach or sermonize but "stimulates the psyche." Drawing its audience not only from among undeservedly maligned young women but from a wide range of male and female readers, the novel was said to have influenced intellectuals and important Meiji writers such as Natsume Sōseki and Mori Ōgai.[53] Kōyō's writing style, with which he had been experimenting for several years, was a factor in its popularity. He wrote the novel immediately before *Konjikiyasha* entirely in colloquial Japanese; in *Konjikiyasha* he drew on colloquial language for the dialogue and classical language for the narrative, skillfully creating a revolutionary literary voice.[54]

Kōyō's health prevented him from keeping up with the demanding schedule of the newspaper and finishing the novel. He was dismissed from the *Yomiuri* in May 1902, the same month his last installment appeared. The removal of *Konjikiyasha* made the paper the target of indignant readers and adversely affected its circulation, a situation from which the paper did not recover until one year later, when it finally found and hired a novelist whose work was able to draw attention.[55] Kōyō died of cancer in October 1903.

The plot of *Konjikiyasha* involves a young woman, Omiya, who is betrothed to her student sweetheart but forsakes him for a wealthy industrialist, blinded by the riches he has to offer. Kōyō successfully played on the sympathies and emotions of his readers by focusing on love and gold, the "two great powers over life." He wrote:

[g]old is temporal.... "Love," on the other hand, is unchanging, eternal, and supports life.... I wanted to write about that. I described the conflict between love and gold.... If Omiya were a prototypical Meiji woman, she would have obliterated memories of her past love as soon as she became the wife of another. However, I wanted to present her as a "transcendant Meiji woman" by describing her remorse. This was my main aim in writing this novel.[56]

And remorse she feels, for Omiya is hounded by it physically and psychologically throughout the novel—from the famous moonlit Atami beach scene in which she tells her sweetheart, Kanichi, of her impending marriage and he, in a rage, kicks her to the ground, to the scene four years later when she espies him from a distance and faints in a heap, unable to restrain her guilt, pain, and confusion.[57] Omiya can never achieve happiness because her actions are based on her unprincipled thirst for the bourgeois life. Kanichi, incited by anger and unrequited passion, submerges himself in the usury business, carrying out the many offensive tasks of the trade for his employer. This occupation makes him intolerable, devoid of feeling, cold, merciless, and self-destructive. He is loathsome to comrades from his student days and milks his victims to abject poverty.

Nevertheless, the reader identifies with and experiences complete sympathy for both characters. Their weaknesses notwithstanding—or rather, *because* of their weaknesses—Kanichi and Omiya are attractive in their anguish. Kōyō presents Kanichi as a person with such magnetism that the reader feels great compassion for him. The same holds for Omiya, who has opted for a life of comfort as an attractive and elegant wife but inwardly suffers great unhappiness and perpetual agony. Hope arises when the reader imagines a reconciliation between Kanichi and Omiya, but this does not happen, for both lives have evolved to depend totally upon the immoral acquisition of wealth. Happiness is beyond their reach as long as they deny their true feelings of love. Their lust for money has destroyed both of them.

In one scene, an avaricious and ambitious female usurer, endowed with beauty and elegance, proposes marriage to Kanichi with the expectation that their union could promise a profitable partnership as well as an enriching personal relationship. To the delight of the reader, he refuses her. In explaining his rejection, Kanichi says:

> I used to be a student but stopped my studies midway, not because of a dissipated life or shortage of funds. Other, more desirable occupations are available for students who decide to give up their education. Why did I choose this brutal, cruel trade, which is the same as stealing in broad daylight; which parches the throats of the sick and kills any semblance of honor, something dearer than life itself? . . . I stooped to this trade after having tasted the bitterest fruits of despair and disappointment fed to me by those whom I trusted. . . . I was betrayed because of money. I was shamed because I had no money. I have forgotten justice and humanity. I am without honor and love. I have no desire except to make money and look forward to the day when my agony will be dispelled. . . . Money is by far more trustworthy and dependable than people.[58]

Kanichi's recitation discloses his self-hate and pain, which, to the reader, diminishes the effects of his most savage and heinous actions as a usurer.

Wealth itself and what it can procure are never criticized in Kōyō's emotion-ridden literary work; nor is it in Shunyō's simplistic fantasy.

The good life, beautiful clothes, the appreciation for Western wine, and other trappings of the bourgeois life are depicted as signs of gentility and grace. This viewpoint is evident from the outset of *Konjikiyasha*, which describes a young gentleman (*shinshi*) who is on his way to join friends for the New Year's festivities.[59] This young man wears over a Japanese kimono a heavy fur-collared greatcoat, which was adapted from the Western double-layered coat with cape. It was popular at the time among men of substance.[60] Aspects of life that the moneyed consider tasteful, can purchase, and enjoy are described in detail in the same way throughout the novel: Omiya's wardrobe, her hairstyle, her upper-class demeanor, the sophisticated conversations of Kanichi's urbane and educated friends. These qualities distinguish the chūryūkaikyū from the rest of society and are not censured. They are the attractive fruits of money and success. Shunyō's hero merits unanticipated riches, status, and love because he proves himself to be an honest and noble gentleman. Kōyō's hero and heroine are doomed to the depths of suffering, loveless and unhappy, because of their misguided lust for money. This lust differentiates Kōyō's characters from Shunyō's. Money is necessary to achieve success, but it has to be acquired in a principled way, with integrity and with regard for humanity. Money-worship corrupts. But the legitimate, rational, and honest acquisition of money can result in the kind of life that the readers of *Konjikiyasha* desire for Kanichi and Omiya.[61]

Among the many ways to acquire money, usury, which is presented in such an ugly way in *Konjikiyasha*, was given some legitimacy in a lengthy article by a *kōrigashi* (usurer) who was "president of a Meiji Finance Company."[62] The article described usurers' lifestyle, motivation, and ambition, as well as the details of loan procedures, methods of collection, interest rates, types of debtors and creditors, and third parties. Readers received what seems to be a practical picture of the trade as well as significant advice. The writer glossed over any strict moral judgment, although he cautioned:

> It is possible that the nature of the usury business cannot prevent the tendency to become excessively brutal, even among the most principled of usurers. However, the quality that is most lacking among usurers is social honor. In order to gain some sense that they have attained honor, they try to buy it and engage in public-spirited actions such as contributing to social welfare agencies or aiding struggling students.... [I]f a contracted debt cannot be collected, its amount increases steadily. Therefore, the usurer hopes that the debtor will uplift himself, amount to something, and ultimately become successful. This is the usurer's eternal prayer. It is a strange

kind of sympathy. Sometimes, by being overly trustful and allowing the debt to increase, terrible disaster can befall the usurer.

He ended his piece with his hopes for his future: Once he has fulfilled his goal of gaining "enough wealth" he can retire, see that his children get an education, and open a pawnshop or some other "profitable" business.

The writer used a convoluted logic to rationalize usurers' activities and portray them as people of humanity and social conscience: Contributing to public causes and infusing debtors with ambition justified the trade. This conclusion relied on the sentimental notion that all people have an innate sense of good in them, even usurers. Articles such as these helped to sanction occupations that thrived under conditions of capital scarcity, a continuing situation through the Meiji years.[63]

From the lofty goals of nobility and honor to the mercenary aim of relentless greed, from pompous analyses of the superiority of the sekkyokuteki American spirit to the adoration of the samurai—success at this time took on many meanings. The Japanese definition of success in the Meiji kindai world had an intimate relationship with the defining of the Meiji kindai identity. Since the incursion of the West, beginning with Perry's mission in 1854 and culminating in the overthrow of a weakened Tokugawa, Japan had acted to rid itself of its minor-power status. Eyeing the west and south for lands to conquer and resources with which to build, Japan infused its capitalistic productive segments with orders for goods to aid in the accomplishment of those ends. The Sino-Japanese War was an important watershed that secured Japan's place as a rising and formidable contender with Western capitalist and imperial powers. Japan's mission to join this community of nations and its desire eventually to supersede the West created ideological contradictions. Pinpointing the essence of the Japanese identity that justified the actions of this expanding, avaricious, power-hungry state was not an easy task.

The recipes for the achievement of success were varied and confusing. They acknowledged American superiority and stressed the importance of acquiring something akin to the American mentality but simultaneously established a strong hold on what were considered desirable "Japanese" traditions. The pre-Meiji behavioral products of harsh living—the results of kinken chochiku—were anathema, but the nobility and strength of the samurai were exalted in this recasting of the Japanese identity. The architects of kindai Japan dissected the American cultural mentality, laid out the ingredients that propelled the United States's surge of economic growth, and presented a picture of Americans as homogeneous, self-sufficient, able, pragmatic, refined, and respectful of labor. Those qualities, combined with the ideals of the pre-Meiji Japanese elite, were said to be crucial in shaping the spirit needed to acquire success. In order to achieve the aims of the ambitious—employment, security, the fruits of hard labor, a good standard of living, and finally, wealth and success—youth had to strike a delicate balance between aspiration and principle, self-fulfillment and concern for humanity, hard work and hard play, specialized endeavors and broad interests, making money and integrity. Young Japanese were inundated with these abstractions.

For members of the generation brought up in this world, the promises and expectations were far beyond their realm of attainment. The many contemporary publications describing simplistic ways to achieve success only served to accentuate the belief among some youth that they were deficient in their efforts. Not realizing success, therefore, meant that a person lacked certain attributes and failed to recognize and practice teachings that, as we have seen, were based on the most narrow and subjective observations and neglectful of the real and unpredictable economic world. Failure meant that the individual misunderstood the lessons of life, work, education, marriage, and family or had been misled into believing that these lessons could be followed easily in Japan. How were success, honor, diligence, romance, and love, the less tangible aspects of life, whose meanings had been transformed from the past, to be acquired? As illustrated by a wide assortment of serialized novels that were avidly followed in the daily newspapers, the answers to these questions concerning the meaning of life were complicated. In addition, myths about living in the West appeared almost as regularly, giving a distorted view of how individuals could or should act. If one could not achieve one's life goals in Japan, perhaps one could do so in the United States. Some educated Japanese expected that their lives in the United States would be more conducive to their aspirations. Furthermore, for the chūryūkaikyū Tokyojin, or those who felt they were on the road to attaining that status, their knowledge and experience might bring them more benefits across the Pacific than in the rigid, mixed-up, and frustrating society that was Japan.

CHAPTER 6

"Go East, Young Man!"

For some, paradoxically, to succeed as the ideal kindai Japanese individual, they had to leave Japan itself. In China, Korea, Manchuria, and the Japanese islands of Hokkaido and Taiwan, propinquity, Japan's imperial interests, and government encouragement eased the process of migration.[1] However, to those most deeply persuaded by the sekkyokuteki consciousness and hungry for an environment that promoted independence and the utilization of "abirete," the dreams reached out far from the Asian continent, across "the great waters beyond."

To understand the reasoning of the hi-imin who made the decision to pursue life in New York City, USA, it is necessary to go beyond purely economic motives. Their expectations may have resembled those of some immigrants to California or Hawaii, but their class, education, and urban background altered the meaning of "living abroad." This was particularly so beginning in the first decade of the twentieth century, when the differences between imin and hi-imin became explicitly defined. Shimanuki Hyōdayū (1866–1912), a prolific writer on matters concerning tobei, lauded the new Japanese passport regulations. He valued them because they restricted "the miscellaneous type of Japanese imin who emigrated to the West Coast when passports were easily obtainable" and who could never advance beyond the status of a laborer.[2] The new regulations guaranteed passports to those "who were trusted by Westerners" and acted in such ways that "anyone could tell their success was assured"[3]—in other words, the hi-imin, who could better understand, appreciate, and acquire the habits, customs, and style of the immigrant country.

In this chapter, I propose to look specifically at tobei publications, which introduced the United States to Japanese desirous of taking the giant step across the Pacific Ocean. The focus will be on the decade before World War I, a time by which the state's dominance and its aspirations for an important international political role had become indelibly printed on the consciousness of the people. Works on tobei originated before this time; they began to appear in the mid-1880s, authored mainly by enthusiastic and admiring students and laborers who had lived in and returned from the United States.[4] However, the tobei publications of this period were qualitatively different, for they no longer merely described the young country. Now they combined Japanese interpretations (or misinterpretations) of the American experience and attitudes toward moneymaking with the ideas of patriotism and internationalism. By examining some tobei works, I hope to gain insight into *tobei netsu* (crossing to America fever), an outlook created by excited and impassioned tobei advocates who informed youth that the United States, despite its racism, labor wars, and immigrant slums, was a paradise.[5]

Two tobei advocates, both Christian, politically liberal, and pro-American, rode the wave of tobei netsu and devoted their lives to preparing would-be emigrants for passage to the United States. In addition to writing articles and books, they managed organizations that introduced prospective travelers to the ways of American life, offered practical advice about the details of daily living, warned them against behavior offensive to their hosts, and preached about the work ethic and the need to experience hardship and deprivation. Both focused upon the work-study route of advancement, which they considered more possible in the United States than in Japan. One—Shimanuki Hyōdayū, Christian minister, head of a tobei school, and beneficiary of well-known and affluent liberals—skillfully and inoffensively treaded the precarious line between Christian beliefs and the conscious self-restraint conditioned by the inflexible ideology of loyalty to the state. The other—Katayama Sen (1859–1933), the Christian socialist—is of particular interest, given his extraordinary political career. A consistent opponent of capitalism, he participated in the founding of the American Communist Party, lived his final days in the Soviet Union, and was the first Asian to be buried in the Kremlin. Analyzing these tobei advocates will help us comprehend the hold tobei netsu had on a generation of youth imbued with a romantic notion of the United States and the hope that the success ethic would work as well for them as it did for the American models they read about in their success magazines.

• • •

Many popular journals included articles presenting the United States as the foreign land in which people could realize their dreams and goals of achievement and accomplishment. The magazine *Amerika* informed its readers, "Success is present in America!"[6] Although acknowledging that such pronouncements could be interpreted as "goading people on," the author's intentions were not such "by any means.... Our nation's population keeps increasing year by year, and land becomes less and less available. Youth are subject to confines which restrict their activity. They must take great leaps forward.... The shortest route to success is to put forth one's efforts and go to America." *Seikō* cautioned that "lingering in small, narrow Japan" hindered the spirit of independence and prevented people from thinking of the whole world as their home.[7] Those who stayed in Japan were victimized by the Japanese family system, "a remnant of the past" appropriate only for a backward civilization. "Family signifies the poetry of life, but poetry cannot feed a people" nor serve as the foundation of an expanding nation. The family system was "barbaric," perpetuated the "outmoded custom of getting married and rearing children in one's father's home," and prevented the taking of risks in business at home or abroad. Statements such as these reinforced the impression that by going to foreign countries one could escape the restraints and restrictions in Japan. In the United States, people enjoyed the freedom to succeed and lived without the family burdens that existed in "unadvanced Japan." Even the educated, the resolute, and the industrious could not find appropriate employment in Japan. But in the United States, the sekkyokuteki spirit worked for everyone.

The tobei publications instructed readers on how to get passports and passage, explained what to expect on shipboard and at immigration offices once in the United States, and described cities and their geography, weather, streets, and buildings. Job opportunities also were described at length. However, the thread that ran through the writings of this period stressed the importance of having the "right kind of people" go to the United States—the businessmen, students, and professionals, who could get passports easily and were treated with lenience once in the United States.[8] These solid and honest Japanese citizens would be joined by their wives and children, be welcomed by Americans, and help solidify good relations between Japan and the United States. *Seikō* urged traveling in second-class accommodations or better to guarantee proper treatment by U.S. immigration officials.[9] Merchants and professionals with hi-imin passports were not governed by U.S. immigration laws and regulations, but all third-class passengers, regardless of occupation, were treated as imin once they arrived in the United States and were subject to the laws.[10] People who traveled in lower-class sections of ships were indistinguishable from "baggage," and the abuse inflicted upon them surpassed even that inflicted in Japan.[11]

The writers made clear class distinctions between the imin, who labored in Hawaii and the West, and the hi-imin, who went to the United States with the intention of becoming businessmen or professionals. They contemptuously described the lowly and "animal-like" imin on the U.S. Pacific Coast, who left the Japanese provinces with barely a high-school education: "They imitate those who have made money and think that success will come easily.... They are coarse and vulgar laboring men, much like the coarse and vulgar Chinese laborers in Japan."[12] They congregated only where Japanese was spoken, "establish Japanese bath houses, noodle shops.... Ignorant country yokels who don't even know the ways of Tokyo act as if they were in their own provinces."[13] For imin, going to the United States was no different from going to Tokyo.[14] They behaved disgracefully and dishonored Japan's victories over China and Russia: "Our countrymen living abroad have learned to swagger and snort and act with arrogance and haughtiness. This tends to offend people. Therefore, from this day forward, we must suppress our confident airs and seek to adopt the manners and customs of the host country. Historically, Americans have held Japanese in high esteem."[15]

Although Japan's outstanding successes on the military front should have guaranteed it big-power status, the immodest, unrefined, and tactless imin's behavior negated their nation's feats.[16] In fact, some imin flaunted Japan's victories with pretentious displays of patriotism, sporting old military uniforms and medals and, for the Fourth of July, selling Japanese-made firecrackers that spewed forth the flag of the rising sun.[17] Such offensive and intolerable acts kindled the flames of American anger and were judged as "threats—like explosives." They provoked conflict and discord such as occurred over the San Francisco schools in 1906.[18] The continuing presence of the "inferior, wretched imin types of Hawaii who indulged in women and wine" could easily precipitate war between the United States and Japan.[19] People had to "assimilate in matters which went beyond the physical to the spiritual," develop the "gentle, mild, or temperate" characteristics of Americans, and rid themselves of the "sharp, clumsy, and rough" characteristics typical of Asians.[20] The litany of contempt was unceasing.

To effect a change in behavior, it was crucial that migrants go to the United States with the intention of becoming permanent residents: "[d]esire to become part of the soil . . . adhere to the customs, socialize with the people, and assume their food and clothing habits."[21] Tobei imin should not stay for only two or three years, for "Americans do not welcome sojourners in the United States";[22] emigrants must resolve to establish "sweet homes" in the United States and stay permanently.[23] "Once in a country, the ways of that country must be observed."[24] Shimanuki optimistically predicted that once the Japanese learned to behave acceptably in all situations in the United States and could "think like Americans," naturalization rights would follow, "the same as [for] Italians."[25] Then they would be free citizens, would be accorded equal treatment, and could even anticipate serving as a chief of police or city councilman. Most important, by becoming permanent residents, they would promote Japanese-American relations and advance Japan's reputation abroad.

As much as anyone, Shimanuki Hyōdayū was dedicated to aiding, educating, and advising Japanese youth anxious to embark on the road to success.[26] The eldest son of a samurai, born and raised near the city of Sendai in northeastern Japan, he became an elementary school teacher at age fourteen. He converted to Christianity, decided to devote his life to the ministry, and entered Tōhoku Gakuin, majoring in theology and English. When he finished his courses he moved to Tokyo, worked with the poor, established a church, and in 1897, at age thirty-one, established an enterprise to help struggling students who moved to Tokyo to attend middle schools and specialized schools rather than the elite government or private colleges.[27] Originally called the Tōkyō rōdōkai (Tokyo labor club), then Tōkyō seireikai (Tokyo diligence club), the institute was overwhelmed by applicants for membership—as many as 500 per day, many more than Shimanuki could advise effectively. The competition for membership resulted in an unprofitable venture, "as if milk had gone sour."

Shimanuki decided to focus his attention on a smaller and more select group—those who desired to go to the United States to study. In

November 1897 he set out on a six-month trip to the United States to learn how American students raised money for schooling. He worked for three months as a pastor in San Jose, California, visited Philadelphia and New York City, and traveled up and down the Pacific coast as far north as Vancouver, Canada. His journey proved to him that "work and study can only be done in America," a realization that became the raison d'être of his Rikikōkai (strenuous action club).[28]

As soon as he returned to Japan in early summer 1898, Shimanuki began to reorganize the Rikikōkai, adding an American section but not designating it formally as such until 1900, after the club became firmly established. He attributed the postponement to criticism by fellow Christians that Shimanuki's activities were inappropriate for a pastor, a surprising perspective inasmuch as many religious leaders, including Christians, Buddhists, and Shintoists, engaged in activities that promoted the guiding of youth during this period.[29] The criticism may have reflected their discomfort with or jealousy about having a man of religion be so aggressively successful in his business efforts. Additionally, conservative religious leaders who believed youth should dedicate themselves to the cause of Japan *in* Japan were angered that Shimanuki taught English and promoted permanent tobei.

Although the key words "determination, hope, perseverance, struggle, and success" were authoritatively and consistently printed on the pages of his many works, the bulk of Shimanuki's prolific writings were pragmatic. Beginning with *Seikōno hiketsu* (Secrets of success), written in 1892, before he began his tobei activities, he followed with *Saikin seikaku tobei annai* in 1901 and *Saikin tobeisaku* in 1904, edited *Jitchi tobei* (Personal stories of tobei) in 1905, wrote *Shintobeihō* and *Rikikōkai towa nanzoya* in 1911, and began publishing the Rikikōkai's monthly, *Tobei shimpō*, in 1907.[30] *Saikin tobeisaku*, which Shimanuki called "the friend of the struggling student," contained 110 questions and answers regarding tobei, each serving as a short chapter. At least one-third of the text concerned money: travel expenses, capital, employment, and ways to save money once in the United States. The rest gave practical advice on passport applications (more than twenty-five questions), English, travel for women, U.S. immigration officials, sponsorships, letters of introduction, transportation, dress, preparations for shipboard, and what to expect upon landing on U.S. shores. Shimanuki did not spend a great deal of time on the abstract and intangible aspects of the success ethic, which typified many Japanese writings for youth of the period.

The Rikikōkai's membership rules and application process give us some idea of the operation of the club. Shimanuki listed the club's goal as helping tobei individuals to gain advantages in every area: "moral, financial, religious, educational, political, commercial, and industrial."[31] He aimed to "show poor students the way to self-supported study" and to teach the ways of a gentleman, "in particular the most indispensable quality, refinement of character." In the back advertisement section of *Saikin tobeisaku*, readers were informed that the club aided more than 950 students, of whom more than 260 had gone to the United States. Membership fees were twenty sen a month, with three months' payment in advance, and members were encouraged to submit "frequent questions," each accompanied by twenty-five sen as an "answer fee." For poor students these sums were not minor. For instance, the average daily wage of a skilled laborer (cabinetmaker, bricklayer, tailor of European clothing) at the time ranged from fifty sen to one yen.[32] In addition to requiring payment for services, the membership application form called for detailed personal information such as registered family domicile, resident domicile, education, family wealth, physical health, conscription status, reason for travel, preparation for travel expenses, and social status. This information helped club leaders to evaluate each student's financial need and family background. In fact, one of the club's stated objectives was to verify "the quality of those wishing to go to the United States."[33] Although evidence does not point to a Rikikōkai–Japanese government relationship, the club's application form resembled the official investigation of a passport applicant's personal history. To further its activities, the organization held fund-raising concerts and claimed support from leading liberal figures such as Ōkuma Shigenobu, Ozaki Yukio, and Shimada Saburō, activists in liberal-progressive politics and promoters of moderate reform, as well as from Shibusawa Eichi, one of the most important industrialists of the Meiji period.[34] It dedicated its publications to American Christians, including "Dr. Harris," who "helped a number of Japanese schoolboys."[35] By 1907 the first issue of *Tobei shimpō* boasted that membership had risen to 3,000 and that the club had received 30,000 visitors and 50,000 requests for information.

"Questions and Answers" became a regular part of *Tobei shimpō*. The answers reveal the level of information given about the United States and the not-altogether-helpful paternalistic assurances the club proffered to its members. Meagerness and mediocrity characterized the advice, as several questions and answers from one issue of *Tobei shimpō* illustrate.³⁶ To one unresolved youth concerned about whether to continue his education beyond middle school in Japan or move to the United States, *Tobei shimpō* optimistically recommended:

Of course, go to America. If you stay in Japan you will have to finish college, then get a low-paying job and depend on your family. In America, you can go through college as a "schoolboy" (domestic worker) in six or seven years, not rely on your parents, and learn English. You will have knowledge that Japanese do not.

....

Ques. I love America. I have no passport and no money. What should I do?
Ans. We will help you raise funds. You will be ready in three months. Send us three sen for our rules and regulations.

....

Ques. I want to go to America with my husband. I want to work, but what should I do if I have a child?
Ans. No problem. But your husband should go first and make arrangements to have your child cared for by Mrs. X or Y.

....

Ques. My daughter has been offered marriage to a successful Japanese in America. What should I do?
Ans. Japanese women are needed. We have a Girls' Section which sends many young women to America. If you are uncertain, have her join our organization and we will train her.

Questions from young women and mothers were infrequent, but Shimanuki did not ignore the problems of male domination within the Japanese immigrant communities in the United States. In *Saikin tobei-saku* he wrote that single women should not go to the United States unless accompanied by missionaries, for traveling alone could only result in loneliness and insecurity. They would be victimized in dangerous all-male situations in which men would coerce them to become unwilling wives or lovers. In *Saikin seikaku tobei annai* Shimanuki recounted the story of a female passenger who was taken to a separate room and forced to disrobe by "red-beards" who "teased her mercilessly"—an ominous warning that left much to the reader's imagination.³⁷

Shimanuki not only cautioned young women but also took it upon himself to help them develop "sound minds and spirits." He established a Rikikō girls' school to prepare graduates of upper high schools or the equivalent to become practical and good wives "who could travel to America and support our brothers."³⁸ He advised women to adopt Western clothing before departing "even if your husband forbids you," for "kimono and obi look unsightly in America."³⁹ He did not flinch from the subject of tobei women, but in keeping with the prevalent Meiji attitudes he regarded them as subordinates and loyal supporters. He presented the family as an institution without which men would find it impossible to live moral lives. The early imin, denigrated as uneducated and uncouth, were beyond rehabilitation because they were wifeless and not able to raise children in family situations.[40] To Shimanuki, an immigrant's success or failure hinged on whether or not he had a family.[41] Missing was a discussion of women's experiences separate and apart from their relationship to men. He did mention menial employment for women such as domestic labor, working in restaurants, or farming but considered it secondary to a woman's primary role as homemaker and mother. The sole purpose of tobei women was to provide companionship to Japanese men and to nurture "sweet homes." Men would then be more likely to develop virtue and principles and thus to be accepted by and develop good relations with Americans.

The club used every means to promote its goals. Rikikōkai-related advertisements appeared in *Saikin tobeisaku*, *Shintobeihō*, and *Tobei shimpō* to promote the club's three magazines (a news magazine, a Christian monthly, and *Tobei shimpō*). One ad listed eighty Tokyo bookstores as distributors of *Tobei shimpō*.[42] A "Rikikō home" was offered as a sanctuary for "bible study and prayer" for lonely travelers in Tokyo at the monthly rate of five to eight yen. A number of small enterprises bought advertisements in *Tobei shimpō* urging readers to buy "the latest and most stylish shoes for going to America"; stay at friendly inns in Kamakura, Tokyo, or Vancouver; use Lion Dentifrice, the Japanese toothpaste that President Roosevelt endorsed; or build their library on Christianity at a bookstore in the Kanda district of Tokyo.[43]

Despite Shimanuki's Christian fervor, however—and there is no reason to assume that he was not devout—the publications with which we are concerned were remarkably free of Christian moralizing or indoctrination. Although the first issue of *Tobei shimpō* listed prayer as one of the "characteristics which made for success" and included an article by the noted Quaker educator Nitobe Inazō, the magazine did not sermonize. Nitobe informed his readers that Japan should have awakened from its isolationist *sakoku* (seclusion) policies fifty years earlier.[44] One article bemoaned the lack of moral principles and religious training among laboring imin.[45] But in *Shintobeihō*, Shimanuki offered the information that neither Rockefeller nor Carnegie was religious.[46] However, both possessed "good character" and counted philanthropy as an important part of their lives. Thus, although Shimanuki acknowledged

Christianity as the ethical core of American behavior, he clearly tolerated nonbelievers. Japanese Christians such as Shimanuki maintained a balanced defensive stance, referring to their religion in the most general terms rather than preaching about the gehenna that awaited those without Christian beliefs. Understandably, restricting membership to Christians, proselytizing, and insisting upon conversion could have limited the club's appeal and discouraged support by members of the elite.

The Japanese state manifested its power more overtly following the Sino-Japanese War, a factor that differentiated the early Meiji years from the late. As long as Christians remained divorced from active political work and focused on education, particularly the teaching of English and other technical and practical matters, the state was tolerant and unthreatening. As a case in point, the mission schools of higher education for affluent and elite young women outnumbered the public higher schools for women.[47] Christian educators worked and acted assiduously in a political atmosphere exemplified by the Imperial Rescript on Education of 1890, a document that identified moral education as the first responsibility of every school in the nation. Its content, however, was not about education but rather about loyalty to the state, obedience to one's parents, unity, and class subservience, emphasizing "the nourishment of the spirit of Reverence for the Emperor and Love of Country." The government demanded that all institutions display an official copy of the document in a place of respect, to be removed only on designated national holidays and read to the students at special ceremonies.[48] Such an environment was hardly conducive to asserting opposition and challenging the authority of the emperor and the state. It is significant that the nationalistic tides of the time were so strong that theories of "Japanese Christianity" or "Shinto Christianity" appeared with the argument that the imperial system and Christianity were not incompatible.[49] Christian thought and Japanese civic morality were conflated to define a religious belief that did not contradict the prevalent ideology of the state but rather served to support it. Although the emphasis of this approach varied with the group or individual, it became the standard for the majority of the small, weak Christian population in Japan. Uchimura Kanzō, who courageously challenged state authority, eventually decided he could no longer teach, resigned from his post at the First Higher School in Tokyo, and became a writer. He opposed Japan's involvement in the Russo-Japanese War but did not engage in antiwar activities.[50] Therefore, Shimanuki's tolerance toward non-Christians was as much a matter of survival as of true openness;

it allowed him to write, recruit, and raise funds for his organization. Regardless of his religious beliefs, he accepted the authority of the state and operated within its dictates.

The Christian socialist Katayama Sen, who was to spend a period of self-exile in New York City before permanently expatriating to the Soviet Union, also devoted a number of years to tobei advocacy. Katayama's case differed from Shimanuki's, however, in that his credentials were enhanced by a twelve-year sojourn in the United States (1884–1895) as a struggling student. Born to poor peasants in Okayama in southwestern Japan, he made his way to the United States with minimal funds supplied by the family of his close friend, Iwasaki Seishichi, a schoolmate from Tokyo and nephew of the founder of the Mitsubishi shipping combine. Starting out in the San Francisco Bay Area, he worked as a houseboy, cook, handyman, and housekeeper, attended English classes at a Chinese mission, and in 1886 enrolled in Hopkins Academy, Oakland, a preparatory school for ministers and university students. His advanced age made him an object of ridicule, and he withdrew. Through the efforts of a teacher at the Chinese mission, he gained admission in 1888 to the preparatory school at Maryville College, Tennessee, and then to the college itself. A year and a half later he transferred to Grinnell College, Iowa, and worked to support himself, first at a farm, then as a housekeeper in the home of a trustee. He received a B.A. in 1892 at the age of thirty-two and an M.A. in history the following year, submitting a thesis on the unification of Germany. In 1894 he entered Andover Theological Seminary, Massachusetts, for a short time, then finished his training at Yale Divinity School in 1895. During his twelve years in the United States, he somehow kept himself fed and clothed, although penuriously, with his meager wages, a twenty-five-dollar monthly stipend from Iwasaki, modest scholarships, loans, and the proceeds from an article he had published in *Harper's Monthly*, a first in his career as a writer. Despite his financial struggles, he was able to remain in elite private institutions and take trips to New York City and the British Isles, an impressive accomplishment.[51]

Although initially exposed to Christianity at normal school in Okayama and at some lectures he heard after migrating to Tokyo as a young man, he was not drawn to the faith until after he arrived in the United States.[52] His socialism began to take form during his student days at Maryville and Grinnell, abetted by his interest in social problems, labor conditions in the United States, his own continued poverty, and the teachings of some of his professors, under whose influence he "developed a worldview."⁵³ His years in the United States witnessed the Homestead labor war and the Pullman strike, which he described in 1897 as having "struck American society with great panic and brought it to the verge of rebellion."⁵⁴

Katayama returned to Japan in 1895 and looked for work in the ministry, but his hopes were unfulfilled. He taught English at Waseda Preparatory School for a short while, although unsuccessfully; then, in 1897, he was invited by the American Congregational Mission Board to direct Kingsley Hall, the first settlement house in Japan. The institution's goal was to promote the "happiness, progress, and development of the citizens of Tokyo," paving the way for "graduates of universities and theological institutes and other interested persons to engage in the study of the actual conditions of society."⁵⁵

Kingsley Hall offered Bible teaching and Sunday school, as well as talks and lectures on socialism, economics, sociology, English, and German. However, neither Christianity nor socialism was the real drawing card. Rather, the English classes were the most popular. Katayama's twelve years as a working student in the United States served as proof for the many who did not have adequate funds that tobei was possible. Katayama wrote in 1901: "[s]everal hundred youth who have the will and desire to go to America have visited me in the past five years. I have written over fifty letters of introduction."⁵⁶ In his autobiography he wrote:

My most successful independent enterprise at Kingsley Hall was advocating tobei. Of course, my original purpose was not to make money, but I had a secretary write up *Tobei annai* ... within one week it sold two thousand copies. Even the haughty Tōkyōdō (Tokyo bookstore), which wouldn't handle my *Rōdōsekai* (Labor world), came running to buy copies.⁵⁷

Indeed, *Tobei annai* (Introduction to America) had its second imprint within twelve days, its third in twenty days, and, by 1906, fourteen imprints and a phenomenal readership of 100,000.⁵⁸ In addition to *Tobei annai* in 1901, Katayama published *Zoku tobei annai* (Introduction to America, II) in 1902 and *Tobei no hiketsu* (Secrets of crossing to America) in 1906.⁵⁹ His writings on tobei were not his only works; by 1906 he had written thirteen books and more than eighty articles, most of them on socialism, labor, and the labor movement. He took a second trip to the United States and Europe from 1903 to 1906 and was about to leave Japan for his third journey to the West.

Katayama's life as a socialist, beginning with his student days in the United States, his participation in the early Japanese trade union movement at the outset of the century, and his endless production of articles for labor and socialist magazines, marked the course the rest of his life was to take. In 1897 he helped found the first labor publication in Japan, *Rōdōsekai*, and became its editor in chief. His socialism and interest in tobei went hand in hand at this time, however, for *Rōdōsekai* eventually became the publication for his *Tobei kyōkai* (Tobei Society), which he established in 1902. In fact, buyers of *Rōdōsekai* automatically became members of the society, and tobei announcements were a regular feature. To no one's surprise, *Rōdōsekai*'s circulation rose, placing it on a stable financial footing. The following year its name was changed to *Shakaishugi* (Socialism), and it was designated the official organ of the Tobei kyōkai. In 1905, during Katayama's trip to the United States, it was renamed *Tobei zasshi* (Tobei magazine), at which time articles on socialism gradually ceased appearing. Claiming that he could not, in good conscience, spend time writing articles for magazines totally devoted to tobei, Katayama then separated himself from the publication entirely.[60] In 1907 he began publishing *Shakai shimbun* (Socialist newspaper), part of which "provided news about former members [of the society] and introduced new ones." Five months later, he concurrently published the magazine *Tobei*, which stopped publication within a few months following the Gentlemen's Agreement and the institution of strict limitations on emigration to the United States.[61] Katayama's business suffered from inactivity; more important, he lost his original enthusiasm for encouraging youth to "go east to America," and he no longer regarded Christianity as the basic principle of his life. He gradually disassociated himself from Kingsley Hall and ceased using his Christian name, Sen Joseph Katayama, for works written in Western languages.[62] Socialism took over the major part of his time and thoughts.[63]

During the period of his tobei advocacy, his advice and teachings did not differ drastically from those of others who counseled prospective emigrants.[64] However, two important factors distinguished his work: his long sojourn as a student in the United States and his primary allegiance to the working class. He criticized the Japanese government for "maltreating" the offspring of the poor:

Yale, Columbia, Chicago, and Stanford have generously offered our poor students tuition-free education.... [T]he [Japanese] government's action is tantamount to condemning capable youth with the penalty of death.... Promising young men who have dared to overcome hardship and completed their preparations to go abroad, ... are rejected by the government for ambiguous reasons, or because they are deemed laborers, or because the government assumes that they have insufficient funds.[65]

Opportunities to emigrate should be given to laborers and "the children of poverty-stricken farmers" instead of wealthy students, who either "gain easy entrance into universities and are excused from military duty" or "are weak-willed and go clutching their money in their hands."[66] Katayama concluded: "With tenacity, perseverance, and determination, nine out of ten youth could expect success. It is people, not money, who overcome the one hundred obstacles and achieve goals. Character and will, not one's capital status, are the crucial ingredients."

Katayama referred to himself as an example, claiming that no one had stood up to as many adversities as he had while in the United States. However, laborers enjoyed greater status and more advantages in the United States than in Japan; they held "positions of esteem," and it was not extraordinary for them to be educated. He encouraged workers to go to the United States to acquire an education, for a Japanese high school diploma was useless. To achieve any status in Japan, one had to enter higher school and "creep through the cramped net called examination," an obstruction surmounted only by 20 to 30 percent of the applicants.[67] Those who failed the examinations were "stigmatized for life through no fault of their own.... The government has deceived them, broken its contract to them.... Is this not oppression?" He described the United States as "the freest land ... which has progressed second to none ... and where wages are the highest in the world."[68]

Like many other writers who guided Japanese youth, Katayama valued migration as a sign of a strong nation with command over its destiny. Citing the Greeks, Romans, and British as "adventurous" peoples who elevated their countries' political and commercial positions, he warned that unless the Japanese purged themselves of their insularism, they could never hope to take on "the heart and soul of a civilized nation." He pointed to the poor Irish immigrants who achieved success in politics, education, and society because they migrated to the United States.[69] Although the relationship between an emigrant nation's economic and political advancement and the upward mobility of an immigrant group is unclear in his analogy (for Ireland did not gain the status

Fig. 8. Cover to Katayama Sen, *Tobei no hiketsu* (1906). The faded colors show red stars, white and blue stripes, and a blue sea.

that he desired for the Japanese state), he insisted that emigration would answer the problems faced by Japan and its people. The long-range solution was "socialized agriculture, industry, and commerce which capitalists and the capitalist system work to prevent."[70] "I say to the promising youth of Japan, 'Go to America!'" he urged, just as "the great newspaperman, Horace Greeley, advocated, 'Go West, young men!' to promising young Americans."[71] (See Figures 8–11.)

Katayama described the Japanese emigrants to Hawaii, how Japanese should and should not deport themselves, the types of people who could or should go to the United States, and what behavior was to be learned from Westerners. His friendship for the working class notwithstanding, he, as other writers, deplored

the truly wretched sight of the emigrants boarding the ship to Hawaii.... Look at them! Their clothing is Japanese. They hoist up the hem. They flap around with hemp-soled straw sandals on their feet ... drape their towels around their heads ... sling carrots and white radishes over their shoulders, and look triumphant as if returning home from the market in the next village.[72]

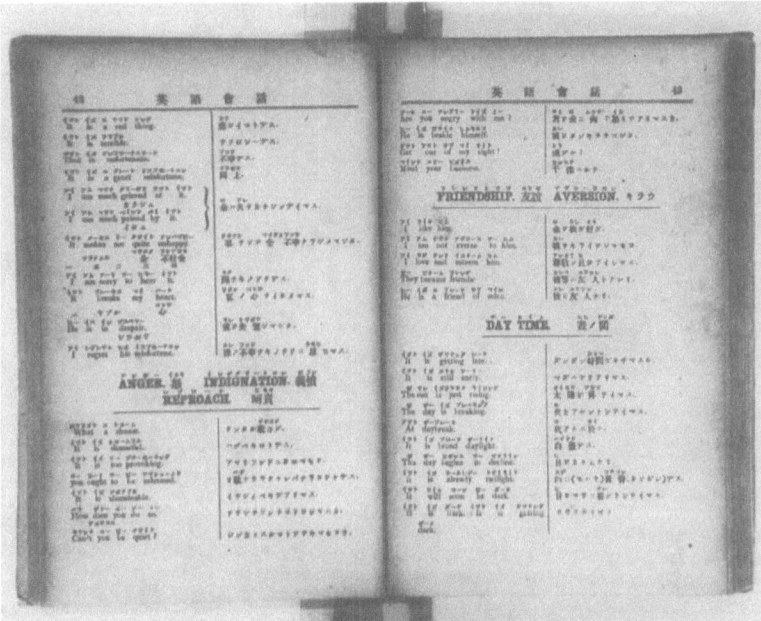

Fig. 9. *Tobei no hiketsu* includes a fifty-four-page appendix of English conversational words and phrases.

Katayama did not mean that expensive clothing was necessary. Secondhand suits, old army shoes, and straw hats or caps were adequate. The main aim was to deport oneself so as not to look "odd" to Westerners, for "clothing manifests one's thinking." Like other tobei writers, Katayama deprecated the customs and habits of the agricultural imin, but he did allow for the possibility that with knowledge and education they could "fit into American society." The list of behavior "don'ts" was long, including adhering to "customary ways" that ranged from "running around the ship partially undressed when the heat is unbearable" to bellowing out folk songs, story dramas, or comic stories. These were inappropriate and undesirable. In order to avoid disapproval and discrimination from Americans, the migrants had to forgo customary behavior, a not-unusual admonition in many tobei publications.[73] Their actions had to be controlled, and they had to conduct themselves so as to be virtually invisible—unless of course, they already understood the ways of the immigrant country.

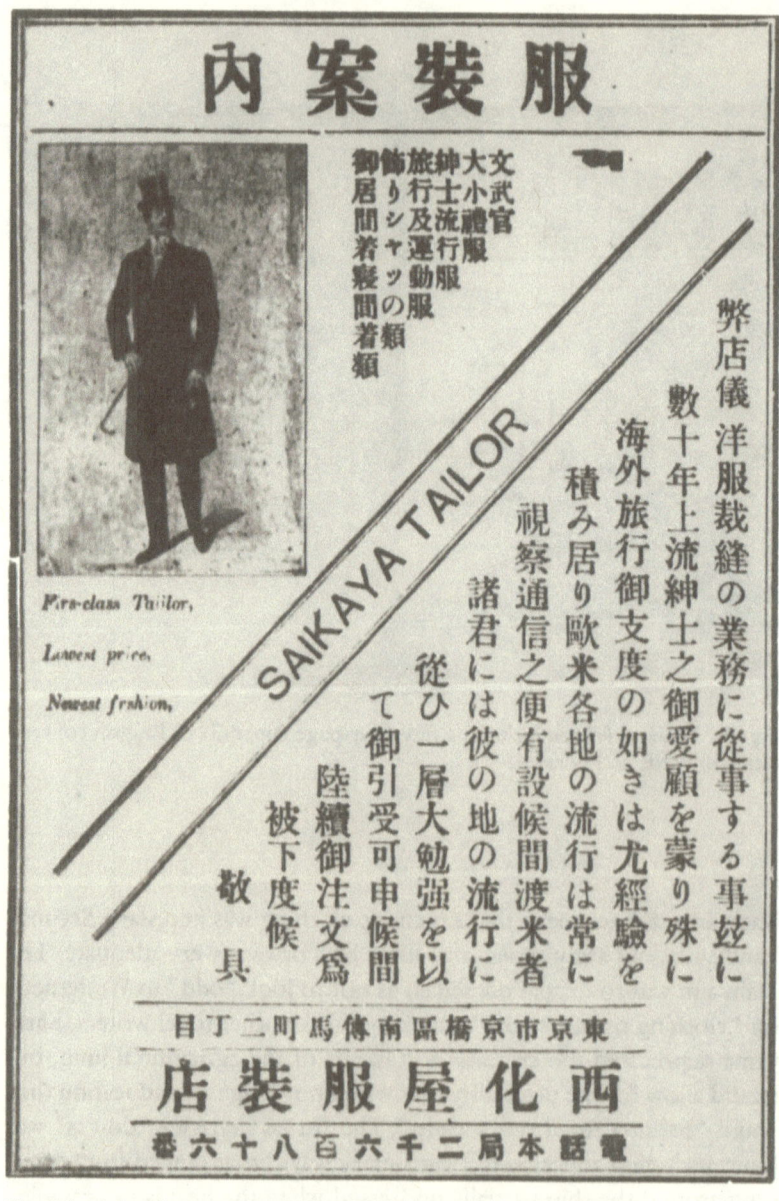

Fig. 10. Advertisement for Saikaya Tailor in *Tobei no hiketsu*. "We have favored patronage from upper-class gentlemen for several decades . . . are up to date on Euro-American fashions. . . . We will adhere to the fashions for our to-bei customers. . . . Makers of suits for civil and military officials, all varieties of formal attire, gentlemen's fashionable apparel, clothing for travel and sports, ornamental dress-up shirts, and at-home clothing or sleepwear."

Fig. 11. Advertisement in *Tobei no hiketsu* for "Yoneda spot-sales store": "One step to progress in the world of Western clothing." Yoneda sold ready-made "first-class merchandise" and forewarned customers that all suits were "price-fixed and to be paid in cash. Positively no bargaining."

Katayama criticized the behavior not only of imin but also of certain hi-imin whom he regarded as obsequious and who catered to Westerners. Describing Aoki Shūzō, consul-general in London, he wrote: "He lowers his hips and scampers [to the mayor of London] as if he were an apprentice summoned by his employer during the Bakufu period."[74] Katayama's criticism of imin and hi-imin, both capable of embarrassing and questionable acts, revealed his disdain for Japanese who thwarted Japan's attempts to gain equality with the West. Significantly, the characteristics he valued most were those held by Americans: "[They are] forthright and defend honesty . . . have dispositions which are without shadow or sun . . . express what comes to their minds. . . . [T]hey hate people who do not express disagreeable thoughts. . . . the double-faced."[75]

During this period of his life, Katayama believed the Christian religion was the crucial element in shaping a character capable of ideal behavior. Without it one could not gain the essence of community and cooperation. To build moral character one had to study religion, go to church, pray regularly, and read the Bible. Churches offered help with employment and inexpensive lodgings and were far more trustworthy than the many confidence men who, under the guise of honesty, "robbed the twenty or thirty dollars one landed with in America."[76] He described Grinnell College appreciatively in his autobiography as an institution where students, Christian gentlemen and ladies all, fraternized as if they were brothers and sisters and maintained stable and close relationships with faculty. Townspeople, parents, and alumni all offered help, support, and warmth. The picture was that of a veritable Christian utopia.[77] Katayama appealed to Japanese students to conduct themselves with humility to ensure Christian communalism. Accordingly, *Tobei annai* did not treat menial labor as an inappropriate form of employment for self-supporting students despite the low pay.[78] Katayama convincingly informed readers that with perseverance and thrift they could eventually begin a small business or get an education. It is interesting that he believed Japanese could never work in "real agricultural industry," which necessitated the operation of large machinery. They should stick with "strawberry picking in the spring or gathering grapes in the late summer," he cautioned, evoking the arguments put forward by American promoters of Japanese labor in the California fruit industry.[79]

Katayama's biases were illuminated further in four sections dealing with who "should" and "could" leave for the United States.[80] He suggested that from Japan's standpoint it would be advantageous to allow "the failures . . . the nonindependent . . . the losers" to emigrate, just as the "beggars and criminals went to America from the European countries." Of course, with the new immigration laws, U.S. authorities would refuse them entry. Therefore, people with hope, courage, and perseverance who could not "properly utilize their advanced skills in Japan" and intended to reside permanently in the United States should migrate. Restrictions in the United States and Japan notwithstanding, those with sufficient finances ("for finances determined the realization of a goal") and holders of first- or second-class transportation tickets were treated as "gentlemen and human beings," not as imin, an important distinction. They could migrate. Administrative policies, not laws, determined emigration and immigration—that is, they were decided by "conventional rules"—so tobei was possible for people who recognized those conventions. Katayama added that he looked forward to answering questions individuals might have on this matter.

One wonders how these words could come from the pen of a socialist convinced that the capitalist system in Japan sacrificed laborers and tenant farmers as "the feed of capitalists and landlords." He blamed Japan's surplus population problems on profiteering capitalists and landlords, who enclosed the people inside the islands of Japan to keep wages down and tenancy rates up.[81] Yet Katayama clearly did not believe in allowing everyone to emigrate. Aspirants must display acceptable behavior, appear conventional, and fit easily into Katayama's idealized American society. They had to assume the characteristics of hi-imin (not the Aoki type), a requirement that was commonly prescribed by other tobei advocates and that, as we have seen, became legalized by the 1908 passport measures sanctioning the use of the term *hi-imin*. Socialist Katayama, by insisting on proper training, inadvertently posed a distinction based on social class.

By considering the nature of Katayama's life in the United States, his associations, and the environment in which he lived, we can arrive at one understanding of this insistence. His initial interest in tobei was an important factor, for he had formed preconceived notions of the United States before he left Japan. During his three years as a domestic worker, toiling long hours (one job was from 5:30 a.m. to 8 p.m.), probably in relative isolation, and learning a language he knew nothing about, and the ten years he spent as a student while working at menial jobs, he had little time to learn about or see much beyond his immediate surroundings. He practiced what he preached: unsparing perseverance. He saved a portion of his inadequate income, which precluded his spending much money on recreation. What leisure time he had was spent in the company of his sponsors or teachers, classmates, and American theological students. His trip to England was with a fellow student from Andover Theological Seminary.

In addition, his years at Maryville, Grinnell, Andover, and Yale (1887–1895) helped formulate his strong allegiance to Christianity and socialism. He was influenced by the liberal theologian William Jewitt Tucker, a professor at Andover and adherent of the social gospel movement in American Protestantism.[82] During the summers of 1891, 1892, and 1895, immediately before he returned to Japan, Katayama worked at Northfield, Massachusetts, and attended religious-student conferences under the leadership of Dwight Lyman Moody, the lay evangelist, and his followers.[83] Katayama closely identified with the new theory of the social gospel, based on the premise that an unjust society caused individuals to sin. Working with the underprivileged and providing them with a more humane and Christian environment would help rid society of inequality and misery.[84] He went to England and Scotland to make firsthand observations of conditions in Manchester, Liverpool, Glasgow, and Edinburgh and to visit institutions set up for reform work: the university settlement, Toynbee House, the Salvation Army, orphanages, and reformatories.[85]

Although he traveled widely, his seriousness and his already unwavering conviction that change would come about through good works by well-meaning people limited rather than broadened his perceptions. Katayama lived, worked, and learned with a particular segment of American society that devoted its energies and thoughts to solving social problems and encouraging the middle class to contribute financially, morally, or physically to Christian causes. His reformist ideas thus took shape. Although he abandoned Christianity as he became more involved in the international socialist movement, he never renounced his conviction that social change could be effected only by reform, not through revolution. Therefore, in keeping with the ideas of the social reformists of progressive America, his views were neither contradictory nor incongruous.

Despite his hardships as a student and his knowledge of the labor wars of the late-nineteenth-century United States, Katayama did not criticize the darker aspects of American life in his tobei writings. Nor did he write at length about racism against blacks or Asians, both of which he probably observed, particularly in Tennessee and California.[86] The closest he came was in recounting a personal experience as a dishwasher, cleaning boy, and waiter in a San Rafael, California, private school. His immediate supervisor held the positions of "matron, servant, and cook, . . . a hard-driving woman who treated me like a slave . . . whose bad mouth uttered words more irrational than those of the worst officials persecuting helpless ignoramuses."[87] He never suggested that his supervisor's attitude was based on racism, nor did he compare the experience to an incident described by Christian educator Niishima Jō, who as a student was kicked "for no reason by some foreigner."[88] Niishima felt "instant fury," burning for "a sword to brandish," but remembered that "striking this one scum of the earth" would be "an act without merit . . . the final act of stupidity." Katayama did not interpret the motives behind this racist act against Niishima but counseled forbearance and nonresistance, as did many other tobei writers. Works that described racism in the United States invariably emphasized the behavior of the victim rather than of the oppressor. For instance, "To get rid of the hateful appellation 'Jap,' it is necessary to be successful like a white person and accepted by white society. 'Character' is attained not by birth but by education, learning behavior, using refined language and acting by observing white families and society."[89]

Given his religious convictions, his belief in the justice of socialism, and the United States's role as leader of the capitalist world, how shall we understand his advocacy of tobei? Why would he encourage "capable" youth, the ones who could assume leadership roles, to seek their futures permanently in United States? Was this not in contradiction to his desire for social reform in Japan? Kinmonth wrote:

As one committed to social reform, Katayama should have been presented with something of a dilemma in his advocacy of emigration. At best, emigration was an avoidance of social problems. At worst, it worked to remove potentially politically active elements from Japan and encouraged a concern with wealth acquired through individual efforts, both tendencies being inherently counterproductive. . . . No such reservations seem to have troubled him.[90]

Of course, Kingsley Hall and the circulation of *Rōdōsekai* were of little importance without the teaching of English and the establishment of Tobei kyōkai. The fact that Katayama capitalized on tobei netsu kept him active and enabled him to reach large numbers of youth. However, these factors alone do not provide an adequate explanation. Although he immersed himself in socialistic activity after returning to Japan in 1895, he also went abroad in 1903–1906 and again half a year later to embark on a Texas rice-plantation enterprise, a pursuit begun during his previous trip. During this time, political conditions in Japan had become increasingly stringent, and the nascent socialist movement, weakened and demoralized, found its intellectuals gradually becoming more isolated from the working class and factionalized into two theoretical camps. One included activists who, like Katayama, believed the practice of socialism was possible within the constitutional framework and the other consisted of anarchists such as Kōtoku Shūsui (1871–1911), the fiery radical and advocate of "struggle with power."[91] In 1900 the government had passed the Public Peace Police Law, which prevented labor from organizing. The following year it dissolved the Social Democratic Party—established by Katayama, Kōtoku, and Abe Isō, among others—within three hours of its founding. Copies of *Rōdō-sekai* that contained the party declaration were confiscated, and three other newspapers were banned for publishing the declaration. The government relaxed its stance somewhat during the following two years, allowing a flood of socialist literature to reappear, but during the Russo-Japanese War it launched intensive suppression of antigovernment, antiwar, and socialist meetings and writings.[92] In 1905, only two years after its first issue, the leftist *Heimin shimbun* (Commoner's newspaper) was banned for publishing the first complete Japanese translation of *The Communist Manifesto*.

In the midst of these events and the antiwar efforts of his socialist friends, Katayama spent three years (including the critical war years) abroad, traveling from the U.S. Pacific coast to Texas, Chicago, St. Louis (to attend the international exposition), Milwaukee, New York, Amsterdam (for the Sixth Congress of the Second Socialists' International), St. Louis (again), and Houston. He spoke at socialist meetings, helped organize Japanese socialists in Seattle and San Francisco, sold ice cream in St. Louis, labored in Texas, later managed a several-hundred-acre rice farm, and made plans to begin a 10,000-acre rice plantation.[93] When questioned if his temporary exile in the United States meant he had abandoned hope for the Japanese labor movement, he replied

with an emphatic no and answered: "I've worked ceaselessly for seven years and need quiet and rest. Furthermore, propagating socialism in a country drunk from the glory of a delusive victory in war is of no use.... My most noteworthy friends are in jail. When these acts of insanity cease and my health is revived, I will once more return to Japan and raise the banner of socialism together with my friends."[94]

Katayama did return to Japan in January 1906 but only stayed for six months to raise capital for his Texas rice plantation, an enterprise planned in partnership with a Japanese restaurant owner in Houston. He approached his liberal and wealthy patron, Iwasaki Seishichi. Mindful of the increasing hardships and oppression socialists faced and wanting to save Katayama from imprisonment, a fate that had befallen other socialists, Iwasaki agreed to invest in the Greater Japan Agricultural Enterprise Corporation, perhaps hoping that, as director, Katayama would become a diligent businessman. However, to Iwasaki's disappointment, Katayama continued associating with his socialist friends and appointed some of them to positions of importance in the firm. His Houston partner, outraged, broke off their relationship and returned to Japan. Katayama, who had gone back to Texas in July 1906, returned to Japan in February 1907. Although the firm survived a scant eight months, it was described as a "success story" in a New York Japanese-language newspaper.[95] In pursuing this ill-fated venture, Katayama operated on his belief that socialism could converge with humanistic capitalism, that capitalists could manage their businesses with morality, cooperate with trade unions, and "treat their workers with kindness and sympathy."[96] His friendship with Iwasaki, one that sustained him and his family for many years, added strength to this view.

His remaining years in Japan were fraught with disagreements with his comrades and dissension within the movement, as well as continued state arrests, prosecutions, and suppression of strikes. This persecution culminated in 1910–1911 with the secret trial and execution of Kōtoku and eleven socialist comrades for conspiring to assassinate the emperor.[97] Nevertheless, Katayama persisted in propagandizing, disseminating, and organizing demonstrations and strikes; he confronted arrest, imprisonment, fines, and the banning of leftist publications. Finally, in 1914, unable to press his activity and suffering from diabetes, he left Japan for good. He worked as a day laborer in San Francisco and continued his writing and organizing efforts, then moved to New York City in December 1916, where he helped to publish and edit *Class Struggle,* worked as a cook, and organized an association for Japanese socialists in the United States.[98] In 1921 he went to Mexico and in 1922 became a permanent resident of the Soviet Union.

Katayama did not pursue his ideals without great sacrifice. He suffered from several illnesses because of overwork and, probably, malnutrition caused by his consistent state of poverty. "He himself stated that at the age of twenty he looked like a man of fifty."[99] The sacrifices of those around him sustained him in his work. His wife, Fude, died shortly before he left Japan in 1903, a lonely and long-suffering woman whom Katayama described as "not having uttered a word or phrase of complaint for seven years."[100] Faced with the prospect of raising two children, Katayama married thirty-three-year-old Tama, a sewing teacher in a girls' high school, in 1907. A child was born the next year. After Katayama's difficult and bitter final years in Japan and his permanent departure in 1914, Tama was supported by part of Katayama's meager earnings in the United States and by Iwasaki, his old friend and patron. In 1923, aided by Iwasaki, Tama obtained a formal divorce from her husband, whom she rarely saw.[101]

Katayama was an active and dedicated socialist, which differentiated him from other tobei advocates. In an increasingly oppressive Japanese world, however, he worked from his conviction of what constituted a progressive and liberal kindai Japanese person—knowledgeable, international, forward-looking, and willing to experiment and to learn about the ways of the West. The official definition of a properly kindai Japanese was far more narrow and nationalistic. Yet, paradoxically, Katayama did not challenge so much as refine and broaden the official definition. Although his tobei writings severely criticized Japan's old provincial customs and habits, he did not condemn the tenets of the emperor system itself. He accepted it and believed it could act as an important unifying factor in shaping a future Japan. Certainly, many of his writings demonstrate that Katayama, like other tobei advocates, was first and foremost a patriotic Japanese citizen: "We must cultivate land that is yet to be cultivated, promote industry wherever we go . . . make it prosper and plan the future of a wealthy and strong Japanese nation which will attain world power."[102] Katayama further emphasized that nothing showed one's "loyalty to the emperor and love of country" more than "defying the waves of the wide ocean, entering another country, and establishing one's livelihood."[103] Sumiya pointed out that Katayama, like most socialists of the period, had no misgivings about the concept of the Japanese state or its constitution.[104] Likewise, the first issue of Shimanuki's *Tobei shimpō* stated that the magazine's goal was to advocate tobei "to establish an imperial beginning in America";[105] and the 1903 book, *Genkon tobei annai*, advanced the position that "[n]ational development and expansion of our population is the goal. . . . [P]lant the seeds of power all over the world. Plant new homelands. America is large, wealthy, and promising."[106]

By the turn of the century, the notion of empire had become an indispensable component in the grand design for a wealthy and powerful Japan. Expansionist writings, reacting defiantly and emotionally to what was perceived as the United States's infantilization of Japan, were as convincing as the encouragement of overseas migration to ease the country's overpopulation and the shortage of land and resources. Writers optimistically alluded to future strongholds of the Japanese empire in the Pacific following the victories in Asia, which ideologically justified a new sense of the prospects of Japanese power. These observers forecasted growing Japanese influence in Asia and close cooperation with the West, particularly the United States, partly to offset the American acquisition of Hawaii and the Philippines and more significantly to prove that Japan had assumed the imperial embellishments of modern civilization as defined by the West. Japan, in fraternal and friendly cooperation with the West, would join in taking possession of the "white man's burden"—the verbiage was not the same, but the concept was—and exploit the world, a responsibility warranted by Japan's advancement.

However, it is important to recognize that large numbers of people never found an outlet outside of the country. Utilizing Foreign Ministry figures for 1907, registered Japanese residents abroad totaled 232,000, less than 1 percent of the total population of 49 million. Migration to the Asian continent and the Japanese territories of Korea and Taiwan amounted to almost 122,000, whereas the figures were 30,000 and 72,000 in North America and Hawaii, respectively.[107] The inadequate amount of capital available for large-scale migration as well as the inability of individuals to raise enough funds made any scheme or desire to establish "imperial beginnings in America" difficult to realize. Japanese business interests had established a foothold in Asia following the Sino-Japanese War and expanded their presence further after the Russo-Japanese War. Such imperial and commercial structures, bolstered and maintained by territorial acquisitions, military activity, and an increasing governmental outlay for armaments and colonial enterprise, hardly existed in the migration to the United States or Canada, a basic and important difference that must not be overlooked. *Seikō* promoted migration to "places closer to our land rather than America" during the Russo-Japanese War.[108] It extolled China's wealth and land mass, represented "many Koreans" as desiring Japanese colonization efforts in agriculture and other enterprises, and prophesied the great prospects offered by Siberian fishing and mining industries: "Before the war China feared Russia; Korea feared Russia . . . but after the war we will be champion leader of Asia."

In Mark Peattie's analysis, Japanese colonialism was characterized first by the European doctrine of treating overseas tropical territories as "separate and distinct." Over time, Japan came to emphasize Asia as a frame of reference and worked to achieve "an integration of rulers and ruled" and "Japanizing" of the colonial subjects.[109] With this in mind, the specific, complex, and intricate brand of patriotism held by tobei advocates such as Shimanuki and Katayama in his early years becomes more apparent. Strongly influenced by their view of the United States as an open and progressive ideal state, they embraced a global concept based on leadership by the Anglo-Saxon nations, of which Japan was fast becoming an active partner and participant. The Japanese communities in San Francisco, Los Angeles, Seattle, and other points in the Pacific states would be part of this internationalist world, in which future Japanese men and women could establish their economic livelihoods, assume the trappings of genteel living, assimilate, and live in harmony with their American brothers and sisters. The notion of permanent settlement did not include territorial takeover and political administration of Japanese ghettoes in the United States but rather the enriching of both the United States and Japan, culturally and economically, a cooperative expansionism bringing enlightenment to the rest of the world.

A useful example of this internationalist and patriotic view is contained in a 1908 work written by a journalist for a Japanese newspaper in Seattle. After giving a historical account of anti-Japanese events in California and attributing them to such differences as Japanese customs, habits, culture, and ethics, the author evaluated racism as "temporary and insignificant":

In the past, Japan and the United States each considered the Pacific Ocean as its own lake. However, with the opening of the Panama Canal, we are now entering the grand new age of the Pacific. . . . The future relationship between our countries is emerging on a large canvas . . . exemplified by Roosevelt's warm message to the Emperor and the Emperor's telegram to Roosevelt.[110]

Masuji Miyakawa, an American-educated lawyer, expressed a similar view.[111] Envisioning a "Congress of the United States of Japan and America" through which the two countries worked "shoulder to shoulder," he wrote that their common interests in Asia could only produce harmony. As late as 1920 Miyakawa Setsurō, internationalist Christian and seven-year resident of the United States, lauded the Japanese contribution to California's growth and used it as an example for the future. Pointing to the breadth and enormity of the United States, from Niagara Falls to the Rockies ("are they not great?") and the spacious plains of Montana, he noted that "north, east, south, and west," this immense land waited to be used.[112]

> With the knowledge that the Japanese rice growers in Texas are not treated as the objects of intolerance, I recommend that the 200,000 [sic] imin in California migrate to this north central region, using Montana as the center, and settle in Wyoming, South and North Dakota, and Idaho . . . transform the dormant plains into an agricultural paradise of golden oranges and red strawberries. How grateful all Americans, high and low, will be! . . . [B]oth the United States and Japan will gain profit, eternal peace, and greatness. . . . I firmly believe that the destiny of our people of Yamato lies in crossing the Rocky Mountains and cultivating the great plains of Montana.

In this light, we can better understand the denigration of imin, the exhortations that prospective emigrants mold themselves to fit American behavioral standards, the insolence toward the Chinese, and the somewhat cavalier attitude toward non-Anglo-Saxon Europeans seen in the previous chapter.[113] The insistence of the tobei advocates that their compatriots comport themselves in a manner worthy of Japan's advancement signified a politicocultural responsibility based on strict regulation of individual behavior and a fervent belief in the common destinies of the Japanese and American nations. Indeed, this internationalist view is best understood in the context of the elite American education the better-known tobei advocates received. They lived their student lives among a group of select and influential Americans, leaders and future leaders, absorbing whatever they could, keenly perceptive of the ways of their mentors and peers. This sensitivity was heightened by their alienation from their surroundings and by the paternalism probably exhibited by their supporters: Dan Takuma at MIT, Abe Isō at Hartford Theological Seminary, Nitobe Inazō at Johns Hopkins, and Katayama, of course. Their understanding of Anglo-Saxons was based on their association with the American elite and its ideology of American manifest destiny. The tobei writers developed this dimension of their internationalist view during their stay in the United States.

However, another important dimension was their pride in Japan's emergence as a world capitalist state. Their consciousness reflected the self-assurance of a people flush from military victories over China and Russia. They desired to construct a coherent Japanese national culture as equal to the Western Other that promoted an international kindai empire and embodied the essence of Japaneseness. The original goal of being accepted by the West as an equal became transformed by time and political/military policies to signify a unique ideology that served as the rationale for paternalism and the subordination of Others of color. The ideology of expansionism—to colonize for the purpose of providing the necessary agricultural base for Japan's self-sufficiency; to act as a big brother to Asian nations; to establish Japan's cultural superiority; to reassert the country's past in rebuilding national loyalty—became more clearly articulated at this time and helped to bring together the contradictory views of patriotism, internationalism, liberal or socialist politics, Christianity, pro-Americanism, and tobei netsu. Tempered by Japaneseness and the desire for a secure partnership between Japan and the United States, the tobei writers, although of varied political bent, presented a united front. All encouraged youth to seek their futures in America, to become educated in Western ways, and to prove that Japan was ready to participate in the global community. Their advocacy of migration to American shores exemplified their hopeful belief in the best of all possible worlds.

CHAPTER 7

Maidens of Japan, Women of the West

Japanese Male Perceptions

Florence Egnus Kelly, daughter of a New York City office worker and wife of Itō Kenzō, received this threatening letter in March 1925 from a Mr. Sano, member of the consular office in Los Angeles:

You tried to double cross me by checking up with Itoh's [sic] how much I had.... You cannot extort money.... Think it over—Flo—and if you care to[,] write me again, if not please don't. Longer this hangs over the fire, it is better for everyone except *you*—and you alone.[1]

Two years earlier Florence and Kenzō met and fell in love; they were married in February 1923, just about the time that Kenzō, a former student at Phillips Academy and Harvard, acquired a "responsible position" at the Standard Gas Light Company.[2] This was Florence's second marriage; her first ended with her husband's death. Florence furnished their New York apartment with furniture that Kenzō estimated to be worth 400 or 500 yen (approximately $200 to $250). However, their honeymoon was short-lived, for when Kenzō's father learned about the marriage in May, he ordered Kenzō to return to Japan without delay. The dutiful son obeyed the command immediately. However, he left New York with every intention of resuming his life with Florence, for he applied for and received a certificate of residency from the Japanese Consulate General of New York, a six-months' guarantee of easy reentry into the United States.[3] Promising Florence that he would return soon, he gave her a number of self-addressed envelopes so she could correspond with him during his absence.[4]

As soon as Kenzō arrived in Japan in August, however, his father forbade him even to think of leaving Japan or to communicate with Florence. Nevertheless, in opposition to his father's wishes, Kenzō wrote to his wife through 1923. His letters were never answered. This situation continued for two years, after which Florence's long silence and his father's uncompromising refusal to consent to the marriage drove Kenzō to submission. In a short formal statement he expressed his wish to carry out divorce proceedings, explaining that his parents did not approve of his marriage and that "there is no way that we could be compatible."[5]

When Kenzō left New York, Florence stored their furniture in a warehouse in Kenzō's name and in June traveled to Los Angeles to wait for him, believing that his return was imminent.[6] However, after six months and the depletion of her funds, she was forced to go back to her father's house in New York City. She wrote three letters to Kenzō's father, begging him to reconsider his position and approve of their marriage. Itō Chūzō, adamant that his family's honor not be sullied by a marriage that crossed class, national, and racial boundaries, ignored Florence's entreaties and kept her letters from reaching Kenzō.[7] Following the great earthquake in Tokyo in September 1923, Florence visited the New York consul general, Saitō Hiroshi, to inquire about Kenzō's safety and whereabouts.[8] The documents do not tell us what she was told, but we know that her efforts were in vain and that the probability of a happy outcome appeared slim.

In December, Saitō met with the elder Itō and a third person in Japan to discuss Kenzō's situation. The three decided that, to bring matters to an expeditious end, a consular official—Sano—would be given power of attorney and entrusted with $1,200 for Florence (the amount her father stated was the value of the furniture).[9] When Saitō returned to the United States in March 1924, he delivered a letter and presents from Kenzō to Florence and advised her that Kenzō would never receive approval to travel to the United States again. She should accept the fact that her marriage was terminated.[10] A distraught Florence attempted to negotiate with the family directly and through a minister, but to no avail. In Saitō's words, Florence was "mentally in pain" and stopped writing to Kenzō in 1925. At about this time she sold pictures and other material to the anti-Japanese Hearst newspaper chain, a transaction in which Frank Egnus, Florence's father, also was involved.[11] Saitō retaliated by initiating an investigation of Florence, which resulted in his allegation that she was a prostitute who "went riding during the day and was at the Biltmore Hotel at night."[12] Itō denounced Florence as a disreputable woman who consorted mainly with Japanese men. Sano's letter to Florence, with which we began this saga, was penned during the heat of this bitter conflict. In it, he also told her: "1,200 is all. . . . You can settle, not fight. Otherwise I refuse to negotiate. You cannot extort money."[13]

The case was finally settled out of court in September 1926, more than three years after Kenzō's return to Japan. By that time, Florence wanted about $5,000.[14] The Japanese side, wanting to finish the case, offered her $3,000, a sum Florence accepted. A contract binding this as the final settlement of all claims was signed on September 28, 1926.[15]

The documents that remain regarding this international case leave a number of questions unanswered. It would seem that Florence was deeply in love with Kenzō and looked forward to a life of middle-class domesticity. She appeared genuinely concerned about her husband's welfare and anxious to be accepted by a father-in-law who showed neither understanding nor sympathy. However, her motives are rendered suspect by her decision to sell what can only be interpreted as scandalous material to the Hearst chain. Compounding this were her demands for money in amounts greater than the worth of her property losses. Were these the actions of a rejected and unhappy woman finally driven to pursue whatever compensation she could from a rudely interrupted marriage? Or were they the final maneuvers of a gold digger? Of all the actors in this international affair, Florence's actions were the least clear-cut, for there was no letter or statement from her in the group of surviving documents. Her intentions were interpreted and conveyed by others, all male, who, in the chronology of events, displayed suspicion, wrath, exasperation, and distortion. They accused her of lying and attempting extortion. Sano accused her of checking with the Itōs about the amount of money they entrusted to him. How aware was she of the Itō family wealth? Judging from the concern and correspondence generated in the Japanese Foreign Ministry, the family possessed both money and status. What is most significant and intriguing, however, is that this American woman received treatment no different than that accorded to Japanese women under Japanese law. The specific site of struggle of this international case resided in its legal and cultural base. It was resolved not in the United States through federal or local U.S. laws but through negotiations mediated by Japanese officials in the United States and Japan. The main concern was to maintain the desires and position of a wealthy Japanese family. The drama involving

Florence and, in a lesser way, her father took place in the United States, but the major decisions were made according to Japanese convention. One can speculate that Florence may have attempted to use the U.S. court system to gain retribution, but from what is known about the Egnus family—her father was a clerk—it is unlikely that they could afford to take legal action. Moreover, their class and lack of status would have worked against them. It is conceivable that Florence assumed that such an attempt would effectively terminate any tenuous hope for reconciliation.

Itō Chūzō's conviction that Florence was an improper and undesirable match for his son hinged on his contempt for love marriages, an attitude based on his class position. Was Itō correct in his accusations that Florence connived and lured his son into the marriage bed? He stated that his son was naïve, a virgin, and had never had any sort of relationship with a woman until he met Florence. Or were his slurs those of an elite and indomitable patriarch? If Kenzō merely had engaged in a temporary love affair with Florence, his father's response, if any, would have been inconsequential. Sexual promiscuity among elite males was condoned and prevalent in Meiji-Taisho Japan.

Kenzō, although aware of the mores of the Japanese family system, played out the role of a well-mannered, well-brought-up, educated young gentleman of the West and married for romantic love, envisioning a life of wedded bliss. He was unexpectedly shaken out of his dreams, first by his father, to whose wishes he obediently submitted, and then by Florence's silence, which he perceived as her abandonment of him. His dreams changed into nightmares. Of the three protagonists in this drama, he had the clearest and most straightforward intentions.

There is a larger question however, concerning the Japanese male attitude toward marriage (be it for love or arranged), Japanese women and wives, and association with American women. These issues were especially acute in relation to the New York hi-imin because of the preponderance of Japanese immigrant males over females. Women made up less than 10 percent of the total New York City Japanese population in any given year from 1896 to 1919. Furthermore, almost 38 percent of the women who came from Tokyo to the United States between 1902 and 1916 were dependent wives of men already in the United States (see Table 5). What happened to the vast majority of the Japanese men who were without Japanese wives? The 756 registration notices filed by Japanese citizens with the consular office in New York from 1909 to 1921 provide a partial picture.[16] During that period eighty-two were notices of marriages, of which twenty-seven, or one-third, were cross-racial. In the early years such unions were sporadic and few, but in 1920 and 1921 the number of cross-racial marriages jumped to five and fourteen, respectively, more than half of the total number of marriages filed at the consulate during those two years (seven and twenty-four, respectively).[17] In 1921 the Japanese government banned the issuance of passports to women emigrating to the United States as "picture brides."[18] The sudden increase of overall marriages can be explained by this ban, as men scrambled to find wives before the measure took effect, but it fails to account for the increase in cross-racial marriages. The only plausible explanation is that, given the unstable world of immigration politics, the ban of 1921 impelled male Japanese immigrants to solidify whatever relationship they may have had with women in the United States.[19] The arbitrary nature of passport and residency regulations created an uneasiness about their legal status as well as the future legal status of their offspring. Marrying an American woman might have dissipated those insecurities somewhat, although bachelorhood continued to be the norm for Japanese males. In the United States as a whole, the ratio of Japanese females to males in 1920 was 1:2.[20]

However one evaluated stories of anti-Japanese racism on the West Coast, Japanese immigrants on the East Coast thought a relationship with an American woman to be within the range of possibilities. As we saw in Chapter 2, living in New York was considered distinctive and special for Japanese. Tobei magazines regarded the East Coast in general, and New York in particular, as places where Japanese would be treated with equality and fairness. Although getting settled was more difficult in New York than in the West, once this was accomplished Japanese immigrants could live full lives, as if "they had the world on their laps."[21] Even more desirable and promising, Americans of the Northeast "were of better quality," making the area a veritable utopia of gentlemen and ladies.[22] In addition, the Japanese who went to New York were the "better sort," "educated" and "serious," qualities that facilitated their acceptance by Americans and helped them become permanent resident and not merely sojourners. The ideal combination of "superior" Japanese hi-imin and "superior" Americans on the East Coast made assimilation easier and thus made union with American women conceivable.

This expectation must be assessed within the context of Japanese men's attitudes toward Western women—such as those expressed by the actions of the Itōs, father and son—and Meiji-Taisho attitudes toward women in general. The actions of Kenzō (he was twenty-eight when the episode began) reflected an outlook probably not uncommon among young bachelors who had the opportunity to broaden their understanding of the world by going to the United States. Given the politics of emigration at the time, we must assume that tobei hi-imin often were unbound by convention, if only temporarily, and harbored special and singular notions about living in the United States. Furthermore, their lives in a changing Japan created contradictions in their minds regarding study, work, and/or social relations (with men and women), and tobei was seen as one solution. The tobei advocates whose writings informed these young men were likewise unconventional—in political outlook, aspirations, views about Japan, and an idealized adoration of the United States.

Fushinchū (Under reconstruction), a short story by the noted Meiji writer Mori Ōgai (1862–1922), presents the not-unusual behavior of a Japanese male involved in a cross-racial relationship.[23] A young government official who had been in Germany and his German lover, an entertainer, meet some time after his return to Japan. The woman is passing through Tokyo on a tour. The reunion is formal and distant, and both consciously suppress their true feelings. They obviously experience pain and regret about a past that cannot be recaptured. The charged situation is suggested by the following sparse description:

She slowly undid the buttons of her long gloves, took them off, and held out her right hand to Watanabe.
It was a beautiful, dazzlingly white hand. He clasped it firmly, amazed at its coldness. Without removing her hand from Watanabe's grasp, she looked steadily at him. Her large brown eyes seemed with their dark shadows to have grown to twice their former size.
"Would you like me to kiss you?" she said.
Watanabe made a wry face. "We are in Japan," he said.
Without any warning, the door was flung open and the waiter appeared. "Dinner is served, sir."
"We are in Japan," repeated Watanabe. He got up and led the woman into the little dining room. The waiter suddenly turned on the glaring overhead lights.[24]

Watanabe ends up choosing the conventional over the exceptional, a proper choice for a promising government official. Interestingly enough, Ōgai himself, while a student in Germany, had an affair with a "small and attractive" woman, Elis, who subsequently followed him to Japan.[25] Unlike his fictional protagonist, however, he did not see his lover until just before her departure for Germany; according to his sister's account, he was "busy with official duties," and his military uniform would have made any meeting "too conspicuous."[26] Ōgai's brother-in-law was given the responsibility of convincing Elis that a future for her in Japan was out of the question.

Anyone would have felt sorry for this young girl who had come so far and was now returning with her hopes dashed.... We thought a lot about the future of the poor girl, for she hadn't had even the common sense to distinguish between truth and falsehood.
Neither Father nor Mother tried to discuss the matter with Kako [Ōgai].
... Everyone in the family was so pleased that our beloved brother had come through unscathed.[27]

In both Ōgai and Kenzō's situations, propriety and conformity prevailed. The process by which that conclusion was reached ranged from coercion and manipulation in Kenzō's case to pragmatic self-restraint in Ōgai's. Initially, Kenzō intended to become a resident of New York; Ōgai's long-term plans were not clear. Regardless of the remorse he may have felt, he misled and deceived, actions that were not unusual among young men who spent time in the West but believed their futures remained in Japan. Kenzō's case is more germane to our discussion, despite its outcome. His decision to marry, live, and work in the United States violated the rigid standards of his father and the social class he represented.

When he left Japan to go to Phillips Academy initially, Kenzō probably did not envision himself as a permanent resident of the United States. Like most students from well-to-do families, he expected and was expected to return to Japan after completing his education. His years in the United States altered those intentions. However Florence may have understood their relationship, Kenzō was prepared to live independently in New York, working for an American company and looking forward to advancement and a stable life. He made his decision to marry Florence away from Japan, his father's influence, and his class and social obligations. It contravened marriage practices observed by middle-class families as criteria of propriety and status that were solidified and ritualized by the late Meiji and early Taisho years.

Yanagita Kunio wrote that during this period the demands of the modern market economy and the concomitant developments in transportation and occupational mobility transformed prenuptial arrangement practices.[28] Before this era, marriages usually took place between individuals from a single community, where geography and common backgrounds helped ease the period of courtship.[29] Choices and relationships between couples and between the families were facilitated, thus assuring familiarity and comfort during what otherwise was a time when "hopes and insecurities fused to create experiences totally different from day-to-day life."[30] In such an environment, couples tended to trust their families' decisions. These were based on and supported by known factors, including the couple's personalities, their preferences, their relationship with the in-laws, and the prospective success of the marriage. In the Meiji period, however, the relative ease that had characterized the earlier period evaporated. As industry expanded and cities grew, people sought work away from their communities and established multiple or temporary residences. As a result, a growing number of marriages occurred between individuals from separate and distant communities. Relatively more open and family-supported endogamous marriages were replaced by a process in which spouse selection gradually became entrusted to outsiders. Exogamous marriage rituals of the former elite—the nobility, samurai, and wealthy landowning class—became accepted over time by the growing urban middle class and by rural families in certain locales. These practices had served to separate the dominant class from the vast majority of society in the pre-Meiji period, but with the upheavals of the Meiji years, important and compulsory social features of the old elite became standard for the general populace. Status and position became the decisive criteria in spouse selection. These could be met within one's own community occasionally, but more frequently individuals had to go outside. Other criteria were judged common and inferior.[31]

Arranged marriage gained widespread acceptance as a tradition, which Eric Hobsbawm defined as "a set of practices, normally governed by overtly or tacitly accepted rules and of a ritual or symbolic nature, which seek to inculcate certain values and norms of behaviour by repetition, which automatically implies continuity with the past. In fact, where possible, they normally attempt to establish continuity with a suitable historic past."[32] Hobsbawm stressed that traditions are "invariant," preclude innovation, and are fixed and formalized. They become "invented" at times "when a rapid transformation of society weakens or destroys the social patterns for which 'old' traditions had been designed."[33]

The invention of tradition—the harking back to practices bearing the ideological legitimation of past worthiness—redefined the rituals of courtship and marriage; cast the family as a social, not an economic, unit; and transformed teachings concerning womanhood. The historic past made newly institutionalized practices seem "unchanging and invariant," justified and extolled them as the traditional means by which common people formed families. The Japanese government encouraged—indeed, pressed—the whole society to conform to this model. The family thus became a component of the political structure of the state, a development that transferred private social affairs into the public realm. Within the family women assumed an essential role as producers of babies and managers of households, but in the social world outside they were denied a political voice.[34] Social and legal constraints were placed on individuals who challenged or questioned the process, and thus, outwardly at least, the whole nation acted in unison. The political-mythic rhetoric of the people as bound together, descendants of a single illustrious imperial line, gave this construction of the family its ideological sustenance.

Yanagita argued that two significant changes regarding premarriage talks took place.[35] These changes served to regulate the procedures, placed inordinate stress on the tie between a couple's families, de-emphasized the human aspects of early socialization, and exacerbated uncertainty and ambiguity—feelings that either or both halves of a couple might experience. The first change was the Civil Code of 1898, under which arranged marriage proposals, most often initiated by the groom's family, became legitimized. The code sanctioned the supremacy of the family and empowered the male head of household, who in many cases represented two or more generations of the household. Sharon Nolte and Sally Ann Hastings have described how official state recognition of the patriarchal, patrilineal, and patrilocal family system affected women.[36] The legal, political, and social articulation of women's inferior status reinforced the koseki laws, which stipulated that when she married her name would be entered into her husband's koseki and struck from her father's. Women were treated as household listings no different from entries inscribed or deleted in account books. In addition, the code required parental consent for marriages, thus legally disregarding even the young groom's wishes. The result was the subordination of any semblance of the choice that had existed in the past and helped to alleviate uncertain feelings held by either the bride or the groom.

The other significant change, according to Yanagita, had to do with the increasing function of go-betweens, or matchmakers. Prior to the

Meiji period, go-betweens negotiated marriages for the elite. Among the peasant class, they were asked to act on behalf of one family when marriage arrangements became cumbersome, complicated, or close to collapsing. The reasons could have been many—weighty or unimportant. As marriages with spouses selected from outside of the community increased, the go-between was "elevated to a primary role" and given a level of respect second only to parents, "often assuming the relationship of a surrogate parent."[37] Go-betweens used photographs as the first step in marriage talks, the sole clue to the personality and character of the future spouse. This device was "not limited only to marriages between a man and woman living on opposite shores of the Pacific Ocean. . . . The use of photographic likenesses to ascertain disposition and temperament reached a level probably unknown in any other country."[38] Couples who knew each other only from photographs met face to face with a single objective—marriage—in mind, a situation replete with "confusion and awkwardness."[39]

In her autobiography, Shidzué Ishimoto, born in 1898, described her courtship and marriage. When she reached seventeen years of age, her father informed her that he wished to make her happy "by arranging a suitable marriage."[40] The young man, "one of the brightest and most serious-minded students" in the mining engineering division of Tokyo Imperial University, was to enter the important Mitsui Mining Company, a bright prospect for an up-and-coming graduate. "Suitable marriage" in this case meant that the prospective groom was from a desirable family and had an economically viable future. Ishimoto's meeting with her future husband took place at the home of the couple who arranged the marriage. The meeting was formal and quiet, but Ishimoto's inner thoughts were racing:

"Do I like him? Does he like me?" I repeated in my mind while a grand dinner was being served. . . . But I could little enjoy this feast, on account of my repeated silent queries: "Do I like him? Does he like me?" In time I found myself reassuring myself: "Yes, my first impression of him is favorable and I hope he is pleased with me!"[41]

After this initial meeting, both sides responded to the go-betweens positively and thus, the young woman and man were formally betrothed to embark on a lifetime of marriage. Writing in 1935, two decades later, Ishimoto described marriage as a "predetermined fate for a Japanese girl":

Today Japanese law solemnly declares that man and woman, high and low, rich and poor, are equal in its eyes. . . . But when we come to the matter of custom rather than statutes, woman is still kept in an inferior position.

. . . My mother did not realize that her dignity was cheated by the discrepancy between our book of civil law and our practices in private, nor did I ever in my youth think for a minute that a definite line divided a woman's rights before and after her marriage. But I discovered in time that she marries to lose her privileges as a person.[42]

Adult authorities in and outside the family took charge of premarriage and marriage rituals. As a consequence, the future husband and wife were effectively removed from the decision-making process, faced great personal risk, and had to adjust to formal and new experiences. Once the marriage ceremony was completed, the bride—particularly of an eldest son—suddenly was responsible to the head of the household (the father-in-law in most cases), the teachings and discipline of her mother-in-law, and her husband.

Etsu Inagaki Sugimoto, who spent many years in the United States, recounted the story of her brother, the only son in the family, who, on his wedding day, refused to marry the young woman to whom he was betrothed.[43] He had fallen in love with "a graceful little maid," a "heart struggle" that ended his relationship with the family, broke "the traditions of his rigid training," and defied "his father's command." "Brother came hurriedly out of Father's room. He passed us with long, swinging strides, never looking at me at all . . . and walked rapidly toward the side entrance. I . . . never . . . [saw] him after that day."[44] Disowned, he went to Tokyo and thence to the United States, returning to Japan and his family only after his father was dead.

The effect of these practices is not difficult to imagine. Marriage often terminated in "ignoble failure."[45] For many it became alienating and rigidly defined—for women certainly, but also for men, in particular those who harbored unconventional aspirations or had experienced new or uncommon situations. Mori Ōgai, whose adherence to social customs and practices led him to reject his German sweetheart, Elis, eventually wed the daughter of an influential statesman. However, the birth of a son notwithstanding, he walked out of the arranged marriage after a year and a half.[46] His second marriage, also arranged, was wracked by domestic unrest caused by conflict between his wife and mother.[47]

The failures of these love and marriage relationships illustrate the experiences of young Japanese from families of status. The Mori and

Inagaki families were formerly of the lower samurai class; the men in the Mori family were traditionally physicians, and Sugimoto's father became a mulberry grove farmer and businessman after the Meiji Restoration in 1868. Neither family was wealthy, but both became part of the new middle class. The pre-Meiji class position of the Itōs is unknown, but it seems certain that they had prestige and probably wealth. In the transforming world of Meiji society, arranged marriages became more common among people of all classes, and the experiences of the Itōs, Moris, and Inagakis reflected the complexities and aggravations of marriage, bound by additional observances. This was particularly true among the growing urban middle class, for in various rural areas, older practices persisted for longer periods of time.[48]

Whereas men were urged to be ambitious and achieve success, other behaviors characterized the proper responsibility of women. Phrases such as *ryōsai kenbo* (good wife; exemplary mother), first coined in the liberal and important *Meiroku* magazine in 1875, became used widely to direct womanly conduct and aspirations.[49] "The elements of a good wife," as ascribed to one "Robert Burns," were dissected into ten parts:

Burns rated affectionate (that is, loving) character at four parts, sound opinions at two parts, and intellect at one part. He valued beauty (beauty of face and elegance of appearance) at one part. Together, these amount to eight parts, and the remaining two parts he accorded to the wife's property, her social contacts, and her superiority in education and the arts.... [W]omen place primary emphasis on affectionate disposition ... based upon or aris[ing] from love. It is said that the loving are invariably genial, that the genial are invariably happy, and that the happy are invariably beautiful.[50]

Articles explaining the ryōsai kenbo formula, most of them written by men, appeared in magazines such as *Seikō*. On the one hand, they urged women to "hunger for the spiritual life as one hungers for food," praising their Spartan qualities but emphasizing that they needed to stretch out beyond the home "as Western women did."[51] Housework was "indisputably the sole responsibility of the woman," but as civilization progressed, working for social causes outside of the home was as important. "Their mission in life could be considered complete" only when they combined those two responsibilities. On the other hand, a medical doctor wrote that "sexual equality as seen in the West was absurd."[52] "As a dumpling-maker sells dumplings and a tōfu-maker sells tōfu," men and women performed specific functions based on the "natural division of labor." Women's roles—working inside the home and bearing and raising children—rendered their use of the intellect and gaining of knowledge inessential. Men's "natural" responsibilities resided outside of the home, forcing them into problem-solving situations in which they had to use their intellects. Sacrifice and love prevailed over the spiritual life of women, ill-preparing them for the realm of logic and learning that naturally fell within the spiritual domain of men.

These prescriptions for womanhood were made somewhat more relevant by Hatoyama Haruko (1868–1938), educator, founder of a women's vocational school, mother of a prime minister, and active promoter of the ryōsai kenbo ideology. In an article entitled "The Main Crisis of a Woman's Life," she wrote:

As one gets accustomed to a married life, the faults of husband and home begin to be noticed. One realizes that the reality of marriage and the ideals one held before marriage are contradictory. . . .
The fearful crisis which women face arises from this contradiction. Women are controlled by emotions.
When their marriage life differs from the hopes they carried in their hearts, they sometimes feel dissatisfaction, disappointment, and despondence.[53]

She offered three suggestions as to how women could combat those feelings. First, a woman should do all within her power to "follow the path of womanhood" and devote herself to her family and husband. If the husband should engage in "misconduct," she should admonish him as gently as possible; if that proved ineffective, she must leave matters to "fate" and give all her powers to wife/motherhood.[54] Second, she was to sympathize with her husband's faults and to focus on his positive aspects, for "without question" all humans (including husbands who engaged in "misconduct") had some "superior virtue." Finally, instead of falling into despondence, she should cultivate her mind by reading the wise sages of the past and present.

Hatoyama was well acquainted with the problems Meiji women faced in marriage, for her article acknowledged the tensions and emotions caused by an unequal domestic life. She delivered her rhetoric with sympathy, skill, and subtlety. Her views fell between the extremes of the articles encouraging middle-class women to engage in homework/voluntarism and those contemptuously rejecting any social role for women that encroached upon the "natural domain" of men. Her teachings were closer to the latter. She advocated education for women, but only as a means to prepare them for the role of "efficient managers" of the household. Women were carefully to shape the home as a refuge to which their husbands could escape from the hardships and pitfalls of the outside world.[55]

Though women were expected to play the central role in the family, men did not escape societal pressures in relation to the family. Shimazaki Tōson depicted the onerous burdens of sustaining a family in his novel *Ie* (see Chapter 4). The eldest brother, Minoru, unable to establish himself in a satisfactory business and repeatedly jailed for illegal transactions, finally is exiled abroad by his brothers. Of the remaining brothers, the Tōson character, Sankichi, supports "weaker members" of the various units in the family—that is, the women and children—by relying on his earnings as a provincial teacher and writer, his wife's dowry, and loans. These obligations take their toll on him:

> "You know, I'm beginning to wonder whether it's really a good thing for us to spend our lives helping relatives. . . .
> "All our help for our family has turned into something completely different from what we originally intended. We saw Oshun through school so that she could earn a living for her mother. But she's grown into a young lady unsuited for teaching. We've pampered Otane and treated her like an invalid, and she's really become one. We've worked hard and long, and what we've done is teach our brothers to depend on us."[56]

Directions and guides for sustaining the family notwithstanding, its continued functioning rested on its members making decisions and taking on financial responsibilities. The feeling for kin was operative, and solidarity and unity remained general goals, but they were concepts legitimated by ideology and law rather than by actual patterns of behavior. In the Shimazaki family, Minoru never acknowledges his demise outwardly. He is anchored into his position as head of the family even as his life disintegrates from recurring failures: "He was like someone maneuvering skillfully through a crowded street. He made no attempt to confide in Sankichi, . . . nor did he offer a single word of gratitude or apology. . . . He sat there, imperious before the youngest therefore least significant of his brothers, and his manner was that of a family head to a subordinate."[57]

Clutching onto shadow positions, asserting authority; upholding prescribed norms, maintaining the semblance of unity, demanding cooperation, expressing obeisance and respect even when reality refuted their legitimacy, the actors learned to play out family dramas faithfully and with competence, making dominance and oppression credible. The families performed what was expected of them by state and society. Their dilemmas and contradictions, rather than rending them apart, tended to cement them, but in rigid, repressive, and unnatural ways.

In that atmosphere, men needed a skewed individualism to succeed, despite the societal emphasis on family and community. To ensure security in life, they had to compete *and* succeed in school and work. I have considered some of the hurdles involved in getting an education, getting a good bureaucratic job, or starting a small business. All of these hurdles necessitated an altered interpretation of pre-Meiji terms for behavior or attitudes. At the same time, positive attitudes regarding the material aspects of life were encouraged, negating the former elite's disdainful notions about the vulgar amassing of wealth. Some tobei writers reacted to the difficulties of getting ahead in Japanese society by combining travel abroad, internationalism, and patriotism to define a new breed of adventurous and ambitious Japanese.

Likewise, reactions to "invented tradition" were operating within the confining world of male/female relationships. Individuals reacted not only to the new rituals of courtship and marriage discussed earlier in this chapter but also to the introduction of new concepts and words that referred to culturally unorthodox behavior and attitudes. One was the translation of the Western word *love,* for which a new term was created: *renai.*[58] Yanabu Akira wrote that *ren* and *ai*, both of which mean "love," when used together to form a compound, came from a Western concept which signified "love from the soul" as opposed to sexual love or lust. Love between a man and a woman was not unknown, of course; the classical *Manyōshū* of the seventh and eighth centuries described the emotion, but the commonly used Japanese ideographs of the past did not connote renai. Referring to an 1890 review essay regarding the translation of a Balzac novel, Yanabu stated: " 'Renai' was not the same as such terms as the Japanese *koi,* which conveyed 'an uninterrupted sense of the base.' . . . Its value was of the highest. The difference was that 'renai' was 'pure and true' because its meaning conveyed 'to love from the depths of one's soul.' "[59]

Yanabu compared "love" with "romance," which he interpreted as originating in the Western medieval tales of knights. It expressed the feelings a man felt for a woman "from afar," an infatuation that tended to keep her remote rather than draw her closer: "Even if physical love was realized finally, romance existed as separate: a love from the soul which was an infatuation of someone distant."[60] Romance was not the pattern in Japanese love stories. In *Manyōshū*, for instance, love was described "almost consistently" as "sadness or joy following intimacy. A male lover's object of desire was not distant nor an object of only the soul, separated from the physical."[61] Of course, Western *love* did not always mean love "of the soul," but *renai* placed emphasis on it and thus could be differentiated from the classical Japanese concept, which did not isolate the emotional from the physical.[62] In other words, love and lust were two different emotions in the West, whereas in Japan a clear distinction had not existed. Yanabu quoted an 1892 article in which renai was considered the "secret lock to life"—"life was possible" only after one had experienced it.[63] One who left this world without renai had never been touched by passion.

Ronald Dore argued that in the upper samurai class, love was considered "an effeminate emotion, for adoration of the superior being and the inability to control emotion were essentially feminine attributes."[64] Renai contradicted that notion. If male-female roles in relationships were rigidly based upon "acting upon" and "being acted upon," they precluded expressions of genuine personal emotion by either partner. Therefore, in the context of being the "secret lock to life," renai was not only a noble value but also a form of subversion, a resistance to the constraints of society, as its free and full realization in Meiji society was improper and improbable.[65]

Resistance can take many forms, and in this case its expression was based on subjective feelings. It was not necessarily a conscious political challenge to Meiji society; rather, it was an individual and sometimes generational or even temporary rebellion, as exemplified by Kenzō's marriage to Florence, Etsu Sugimoto's brother's refusal of an arranged marriage, or Ōgai's love affair and the breaking off of his first marriage. The personal-emotional attraction implicit in renai led to the hoped-for gratification of "pure and inviolable" emotions. This desire contradicted the socially valued relationship between a man and a woman, which guaranteed a strong and secure family structure with a dominant, unhesitating, and self-controlled male and a passive, sacrificing, and self-effacing female. By focusing on feelings and choice, renai exposed the orthodox and approved power relationship between men and women. Thus it became political—a "criterion by which reality was judged," an abstraction, a wished-for relationship between a man and a woman.[66]

The bland traits that made for a "good wife" included the "genial" love that could engender benevolence in the husband. But it did not account for renai. Hatoyama's piece on the difficulties women faced as ryōsai kenbo certainly did not touch on it. However, the novel *Futon* [The quilt] by Tayama Katai (1872–1930), first published in 1907, described the emotional content of the longing for renai as revealed by the main character, Tokio, a middle-aged teacher of literature.[67] He falls in love with his protégé, Yoshiko, a young woman who independently has sought him out as her mentor. Katai's own relationship with a student formed the basis of this story. The novel is a series of confessions by Tokio about his feelings and yearnings for Yoshiko.[68] Although the two never act on their passion, the descriptions of Yoshiko and of Tokio's wife inform us about the differences between two prototypes of women: one who is perceived as an ideal renai partner and another who tries to comply with the societal concepts of womanhood.

Yoshiko's parents are wealthy, Christian, and educated, and they send her to one of the better-known Christian mission girls' high schools. She becomes familiar with "novels such as *Konjikiyasha*, . . . which was banned, . . . but as long as banned books were not brought into the class room, anything could be read."[69] Living in a dormitory away from her parents, she loses the naïveté that characterized girls raised at home with their families. She develops "an excessive vanity" and becomes part of a group that "ignored the vileness of human beings and advocated their beauty." Tokio comments: "The sudden rise of women's education in the past three or four years, the new women's colleges, . . . not one of these women [students] felt self-conscious about walking side by side with a man."[70]

Tokio's wife, however, "his lover of the past, his wife of the present," has an old-fashioned hairstyle, walks "like a muddy duck," and except for her "docility and faithfulness" has no positive features. She is the nameless wife, *kanai* (literally, within the house), the term to which she is referred throughout the novel.

[S]he did not attempt to read the novels he wrote with such pain, was indifferent to his anguish and agony, and thought that only if her children were raised well she was satisfied. . . . [H]is loneliness welled up within him. . . . [B]ut when the fashionable, modern, and beautiful woman disciple called him *sensei!* [teacher] *sensei!* as if she were addressing someone eminently famous, who could not but be moved by such adoration?[71]

Although the story can be dismissed as a series of "confessions" by a middle-aged and egotistic male captivated by an ebullient young female, the descriptions of this kindai woman who has acquired a broad Western cultural knowledge without having left Japan is significant. She is educated, able to discuss matters of the intellect, inquisitive, and anxious to shed the prescribed traits of submissiveness; she independently seeks an equal renai relationship. Of course, much of Yoshiko's understanding of this new way of thinking and acting comes from Tokio's teachings about Western literature. She learns the meanings of independence and equality and cherishes images of a kindai woman's life. Ironically, however, Tokio's instructions about love and literature do not benefit him, for Yoshiko becomes the intimate of another younger man. Furthermore, because their real relationship is the unequal one of a teacher and student, Tokio's visions of a renai relationship and Yoshiko as a renai partner are unreal, a dream, a yearning, for Tokio never hints at relinquishing his male prerogatives.[72] The burden of change falls upon the woman, who must abandon submission and blind devotion to husband and family in favor of the male-defined qualities of companionship, sexuality, sympathy, and support. The male remains a neutral observer and shaper of womanhood. Yet, the shallowness and inequity of Tokio's vision notwithstanding, his desire for a renai relationship reveals the extent to which conventional marriage practices were not satisfying to him or to other Japanese like him.

The qualities Tokio craves and nurtures in Yoshiko were expressed in the descriptions of American women by Japanese who lived or visited in the United States. Their observations, impressions, and judgments of American women provided physical and mental representations, which might be negative or positive. One significant trait was that, in the words of Masuji Miyakawa, American women possessed "the privileges of a moral being, that is, the privileges of unrestricted action."[73] That unrestricted action was closely related to the Japanese male perception of American women as potentially ideal renai partners.

Miyakawa's pairing of morality and human behavior as privileges seems incongruous at first glance. However, his emphasis on the "complete equality of individual condition and opportunity" in the United States is based on the confident understanding that certain rights accorded to American citizens provided the framework that enabled them to act responsibly and with principle. His work, a glowing account in English of the U.S. Constitution, imparted a serious and studied Japanese appreciation of the political process by which American men and women enjoyed equality and freedom. Miyakawa was educated at the University of Indiana Law School and had the distinction of being the first Japanese admitted to the U.S. bar. His observations about American women contrast sharply with his earlier remarks about the role of Japanese women, written for an American audience. Though avoiding self-deprecation, Miyakawa presented a propagandistic and patriotic picture of Japanese womanhood as based on the nation's particular history, customs, and modern development.[74] He stated that "part of the wife's grace [is] to be obedient to her husband in all things right and reasonable," repeating the ryōsai kenbo ideology and expressing a vague notion of right and reason without clarifying who was to define it. In cases where the husband was at fault, "her duty was to rescue him and turn him right by mild and effective means." Unlike the "cloistered" women of Europe or Asia, American women were not held to standards separate from those of men. Therefore, they accepted the "higher responsibility" that society thrust upon them and tenaciously held on to their "resulting rights under it."

We see everywhere in America, young girls struggling to learn to stand upon their own ground.... The vices and dangers of society are early discerned by the young American girl. She wants to understand the corruption of the world.... There are many unmarried men, as there are many unmarried women. These do not marry, and cannot be made to marry, like in some foreign countries where parental authority forces marriage upon their sons and daughters. But if an American girl marries, she is mistress of her own action. She is not like some European or Oriental girls, bashful, childish, or excited.[75]

Miyakawa regarded American women as rational controllers of their own destinies. Though he presented his political understanding of freedom as it affected American women, he did not censure the lack of "free social intercourse" for Japanese women. Rather, he claimed that "at the present stage," giving Japanese women more social leeway would present "greater disadvantages than advantages."[76]

A more personal and expanded account of the freedom enjoyed by American women appeared in Etsu Sugimoto's sentimental autobiography. She was betrothed at the age of fourteen to a Japanese businessman stationed in the United States. To prepare her for married life abroad, her parents enrolled her in a Tokyo mission school, "the best girls' school," where she experienced her first contact with foreign women, who taught English and Bible lessons. They were "young, lively, most interesting and beautiful." "I admired them greatly, but their lack of ceremony surprised me.... [T]he free actions of the teachers with the pupils . . . shocked me."[77] Her continued association with her teachers cultivated a metaphoric idealization that she "never regretted":

> I came to realize the tragic truth that the Japanese woman—like the plum blossom, modest, gentle, and bearing unjust hardship without complaint—is often little else than a useless sacrifice; while the American women—self-respecting, untrammeled, changing with quick adaptability to new conditions—carries inspiration to every heart, because her life, like the blossom of the cherry, blooms in freedom and naturalness.[78]

She subsequently crossed over to the United States after close to six years of preparatory education, met her husband, and lived with him and their American-born children at the home of a "stern, high-principled" woman of "gentle Virginia" and New England stock, whom she eventually called "mother." Her impressions and thoughts about the United States were moral and proper, reflecting the social environment in which she lived (in an unmentioned eastern state), but that environment nevertheless altered her relationship with her husband. He was "more demonstrative . . . than would have been polite in Japan. . . . [S]uddenly I saw Japanese men in a new light. 'They have no chance!' . . . An American man can show his feelings without shame, but convention chains a Japanese man."[79] This growing awareness of and adaptation to life as a woman in the United States incited her reproach of life in Japan:

> "Our conventionality is too extreme. It is narrowing to the soul. I hate to be so happy here—and all those patient subdued women sitting hushed in their quiet homes. Our lives in Japan—a man's as well as a woman's—are like our tied-down trees, our shut-in gardens, our—"
> I stopped abruptly; . . . "I am growing too outspoken and American-like."[80]

Her idyllic life in the United States came to an unanticipated halt with her husband's sudden death, and she was forced to leave the "wonderful, busy, practical country." She assumed the life of a mother in Japan and raised her two daughters in an environment that had become alien to her. The older daughter lost the "joyous eagerness" and "vivid interest in life" she had displayed in the United States. When this daughter turned fifteen, the conventional year of betrothment, Sugimoto took it upon herself to leave Japan with her daughters so they could have "a few more years of study in America." The book ends with their departure.[81]

Despite the class orientation of this autobiography, its significance lies in Sugimoto's description of her understanding of life in the United States. She observed and experienced the role of middle- and upper-middle-class American housewives and concluded that it differed in important ways from the roles generally accepted for women in Japan: arranged marriages, subservience, formal relationships with men, and stultifying married life. For her, equality and freedom meant that couples could express mutual and genuine feelings and that women could behave with openness. Sankichi and his former teacher refer to this vaunted American openness matter-of-factly in the novel *Ie:* "American women are very sophisticated. They introduce their former boyfriends to husbands and form a new, clean friendship. 'He was my sweetheart,' they say. They're so open. Japanese women should learn something from them."[82] These were the conditions that allowed the kind of renai relationship that Tokio dreamed about in *Futon* and that found expression in some of the impressionistic handbooks, guides, and recollections of male travelers to the United States.[83]

The latter works were not as reverential of American womanhood as Sugimoto's, but they portrayed American women as independent, imbued with an "American spirit," lively, and talented—qualities that were evident in their mental capabilities as well as their physical characteristics:

There is no other place in the world where women have a strong sense of their own ideas and have developed personalities.[84]

American women nurture their intellect.... Women readers are superior to men.... When foreign scholars such as Tagore or Gorky visit, it is the women who organize their lectures.[85]

It is said that a fair complexion hides many blemishes, but not only do American women have white skin, but the arrangement of their eyes and noses is much more pleasing than in Japanese women.... There are many good horses and beautiful women in California, a well-known fact in the U.S.[86]

American women are educated.... [T]hey excel in social relations, are talkative, but courteous and gracious.[87]

Some descriptions, however, criticized and complimented simultaneously. One writer stated that women in New York were "aggressive, but very feminine and sweet," "conceited," "rebellious and obstinate ... without etiquette," "gentle, but wise and pragmatic."[88] Another, comparing Japanese and American standards, confessed his abhorrence of the Japanese *danson johi* (respect for men; reviling women) but admitted that its opposite in the United States, *joson danpi* (respect for women; reviling men), was "difficult for people like me who are timid with women."[89] Therefore, although his personal preference was for the "modest and feminine" Japanese woman, he admired the freedom with which American men and women were able to socialize. This freedom was "never self-indulgent, . . . but strictly disciplined."[90]

The potential for *renai*, then, hinged on the freedom under which social relationships between men and women took place. With this understanding of social and political freedom, men could venture beyond their circumscribed roles and express emotions, and women could conquer shyness and escape the confines of the modest, gentle, uncomplaining plum blossom described in Sugimoto's autobiography. For most middle-class young men, the kind of freedom that allowed for genuine and unaffected relationships with properly brought-up middle-class young women was not easily obtainable, nor could an ambitious young person seek it out in a country that set strict social boundaries and rules to assure his future as a worthy citizen.

As a young man Nagai Kafū (1879–1959), an important Meiji literary figure, struggled with social customs and worldviews and attempted to come to terms with *kindai* Japan and its attitudes toward the West. Kafū grew up in a household dominated by a father who strove to maintain a lifestyle that accorded with his understanding of the United States and the West.[91] Kafū's father had moved to Tokyo after the Restoration, learned English at the age of nineteen, and studied under government sponsorship at Princeton and Rutgers for two years. He entered the bureaucracy in 1873 and served various ministries as an engineer and technician, planning libraries, constructing water-supply and drainage systems, and helping to draft the Imperial Rescript on Education. He left the government in 1897 and joined Nippon Yūsen Kaisha, the important shipping monopoly.

Like Ōgai, Natsume Sōseki, and other writers who went abroad as young men, Kafū became well versed in Western literature, but his upbringing contrasted sharply with Ōgai's and Sōseki's. His peers in high school jeered at him for wearing short pants like a European child (rather than the regulation trousers worn by his schoolmates) and for having longer hair than the other boys.[92] However, much to his father's distress, Kafū was not successful in the Meiji educational environment, failed abysmally in school, was unable to pass entrance examinations, and was expelled from the Foreign Languages School in 1899, just when he began to seek out mentors from among the Meiji literati.[93] At this time of his life he was already beginning to write and was intensely engrossed in the works of Emile Zola.[94]

When he left Tokyo for the United States in 1903 at the age of twenty-four, Kafū had received training in Western thought and living, but it had been decoded and recoded in Japanese terms by his father, his Meiji mentors, and his own self-education. These experiences had helped him to formulate, in Japan, a distinct understanding about what was Western, kindai, as well as what was historically basic to Japanese culture. Kafū's father, a writer of Chinese poetry, a lover and collector of Eastern antiques, and a *bonsai* (dwarfed plants) aficionado, had him tutored in Confucianism and classical Chinese. His mother imparted an appreciation for the popular culture of Edo.[95] These formed fundamental parts of his consciousness.[96]

Kafū's early works depicted the "dark side of society" and constituted "an indictment of human misery," an approach apparent in a number of the pieces in *Amerika monogatari* (Stories from America)," based on his four-year stay in the United States (see Figure 12).[97] Published in 1908, it is a series of stories about a multifaceted and diverse nation, with a wide range of Japanese and American characters: immigrant workers, businessmen, housewives, pimps, amusement-park hawkers, male and female students, literati, blacks, Italian musicians, Irish, Italian, and Canadian prostitutes—all representing divergent aspects of the United States from Tacoma, Washington, to Kalamazoo, Michigan, Chicago, and New York City. However, Kafū's outlook changed over time to reflect his love for French literature, from the works of Zola to Maupassant and, later, Baudelaire. This evolution began toward the end of his American years. Some stories in *Amerika monogatari* suggest this literary transition. They describe the meaning of life as sought in evil, dissipation, sensual pleasures—all outcomes of dissatisfaction with society—which symbolize Kafū's increasing detachment from his early role as a critic of society's inequities.[98]

Ōkubo Takaki argued that Kafū's early work represents a point of view directly contradicting that of Meiji authors such as Ōgai or Sōseki, whose writings he considered representative of the cultural milieu of intellectuals.[99] By contrast, Kafū's writings were based on the assumption that intellectuals constituted only one group among many in society and that they, like farmers and laborers, held distinct individual views influenced by their social position. Therefore, his depictions of the United States and France do not constitute a generalized view of Western civilization such as Ōgai's—that of an outsider looking in. His

Fig. 12. Cover to Nagai Kafū, *Amerika monogatari* (1908).

regard for the particular as an important part of the whole gives his observations of the United States a singular attribute. He represents the diverse classes, lifestyles, and personality types woven into society. His characters meet with a variety of experiences—work, leisure, poverty, exploitation, insanity, love, rejection, friendship, rape—in a range of urban, rural, backwoods, or small-town surroundings. Kafū's class background notwithstanding, the breadth of life in this early work is impressive and often moving.

Two aspects of Kafū's youth are of particular interest to us: his alienation from life in Japan and his attitudes toward relationships with women. We have considered both themes as they affected emigration: urban educated individuals caught in the waves of social change in modern Meiji Japan moved to the United States seeking to overcome the insecurities they faced at home. Kafū's intellectual detachment from Japanese life was reinforced by his distaste for the East/West cultural framework relished by his upper-middle-class father.

To Kafū, his father, despite the latter's Western leanings, personified governmental bureaucracy and the state, forces that constricted individual action, and the "most hidebound Confucianism."[100] He first journeyed to the United States in October 1903 because his father wanted him "to learn English and something of business." He did not want to send his son to France, believing the young man would succumb to dissipating influences there.[101] But Kafū's original wish was to go to France, so he did not bother with English or business courses. Instead, he studied French at a high school in Tacoma for one year and then enrolled in Kalamazoo College in Michigan for half a year to become proficient in reading the language. In June 1905 he crossed the North American continent via Chicago and ended up in New York and Washington, D.C.[102] In New York, he initially lived on Concord Place in Brooklyn and placed an employment-wanted ad in the *New York Herald* for work as a "houseworker in small family." But his cousin, an employee at the New York Consul General's office, found him work as a clerk at the Japanese Embassy in Washington, D.C., a job he held for five months.[103] For his remaining year and a half in the United States, Kafū held an unstimulating job in a New York City branch of a Japanese bank, spent whatever extra money he had on opera and concert tickets, had a romantic affair with a prostitute named Edith (whom he met in Washington and who moved to New York to be with him), read voraciously, and finally embarked on his voyage to the land of his dreams, France.[104]

Kafū's attitudes toward women in his later years hardly exemplified renai. In fact, his transformation from an admirer of Zola to a Baudelaire devotee is apparent in his stories about prostitutes in New York City, in which he expressed heartfelt sympathy for them and lamented their inhuman existence yet luxuriated in the physical pleasures he derived. Recalling an evening with "Bessie," he wrote, "[W]e drank, sang, and then kissed and explored each other's bodies. If you want to engage in the most insane pleasures, you need a Western woman, not a reticent Japanese woman."[105] The physical freedom of these women excited and impressed him. In addition, he admired what he interpreted as their liberated quality. They were able to discuss matters of the intellect as equals with men and could reject marriage as their supreme goal in life.

His final story in *Amerika monogatari* centered on Rosalind, a young woman whose friendship and love he treasured during his month's vacation stay on Staten Island before departing for France.[106] Like Kafū, she loved classical music and the opera and was self-assured and independent, both qualities belied by her "petite and fragile looks." Of the many women described in the book, Rosalind was the only one to whom Kafū felt free to communicate his "dreams."

My experience with American women during these years and months has been that I am unable to talk about things I am interested in to them. They are too lively to engage in conversations about radical theories of art or the violent problems of life. So much so that when I am introduced to them, I do not expect either genuine conversation or pleasurable joking. My goal at such times is to practice my English or observe human nature.[107]

When he first met Rosalind, he was ready, "being a polite young man," to carry on a mundane conversation about automobiles (which he hated) or going to church, anything that came to mind. To his surprise and delight, the first question she asked was whether he liked the opera. Conversations about music and musicians followed, "practically bringing tears" of happiness to his eyes. His experience with her prompted him to confess: "To tell the truth, I like Western women.... My odd understanding of American women was because I was expecting too much of them in the beginning."[108] They not only talked about cultural topics but also shared opinions about marriage and love. Following a discussion about Japanese women, Kafū "nonchalantly" asked Rosalind if she believed in remaining single "as most American women seemed to." Rosalind, "indignant" at being placed in the category of "most American women," nevertheless replied that she would probably remain single: "It's not because I'm passive. I'll never become hopeless like a pitiful, wretched French widow, nor end up a narrow-minded and stern American old maid."[109] Although she had lived in the United States since the age of five, Rosalind took pride in her English birth and background, which she claimed endowed her with an optimistic and lighthearted stoicism about life. The English, she said, "fight laughing until they are beaten."

Through the weeks in Staten Island, the two spent whatever time they could together until Kafū's departure for France approached. He considered living "forever" in the United States or asking Rosalind to leave "for love of a man" but decided that neither was possible. He could not ask Rosalind to make such a momentous decision. He characterized both of them as "extremely practical," a quality he attributed to their living in the United States. The two separated, and thus the "short, beautiful dream turned into a lifetime of sad tears." Although Kafū was never able to enter into a lifelong renai relationship because of his commitment to art ("men are selfish and sinful") and his changing attitudes regarding renai's permanence, it was his ideal.[110] He "desired love" but was convinced that reality would make it "disappear like smoke": "I felt despair about anything that was real. . . . I would rather spend my life dreaming about a love that was true."[111] His relationship with the prostitute Edith had, at one time, prompted him to "become an American" and manage a brothel with her in New York City, but, like his summer in Staten Island with Rosalind, this was a temporary dream.[112]

American women's lack of formality and freedom of behavior were attractive to Kafū, the young Etsu Sugimoto, and Masuji Miyakawa. All three compared American women to Japanese women. Sugimoto's descriptions were full of envy and adulation; Miyakawa intimated that, with progress, Japanese women could learn to achieve a comparable position of equality. Kafū indicated that they were confined in more ways than one. In a paragraph praising the physical beauty of Western women he wrote:

The beautiful curves of their pronounced hips, eyes full of expression, sculptured shoulders, full arms, ample bosoms, I cannot but marvel at the skill and taste with which they use cosmetics. The color and design of each woman's dress is chosen according to her hair, complexion, and body, and even the most average-looking woman tends to attract men. Japanese women lack these talents. Of course, the Japanese are a people who criticize and interfere, so that weak women brought up in such a society shrink in fear and cannot decorate their natural features as they wish.[113]

In one short story, Kafū remarked on the openness between American men and women. Observing their natural relationship and cooperation, he felt "extraordinary happiness": "I see women bite into huge sandwiches or whole apples, peel and all, drink champagne at restaurants late at night after the theater or opera, converse with their husbands or male friends with frankness. . . . That kind of happiness was never shown by . . . my mother."[114] Statements such as these reveal the Japanese perception that womanhood and male/female relationships were unconstrained in the United States. The authors expressed the desire to escape beyond the constricting Japanese world of marriage practices, a world that ignored freedom of choice and lacked an emotional element that could give meaning to a relationship. In the renai relationships common in the United States, individual choice was important; men could express feelings toward their partners without embarrassment or humiliation, and women could develop independently, becoming more than passive and obedient maids, wives, and daughters-in-law. These effects produced qualitative differences in men and women's day-to-day lives together, promoting cooperation, frankness, and equality. Although going to the United States did not enable most young people to overcome the restrictions they experienced in Japan, the widespread illusions about American behavior in relationships and marriages created a compelling expectation of fulfillment and genuine companionship.

I am not suggesting that urban hi-imin left Japan solely because they yearned for a renai relationship. However, the perception of renai as an essential part of American courtship and marriage was another in a wide assortment of appealing notions about the United States. It was important not as a conscious motivating force but as a vague and subjective sense of how one's personal life could enfold in the United States. Among the more educated hi-imin, it found expression in works such as Nagai Kafū's. It did not find expression among the less erudite, but it is not far-fetched to assume that their dreams were not far from those of a Kafū. Those who decided to go to the United States and become permanent residents probably did not ponder the problem of a population dominated by single Japanese males. Perhaps they thought women would follow them across the Pacific or that relationships with American women would ensue. This was conceivable for the hi-imin, whose passport designation granted both privilege and status and who presumed that their lives could be as free and equal as the Americans'. It was even more conceivable for those who were acquainted with stories about American women and knew that gender relations in the United States differed from those in Japan. This knowledge elicited the fantasy that one could reject the arbitrary marriage rituals and social customs of Japan and anticipate free and open relationships with women in America. One could discover renai, a pure and true love "from the depths of one's soul."

CHAPTER 8

Conclusion

The Metro section of a Sunday *New York Times* in February 1994 prominently displayed several photographs of young Japanese visitors to Manhattan wearing oversized soccer coaches' field coats embellished with Adidas and Nike logos. At first glance these coats might appear to be products of the visitors' shopping spree in the city, but in reality they were from Japan and could be purchased in Tokyo department stores for $150. According to the *Times*, American tourists to Tokyo brought back similar purchases, creating a "new status symbol and demand in New York City."[1]

Contemporary cultural products such as these field coats all tend to look alike. However, that "sameness" is only superficial, for if we start to scrutinize the *Times*' designation of the coats as "status symbols," we are forced to consider what status means in Japan and in the United States. The word has subtle and distinct connotations in each country. In Japan *status* could mean "positioned better than" or, conversely, "familiarity with the Other," "cosmopolitan," and "free of insularism." In the United States, status involves being "cool," "casually superior," "in the know," and "fashion-setting."[2] The motives, impulses, and effects of status on self-image derive from individual cultural lives and social situations.

I began this study by posing the question of how the Japanese Other, the United States, was constructed in the minds of urban and literate Japanese of the Meiji-Taisho era. A wide assortment of individuals visited, resided, or worked in the United States—people ranging from vacationers to temporary laborers, students to teachers, official representatives to independent travelers, sons and daughters of the elite to youth anxious to learn and curious about "the Occident." All were raised and educated in an era of dislocating social and economic change and ever-intrusive political demands on their lives. These individuals produced a large collection of writings on the United States during an era when large sections of the world were experiencing the volatile effects of economic and territorial imperialism. Japan, the sole non-Western power, brandished its chrysanthemum and sword to accomplish its imperial objectives, an important one being to gain membership in the fraternity of the Occident.

It was in this context that Japanese "Occidentalism" was formed and projected into the national consciousness.[3] The construction was not identical to Orientalism, which has been analyzed in recent times as the product of power combined with knowledge to justify imperialist projects.[4] But neither was it totally dissimilar. The nineteenth-century Japanese notion of the Occident augmented and extended the Western notion of the Orient. It constituted the other side of the coin. Like Orientalism, Occidentalism was binary, homogeneous, and essentialist—constructed in terms of culture and social behavior. It had strong political connotations, intimately associated with power, which rendered the concrete lives of the Occidental Other irrelevant. It reduced understanding to products of the imagination. As the future unfolded and Japan's capitalist wealth increased, the country unfolded its past, to advancing the expectation that a unique and unadulterated folk strain, existent for over two and a half millennia, would yield noble and glorious supremacy. The government attempted to change history by controlling it.

However, Japan's Occidentalism differed from Orientalism in that its contours were shaped with the acute awareness that the West had positioned Japan in the unenvious role of simultaneously being advisee, imitator, competitor, inferior, collaborator, and opponent. As time elapsed, Japan challenged and contested this position, increasingly constructing itself, the viewer, as pure, sagacious, old, and civilized and the West, the viewed, as juvenile, abrasive, tactless, and materialistic and therefore not as (or un-) civilized. Persevering, benevolent, courageous, and cultured warriors, youth, and poets of the past, taken from traditional folk tales and the classics, were evoked as representatives of the viewer. The representatives of the viewed were entrepreneurs, fly-by-night money makers, crass movers of capital who lacked a consistent, continuous, and ancient history and an untainted blood stock. Japan's colonial ambitions were frustrated in the 1920s, and depictions of the immaturity and brashness of the West, in particular the United States, began to intensify in the mid- to late 1930s, finally including a portrayal of cowardice in the 1940s.[5] In our period of concern, however, this was not yet significant.

Japanese Occidentalism was not the model for the Orient as a whole. Rather, it was nation-specific, more telling about the Japanese self than about the Occidental Other. It reflected the desires, fears, and misapprehensions of a nation-state that only recently had entered into the competitive capitalist arena. Like the capitalist colonialist powers of the United States and Europe, it subordinated the Oriental Other—the colonized and colonizable territories and people in Asia (China, Korea, India, Burma, Indonesia). None of Japan's Asian neighbors was to escape this secondary status. Like the Western imperialist powers, Japan cultivated an increasingly strident nationalism, solidified by the colonialist creation of the Oriental Other. Looked upon in this context, Japanese Occidentalism was constructed with a strong component of Orientalism and the recognition that active and aggressive competition, the "sekkyokuteki spirit," was necessary. Additionally, it contained the uncomfortable and awkward perception that Japan had yet to gain total acceptance as an equal in the world of the Western powers. Irritating ingredients of self-doubt and uncertainty were as definitive as the more obvious indispensable elements crucial to the formation of power. The task was complicated and intricate: Japan sought to forge a superior and exceptional combination of old and new that would triumph over the weak and establish a formidable confederation with the strong.

These factors informed and influenced the literate, urban, and aspiring youth in their constructions of "imagined communities,"[6] not only in relation to nationalist patriotic aspirations for their own country but also in a consolidation with the outside, the Occidental Other, which fundamentally encompassed an international and global element. With this in mind, we can come to some understanding about the impulses behind the tobei hi-imin's ultimate decision to move outside their native borders. They prepared to orient their lives to new situations, places, and relationships that could not be predicted. Laudatory explications of the American spirit of success or the hopeful expectations of greater flexibility in their public and private lives withal, the emigrants' unarticulated feelings and thoughts, which had cultural origins in their individual lives and social situations at a specific time in history, helped to create their images, fantasies, and dreams of the unknown, however impermanent and unfixed. It is difficult to point to these factors as facts and to define them in clear-cut terms; as Renato Rosaldo indicated, "change rather than structure becomes society's enduring state, and time rather than space becomes its most encompassing medium."[7]

In attempting to reconstruct a social past, we must consider the unexpected, the unforeseen, and the unintended, which are just as vital as "conventional wisdom" and codes and norms to the formation of cultural practices. Thus, we must look upon the migration process as more than a physical and mental movement from one place to another. It was controlled and dominated by the ideologies and worldviews of Japan and, indirectly, the United States. More important, it reflected the specific circumstances of the migrants, who acted according to convention, against convention, or, as the case may be, by trial and error. The hi-imin cannot be placed en masse into a coherent and unified social drama, only into a superficial structural context. Each individual had different motivations and different experiences and effected change according to the circumstances of their everyday lives. Etsu Sugimoto's desire to raise her daughters in a place where men were not "chained" by convention; her brother's escape to the United States from an undesired marriage; "Henry's" comparisons of the social training of American and Japanese children; Abe Isō's comparative ranking of leisure activities by country; the coincidences in Toyohiko Takami's life that took him from stewardship on ships in Wallabout Bay to a lucrative medical practice in Brooklyn; Kafū's observation that his mother never showed the free behavior of American women; Katayama Sen's creation of a bizarre and conflated capitalist-socialist world—all of these exemplify myriad cultural practices and thoughts that in themselves only partially explain the reasons behind the imprecise and sweeping process of immigration.

Japanese immigrants to New York sought to unshackle themselves, perhaps escape, from a past in which relationships with kin, authority figures, and peers hindered desires for individual development; to prove that an alternative life was possible; to explore subjective feelings, new relationships and ties, new sensations, advancement and knowledge; to experience untried ways of living; to fantasize about new realities. These intangible emotional and attitudinal factors redefine the conventional reasons of economic and political push and pull with distinctive, interesting, complicated, nonessentialist aspects that more accurately reflect the complexities of human life. The tobei hi-imin combined elements of their past and the realities of their lives in Japan, consequences of their nation's industrial capitalism and participation in the new world order, with what they perceived as kindai to produce their own cross-national, or wayō, culture. They joined a patriotic desire for Japan's rise in the community of world powers with the ideal of building an exceptional, enlightened, and integrated world guided by the educated, refined, and cosmopolitan segment of society. These ideas surpassed narrower racial or national identities.

The invention of this kindai wayō mentality reflected the hi-imin's deep desire to negotiate their selfhood, having experienced an incomplete and less than satisfactory process in their own home environment. They believed that East Coast Americans (the "better sort") and more knowledgeable and cosmopolitan Japanese would together orchestrate a genuinely collaborative and innovative culture, enhancing the quest for self-identity. This perspective was linked to interactions and social relations that could not yet take place in Japan. It included a somewhat narcissistic vein, a certain dilettantism, in which openness to unknown experiences was to bring exhilaration and new sensibilities. As boundaries were eliminated in the new world culture, the hi-imin and Japan as a whole would emerge from the repugnant state of subordination and inferiority.

In one sense, this cultural integration would occur because of cultural disintegration—not necessarily a negative process, but one that made provincialism obsolete. It looked to a form of globalization as the goal—the notion that people with comparable aspirations and upbringings could achieve a single society. Roland Robertson stated that historically, such a society has taken on forms of various theoretical possibilities:

The world could in principle have been rendered as a "singular system" . . . via the imperial hegemony of a single nation or a "grand alliance" between two or more dynasties or nations; the victory of "the universal proletariat"; the global triumph of a particular form of organized religion; the crystallization of "the world spirit"; the yielding of nationalism to the ideal of "free trade"; the success of the world-federalist movement; the world-wide triumph of a trading company; or in yet other ways.[8]

Although the tobei hi-imin did not participate in or initiate any meaningful world-order analysis, each individual's migration process signified unarticulated, imprecise, and hopeful longings that a different world could better promise freedom, equality, well-being, and refinement. The "crystallization of 'the world spirit' " emanated from a class-bound, kindai, wayō, capitalist mentality, but it proved inconsequential and alien in an environment where a class-based, modern, American capitalist mentality flourished. Both mentalities possessed basic similarities in intent and execution, but differences in sensibility and understanding stemming from power relations rendered them remote and irrelevant.

In contemporary times, we are experiencing the conceptualization of a decontextualized transnational culture that "operates in *relative* independence of strictly societal and other more conventionally studied sociocultural processes."[9] Mike Featherstone pointed out that the formation of this transnational cultural world does not represent a homogenization and integration into a "third culture" caused by the weakening of sovereignties and their absorption into units transcending the state-society unit. Rather, its conceptualization, in postmodern theoretical terms, focuses on "the diversity, variety and richness of popular and local discourses, codes and practices which resist and play-back systemicity and order. Modes of understanding which operated within a strict symbolic hierarchy and a bound context are now asked to accept that all symbolic hierarchies are to be spatialized out and that the context is boundless."[10] Featherstone warned that this escape from a "bounded nation-state society" is narrowly Eurocentric and is encapsulated in the terms *premodernity, modernity,* and *postmodernity*—a "Western continuum" into which Japan does not fit.[11] Masao Miyoshi and H. D. Harootunian offered the compelling argument that, historically, Japan was engaged in a "constant practice" to locate "the insular society on the international map of progress," a process that was not without disagreements. It was informed by its position of privilege, "distant enough from modernism but close enough to it to be in the know." In other words, Japan was well aware of the consequences of Western encroachment and colonialism in Asia and operated from this premise.[12] It played "modern" and "patriotic/national," Western and Japanese, shifting and changing from one to the other depending on the time in which it was meeting the demands and needs of historical change. I would also add that this play was peopled by an assortment of characters, givers and takers, initiators and translators, producers and consumers, decoders and misinterpreters, each of whom conferred on it a particular stamp of intention, meaning, and use. This reasoning allows me to correlate the story of the Japanese-made field coats with the migratory impulses and motives of the tobei hi-imin.

One hundred years of history separate the present-day fashion fads of young Americans and Japanese from the imaginary social world of the literate, urban Japanese of the Meiji and Taisho periods. However, that separation does not negate the idea that the world is global where relations, exchange, and communication are not exceptional but rather the norm. Nor does it negate the transience, dynamism, movement, and vigor of cultural agents, and of culture itself (that culture is "a process" with people playing vital roles). These ideas assume overpowering and complex meanings when placed in the context of the last four centuries, which began with the West reaching out to acquire trade routes and territories. The projection of the West and Western ideas on the non-Western world has continued apace, with unprecedented cultural consequences. Today we see innumerable material products from various corners of the earth, ranging from mundane everyday items to leisure-time goods and services—all assumed to have been generated by the West. Architects of this view regret the loss of a past in the colonial non-Western world and, as Rosaldo aptly worded it, refer nostalgically to cultural objects as well as to cultural time and space, which have become irrelevant and alien in industrialized societies.[13] The nostalgia also allowed William Westmoreland to say, in the mid-1970s film *Hearts and Minds*, that the Vietnamese place little value on life and, more recently, Karel van Wolferen to open his appropriately titled *The Enigma of Japanese Power* with the words: "Japan perplexes the world . . . , yet it does not behave the way most of the world expects a world power to behave; sometimes it even gives the impression of not wanting to belong to the world at all."[14] This nostalgia, exoticism, and mystery place importance on the generalized concept of Westernization and ignore the specificities that make for divergence.

The process by which goods, ideas, and people traverse international boundaries and are embodied and represented cannot escape the particular, whether it be geographic, national, societal, ethnic, or individual. The particular reinforces, supplements, and alters meanings that affect people's experiences, and at times it takes on struggles against forms of power. The urban hi-imin's struggle was against the hegemonic elements of their own society and toward what was told to them about an unknown society. They utilized the images from information they gathered and constructed a kindai, wayō vision of how they might accommodate to that other world.

I will end this study by recounting an experience I had in Japan at the forty-ninth-day memorial service on the occasion of the interment of my mother's ashes. As fate would have it, I did not own the correct attire. Everyone was dressed in the expected black. I wore my "formal" American outfit—white slacks, linen jacket, and linen blouse—and was worried that I would feel awkward and humiliated. However, to my great relief, the event ended without discomfort. Rather, it was a congenial time with many anecdotes, stories of childhoods, jokes interspersed with gossip, much laughter, and food. My being accepted had nothing to do with what I knew—or thought I knew—about my host country.

Appendix 1

Statistical Conclusions Concerning the Profile of the Japanese in New York

1. Japanese from Tokyo outnumbered those from any other area in Japan. Over half came from twelve ken and fu; the rest came from thirty-four ken scattered throughout the three main islands of Japan (see Tables 1, 2, and 3).

In sharp contrast, 60 percent of the California issei came from only four southwestern agricultural ken in Japan.[1] The largest group of New York Japanese listed honseki in Tokyo-fu and the city of Tokyo—8.9 to 12.3 percent from Tokyo-fu and 11 percent from the city.[2] Altogether, 17.9 percent came from the five major cities of Japan: Tokyo, Yokohama, Osaka, Kobe, and Kyoto. Approximately half as many were from Hiroshima-ken as from Tokyo.

The figures on New York Japanese with Tokyo origins need further explanation. A person's official honseki was not necessarily his or her place of residence. One could move to another part of Japan but still maintain the honseki as the registered domicile.[3] It was not unusual, for instance, for an individual to migrate to Tokyo, live there, even die there, and still be registered officially as having the former honseki address. Thus, in analyzing the geographic origins of the New York Japanese, it is necessary to consider migration inside Japan, particularly from rural areas to the cities, a movement not accurately reflected in the honseki listings. Based on the annual statistics of Tokyo, the official honseki population of Tokyo hovered between 52.1 and 67.3 percent during 1891–1920.[4] Demographic studies of the pre–World War I years estimated that in 1911 only 40 percent of the population was born in Tokyo.[5]

Therefore, we can assume that the figures listed in Tables 1, 2, and 3 are conservative ones, as some of the New York Japanese, although maintaining honseki in other ken, probably were de facto residents of Tokyo. Their orientation, if not their origins, were urban.

2. Hi-imin constituted 73.5 percent of the Japanese residents in New York. Between April 1912 and July 1916 the New York Consul General issued 446 certificates of residency, of which 328 were classified as hi-imin.[6] This is an extraordinary number, particularly when we consider the occupational makeup of all immigrants to the United States at this time. Thomas Kessner calculated that between 1899 and 1910, 1.4 percent were "professional," 20.2 percent were "skilled," and 78.4 percent were "miscellaneous."[7] Consequently, if all immigrants were defined according to Japanese government classifications, close to 99 percent of the immigrants to the United States during those years would have been imin. Likewise, the imin/hi-imin ratio of the West Coast Japanese was the exact opposite of that in New York. As listed in the monthly consular reports from Seattle and Portland, for instance, more than 75 percent of the Japanese residents of those cities were imin. Chicago also showed a greater number of imin than hi-imin. The New York Japanese community constituted an exception to the rule.

A listing of the Tokyo honseki residents who applied for passports to the United States offers further information on the imin/hi-imin breakdown (see Table 4). Over 75 percent were hi-imin; close to 7 percent, imin; and 18 percent, "indeterminate." Two-thirds of the women were in the "indeterminate" category—neither imin nor hi-imin, laborer nor lady—and officially had no singular attribute other than their femaleness. The majority were wives who came to the United States to join their husbands.

Students constituted a little more than 34 percent of the total (Table 4), a ratio that exceeded any other category. Merchants and businessmen made up over 29 percent, and those who represented Japanese companies, banks, or the government made up 2.5 percent.

Were the stated objectives of students and merchants the real reason for travel, or were they simply means to obtain passports? Yasuo Wakatsuki states that students often emigrated "to work under the pretext of studying, rather than to work to meet any deficiency in school expenses."[8] For instance, persons who professed to be taking inspection tours of poultry farms or carrying out research in vegetable cultivation did not differ from "the workers going abroad to engage in poultry raising or agriculture." Whatever their intentions, in order to get hi-imin passports, students had to have completed eleven years of schooling, and merchants were expected to have considerable education or experience.

3. For every Japanese female in New York, there were thirty-one Japanese males in 1904 and twelve in 1919.

The official annual statistics of Japan were the only source that accounted for the number of women in New York (Table 5). Up to 1919 less than 10 percent of the Japanese in New York were women. In 1920 the figure rose to 16.3 percent and in 1922 jumped to 23.5 percent. This increase is significant, because the Japanese government curtailed the entry of imin wives with its ban on picture brides in 1921. The overall number of passports for women destined for the United States decreased by 31.2 percent in that year and by 15.4 percent in 1922. The New York figures, on the contrary, increased.

Of all Tokyo honseki residents who came to the United States between 1902 and 1916, women made up 15.9 percent; of that total, 37.8 percent came as wives of males already in the United States (Table 4). More women who left Tokyo were in this category than any other, and consequently we can infer that, given the large percentage of hi-imin males in New York, the steady increase of Japanese women reflected the arrival of hi-imin wives. Students constituted the next largest group of women with honseki in Tokyo, at 10.5 percent.

4. The age range of the largest number of both males and females was 21-40 (Tables 6 and 7).

Women of the 21-30 age group constituted more than 50 percent of all women. Males were almost equally represented in the 21-30 and 31-40 age groups (Table 7). According to Yamato Ichihashi, 75 percent of all Japanese who arrived in the United States were under the age of twenty-five.[9] Therefore, in comparison with Japanese males in the United States and Hawaii as a whole, the New York Japanese were older.

The age and hi-imin status of the New York Japanese suggests that merchants and entrepreneurs, not including the 2.5 percent who were government and Japanese company representatives, came independently to the United States intending to establish a business and probably had had some experience in Japan. Students probably were older, had acquired schooling in Japan, and came to the United States with the intention of furthering their education.

Information on Sources for Tables 1, 2, and 3

Three sources give conclusive evidence about the geographic origins of the New York issei. First are the monthly reports the New York Consul General submitted to the Foreign Ministry in Tokyo from 1909 to 1921.[10] Essentially, these were notices concerning births, marriages, deaths, and divorces that indicated a change in family status and included the individual's honseki. The lists were painstakingly written in calligraphy by clerks in the earlier years, but as time elapsed, particularly after World War I, the writing became careless, and the records lacked complete addresses. However, ken and fu and, in the case of urban residents, the city of origin were recorded for each entry.

The second important documentary source comprises the New York Consul General's reports to the Foreign Ministry, 1912–1924, regarding the issuance of certificates of residence.[11] These certificates enabled the citizen to apply for passports for themselves, their wives and children, or their employees. Legally, only people with certificates could travel back and forth between the United States and Japan or bring relatives or employees. This group of documents included the resident's honseki and imin/hi-imin status.

A third important source is Shōzō Mizutani's *Nyūyōku nihonjin hattenshi* (History of the Japanese in New York), published in 1921.[12] Sponsored by the Japanese Association of New York, the book listed statistical information based on an "accurate account" of the New York Japanese population in 1919. The material probably is more reliable than the official figures, because the association's role as the major organization for Japanese in New York and its close connection with the Japanese government placed it in a position to keep the most comprehensive information.

Appendix 2

1 *Geographic Origins*
   Honseki of 553 Japanese Citizens Registered at the New York Consulate General, 1909–1921

Ken/fu	Number	Percent
Tokyo	68 (61 from Tokyo city)	12.3
Hiroshima	36	6.4
Kanagawa	31 (15 from Yokohama)	5.6
Yamaguchi	29	5.2
Fukuoka	28	5.0
Kumamoto	25	4.5
Osaka	18 (11 from Osaka city)	3.3
Hyōgo	18 (7 from Kobe)	3.3
Niigata	18	3.3
Kyoto	17 (5 from Kyoto city)	3.1
Nagasaki	17	3.1
Ehime	16	2.9
Remaining 34 ken and Hokkaidō[a]	232	42.0

[a] Number of people ranged from 13 from Saga, Mie, and Kagoshima to 0 from Akita.

2 Geographic Origins
Honseki of 1,956 Japanese Citizens Issued Certificates of Residency by the
New York Consulate General, 1912–1924

Ken/fu	Number	Percent
Tokyo	230	11.8
Hiroshima	114	5.8
Kanagawa	107	5.5
Hyōgo	106	5.4
Osaka	83	4.2
Fukuoka	70	3.6
Wakayama	64	3.3
Yamaguchi	62	3.2
Kyoto	61	3.1
Shizuoka	59	3.0
Aichi	57	2.9
Ishikawa	57	2.9
Remaining 34 ken and Korea and Taiwan[a]	886	45.3

[a]Numbers of people ranged from 56 from Nagasaki to 3 from Akita. Taiwan was annexed in 1895; Korea in 1910.

3 Geographic Origins
Birthplaces of 2,992 Japanese Male Residents of New York, 1920 (based on Mizutani)[a]

Ken/fu	Number	Percent
Tokyo	265	8.9
Hiroshima	174	5.8
Fukuoka	136	4.5
Niigata	131	4.4
Kumamoto	127	4.2
Kanagawa	118	3.9
Yamaguchi	113	3.8
Kagoshima	111	3.7
Hyōgo	98	3.3
Osaka	96	3.2
Okayama	83	2.8
Ehime	80	2.7
Remaining 33 ken, Hokkaidō, Korea and Taiwan	1,434	47.9
United States	26	0.9

[a]Mizutani, Nyūyōku nihonjin hattenshi, 1:366–69.

4 Passports Issued for Travel to United States, Tokyo Honseki Residents:[a] 1902–1914 and 1916

Objective	Number		Percentage	
I. *Hi-imin*	M	F	M	F
1. Religious Study	12	1		
2. Study	870	45	32.2	1.7
3. Physician	1			
4. Instructor	8	2		
5. Reporter	10			
6. Performer	25	6		
7. Photographer	11			
8. Commercial	634	26	23.5	1.0
9. For Industry	114		4.2	
10. Emigration Business	1			
11. Contract Building	10			
12. Study Railroad	2			
13. Investigation of Condition of People	110	2	4.1	
14. Member of Company	41	1		
15. Shipping Business	2			
16. Official Mission	22	1		
17. Interviews	8	8		
18. Pleasure	52	7	1.0	
TOTAL	1,933	99	71.6	3.7
II. *Imin*	M	F	M	F
1. Agriculture	36	1		
2. Tailoring	18	5		
3. Gardening	3			
4. Laborer	14			
5. Servant	10	4		
6. Attendant	39	23		
7. Invited	15	5		
8. Accompanied	6	7		
TOTAL	141	45	5.2	1.7
III. *Indeterminate Classification*				
1. Others	198	122	7.3	4.5
2. To Husband's House		161		6.0
3. For Marriage		1		
TOTAL	198	284	7.3	10.5

[a] *Tōkyōshi tōkei nenpyō* (Annual statistics of the city of Tokyo), 1902–1917.

5 *Japanese Population in New York City, 1890–1924*

		Japanese Figures[b]		American Figures	
	Mizutani[a]	Male	Female (Percent)	U.S.[c]	N.Y.C.[d]
1890				123	164
1891		600			
1896		408	28 (6.4)		
1897		596	26 (4.2)		
1898		619	39 (5.9)		
1899			n.a.		
1900		1,097	73 (6.2)	286	311
1901		974	56 (5.4)		
1902		977	64 (6.1)		
1903		1,316	87 (6.2)		
1904		1,830	60 (3.2)		
1905		2,067	121 (5.5)		
1906		1,966	87 (4.2)		
1907			n.a.		
1908			n.a.		
1909	3,000		n.a.		
1910		1,174	—	1,037	957
1911		1,788	170 (8.7)		
1912		1,962	186 (8.7)		
1913		1,976	187 (8.6)		
1914			n.a.		
1915		2,552	246 (8.8)		
1916		2,386 (total)			
1917		"			
1918		3,320	284 (7.9)		
1919		3,735	318 (7.8)		
1920	4,652	3,286	640 (16.3)	2,312	2,073
1921			n.a.		
1922		3,013	925 (23.5)		
1923		n.a. (Tokyo earthquake)			
1924		2,602	745 (22.3)		

[a] Mizutani, *Nyūyōku nihonjin hattenshi*, 1:363–66.
[b] *Nihonteikoku tōkei nenkan*, 1891–1924.
[c] U.S. Department of Commerce, Bureau of the Census, *Census of the United States*, 1890–1920.
[d] *Population of the City of New York, 1890–1930*, comp. and ed. Walter Laidlaw (1932).

6 *Age of Travelers to the United States, Tokyo Honseki Residents, 1907–1916*

	11–20		21–30		32–40		41+	
	M	F	M	F	M	F	M	F
1907	73	13	239	24	98	10	42	2
1908	11	7	71	27	20	9	43	6
1909	9	9	101	20	60	11	47	12
1910	11	10	102	23	101	14	98	8
1911	18	5	63	21	36	12	47	4
1912	16	1	79	29	98	8	43	7
1913	6	6	58	28	83	15	46	6
1914	3	12	83	37	90	12	81	6
1915	14	8	126	33	100	16	76	6
1916	15	16	131	49	165	9	82	7
Total	176	87	1,053	291	851	116	605	64
Percentage of Gender								
Total	6.5	15.5	39.1	52.0	31.9	20.7	22.4	11.8

7 *Age of 2,992 Japanese Male Residents of New York, 1920 (based on Mizutani)*[a]

	to 20	21–30	32–40	41+	unknown
	159	1,102	1,172	468	91
Percent	5.3	36.8	39.1	15.7	3.1

[a] Mizutani, *Nihonteikoku tōkei nenkan*, 1:372–76.

8 *Japanese Immigrants to the United States, 1891–1924*

	Japanese Figures[a]		American Figures	
	Passports Issued	Returned	Immigrants	Emigrants
1891	1,461	168	1,136[b]	
1892	2,344	243	—	
1893	1,978	356	1,380	
1894	1,497	391	1,931	
1895	1,049	347	1,150	
1896	1,764	367	1,110	
1897	1,945	388	1,526	
1898	2,936	671	2,230	
1899	6,942	833	2,844	
1900	10,562	1,006	12,635	
1901	1,986	866	5,269	
1902	5,096	1,013	14,270	
1903	5,215	1,028	19,968	
1904	3,490	922	14,264	
1905	3,124	1,791	10,331	
1906	8,466	2,881	13,835	
1907	9,618	1,903	30,226	
1908	3,214	2,273	15,803	
1909	2,002	1,600	3,111	
1910	2,900	1,548	2,720	
1911	3,895	1,387	4,282[c]	5,869
1912	6,021	2,013	5,358	5,437
1913	6,460	1,614	6,771	5,647
1914	8,398	2,264	8,462	6,300
1915	8,537		9,009	5,967
1916	8,736		9,100	6,922
1917	9,962		9,159	6,581
1918	10,897		11,143	7,691
1919	11,305		11,404	8,328
1920	11,142		12,868	11,662
1921	8,557		10,675	11,638
1922	7,454		8,981	11,173
1923	n.a.		8,055	8,393
1924	8,723		11,528	9,248

[a] *Nihonteikoku tōkei nenkan.*
[b] U.S. Congress, Senate, *Reports of the U.S. Immigration Commission*, 3, *Statistical Review of Immigration, 1820–1910*, 61st Congress, 3d sess., 1910.
[c] Michael David Albert, "Japanese American Communities in Chicago and the Twin Cities" (Ph.D. dissertation, University of Minnesota, 1980). Based on the U.S. Immigration Commission *Reports*, 1, and Dorothy Swaine Thomas, *The Salvage* (Berkeley: University of California Press, 1952).

9 *Points of Entry into North America of 2,992 Japanese Male Residents of New York City, 1920 (based on Mizutani)*[a]

	Number	Percent
New York	881	29.4
Philadelphia	67	2.2
Baltimore	28	
Boston	24	
New Orleans	12	
Norwalk	8	
New Portsmouth, Bahamas	7	
Portland, ME	2	
Bayonne, NJ	2	
Key West, FL	1	
Portsmouth	1	
Nova Scotia, Acadia	1	
Montreal	2	
St. Johns, Acadia	1	
Cuba	281	9.4
TOTAL, EAST COAST	1,318	(44.1 percent)
Seattle	774	25.9
Tacoma	34	
Portland, OR	10	
San Francisco	595[b]	19.9
Vancouver	89	3.0
Victoria	19	
Mexico	11	
TOTAL, WEST COAST	1,532	(51.2 percent)
U.S.-born	63	2.1
Unknown	78	2.6

[a] Mizutani, *Nyūyōku nihonjin hattenshi*, 1:370–71.
[b] Error in Mizutani's table. Actual number is 596.

Notes

Chapter 1

1. Major historical works according to year of publication are Yamato Ichihashi, *The Japanese in the United States* (Stanford: Stanford University Press, 1932; New York: Arno Press, 1969); Masakazu Iwata, "The Japanese Immigrant in California Agriculture," *Agricultural History* 36 (January 1962), 25–37; Roger Daniels, *The Politics of Prejudice: The Anti-Japanese Movement in California and the Struggle for Japanese Exclusion* (Berkeley: University of California Press, 1962; Gloucester, MA: Peter Smith, 1966); Hilary Conroy and T. Scott Miyakawa, eds., *East Across the Pacific* (Santa Barbara, CA: ABC-CLIO Press, 1972); John Modell, *The Economics and Politics of Racial Accommodation: The Japanese of Los Angeles, 1900–1942* (Urbana: University of Illinois Press, 1977); Yasuo Wakatsuki, "Japanese Emigration to the United States, 1866–1924: A Monograph," *Perspectives in American History* 12 (1979), 389–516; Evelyn Nakano Glenn, *Issei, Nisei, War Bride* (Philadelphia: Temple University Press, 1986); Yuji Ichioka, *The Issei* (New York: The Free Press, 1988); and Valerie J. Matsumoto, *Farming the Home Place: A Japanese American Community in California, 1919–1982* (Ithaca: Cornell University Press, 1993). The following also should be noted: Emma Gee, ed., *Counterpoint: Perspectives on Asian America* (Los Angeles: Asian American Studies Center, UCLA, 1976); Roger Daniels, ed., *The Asian Experience in North America*, 47 vols. (New York: Arno Press, 1979); Lucie Cheng and Edna Bonacich, eds., *Labor Immigration Under Capitalism: Asian Workers in the United States Before World War II* (Berkeley: University of California Press, 1984); Ronald Takaki, *Strangers From a Different Shore: A History of Asian Americans* (Boston: Little, Brown & Co., 1989); Sucheng Chan, *Asian Americans: An Interpretive History* (Boston: Twayne Publishers, 1991); Gary Y. Okihiro, *Margins and Mainstreams: Asians in American History and Culture* (Seattle: University of Washington Press, 1994); and Lloyd H. Fisher, *The Harvest Labor Market in*

California (Cambridge: Harvard University Press, 1953). Important works in other fields include Sylvia Junko Yanagisako, *Transforming the Past: Tradition and Kinship Among Japanese Americans* (Stanford: Stanford University Press, 1985); S. Frank Miyamoto, *Social Solidarity Among the Japanese in Seattle* (Seattle: University of Washington Press, 1984; first published 1939); Akemi Kikumura, *Through Harsh Winters: The Life of a Japanese Immigrant Woman* (Novato, CA: Chandler & Sharp, 1981); Harry H. L. Kitano, *Japanese Americans: The Evolution of a Subculture* (Englewood Cliffs, NJ: Prentice-Hall, 1976); and Frank F. Chuman, *The Bamboo People: The Law and Japanese-Americans* (Del Mar, CA: Publishers Inc., 1976).

2. See his book *The Issei*. Two significant listings of Japanese language sources are Yuji Ichioka, Yasuo Sakata, Nobuya Tsuchida, and Eri Yasuhara, comps., *A Buried Past: An Annotated Bibliography of the Japanese American Research Project Collection* (Berkeley: University of California Press, 1974); and Yasuo Sakata, comp., *Fading Footsteps of the Issei: An Annotated Bibliography of the Manuscript Holdings of the Japanese American Research Project Collection* (Los Angeles: UCLA Asian American Studies Center, UCLA Center for Japanese Studies, and Japanese American National Museum, 1992).

3. *Kaigai ryoken kafu hennōhyō shintatsu* (Passports issued and returned for travel abroad), 204 unbound vols. (1879–1921), Record Group (hereafter, RG) 3.8.5.8, Diplomatic Record Center, Foreign Ministry of Japan, Tokyo (hereafter, DFMJ), is a listing by ken of persons who applied for passports according to country of destination. A quick perusal of the "reason for travel" of individuals indicates that particularly after 1900, when the Japanese government more actively began to limit the number of passports issued to laborers, there was an increase of persons traveling as "other than laborers" from all areas of Japan to the United States. Based on Japan's annual statistics, Yuji Ichioka states that between 1901 and 1907 approximately one-seventh of all passports to the continental U.S. were issued to people classified as nonlaborers (Ichioka, *The Issei,* 52). According to a UCLA Japanese American Research Project survey of issei in the continental U.S., 36 percent of the male and female respondents immigrated with more than eight years of education in Japan. Cited in Yanagisako, *Transforming the Past,* 3, fn 3.

4. T. Scott Miyakawa, "Early New York Issei: Founders of Japanese-American Trade," in Conroy and Miyakawa, eds., *East Across the Pacific,* 156–86; Haru Reischauer, *Samurai and Silk* (Cambridge: Harvard University Press, 1986).

5. Anthropologist Dorinne Kondo presents a different experience in which she was expected to act Japanese because of her Japanese ancestry. *Crafting Selves: Power, Gender and Discourses in a Japanese Workplace* (Chicago: University of Chicago Press, 1990).

6. William I. Thomas and Florian Znaniecki, *The Polish Peasant in Europe and America,* 5 vols. (1918–1920), ed. and abridg. Eli Zaretsky (Urbana: University of Illinois Press, 1984).

7. Jon Gjerde, *From Peasants to Farmers: The Migration from Balestrand, Norway, to the Upper Middle West* (New York: Cambridge University Press, 1985).

8. Virginia Yans-McLaughlin, *Family and Community: Italian Immigrants in Buffalo, 1880–1930* (Ithaca: Cornell University Press, 1977); Josef J. Barton, *Peasant and Strangers: Italians, Rumanians and Slovaks in an American City, 1880–1950* (Cambridge: Harvard University Press, 1977); Dino Cinel, *From Italy to San Francisco: The Immigrant Experience* (Stanford: Stanford University Press, 1982). See also Ewa Morawska, *For Bread with Butter: The Life-Worlds of East Central Europeans in Johnstown, Pennsylvania* (New York: Cambridge University Press, 1985); Kerby A. Miller, *Emigrants and Exiles: Ireland and the Irish Exodus to North America* (New York: Oxford University Press, 1985); John W. Briggs, *An Italian Passage: Immigrants to Three American Cities, 1890–1930* (New Haven: Yale University Press, 1978); John Bodnar, *Immigration and Industrialization: Ethnicity in an American Mill Town, 1870–1940* (Pittsburgh: University of Pittsburgh Press, 1977); Kathleen Neils Conzen, *Immigrant Milwaukee, 1836–1860: Accommodation and Community in a Frontier City* (Cambridge: Harvard University Press, 1979). Important earlier works are Herbert G. Gutman, *Work, Culture and Society in Industrializing America* (New York: Alfred A. Knopf, 1966); Marcus Lee Hansen, *The Atlantic Migration, 1607–1860* (Cambridge: Harvard University Press, 1940); and Brinley Thomas, *Migration and Urban Development* (London: Methuen & Co., 1972), which presents migration in relation to economic cycles in both the immigrant U.S. and emigrant Great Britain.

9. Virginia Yans-McLaughlin, "Introduction," in Virginia Yans-McLaughlin, ed., *Immigration Reconsidered: History, Sociology, and Politics* (New York: Oxford University Press, 1990), 6–7.

10. Sucheng Chan, "European and Asian Immigration into the United States in Comparative Perspective, 1820s to 1920s," in Yans-McLaughlin, ed., *Immigration Reconsidered*, 38. See also, Chan, *Asian Americans*, chapter 1.

11. The Meiji period lasted from 1868 to 1912. The following period, the Taisho, lasted from 1912 to 1926. The Japanese method of enumerating each calendar year is by the year of the emperor's reign. Thus, 1912 was both Meiji 45 and Taisho 1.

12. John L. Caughey, *Imaginary Social Worlds: A Cultural Approach* (Lincoln: University of Nebraska Press, 1984).

13. Ibid., 9–30.

14. Ibid., 136.

15. Yanagisako, *Transforming the Past*, 17.

16. Miriam Silverberg, "The Modern Girl as Militant," in Gail Lee Bernstein, ed., *Recreating Japanese Women, 1600–1945* (Berkeley: University of California Press, 1991), 239–66. Silverberg placed the "modern" Japanese woman of the 1920s in the ideological constructs of the period, a "recasting" that challenged Western notions of "modern" as well as various contradictory and ambiguous Japanese attempts to display the "new woman" as apolitical, romantic, passive, promiscuous, communist, and consumerist, among other unflattering definitions. See also her "Constructing the Japanese Ethnography of Modernity," *Journal of Asian Studies* 51:1 (February 1992), 30–54.

17. See Masao Miyoshi, *As We Saw Them: The First Japanese Embassy to*

the United States (1860) (Berkeley: University of California Press, 1979) for impressions of an earlier era.

18. Sasaki Shigetsu, *Beikoku o hōroshite* (Wandering in America) (Tokyo: Nihon hyoronsha, 1921), the result of the author's fifteen years in the United States.

19. Kuriyagawa Hakuson, *Inshōki* (Impressions) (Tokyo: Sekizenkan, 1918). Hakuson was a Meiji writer-critic.

20. Katayama Sen, *Tōbei annai* (Introduction to America) (Tokyo: Rodo-shimbunsha, 1901?).

21. Compulsory education was four years, extended to six in 1908. The nationwide compulsory attendance rate was consistently over 90 percent for boys from 1900 and for girls from 1904. See *Japan's Modern Educational System: A History of the First Hundred Years* (Tokyo: Research and Statistics Division, Ministers' Secretariat, Ministry of Education, Science and Culture, 1980), 106–8.

22. On the process of ideology building, see Carol Gluck, *Japan's Modern Myths: Ideology in the Late Meiji Period* (Princeton: Princeton University Press, 1985) and Earl H. Kinmonth, *The Self-Made Man in Meiji Japanese Thought: From Samurai to Salary Man* (Berkeley: University of California Press, 1981).

23. Hakubunkan dominated the publishing world from the mid-1890s up to the early 1920s, a time called the *Hakubunkan jidai* (Hakubunkan period). See *Ōhashi Sahei to Hakubunkan* (Ōhashi Sahei and Hakubunkan) (Private collection, n.d.), 211–14. I am indebted to Professor Sugimoto Teruko (née Ōhashi) for making this work available to me.

24. James A. Fujii, *Complicit Fictions: The Subject in the Modern Japanese Prose Narrative* (Berkeley: University of California Press, 1993).

25. Ibid., 18 and 23. One of Fujii's major purposes was to critique the heretofore accepted interpretation of the West's influence on modern Japanese literature.

26. Gluck, *Japan's Modern Myths*, 10 and 29.

27. One of the few books in English about the small group of Meiji-Taisho women who received higher education in the United States is Barbara Rose, *Tsuda Umeko and Women's Education in Japan* (New Haven: Yale University Press, 1992).

Chapter 2

1. The Imperial Edict of 1871 restructured the 76 former feudal domains of the Tokugawa period into 46 prefectures, of which three were *fu*—Tokyo, Kyoto, and Osaka, named after the three major cities.

2. *Ryokenkafu shutsugan ni yōsuru zaigaikōkan hakkyū kakushu shōmeisho-kōfu jinmeihyō* (List of persons issued official certificates by overseas consular offices for passport application), *Nyūyōku no bu* (New York section), 2 vols., 1912–1924, RG 3.8.2.283, DFMJ.

3. I will treat the development of the hi-imin/imin passport categories in Chapter 3.

4. Shōzō Mizutani, *Nyūyōku nihonjin hattenshi* (History of the Japanese in New York), 2 vols. (Tokyo: PMC Publishing Co., 1984; New York: Japanese Association of New York, 1921), 1:356-58.

5. Ibid., 1:400.

6. Ibid., 1:358-59.

7. Ibid., 2:617-20; *Amerika* 11:7 (July 1907), 49-51.

8. Kuroki "just loved" American women. They were "lovely, gracious, graceful, self-reliant, yet tactful, healthy yet dainty, and—and—he liked brunettes the best." *New York Times*, 17 May 1907.

9. Okamoto Yonezō, *Nyūyōkushi naigaino jisho* (Property in the New York City area) (Tokyo: Hakubunkan, 1912).

10. For instance, *Amerika* 11:6 (June 1907), 11:10-12 (October-December 1907), and 12:7-8 (July-August 1908); *Tobei shimpō* (News on crossing to America) 6:11 (15 November 1908); *Seikō* (Success) 10:3 (1 November 1906); Katō Jūshirō, *Zaibeidōbō hattenshi* (The history of our compatriots in America) (Tokyo: Hakubunkan, 1908), 39-61.

11. On conditions in New York see David C. Hammack, *Power and Society: Greater New York at the Turn of the Century* (New York: Russell Sage Foundation, 1982), especially chapters 2 and 3; John Higham, *Strangers in the Land: Patterns of American Nativism, 1860-1925*, 2d ed., (New Brunswick, NJ: Rutgers University Press, 1963; New York: Atheneum, 1975); Bayrd Still, *Mirror for Gotham: New York as Seen by Contemporaries from Dutch Days to the Present* (New York: New York University Press, 1956), chapters 8 and 9; Jacob A. Riis, *How the Other Half Lives* (1890; New York: Dover Publications, 1971).

12. *Amerika* 11:11 (November 1907), 26-30.

13. Mizutani, *Nyūyōku nihonjin hattenshi*, 1:411.

14. Jōkichi Takamine (1854-1922), chemist, entrepreneur, and publicist, received his early training in physics and chemistry in Japan. In 1881 the Japanese government commissioned him to study and apprentice in England for three years under the sponsorship of a leading trading firm. Upon his return he applied his scientific knowledge to improve Japan's indigenous industries and initiate the artificial fertilizer industry. He made a number of trips to the United States during the course of his scientific work and in 1887 married a southern woman, Caroline Hitch. The marriage coincided with an invitation from her father to engage in research at a distillery company in Chicago. His research resulted in the shortening of the six-month distillery process to forty-eight hours through the use of an artificial fungus culture. In 1897 he established the Takamine Research Center in Clifton, New Jersey, where he perfected a digestive medicine, "Taka-Diastase." A permanent resident of the United States, he built an elaborate home on Riverside Drive in New York City. Originally, each of its five floors was to represent a school of Japanese art. However, the plan proved impractical, and only the first two of the five stories had Japanese motifs. Takamine devoted the rest of his life to promoting Japanese-American friendship by helping to establish the Nippon Club in 1905 and a Japanese news bureau in 1908 "to disseminate authentic information about Japan." He served as vice president of the Japan Society in 1907 and was a founding member and four-term president of the Japanese Association of New

York. K.K. Kawakami, *Jokichi Takamine: A Record of His American Achievements* (New York: William Edwin Rudge, 1928), and Mizutani, *Nyūyōku nihonjin hattenshi*, 1:413–19 and 2:733–53.

15. Mizutani, *Nyūyōku nihonjin hattenshi*, 1:4.

16. The other two are Ryōichirō Arai, considered founder of the Japanese-American silk trade, and Yasukata Murai, driving force behind Morimura Bros. and Co., a leading wholesaler and importer. Both came to New York in the 1870s. In 1893 Arai and the Morimura brothers joined to form a trading company that extended to China, Italy, and France, and by 1908 dominated Japanese silk imports to the United States. On the early Japanese traders in New York, see Miyakawa, "Early New York Issei."

17. On early anti-Japanese prejudice and agitation in the western states see Ichioka, *The Issei;* Daniels, *The Politics of Prejudice;* Paul Jacobs and Saul Landau with Eve Pell, "The Japanese," in *To Serve the Devil: A Documentary Analysis* (New York: Vintage Books, 1972), 2:166–250; Chuman, *The Bamboo People;* Yamato Ichihashi, "Anti-Japanese Agitation," in Roger Daniels and Spencer C. Olin, eds., *Racism in California* (New York: Macmillan, 1972), 105–15; Donald R. Hata, *"Undesireables": Early Immigrants and the Anti-Japanese Movement in San Francisco, 1892–93* (New York: Arno Press, 1978); Daniels, "Japanese Immigrants on a Western Frontier: The Issei in California, 1890–1940," in Conroy and Miyakawa, eds., *East Across the Pacific,* 76–91; and Daniels, ed., *The Asian Experience,* which includes primary sources describing contemporary anti-Japanese events and writings.

18. *Japanese-American Commercial Weekly* (New York), 2 June 1906.

19. *Tōbei shimpō* 1:2 (10 June 1907), 15.

20. Mizutani, *Nyūyōku nihonjin hattenshi,* 1:358.

21. Ibid., 1:359–60. The Japanese population of New York was 3,000 in 1909 and 4,652 in 1921. Ibid., 364–65.

22. When Japanese firms first came to New York in 1876, Japan's foreign trade was controlled by resident Westerners in Japan. There was no trans-Pacific cable (communication had to be directed via Europe and Asia), and Japanese firms negotiated for capital funds through the consulate in New York, because U.S. banks did not give credit to Japanese. By 1896 the situation had changed considerably. The Yokohama Specie Bank had established a New York office in 1880, Japan and the United States were linked with a telegraph service and a passenger liner, and a number of Japanese firms (including Mitsui Company and Nippon Yūsen Kaisha [NYK], the shipping firm) had New York branches. See Miyakawa, "Early New York Issei," 167, 175–76; also *Zaibei nihonjinshi* (History of the Japanese in America) (San Francisco: Japanese Association of America, 1940), 1054–55. The *Japanese-American Commercial Weekly* proudly noted that Japanese shipping was the fifth largest in the world in 1908 and that ninety-five NYK vessels were scheduled to come to New York via the Suez Canal starting in November (22 August 1908).

23. Toyohiko Campbell Takami, *The Shining Stars: The Autobiography of Dr. Toyohiko Campbell Takami,* ed. Masahiko Ralph Takami (Cold Spring Harbor, NY: n.p., 1945). I am indebted to Mitsuye Ōhori Katagiri for making this work available to me.

24. Through Takami's initiative the Japanese Mutual Aid Society, precursor to the Japanese Association of New York (1914), was formed as an independent organization in Brooklyn in 1907 (*Japanese-American Commercial Weekly*, 1 June 1907). Takami later wrote that during his medical studies, he came across the body of a young Japanese man "who probably came to this country, just as I did, full of ambition and hope." After opening his medical practice, Takami enlisted support to establish the society as his first community welfare action. Its purpose was to assure "that no Japanese person would die a pauper's death or need to fear illness or adversity." In 1912 the organization purchased a 2,500-square-foot plot at Mt. Olivet Cemetery in Maspeth, Long Island. The society also conducted lectures and entertainment programs. Its membership was 400 in 1912 (Takami, *Shining Stars*, 41 and 45; Mizutani, *Nyūyōku nihonjin hattenshi*, 2:438–43).

25. Takami, *Shining Stars*, 8.

26. Ibid., 13.

27. Ibid., 15.

28. From Cushing Academy, Takami transferred to Lawrenceville School, New Jersey, then enrolled as a premed student at Lafayette College, Pennsylvania, and Brooklyn Polytechnic Institute. He entered Columbia University and transferred to Cornell University Medical College, from which he graduated in 1906 (Ibid., 22–42). He advertised two offices during his first three months of practice: South Elliot Place, Brooklyn, within walking distance of the Navy Yard, and a Japanese boardinghouse on East 27th Street in Manhattan (*Japanese-American Commercial Weekly*, 14 July 1906).

29. It was Takami's "privilege to support . . . Miss Campbell" until her death in 1907 (Takami, *Shining Stars*, 43–44). Campbell's obituary stated that she was an aunt of Alexander Graham Bell, of "English aristocratic blood," and began ministering to Chinese immigrants beginning in 1882, when she was fifty-seven years old (*Japanese-American Commercial Weekly*, 12 January 1907).

30. *Plans of the U.S. Navy Yard, New York, Showing Improvements up to July 1, 1894; Map of the Enlarged City of Brooklyn* (New York: J. B. Beers and Co., 1894).

31. Mizutani, *Nyūyōku nihonjin hattenshi*, 1:396.

32. Ibid., 1:364.

33. Ibid., 1:396–97. The earliest boardinghouse for Japanese seamen was established on Gold Street in 1886. Subsequently, in the 1890s, more Japanese-run houses began to appear in Brooklyn, including one run by two women from Hyōgo-ken, which catered mainly to Japanese businessmen.

34. Ibid., 1:397. Later, in 1915, responding to the Bricklayers' Association complaint regarding subway-building labor, a New York state law was passed stating that citizens be given preference over aliens as workers in the construction of public works. See *Beikoku ni okeru hainichimondai zakken. Nyūyōkushū hainichi kankei* (Miscellaneous documents concerning the anti-Japanese problem in the United States: New York state), 1915, RG 3.8.2.288, DFMJ.

35. See Ichihashi, *Japanese in the United States*, chapter 8. In a survey in 1927, the Japanese consul estimated that 53.4 percent of the gainfully

employed in Los Angeles were domestic servants (Ibid., 112). In the Western states, Asian men, mainly Chinese, provided the bulk of domestic servants up to the turn of the century. (David M. Katzman, *Seven Days a Week: Women and Domestic Service in Industrializing America* [New York: Oxford University Press, 1978], 45, 221–22). On Pacific Coast domestic workers, see Ichioka, *The Issei*, 24–28; and Evelyn Nakano Glenn, "The Dialectics of Wage Work: Japanese-American Women and Domestic Service, 1905–1940," *Feminist Studies* 6:3 (Fall 1980), 432–71, an analysis of the relationship between issei women's family life and domestic work as employment.

36. "The Life Story of a Japanese Servant," in Hamilton Holt, ed., *The Life Stories of Undistinguished Americans as Told by Themselves*, 2d ed., New York Young People's Missionary Movement (New York: J. Pott and Co., 1906; reprint, New York: Routledge, Chapman and Hall, 1990), 159–73. Hamilton Bowen Holt (1872–1951), progressive reform activist and internationalist, helped found the Japan Society as well as the National Association for the Advancement of Colored People, the World Federation League, the Carnegie Endowment for International Peace, and the American Scandinavian Foundation.

37. Ibid., 160–61.

38. Ibid., 164. He is referring to *Henry Esmond* by William Makepeace Thackeray, first published in 1852, about a young man who fell in love with two women, one of whom was his guardian, Lady Castlemond.

39. Ibid., 171–72.

40. Ibid., 172.

41. Shibuta Ichirō, "Nyūyōku ni okeru nihonjin no shokugyō" (Employment for Japanese in New York), in Yamane Goichi, ed., *Saikin tobei annai* (Introducing contemporary America) (Tokyo: Tobei zasshisha, 1906), 52–59. The various essays in *Saikin tobei annai* include topics such as the wealth of the United States, the shoemakers union in San Francisco, travel from Yokohama to New York, industrial education, management of business, university life, agriculture and mining in Colorado, and a vocabulary of useful English words.

42. Ibid., 53–54.

43. Ibid., 56.

44. Ibid., 56–57. Other publications had varying figures. In 1907 housework in New York was said to have paid Japanese $20 to $25 a month; *Tobei shimpō* 1:2 (10 June 1907), 16; *Tobei shimpō* 6:11 (15 November 1908), 6. In Chicago weekly wages for all domestic workers averaged $5.77, or about $24 a month (Katzman, *Seven Days a Week*, 310).

45. Mizutani, *Nyūyōku nihonjin hattenshi*, 1:380.

46. Ibid., 1:381.

47. *Japanese-American Commercial Weekly*, 14 July 1906.

48. Ichioka, *The Issei*, 24.

49. Takami, *Shining Stars*, 29.

50. Ibid., 26.

51. In 1880 more than half of the New York City working population was foreign-born. See Thomas Kessner, *The Golden Door: Italian and Jewish Immi-*

grant Mobility in New York City, 1880–1915 (New York: Oxford University Press, 1977), 48 and fn 8. Jews dominated the clothing industry until the 1890s, when the Italians began to move in (Ibid., 69).

52. Mizutani, *Nyūyōku nihonjin hattenshi*, 1:381–82.
53. Ibid., 1:390.
54. Ibid., 1:391–92.
55. Ibid., 1:408.
56. Ibid., 1:408–11. Japanese newspapers published in New York prior to World War II are nonexistent in both U.S. and Japanese libraries and archives. The only exceptions are the *Nyūyōku shimpō* (1940–41) at the Library of Congress and random copies of the *Japanese-American Commercial Weekly* (1905–08) at the Research Library, New York Public Library.
57. Takami, *Shining Stars*, 19–20; Mizutani, *Nyūyōku nihonjin hattenshi*, 2:477.
58. Mizutani, *Nyūyōku nihonjin hattenshi*, 2:470.
59. E. A. Ōhori, *Hopes and Achievements* (New York: Women's Board of Domestic Missions of Reformed Church in America, n.d.); Reformed Church in America, Board of Domestic Missions, Women's Executive Committee, *Annual Reports*, 1909–19; Mizutani, *Nyūyōku nihonjin hattenshi*, 473–75. On churches see also Alfred Saburo Akamatsu, "The Function and Type of Program of a Japanese Minority Church in New York City: A Proposal for the Establishment of the Japanese American United Church of Christ in New York" (Ed. D. dissertation, Teachers College, Columbia University, 1948), 50–52.
60. Kamide Masataka, *Kuwayama Senzō-ō monogatari* (The story of the venerable Kuwayama Senzō) (Kyoto: Tanko shinsha, 1963). This biography, the result of interviews and discussions the writer had with Kuwayama twice a week, is written as if it were an autobiography. I am indebted to Kuwayama's son, Yeiichi, for making the work available to me.
61. Ibid., 76–77.
62. Ibid., 79.
63. Ibid., 81.
64. Ibid., 118–20.
65. Takami, *Shining Stars*, 45.
66. Mizutani, *Nyūyōku nihonjin hattenshi*, 1:388.
67. This "rolling ball game" proved to be a successful venture for Japanese for a considerable period of time, for in addition to Mizutani's history, at least three tobei publications covering a span of thirteen years mentioned it: *Tobei shimpō* 1:2 (10 June 1907), 16; Harada Tōichirō, *Nyūyōku* (Tokyo: Seikyosha, 1914), 257; Miyakawa Setsurō, *Beikoku no uraomote* (The U.S. inside and out) (Tokyo: Kobundo, 1920), 81.
68. Mizutani, *Nyūyōku nihonjin hattenshi*, 1:388–89.
69. Ibid., 1:398–99. For accounts of Coney Island at the turn of the century, see John F. Kasson, *Amusing the Millions* (New York: Hill & Wang, 1978); Oliver Pilat and Jo Ransom, *Sodom by the Sea* (Garden City, NY: Doubleday, Doran & Co., 1941); and Kathy Peiss, *Cheap Amusements* (Philadelphia: Temple University Press, 1986), especially chapter 5.
70. Nagai Kafū, *Amerika monogatari* (Stories from America). Vol. 3 of

Nagai Kafū zenshū (Complete works of Nagai Kafū) (Tokyo: Chuokoronsha, 1949; first published, 1908), 211-33.

71. Ibid., 211-12. This description is similar to that of Coney Island's Luna Park by Maxim Gorki in 1907: 250,000 electric lights transformed the Park into "a fantastic city . . . [with] shapely towers of miraculous castles, palaces and temples" (cited in Pilat and Ranson, *Sodom*, 148). One Japanese author sneered at this display, deeming it a waste of electricity for disreputable amusement purposes, but obviously was impressed by the illumination, which was "not unlike walking into fire." He dubbed it a product of the "capitalism of insanity" (Harada, *Nyūyōku*, 256-58).

72. Kafū, *Amerika monogatari*, 212. Kafū's observation evokes another, which described the irresistible attraction to the "graceful romantic curves of the Oriental" and characterized Luna Park as an exotic fantasyland for Coney Island visitors. Cited in Kasson, *Amusing the Millions*, 63.

73. Kafū, *Amerika monogatari*, 212-13.

74. Ibid., 215.

75. Haru Kishi, interviews by author, New York, 21 November 1981 and 7 August 1985. See also *New York Nichibei*, 2 May-23 May 1985. Transcriptions of interviews with four New York issei conducted by Yasuko Nakanishi appeared in the Japanese section of the weekly *New York Nichibei*, 28 March-18 July 1985.

76. The interviews were conducted in Japanese, but Haru occasionally interspersed English words or phrases.

77. Much later, just before the outbreak of World War II, Haru had a chance to leave her husband and return to Japan, but since they had stuck it out for so long she decided to stay in New York. ("Anyway, I was used to life in America by then.")

78. Haru Kishi is healthy and active today and lives with one of her sons in Manhattan. ("This is the happiest time of my life," she says) She visits her other children occasionally. When I spoke to her last, she was going to California to attend the wedding of one of her grandchildren.

79. *New York Nichibei*, 28 March 1985. The conditions for men on the West Coast tend to be idealized. The number of married Japanese women in the whole United States was as follows:

Japanese Population in the United States

	Total	Males	Females	Married Females
1900	24,326	23,341	985	410
1910	72,157	63,070	9,087	5,581
1920	111,010	72,707	39,303	22,193

United States, Department of Commerce, Bureau of the Census, *Abstracts of the Census*, 1900, 1910, 1920.

The interviewee's statement that Japanese could buy property in California is misleading, for the Alien Land Laws were passed in 1913 and 1920 in California and in 1921 in Washington state prohibiting Japanese from owning, leasing, or farming under cropping contracts. The laws were upheld by the Supreme Court in 1921 (Ichioka, *The Issei*, 226–43).

80. Some marriages were not registered. For instance, Eikichi Kishi never registered with the Japanese consulate as Japanese nationals were required to do. Haru explained that he preferred to "be independent" and did not even join the Japanese Association.

81. Based on the U.S. census figures, if all the married Japanese women were married to Japanese males, the percentage of married Japanese males in the United States would have been 1.7 percent in 1900; 8.8 percent in 1910; and 30 percent in 1920. However, the accuracy of census figures is questionable. For instance, in the period 1890–1920, 45 percent of births in the United States were not officially registered (Hyman Alterman, *Counting People: The Census in History* [Harcourt Brace, 1969], 314).

82. *New York Nichibei,* 20 June–11 July 1985.

83. Sona Oguri came to the United States in 1905 and married Takami in 1909.

84. Mrs. Francis J. Swayze, *Finding the Way in a New Land* (New York: Reformed Church in America, Women's Board of Domestic Missions, n.d.), 10.

85. Takami was thirty-four; Takamine, thirty-three; Ōhori, thirty; and Iwamoto, thirty-five.

86. Kafū, *Amerika monogatari,* 319–29.

87. Ibid., 325. Kafū's writing reflected the widespread anti-Chinese bias prevalent among Japanese.

88. *Amerika* 11:10 (October 1907), 658–62.

89. Kafū also wrote about an evening in a bar "four or five blocks up along Third Avenue where the 'el' runs to Chatham Square. Jewishtown is to the left. Chinatown to the right, next to Italian town. . . . an area which is called 'the Bowery' " (Kafū, "Yahan no sakaba" [A night-time bar], 271–80).

90. "Dark-skinned Japanese" connotes laborers or imin who worked in the sun. In the passport records at the Foreign Ministry Diplomatic Record Office in Tokyo, Katagiri was listed as "hi-imin."

Chapter 3

This chapter is a revised version of the article that appeared in *Pacific Historical Review* 60:3 (August 1991), 339–59.

1. Japanese Consul, San Francisco, to Foreign Ministry, Tokyo, 22 and 25 April 1891, *Hokubeigasshūkoku ni okeru honpōjin tokōseigen oyobi haiseki ikken* (Records concerning travel restriction and exclusion of Japanese citizens in the United States) (hereafter cited as *Haiseki ikken*), 19 unbound vols. (1891–1912), 1, RG 3.8.2.21, DFMJ; *Statutes at Large* 23:332–33 (1885).

2. *Haiseki ikken,* 1; *Statutes at Large* 26:968 (1891). This amendment, passed 3 March 1891, specifically authorized the Treasury Department to inspect alien immigrants at the borders of British Columbia and Mexico, entry

points used by some Japanese to circumvent immigration procedures at U.S. port cities on the West Coast.

3. D. W. Stevens to Tateno Gōzō, Minister to the United States, 12 Oct. 1891, *Haiseki ikken*, 1. On Stevens, see *Gaimushō no hyakunen* (One hundred years of the Foreign Ministry), 2 vols. (Tokyo: Foreign Ministry, 1969), 1:592.

4. Japanese Consul, San Francisco, to Foreign Minister, Tokyo, 12 May 1892, *Haiseki ikken*, 1.

5. Chief, Emigration Bureau, Foreign Ministry, to Ken and Fu Governors, 16 May 1892; Chief, Emigration Bureau, Foreign Ministry, to Governors of Hiroshima-, Wakayama-, and Kumamoto-ken, 25 May 1892, *Haiseki ikken*, 1.

6. The major works are Thomas A. Bailey, *Theodore Roosevelt and the Japanese-American Crisis* (Stanford: Stanford University Press, 1934); Howard K. Beale, *Theodore Roosevelt and the Rise of America to World Power* (Baltimore: Johns Hopkins University Press, 1956; New York: Collier Books, 1973); William L. Neumann, *America Encounters Japan* (Baltimore: Johns Hopkins University Press, 1963); Raymond A. Esthus, *Theodore Roosevelt and Japan* (Seattle: University of Washington Press, 1966); Charles E. Neu, *An Uncertain Friendship: Theodore Roosevelt and Japan, 1906-1909* (Cambridge: Harvard University Press, 1967); and Akira Iriye, *Pacific Estrangement: Japanese and American Expansion, 1897-1911* (Cambridge: Harvard University Press, 1972).

7. Daniels, *The Politics of Prejudice*, 1-2. The following illustrates Japanese immigration as compared to countries which provided the most immigrants to the U.S. and those whose figures were comparable to Japanese figures. Leonard Dinnerstein and David M. Reimers, *Ethnic Americans* (New York: Harper and Row, 1975), app. 1.

Immigration to U.S. from Nation of Origin, 1891-1930

	1891-1900	1901-1910	1911-1920	1921-1930
ALL COUNTRIES	3,687,564	8,795,386	5,735,811	4,107,209
EUROPE	3,555,352	8,056,040	4,321,887	2,463,194
Austria	592,707[a]	2,145,266[a]	453,649	32,868
Hungary			442,693	30,680
Germany	505,152	341,498	143,945	412,202
England	216,726	388,017	249,944	157,420
Scotland	44,188	120,469	78,357	159,781
Greece	15,979	167,519	184,201	51,084
Italy	651,893	2,045,877	1,109,524	455,315
Netherlands	26,758	48,262	43,718	26,948
Portugal	27,508	69,149	89,732	29,994
Russia	505,290	1,597,306	921,201	61,742
ASIA	74,862	323,543	237,236	112,059
Japan	25,942	129,797	83,837	33,462

[a]From 1891 to 1910, figures include both Austria and Hungary.

8. Sucheng Chan analyzes the role of international politics as being "particularly salient" in Asian emigration and immigration. She writes of the "more subtle and complicated" exclusion approach the United States took toward Japan in comparison to its approach toward other nations (Chan, "European and Asian Immigration into the United States in Comparative Perspective, 1820s to 1920s," in Yans-McLaughlin, ed., *Immigration Reconsidered*, 48 and 62). On U.S. and Japanese foreign policy, see Richard W. Van Alstyne, *The Rising American Empire* (Oxford, England: Blackwell & Mott, 1960; New York: W. W. Norton & Co., Inc., 1974); Walter LaFeber, *The New Empire* (Ithaca, NY: Cornell University Press, 1963); Akira Iriye, *Across the Pacific: An Inner History of American-East Asian Relations* (New York: Harcourt, Brace & World, Inc., 1967); Iriye, *Pacific Estrangement;* Mikiso Hane, *Modern Japan: A Historical Survey* (Boulder, CO: Westview Press, 1986); Jon Livingston, Joe Moore, and Felicia Oldfather, eds., *Imperial Japan* (New York: Pantheon Books, 1973); E. H. Norman, *Japan's Emergence as a Modern State* (1940), in John W. Dower, ed., *Origins of the Modern Japanese State: Selected Writings of E. H. Norman* (New York: Pantheon Books, 1975); Jon Halliday, *A Political History of Japanese Capitalism* (New York: Pantheon Books, 1975); Hilary Conroy, *The Japanese Frontier in Hawaii* (Berkeley: University of California Press, 1953).

9. The literal translation of the term *imin* is "a citizen who moves or migrates" and includes both emigrants and immigrants. *Hi* means "non-" or "other than." After 1908 the Foreign Ministry recorded the ideographs *hi* or *i* to designate the imin or hi-imin category of citizens who were issued passports. See *Kosekihō ni yori zaigaihonpōjin shotodokesho sono honsekichi kosekiri e sōtatsu no ikken* (Documents concerning notices filed by citizens abroad to be sent to household registry in registered family domicile areas according to household registry law), 43 vols. (1909–1921), RG 3.8.7.21, DFMJ.

10. *Statutes at Large* 22:58–61 (1882). Chinese government protests against the exclusion acts as well as individual suits in the lower courts and the Supreme Court spanned three decades but failed to pacify anti-Chinese sentiments in the United States (Chan, *Asian Americans,* 91–92). Takaki interprets this failure as being "symptomatic" of the conflict between white labor and white capital (Takaki, *Strangers from a Different Shore,* 110–111). By 1895 the Chinese government "fully acquiesced" to U.S. policies (Michael H. Hunt, *The Making of a Special Relationship: The United States and China to 1914* [New York: Columbia University Press, 1983], 85–114). See also Delbert L. McKee, *Chinese Exclusion versus the Open Door Policy, 1900–1906: Clashes over China Policy in the Roosevelt Era* (Detroit: Wayne State University Press, 1977).

11. For instance, see Consul General, New York, to Foreign Ministry, 5 May 1900, *Haiseki ikken,* 3.

12. Emigration "siphoned off a small stream," not to relieve population pressure but to develop "markets and materials for Japanese industry" (William W. Lockwood, *The Economic Development of Japan* [Princeton: Princeton University Press, 1968], 157). Between 1890 and 1924, 1.1 million people, of whom half were imin or seasonal workers, went abroad. The population of

Japan was 39.9 million in 1890 and 59.7 million in 1925. Comparative figures of some destinations of Japanese travelers based on travel permits are as follows:

Japanese Travelers by Destination

	China	Korea	Russia & terr.	U.S. cont.	Brazil	Total (all nations)
1890–99	17,903	44,159	28,481	15,585	43	220,485
1900–09	47,709[a]	21,617[a]	41,534	62,615	740	320,341
1910–19	19,546	—	183,540	74,211	17,364	430,869
1920–26[b]	18,238	—	45,050	40,123	21,018	199,484

[a] After 1904 travel permits for Korea and Manchuria were unnecessary.
[b] No figures for 1923 (Tokyo earthquake).

Inoma Kiichi, "Senzen rokujūhachinen no waga imin tōkei no gaikan" [Overview of Japanese emigration statistics for 68 years prior to World War II], *Keishō ronsan* 60 (February 1955), 100.

13. For instance, the magazines *Amerika*, *Tobei zasshi* (Crossing to America magazine), and *Tobei shimpō* (Crossing to America news); articles in *Seikō* (Success); and Shimanuki Hyōdayū and Katayama Sen's tobei publications, among many others. I will consider these works in chapters 5 and 6.

14. *Amerika*, 12:6 (June 1908), 30.

15. *Tobei shimpō*, 1:2 (June 1907), 9.

16. Tabata Kisaburō, *Zaibeisha seikō no tomo* (The guide to success for Japanese in America) (Tokyo: Shimizu shoten, 1908), 29–30.

17. *Imin hogokisoku* (Emigrant protection ordinance), 12 April 1894, *Hōrei zensho* (Compendia of laws), 5 vols. (1894), 2, *Chokurei* (Imperial decrees), 112–15; *Imin hogohō* (Emigrant protection law), 7 April 1896, *Hōrei zensho*, 7 vols. (1896), 2, *Hōritsu* (Laws), 116–20. See also Alan Takeo Moriyama, *Imingaisha: Japanese Emigration Companies and Hawaii, 1894–1908* (Honolulu: University of Hawaii Press, 1985), 33–42.

18. *Kaigai ryokenkisoku*, 1878, *Hōrei zensho* (1878), 193–94. The Passport Law was revised in 1897, 1900, and 1908.

19. *Gaikoku ryokenkisoku* (Passport regulations for travel abroad), rev., 1897, *Hōrei zensho*, 8 vols. (1897), 4, *Shōrei* (Ministerial ordinances), 353–54. All individuals engaged in farming, ranching, fishing, mining, manufacturing, engineering, construction, transportation, and domestic services were classified as laborers.

20. Edwin Dun, Tokyo, to W. Q. Gresham, Washington, 13 October 1893, U.S. Department of State, *Japanese Emigration and Immigration to American Territory, Correspondence from 1892 to January 29, 1908* (Washington, 1908–09), 9.

21. Ibid., 11. T. V. Powderly, commissioner-general of immigration, wrote that large profits were derived "from commission paid either directly by the immigrant or through the agency of the steamship lines" as well as "solicitations of citizens in this country who wished to avail themselves of cheaper labor." Congress, House of Representatives, *Immigration of Japanese*, House Doc. 686, 56th Cong., 1st sess., 15 May 1900, 3.

22. Ten thousand yen was equivalent to $5,100. The dollar value of the yen was 51 cents in 1895 and fluctuated around 49.5 cents from 1896 to 1919 (Lockwood, *Economic Development*, 257, table 21, note a).

23. *Kaigai ryokenkisoku ihan zakken* (Miscellaneous documents on overseas passport regulation violations), 4 vols. (1900–15), RG 3.8.5.21, DFMJ. This series records approximately 200 official passport offenses, the majority concerning travelers to the United States. The number of offenses by imin to China, Russia, Korea, and Canada is inconsequential. In 1900–02 (vol. 1) for instance, 33 of 42 recorded passport violations related to imin seeking to emigrate to the United States.

24. Watanabe Kanjirō, *Kaigai dekasegi annai* (Guide for workers going abroad) (Tokyo: Tokyo naigai shuppankyokai, 1902), app. 9–15. The literal translation of *dekasegi* is "earning away from home" and connotes temporary work. There is no English equivalent. Early immigrants to the United States were considered dekasegi, which often is interpreted as "sojourner."

25. Ichihashi, *Japanese*, 86.

26. Slightly more than 27 percent of the total passports for the United States issued 1891–1914 were returned to the Foreign Ministry. The ratio ranged from a low of 9.5 percent in 1900 to a high of 80 percent in 1909, the year following the Gentlemen's Agreement. These returned passports were the official means by which the government kept track of citizens who remigrated (*Nihonteikoku tōkei nenkan* [Annual statistics of the empire of Japan] [hereafter NTN], 1891–1914). Sucheng Chan gave the crude remigration rate of Japanese immigrants, 1909–24, as 33 percent (Chan, "European and Asian Immigration," 38).

27. Aoki Shūzō, Foreign Minister, to Sugimura, Commerce Section, Foreign Ministry, 22 March 1900, *Haiseki ikken*, 2.

28. According to federal statistics, migration of Japanese from Hawaii to the mainland United States, 1902–05, totaled 20,266. In 1906 the number was 13,578; in 1908, 755; and 1909, 1,106 (cited in Moriyama, *Imingaisha*, 133). The 1907 order did not specify a country, but its intent was to restrict Japanese with passports to the United States, its territories, or other nations from entering the continental United States (Bailey, *Japanese-American Crisis*, 142–49).

29. According to Foreign Ministry records, emigration companies supplied only 165 jiyū-imin to the United States between 1894 and 1898. See Commerce Section, Foreign Ministry, *Imin toriatsukainin ni yoru imin no enkaku* (History of emigrants using emigrant agents) (Tokyo: 1909), 96–97.

30. William D. Wray, *Mitsubishi and the N.Y.K., 1870–1914* (Cambridge: Harvard University Press, 1984), 255–58, 491–504 on government subsidies and 261–66, 408–20 on trans-Pacific route.

31. Wakatsuki, "Japanese Emigration," 478–79.

32. For a contemporary American report on Japanese "money making enterprises," see House of Representatives, *Immigration of Japanese*, 7–9.

33. NTN, 1896–1900. Moriyama states that as the number of emigrant workers increased, "efficient enforcement" of the law became more difficult (Moriyama, *Imingaisha*, 41).

34. Aoki to Fu and Ken (excluding Tokyo-fu), 2 Aug. 1900, *Haiseki ikken*, 3.

35. Head, Commerce Section, Foreign Ministry, to Japanese Consuls, Vancouver BC, San Francisco, Tacoma, and Seattle, 31 July 1900, *Haiseki ikken*, 3.

36. NTN, 1901. U.S. immigration figures for 1900 and 1901 were 12,628 and 5,269, respectively (Bureau of Immigration, *Annual Report*, 1900 and 1901).

37. NTN, 1902-1908.

38. Chinda Sutemi to Governor of Hokkaidō, Chief, Tokyo Metropolitan Police Headquarters, and Ken and Fu Governors, *Beika tokōsha ni kansuruken* (Regarding travelers to the United States and Canada), 7 July 1904, *Haiseki ikken*, 3. Emigrants in Tokyo-fu had to apply for passports at the Metropolitan Police Headquarters (Gaikoku ryokenkisoku, 1900, *Hōrei zensho*, 11 vols. (1900), 5, *Shōrei*, 335-38.

39. Compulsory education in Japan was four years, then extended to six in 1908 (*Japan's Modern Educational System*, 107-8).

40. Vice-Minister, Foreign Ministry, to Ken and Fu Governors, *Gakujutsu shūgyō mokutekitosuru kaigai tokōsha ni kansuruken* (Regarding travelers who go abroad as students), 8 November 1905, *Haiseki ikken*, 3. On early Japanese student emigrants to the United States see Hata, *"Undesireables,"* 43-67, and Wakatsuki, "Japanese Emigration," 485-95.

41. McKee, *Chinese Exclusion*, 24.

42. Frank L. Coombs, U.S. Legation, Tokyo, to Mr. Foster, Washington, 7 Oct. 1892, U.S. Department of State, *Japanese Emigration*, 5.

43. House of Representatives, *Immigration of Japanese*, 4.

44. Lockwood, *Economic Development*, 252-58 and 328-34. The British first, then the United States dominated Japanese trade until after World War I.

45. Hayashi Tadasu, Foreign Minister, to Luke E. Wright, Acting Ambassador to Japan, 6 Feb. 1907, *Haiseki ikken*, 5.

46. Thomas J. O'Brien, American Ambassador to Japan, to Hayashi, 26 November 1907, *Nihon gaikō monjo* (Records of the Foreign Ministry of Japan), 40, doc. 2082, 634-37. At the time there were four Japanese consular areas in the United States: New York, which was responsible for seventeen states; Chicago, twenty; San Francisco, four; and Seattle, six.

47. Hayashi to O'Brien, 30 Dec. 1907, *Haiseki ikken*, 13.

48. Hayashi to O'Brien, 18 Feb. 1908, *Haiseki ikken*, 13.

49. "... all recent war talk has started at the White House" (Aoki, Japanese Ambassador to the United States, to Hayashi, 5 Feb. 1907, *Haiseki ikken*, 5).

50. "To save face the Japanese now had to attack the fleet, make a counter demonstration, or proclaim their satisfaction with the President's decision as though it had no meaning for Japan. They chose the latter alternative" (Esthus, *Theodore Roosevelt*, 185).

51. *Gaikoku zairyū teikoku shinmin tōroku kisoku* (Regulations regarding registration of imperial citizens abroad), 7 May 1909, *Genkō hōreishūran* (Existing laws), 2 vols. (Tokyo, 1925), 1, 755. The regulation went into effect on April 1, 1910.

52. *Gaikoku ryokenkisoku,* 1907, *Hōrei zensho,* 4 vols. (1907), 2, *Shōrei,* 43–47.

53. *Kaigai ryokenkafu hennōhyō shintatsu* (Passports issued and returned for travel abroad), 204 unbound vols. (1879–1921), RG 3.8.5.8, DFMJ.

54. *Gaikoku zairyū teikoku shinmin tōroku kisokuseitei narabini kaiseijisshi ikken* (Documents regarding the enactment and revised enforcement of registration regulations of imperial citizens residing abroad) (1908–1910) RG 3.8.7.20, DFMJ; *Gaikoku zairyū teikoku shinmin tōroku kankei zakken* (Miscellaneous documents regarding the registration of imperial citizens residing abroad), (1910) RG 3.8.2.268, DFMJ.

55. Japanese males could be drafted for a three-year military term from ages twenty to thirty-two (revised to thirty-seven in 1910). In order to avoid service entirely, they had to remain abroad twelve years, and after 1910 seventeen years. See Ueda Ryōzō, *Kaigaitokō hōsoku* (Laws regarding travel abroad) (Kishiki-gun, 1902), 71; Wakatsuki, "Japanese Emigration," 421–26; Ichihashi, *Japanese,* 87–88.

56. The Berkeley branch of the Japanese Association protested the institution of fees. Yuji Ichioka, "Japanese Associations and the Japanese Government: A Special Relationship, 1909–1926," *Pacific Historical Review* 46 (August 1977), 421–22.

57. *Hokubeigasshūkoku ryōdo oyobi eiryō kanada ni tokōsuru imin ni taisuru ryoken kafuhōni kansuruken* (Regarding the issuance of passports to imin who travel to the United States and British Canada), 16 November 1908, *Haiseki ikken,* 12.

58. Mizuno Kōkichi, Japanese Consul, New York, to Terauchi Masataki, Foreign Minister, 12 Aug. 1908, *Haiseki ikken,* 12.

59. O'Brien to Hayashi, 25 Jan. 1908, *Haiseki ikken,* 13.

60. Hayashi to O'Brien, 18 Feb. 1908, *Haiseki ikken,* 13.

61. In March 1905 approximately 3,000 Japanese, who had purchased about "35,000 acres of land" to cultivate rice, resided near Houston, Texas. U.S. newspapers reported that they were of the "best class, all of them have money" and "superior to much of the white immigrants . . . from Europe during the past five years, more intelligent, more orderly, more industrious and less offensive." See *New York Tribune,* 22 March 1905; *Houston Post,* 17 March and 27 April 1905; and *Nihonjin kikaishi todoke ni kanshi zainyūyoku ryōji yori gujō ikken* (Reports from New York consul concerning notices of intention of naturalization), (1905) RG 3.8.7.15, DFMJ. See also *Nyūyoku ryōjikan hōkokusho* (Reports of New York Consul General), 6 unbound vols. (1885–1911), 4, *Shisatsu hōkoku* (Investigative reports), (1902) RG 6.1.6.6, DFMJ; Kiyoko T. Kurosawa, "Seito Saibara's Diary of Planting a Japanese Colony in Texas," *Hitotsubashi Journal of Social Studies,* 2 (August 1964); and Kazuhiko Orii and Hilary Conroy, "Japanese Socialist in Texas: Sen Katayama," *Amerasia Journal* 8 (Fall/Winter 1981), 163–70.

62. On a petition demanding the elimination of the imin/hi-imin categories, see Consul General, San Francisco, to Foreign Minister, *Zaibei nihonjinkai seigansho shintatsu no ken* (Regarding submission of written petition by the Japanese Association of America), 4 December 1911, *Kaigai tokō kankei*

zakken (Miscellaneous documents concerning travel abroad), vol. 6 (unbound), DFMJ.

Chapter 4

1. Yanagita Kunio, *Meiji Taishōshi sesōhen* (History of the Meiji-Taisho era: social conditions), 2 vols. (Tokyo: Kodansha, 1976; first published, 1930), 1:46. The works of Yanagita (1875–1962) stress the dichotomy of the Tokugawa and Meiji worlds in relation to community, culture, customs, habits, nature, politics, and economics. Although nostalgic and glorifying of the past, his descriptions are important for our understanding of social change in the Meiji period.

2. Yanabu Akira stated that *kindai* was a term first used (as either noun or adjective) in English-Japanese and French-Japanese dictionaries in 1873 and 1887 as the translation for "modern," denoting "a chronological historical era" as in "prehistoric, ancient, medieval (feudal)." Beginning in 1890 the term was combined to form new compound phrases such as *kindaijin* (modern person) or *kindaibungei* (modern literary arts). By 1910 *kindai* was widely used among scholars and writers. In a compilation of essays in a literary magazine that addressed the question, "What is a kindaijin?" one writer listed such qualities as "pragmatic," "scientific or materialist," "individualistic," "gaining higher standards by developing greed," and "highly sensitive," among others. Thus, Yanabu wrote, kindai developed *ura* (shadow) meanings that ascribed value and went beyond the mere description of a specific historical time period. Yanabu Akira, *Honyakugo seiritsujijō* (On the development of translation) (Tokyo: Iwanami shoten, 1982), 49–62.

3. *Tōkyō hyakunenshi* (One hundred years of Tokyo), 6 vols. (Tokyo: Tokyo Metropolitan Government, 1972–73), 3, *"Tōkyōjin" no keisei* (The making of the people of Tokyo), 871–73. See also Edward Seidensticker, *Low City, High City: Tokyo from Edo to the Earthquake* (New York: Alfred A. Knopf, 1983), 92; G. B. Sansom, *The Western World and Japan* (New York: Alfred A. Knopf, 1950), 384–86.

4. *Tōkyōshi tōkei nenpyō* (Annual statistics of the city of Tokyo), 1924. In 1889 40 percent, and in 1907 one-half of Tokyo's population migrated from other areas of Japan, mainly from ken near the Kantō section and Niigata-ken (Ishizuka Hiromichi, *Tōkyō no shakaikeizaishi* [Social and economic history of Tokyo] [Tokyo: Kinokuniya, 1977], 101–3). As expected, however, the accuracy of the statistics is open to question. The first comprehensive national head count was taken in 1872, but the next was not taken officially until the census of 1920. During the interim years, population migration figures were based on individual exit notices, which people had to submit to their registered prefectural offices, or entry notices, which they had to submit to the offices in their new residential areas. In many cases only one requirement was followed, usually the latter. Additionally, registration occurred in only a few cities up to 1914 (Itō Shigeru, "Senzenki nihon no toshiseichō, jō" [Urban growth in prewar Japan, part 1], *Nippon rōdō kyōkai zasshi* [Journal of the Japan Labor Institute]

280 [July 1982], 26-27). See also Irene B. Taeuber, "Population and Labor Force in the Industrialization of Japan, 1850-1950," in Simon Kuznets, Wilbert E. Moore, and Joseph J. Spengler, eds., *Economic Growth: Brazil, India, Japan* (Durham, NC: Duke University Press, 1955), 320-26.

5. Gluck, *Japan's Modern Myths*, 159.

6. Nakamura Takafusa, *Economic Growth in Prewar Japan*, trans. Robert A. Feldman (New Haven: Yale University Press, 1983), 128. By 1920 only 23 percent of Tokyo's population was native-born (*Tōkyō hyakunenshi* 4, Taishōki [The Taisho period], 47). In 1898, 82 percent of Japan's population lived in rural areas of under 10,000; in 1920, 66 percent (Lockwood, *Economic Development*, 18 and 158). See also G. C. Allen, *A Short Economic History of Modern Japan* (New York: Frederick A. Praeger, 1963), 62. Comparisons of urban migration in Europe are in order. In Germany in 1907, only half the citizens resided in their place of birth, and the population percentage in cities over 100,000 grew from 4.8 percent in 1871 to 21.3 percent in 1910 (Wolfgang Kollmann, "The Population of Germany in the Age of Industrialism," in Herbert Moller, ed., *Population Movements in Modern European History* [New York: Macmillan, 1964], 102-3). London census figures from 1861 to 1881 showed 37 to 39 percent of the London population coming from outside the city (Gareth Stedman Jones, *Outcast London* [New York: Pantheon, 1984], 139). In England and Wales 58 percent of the population was living in cities of 20,000 or more in 1901, whereas it had been less than 10 percent in 1801 (Kingsley Davis, "The Origin and Growth of Urbanization in the World," Moller, ed., *Population Movements*, 70). See also E. J. Hobsbawm, *The Age of Capital, 1848-1875* (New York: Charles Scribner's Sons, 1975), 193-207.

7. The migration was not merely rural to urban but was predominantly "rural to industrial-urban." See Thomas O. Wilkinson, *The Urbanization of Japanese Labor, 1868-1955* (Amherst, MA: University of Massachusetts Press, 1965), especially chapter 4.

8. Yanagita Kunio, *Toshi to nōson* (The city and the rural village), vol. 16, *Teihon Yanagita Kunioshū* (Authentic collection of works by Yanagita Kunio) (Tokyo: Chikuma shobo, 1962), 272-73.

9. Cities such as Nanotsu (Hakata) in Kyūshū, Sakai (Osaka), and Anotsu in Mie-ken grew to thrive as merchants gained profit from their foreign transactions (Yanagita, *Toshi to nōson*, 244). Yanagita conflated historical time in his references, which ranged from the Mongol invasions in the thirteenth century through the Ashikaga period of the fourteenth and fifteenth centuries and up to the sixteenth and early seventeenth centuries, when Europeans first began to compete for trade privileges.

10. Yanagita, *Toshi to nōson*, 273.

11. This is not to subordinate Tokugawa merchant culture, as it set the terms of standards of taste, first in Osaka and then, by the eighteenth century, in Edo. It was separate and distinct from the sophisticated elite Tokugawa culture, as well as the provincial rural culture of the peasants. It had a life of its own and its own artists and craftspeople, who held high positions (among elites and merchants alike) without respect to social origins. This culture produced significant cultural art forms that have survived as important aspects of Japan's

artistic heritage, including *kabuki*, *hanga* (woodblock prints), and *bunraku* (puppet theater). See Robert J. Smith, "Pre-Industrial Urbanism in Japan: A Consideration of Multiple Traditions in a Feudal Society," Research Center in Economic Development and Cultural Change, University of Chicago, *Economic Development and Cultural Change* 9:1, part 2 (October 1960), 241-57.

12. Katō Hidetoshi and Maeda Ai, *Meiji medeakō* (Thoughts on media during the Meiji period) (Tokyo: Chuokoronsha, 1980), 152.

13. *Tōkyō hyakunenshi* tells us that during the Edo period the popular belief was that to become an authentic Edokko, one had to come from a family that had lived in Edo for three generations. However, in the Meiji period this idea began to lose its significance as people moved into the city from the provinces and the term *Tokyojin* began to take on greater importance. By the Taisho years the Edokko was devalued to a "minority" position (*Tōkyō hyakunenshi*, 4:35-36).

14. During the Taisho period (1912-26), none of Tokyo's eight mayors was born in the city. Only one of Tokyo-fu's six governors was a native. Leading business, political, and literary figures migrated to Tokyo and became permanent residents (*Tōkyō hyakunenshi*, 4:39).

15. Natsume Sōseki, *Botchan*, trans. Alan Turney (Tokyo: Kodansha, 1972).

16. Ibid., 23. Ōmori was a suburban section of Tokyo.

17. Takeo Yazaki, *Social Change and the City in Japan* (Tokyo: Japan Publications, 1968), 468-69; *Tōkyō hyakunenshi*, 3:371-91.

18. This fire destroyed 235 acres and left close to 20,000 residents homeless (Yazaki, *Social Change*, 336). Forty-seven major fires swept across the city, located on a windy plain, between 1887 and 1912 (*Tōkyō hyakunenshi*, 3:734-78).

19. Ishizuka, *Tōkyō no shakaikeizaishi*, 137. Seidensticker, *Low City, High City*, 198-206, tells us how the Ginza developed as the district of "business and fun."

20. Seidensticker, *Low City, High City*, 75-79.

21. Various laws concerning local government were passed in 1869, 1871, 1878, and 1888, but it was not until 1898 that Tokyo had it own mayoral administration. However, the mayor was appointed by the emperor from a list submitted by the powerful Ministry of Home Affairs (Yazaki, *Social Change*, 334).

22. In 1891 there were six cities in Japan with populations of more than 100,000. Until 1910, approximately 15 percent of the population resided in those areas. See Asō Makoto, "Nihon no kyōiku to kigyō seichō" (Education and the growth of business in Japan), in Hazami Hiroshi, ed., *Nihon no kigyō to shakai* (Japanese business and society) (Tokyo: Nihonkeizai shimbunsha, 1977), 71. In 1887, 12 percent of the population resided in cities of over 10,000; that figure rose to 18 percent in 1898, 25 percent in 1908, and 32 percent in 1920 (Yazaki, *Social Change*, 391).

23. During the height of the Tokugawa period in the late 1780s, Edo was the most populous city in the world, with more than one million residents. In

1898 Tokyo's population was 1.4 million, far surpassing that of Osaka, the second-largest city, with a population of 820,000. Yazaki included the suburban population in his calculations, making Tokyo's population 1.9 million in 1901 and 3.4 million in 1924 (*Social Change*, 451).

24. *Shita* has various meanings, including "low," "below," "underneath," and "plebian." *Shitamachi* describes the flatlands that made up part of Edo. The term also serves as a geographic reminder of the low status given to merchants during the Edo period. Seidensticker tells us that Shitamachi's boundaries were not clearly defined but shifted during the Meiji period (*Low City, High City*, 8–11, 206).

25. *Tōkyōshi tōkei nenpyō*, 1907 and 1924.

26. Yui Tsunehiko, "Introduction," in Yui Tsunehiko, ed., *Kōgyōka to kigyōsha katsudō* (Industrialization and the role of the businessman) (Tokyo: Nihonkeizai shimbunsha, 1976), 26–28.

27. On Echigoya, the early Mitsui dry goods enterprise, see John G. Roberts, *Mitsui: Three Centuries of Business* (New York: Weatherhill, 1973), 17–22. On the development of department stores, see Seidensticker, *Low City, High City*, 109–13.

28. This term is from a 1909 publication, *Tōkyōgaku* (Tokyo learning). See Miriam Silverberg, "Constructing a New Cultural History of Prewar Japan," *boundary 2* 18:3 (1991), 78.

29. Yazaki, *Social Change*, 339–43.

30. *Tōkyō hyakunenshi*, 3:682–83, and Seidensticker, *Low City, High City*, 11 and 250–51.

31. Ishizuka, *Tōkyō no shakaikeizaishi*, 129–36. By 1880 there were at least seventy slum areas of assorted size and population in Tokyo.

32. *Tōkyō hyakunenshi*, 3:719–20, and Ishizuka, *Tōkyō no shakaikeizaishi*, 171. Preposterous physical therapy was conjured up for victims of tuberculosis, such as deep-breathing exercises, an excruciatingly painful procedure. In 1904 the city instructed factory owners to install spittoons to prevent the disease from spreading (Ishizuka, *Tōkyō no shakaikeizaishi*, 172). The abuses of industrialization—"the sweatshops and dormitory, of child labor and slum living, of long hours, widespread tuberculosis, and high accident rates"—were neglected to the extent that as late as 1925, turnover of factory labor was 40 to 60 percent annually (Lockwood, *Economic Development*, 486). The sixty years or more separating industrial capitalism in Japan and England notwithstanding, the similarities in the human condition of both countries are striking. See Jones, *Outcast London*, and E. P. Thompson, *The Making of the English Working Class* (New York: Vintage, 1963), especially chapter 10.

33. *Tōkyō hyakunenshi*, 3:374 and 377. The household industries, too tiny to be considered factories, were an important part of the industrial picture. Even in 1920, for instance, close to 55 percent of all employees in the manufacturing industries worked in enterprises with only one to four workers. Many were unpaid family workers (Lockwood, *Economic Development*, 191–201). See also Mikio Sumiya, *Social Impact of Industrialization in Japan* (Tokyo: Japanese National Commission for UNESCO, 1963), 125.

34. Yanagita, *Meiji Taishōshi*, 2:131–32; Andrew Gordon, *The Evolution of*

Labor Relations in Japan (Cambridge: Harvard University Press, 1988), 36–37.

35. Nakamura, *Economic Growth*, 129–36.

36. Even in 1921, 1,783 of the 2,033 factories in Tokyo were situated in Shitamachi (Ishizuka, *Tōkyō no shakaikeizaishi*, 202).

37. Between 1870 and 1873, Japan had two small European loans. Thereafter, for a quarter of a century until 1897, aside from small investments in foreign trading companies, foreign capital played no role. Intensive foreign borrowing occurred during 1897–1913. Subsequent to this period, it ceased for a short time until the post–World War I era and then resumed, but never to the extent that it had previously. See Edwin P. Reubens, "Foreign Capital and Domestic Development in Japan," in Kuznets, et al., eds., *Economic Growth*, 185–89; Lockwood, *Economic Development*, 253–54. See also Norman, *Japan's Emergence*, 221–24.

38. Army and navy spending in 1893, the year before the outbreak of the Sino-Japanese War, was 27 percent of overall national expenditures. In 1898 it skyrocketed to 51.2 percent and was maintained at one-third up to 1923 (Lockwood, *Economic Development*, 292n). Military commitment in 1898 was 51.79 percent as compared to Great Britain's 31 percent (Yazaki, *Social Change*, 379).

39. Halliday, *Political History*, 58. Power looms were adopted first in 1910; see Tokutarō Yamanaka, *The History and Structure of Japan's Small and Medium Industries* (Tokyo: Science Council of Japan, 1957), 38.

40. Yamanote was also the name of the loop line encircling the city, which was completed in the main in 1905. It did not service Shitamachi, for which public transportation consisted of horse-drawn streetcars, then electric streetcars. Before electric streetcars were introduced in 1903, the rickshaw, which had a short but indispensable lifetime, and horse-drawn vehicles were the major forms of transportation for a large number of Tokyo citizens (Yazaki, *Social Change*, 444; Yanagita, *Meiji Taishōshi*, 1:197–201; and Ishizuka, *Tōkyō no shakaikeizaishi*, 97–100).

41. Other terms, such as *chūtōkaikyū*, *chūkankaikyū*, or *chūsankaikyū*, were used in popular magazines up to 1929 (Kinmonth, *Self-made Man*, 290–91). The terms are all synonyms for "middle class," although *chūsankaikyū* translates specifically as "middle-income class." Statistician and class analyst Ōhashi Ryūken listed bureaucrats, independent farmers owning less than five *chō* (approximately eleven acres), business proprietors liable for the payment of taxes, professionals (doctors, teachers, religious ministers, and priests), and retired junior bureaucrats as falling within the middle class. He stated that this population grew rapidly between 1888 and 1920, simultaneously with the decrease of the agricultural population. The percentage of the population he defined as "middle class" ranged between 25 to 37 percent during those years. See Ōhashi Ryūken, *Nippon no kaikyūkōsei* (Japan's class formation) (Tokyo: Iwanami shoten, 1971), 25–28.

42. In 1897 the traditionalist writer Kōda Rohan criticized the private homes as not being conducive to "agile and cheerful" work habits (*Tōkyō hyakunenshi*, 3:181). From the Edo to early Meiji periods the typical form of rental

in cities was the *nagaya*, or tenement building, supervised by a superintendent hired by the landlord. Ishizuka wrote that the tenant was called *tanako*, written with the ideographs for "store" and "child." However, "store" did not connote a place to sell but rather a place to rent. The responsibilities of the superintendent to maintain property, choose appropriate tanako, evict undesirable tenants, engage in the political life of a district at times, and exhibit kindness as well as authority indicated a "feudal master-servant relationship." "An *ōoya* [landlord] is like a parent, a tanako like a child," was a saying in *rakugo*, the popular form of storytelling (Ishizuka, *Tōkyō no shakaikeizaishi*, 124–27).

43. Yanagita, *Meiji Taishōshi*, 1:103–4.

44. Silverberg, "New Cultural History," 65. Silverberg analyzed the formation of a Japanese consumer culture, taking into account the process of consent as well as challenge in relation to Japanese state ideology. She dated this process to the 1920s but through a close reading of *Tōkyōgaku* stressed that its noticeable beginnings occurred in the mid-Meiji era as "new, specialized techniques" began to be utilized in urban Tokyo. See also Silverberg's discussion of the construction of cultural identity in 1920s Japan ("Ethnography of Modernity," 30–54).

45. Quoted in *Tōkyō hyakunenshi*, 3:181. Yanagita, *Meiji Taishōshi*, 1:96–132, gives a vivid description of the changes in residential living.

46. Seidensticker, *Low City, High City*, 236–41.

47. For instance, Samegahashi in Yotsuya and Tanimachi in Azabu (Ishizuka, *Tōkyō no shakaikeizaishi*, 129). See also Yazaki, *Social Change*, 365; Seidensticker, *Low City, High City*, 241. In the late 1880s, the three largest slum districts were in Shiba-, Yotsuya-, and Shitaya-ku (Ishizuka, *Tōkyō no shakaikeizaishi*, 130).

48. However, in Tokugawa days, plebian did not mean "poor." The merchant, despite his inferior class status, was dominant financially and economically.

49. *Kosekihō ni yori zaigai honpōjin shotodokesho sono honsekichi kosekiri e sōtatsu no ikken* (Documents concerning notices filed by citizens abroad to be sent to household registry officials in registered family domicile areas according to household registry law), 43 vols. (1909–1921), RG 3.8.7.21, DFMJ.

50. The political redistricting of the country was administered in various stages from 1871 to 1888, the year when the final reorganization created three fu and forty-three ken (Hane, *Modern Japan*, 89–90). See also Tōyama Shigeki, *Kindai nihonshi* (History of modern Japan) (Tokyo: Iwanami shoten, 1975), 1:33–37, in which the passage of three major measures—the reorganization of counties, wards, and villages; regulating of local taxation; and the establishment of fu and ken—is discussed as an antidote to progressive political trends and a means to consolidate central government power.

51. Yanagita, *Meiji Taishōshi*, 1:170–1. Community participation in preindustrial Japan's wet-rice agriculture provided the framework for community solidarity and self-sufficiency. People could be mobilized for a variety of day-to-day functions, including not only raising and harvesting crops but also building farmhouses, reroofing, repairing, storage, and so on. Communal ownership of nonfarm land was an important source of fuel and fertilizer. Early in the Meiji

period, the government confiscated communal property for distribution among the new political units. This placed the agricultural sector in an untenable situation and meant that any use of this land became a privilege bestowed by public servants. See Thomas C. Smith, *The Agrarian Origins of Modern Japan* (Stanford: Stanford University Press, 1959), especially chapters 5–7; Fukutake Tadashi, *Japanese Rural Society*, trans. R. P. Dore (Ithaca: Cornell University Press, 1967), 82–84; and Sumiya, *Industrialization*, 22–23.

52. During the Tokugawa period the samurai ranked second after the *daimyō* (feudal lord) in the social class structure. On the 6 percent who constituted the warrior class at the beginning of the Meiji period, see E. H. Norman, *Feudal Backgrounds in Japanese Politics*, in Dower, ed., *Origins*, especially chapter 3.

53. The electorate numbered 460,000; the population of Japan was 40.5 million. Voting laws were revised in 1900 and 1920, the number of voters being increased by about three times with each revision. Universal manhood suffrage was instituted in 1925.

54. An important form of Tokugawa hegemonic control that the shogun instituted (official and compulsory in 1634), the *sankin kōtai* system, required each feudal lord to maintain two residences, one in Edo and one in the feudal domain. This was part of a complicated and perpetual martial law system accompanied by minute rules as to behavior, residential orders concerning family members, number of followers, gifts to the Tokugawas, and so on. The higher the status of the lord, the more ostentatious his estate in Edo; the more prone to independence, the greater the demands made upon him. The system's relationship to the spread of the money economy and the subsequent nationwide economy is discussed in Charles David Sheldon, *The Rise of the Merchant Class in Tokugawa Japan, 1600–1868* (New York: Russell and Russell, 1958), 18–19.

55. Shorn of their status and privileges, former samurai led four uprisings between 1873 and 1877, the last and major one being the Satsuma rebellion. The government's solution to the problem of discontented former samurai was "based almost exclusively on officeholding, and this monopoly was not immediately in danger because no other class had yet the experience, education, and confidence to displace warriors in administration" (Thomas C. Smith, "Japan's Aristocratic Revolution," in Smith, *Native Sources of Japanese Industrialization, 1750–1920* [Berkeley: University of California Press, 1988], 142). In 1876 the Meiji government put forward a scheme whereby members of the former feudal class received compensation that had varying effects. The average stipend paid to lower samurai was 415 yen, a paltry sum compared to the 97,000 yen for daimyo and 14,000 yen for former court nobles (Ōhashi, *Nippon no kaikyūkōsei*, 16). See also Norman, *Japan's Emergence*, 201–5.

56. The number rose from 40,000 to 308,000 in three and a half decades (Yazaki, *Social Change*, 425). This was a little more than 1 percent of the total work force of 27 million (Lockwood, *Economic Development*, 462). In Tokyo, public and self-employed males constituted 11.6 percent of all males employed in 1918 and 10.8 percent in 1920 (Nakamura, *Economic Growth*, 126).

57. Nobutaka Ike, *Japanese Politics* (New York: Alfred A. Knopf, 1957), 145–46.

58. Tokyo (1886) and Kyoto (1897) Imperial Universities were the only two institutions given university status until 1903. Imperial universities established after the turn of the century were Tōhoku (1907), Kyūshū (1910), and Hokkaidō (1918). See *Japan's Modern Educational System*, 128–30.

59. Ike, *Japanese Politics*, 146.

60. Kinmonth, *Self-made Man*, 184.

61. Although universal education was established in 1872, it was not until 1886 that comprehensive ordinances were instituted that unified and controlled educational content for all youth (Hane, *Modern Japan*, 101–5). See also Herbert Passin, *Society and Education in Japan* (Tokyo: Kodansha, 1982; New York: Columbia University Press, 1965), chapter 4.

62. Kinmonth, *Self-made Man*, 131. In 1892 approximately 15 percent of the over 2,000 reported college graduates were from Tokyo Imperial University (ibid., 132n).

63. *Tōkyō hyakunenshi*, 4:512.

64. Asō, "Nihon no kyōiku to kigyō seichō," 73. Keio developed networks with leading firms in trade and industry. Within seven years it was the major educational institution feeding into the Mitsubishi combine; see Kageyama Kiichi, "Howaito karaa no suii" (The transition to white-collar work), in Hazama, ed., *Nihon no kigyō*, 182. By the turn of the century, Tokyo Higher Commercial College had entrance ratios higher than those of the First Higher School of Tokyo. Of its 2,692 graduates before 1911, more than one-third had entered commercial firms, 578 had positions in small businesses, and 359 were in banks. Its network with the Mitsui combine was impressive, for over 10 percent, or 346, of its alumni were in that concern alone (*Tōkyō kōtō shōgyōgakkō dōsōkai kaiinroku* [Alumni list of Tokyo Higher Commercial College], 1911). Permanent status in the college could not be achieved until after a preparatory course and examination had been completed; see *Seikō* 19:6 (1 December 1910), 93.

65. The College of Medicine required four years, the others (Law, Engineering, Literature, and Science), three (*Japan's Modern Educational System*, 122). Significantly, public middle schools were originally established (1887) for boys only. In 1894 only 2,000 girls were enrolled in public girls' high schools, more in private schools, many of which were mission schools. See Passin, *Society and Education*, 97–98; Thomas P. Rohlen, *Japan's High Schools* (Berkeley: University of California Press, 1983), 59.

66. *Japan's Modern Educational System*, 125–27.

67. Kinmonth, *Self-made Man*, 187.

68. Ibid., 218.

69. Asō, "Nihon no kyōiku to kigyō seichō," 73.

70. Kinmonth, *Self-made Man*, 133. Kinmonth stated that most histories present unemployment among educated youth as commencing after World War I, but, quoting a number of contemporary sources, he concluded that the condition existed at least two decades earlier. Lockwood pointed out that although there was sustained geographic and occupational mobility, the "unequal distribution of educational opportunity among the people, the cultural and technological lag of rural Japan, the technical and political factors which made certain

industries the preserve of big financial cliques, the controls and subsidies applied by the State in the strategic realm, etc.," contributed to an "imperfect utilization of the country's manpower" (Lockwood, *Economic Development*, 480–81).

71. Nakamura, *Economic Growth*, 8, and *Tōkyō hyakunenshi*, 3:453–56.

72. Compulsory education was four years in 1886, then extended to six in 1908, but the number of students who continued on to middle school was considerable. This pattern was mainly found in the urban areas, particularly Tokyo, where the majority of elite and nonelite schools were concentrated (*Japan's Modern Educational System*, 165; Passin, *Society and Education*, 73). In 1900 compulsory education became free, and consequently the nationwide compulsory attendance rate rose to more than 90 percent for boys from 1900 and girls from 1904 (Passin, 79; *Japan's Modern Educational System*, 106). In the early 1900s 40 percent of the nation's "productive-age population" finished elementary school. By 1920 the number increased twofold (Sumiya, *Industrialization*, 77 and 129).

73. Futabatei Shimei, *Ukigumo*, trans. Marleigh G. Ryan, *Japan's First Modern Novel: "Ukigumo" of Futabatei Shimei* (New York: Columbia University Press, 1965), 193–356. Regarding Shimei, see Nakamura Mitsuo, *Nihon no kindaishōsetsu* (Japan's modern novels) (Tokyo: Iwanami shoten, 1954), 45–51. See also Masao Miyoshi, *Accomplices of Silence: The Modern Japanese Novel* (Berkeley: University of California Press, 1974), 17–37, on Shimei and *Ukigumo*, which Miyoshi placed in the context of early Meiji literary struggles and practices. He also noted instances of Ryan's "imprecise" translation.

74. Shimei, *Ukigumo*, 207–8.

75. Ibid., 208 and 224.

76. Ibid., 247.

77. Ibid., 247–48.

78. Kinmonth described the conceptual development of risshin shusse, placing it as early as the Tokugawa period, when it denoted a samurai's excellence in battle. The term underwent a number of changes in meaning and usage and in the Meiji years referred to achieving "publically recognized success" (Kinmonth, *Self-made Man*, 56–58).

79. Kinmonth argued that *nintai* developed different conceptual meanings: moral steadfastness, which necessitated time to achieve a goal of "discovery and innovation"; and chipping away to advancement, a reflection of the bureaucratic ethos (Kinmonth, *Self-made Man*, 69–71).

80. R. P. Dore, *City Life in Japan* (Berkeley: University of California Press, 1958), especially chapter 4. Dore compared standards of moral conduct and principles in Tokugawa society to those in the Meiji society, which were more generalized and dependent upon an individual's internal conscience. He described the "individuated person" as wanting most things "for himself or for specific individual others, not for some group," although this trait was not as accentuated in Japan as in Western societies.

81. Shimei's description forecasts the *sarariiman* (salary man). Kinmonth (*Self-made Man*, 277–80 and 289–90) discussed the term *sarariiman* as having taken hold by the late 1910s. The earlier colloquialisms for low-salaried clerks

were *koshibentō*, a Tokugawa term that literally meant "hanging a lunch from one's hip" (the male's *obi*, which was worn lower than the waist), and *yōfukusaimin*, the poor in Western clothing.

82. Yazaki, *Social Change*, 425; Gluck, *Japan's Modern Myths*, 60–61. However, bureaucratic authoritarianism should not be interpreted as a simple and direct descendant of samurai authoritarianism.

83. *Botchan* is a term of respect used by people of lower status (such as servants and storekeepers) to address sons of employers, customers, and other people of authority or higher station.

84. Sōseki, *Botchan*, 35–36.

85. The usage of standardized Japanese was stressed in the schools and other public institutions. Dialects were considered backward. In some workplaces, debates were initiated and scheduled daily so that employees could learn the new standardized language (Yanagita, *Meiji Taishōshi*, 1:170). The variety of dialects was extreme for a country as small as Japan. Furthermore, they were often incomprehensible in places other than where they originated. This was compounded by language protocols based on class, gender, and occupation. The differences are not as pronounced today, although they still exist; see Kindaichi Haruhiko, *Nihongo* (The Japanese language) (Tokyo: Iwanami shoten, 1957), 31–38. In the Taisho era Yamanote speech was considered the more refined form of speech, differentiating it clearly from Shitamachi speech. It included the use of appropriate honorifics when addressing people of greater authority—parents or older brothers and sisters—as well as Western terms such as "papa" and "mama" in Yamanote middle-class families (*Tōkyō hyakunenshi*), 4:346–48.

86. Sōseki, *Botchan*, 140–41.

87. See Gluck, *Japan's Modern Myths*, 73–101, for a discussion of the imperial institution as the symbol and Emperor Meiji as the personal manifestation of national unity.

88. Dore, *City Life*, 115.

89. Silverberg, "New Cultural History," 79.

90. Conflicts, turbulent action, and contestation constituted the regrounding of Meiji society. Peasant revolts in the early Meiji years, opposition to conscription, numerous workers' actions which began in the 1870s, protest actions at Tokyo Hibiya Park in 1905, the rice riots of 1918, and underground socialist/anarchist activities were some of the better-known political attempts to challenge authority in Japan. See Tetsuo Najita and J. Victor Koschmann, eds., *Conflict in Modern Japanese History* (Princeton: Princeton University Press, 1982); Mikiso Hane, *Peasants, Rebels, and Outcasts: The Underside of Modern Japan* (New York: Pantheon, 1982); E. H. Norman, *Soldier and Peasant in Japan* (New York: Institute of Pacific Relations, 1943); Norman, *Japan's Emergence*, 178–87.

91. *Tōkyō hyakunenshi*, 3:847–48.

92. Ibid., 3:871–73.

93. Quoted in Kageyama, "Howaito karaa no suii," 176.

94. Shimazaki Tōson, *The Family*, trans. Cecilia Segawa Seigle (Tokyo: University of Tokyo Press, 1976).

95. Ibid., 29.
96. Ibid., 30.
97. Ibid., 179.
98. The translator, Cecilia Segawa Seigle, informed us that the novel is less a novel than a Shimazaki family history, for it closely followed the lives of each member of the family as far as the facts are known (Ibid., vii–xix).
99. Ibid., 151.
100. Ibid., xviii.
101. Prior to World War I, migrants into the cities, after initially experiencing employment in a trade, often would open their own businesses. These ranged from small enterprises such as noodle or sake stands to shops and putting-out households. "The scale of operation in many activities were almost infinitely divisible" (Koji Taira, *Economic Development and the Labor Market in Japan* [New York: Columbia University Press, 1970], 3–4).
102. In his short but important monograph on Japan's small and medium industries, Tokutaro Yamanaka stated that modernization could not have occurred without the dual existence of government-sponsored heavy industry and the small business sector, which produced foreign-exchange-earning exports and domestic consumer goods and services. "The imported industries [munitions, iron, steel, shipbuilding, spinning, etc., which utilized imported machinery] needed the native industries to pay for their equipment, and the native industries could only develop under conditions of economic independence which the imported industries helped to preserve. These two segments—westernized and indigenous—formed, so to speak, the 'two inseparable related wheels' of the Japanese economic structure. It was on these two wheels that Japan's Industrial Revolution rolled forward" (Yamanaka, *History and Structure*, 34).
103. Ibid., 7. See also Lockwood, *Economic Development*, 210–11.
104. The government encouraged the formation of trade associations in 1884, 1898, and 1900, but these efforts fell short of helping. Rather, quality controls were placed on goods for exports, creating negative results (Yamanaka, *History and Structure*, 35).
105. Interest rates varied depending upon the amount of loan and where it was secured. The less the loan, the higher the interest rate; small agricultural loans cost more than nonagricultural loans. A law to ban usury was passed in 1877, but it remained "a dead letter" (Lockwood, *Economic Development*, 288). On small businesses, see Lockwood, 206–12.
106. Yamanaka, *History and Structure*, 18–19.
107. "Without breaking ties with their traditional callings, they took on two or more activities and invested their total income where most beneficial to themselves. At times they even funded and managed enterprises in the modern sector the better to carry on traditional businesses. Cold calculations of rates of return and of risk led to the diversification and dispersion of capital. Naturally, these small capitalists did not indulge in objective assessments of the contribution that the resulting new industries would make to economic growth. They just followed the path to wealth" (Nakamura, *Economic Growth*, 109–10).

108. The economic status of a large number of small businessmen "was no higher than that of the male factory hand . . . and even less in the way of capital resources or modern skills" (Lockwood, *Economic Development*, 210).
109. Dore, *City Life*, 210.
110. Tōson, *The Family*, 42–43.
111. Dore, *City Life*, 210.

Chapter 5

1. *Seikō* 5:1 (1 July 1904), 52.
2. Many words of Portuguese and Dutch origin of the Tokugawa period have remained to this day: Portuguese terms such as *velludo* (velvet), *pão de Castella* (sponge cake), and *tabaco* (tobacco) for the Japanese *birōdo, kasutera,* and *tabako;* and the Dutch *oblaat* (a wrapper for powdered medicines), *alcohol, bier* (beer), and *jak* (vest), which converted to the Japanese *oburaato, arukōru, biiru,* and *chokki.* The Dutch conversions were by far the most numerous, noticeably so in the fields of science and medicine (Yazaki Genkurō, *Nihon no gairaigo* [Japanese words of foreign origin] [Tokyo: Iwanami shoten, 1964], 53–79).
3. Ibid., 87–88.
4. Ibid., 84.
5. Mori Arinori (1847–1889), envoy to the United States, England, and China and the first minister of education in 1885, suggested early in his career that Japanese be replaced by English and corresponded with American educators in 1872 asking their views on the subject (Roy Andrew Miller, *Japan's Modern Myth* [New York: Weatherhill, 1982], 108). Mori's political position in the Meiji government was far from radical, however; he preached absolute and conservative statism and viewed education as the important vehicle by which to disseminate state ideology.
6. The middle school was reorganized in 1899, deemphasizing its former vocational aspect and establishing entrance and teacher qualification requirements (*Japan's Modern Educational System*, 117). Between 1902 and 1906 the average enrollment of middle school students was 100,000, a tenfold increase in ten years (Kinmonth, *Self-made Man*, 1981, 180).
7. A vast assortment of magazines for different interests, age and gender groups, predominantly for the rapidly forming middle class, poured out from the Hakubunkan presses, as did government primary school textbooks, encyclopedia, and books for a general audience on current affairs, economics, law, and politics. Two of its best-sellers were popular treatments of the Sino-Japanese and Russo-Japanese wars. In 1897, ten years after issuing its first publication, Hakubunkan had published twenty-nine magazines and more than 1,000 books; it controlled bookstores, printing shops, paper plants, and subsidiary publishing houses in a comprehensive enterprise that combined all aspects of the publishing business. See *Ōhashi Sahei to Hakubunkan* (Ōhashi Sahei and Hakubunkan) (Private collection, n.d.), 211–14. Yanagita wrote about the rapid appearance of a large variety of published works, the growing "avarice of

a reading public," and the phenomenal development of the publishing industry (Yanagita Kunio, *Meiji Taishōshi*, 2:214–16).

8. See Kinmonth, *Self-made Man*, chapter 1, for a discussion of Samuel Smiles's work.

9. For instance, *Eisai shinshi* (Talent magazine), *Kokumin no tomo* (Friend of the people), *Shōnenen* (Garden for youth), and *Chūgaku sekai* (World of the middle school); see Kinmonth, *Self-made Man*, 62, 108, 123, and 164. Kinmonth analyzed more than thirty self-advancement magazines for youth published from the 1870s to 1920s in his study on the ethos of the Japanese white-collar worker. See also *Shimbun no ayumi* (Development of newspapers) (Tokyo: National Diet Library, 1972).

10. Katō and Maeda, *Meiji medeakō*, 56.

11. Kinmonth, *Self-made Man*, 159.

12. Quoted in Yoshitake Oka, "Generational Conflict after the Russo-Japanese War," in Najita and Koschmann, eds., *Conflict in Modern Japanese History*, 198–99.

13. Kinmonth, *Self-made Man*, 166. R .P. Dore wrote that *Seikō* promoted individual self-attainment, encouraging a person "of character who helps himself and respects himself, lives by his own enterprise and his own toil, and creates his own fate" (Dore, "Mobility, Equality, and Individuation in Modern Japan," in R. P. Dore, ed., *Aspects of Social Change in Modern Japan* (Princeton: Princeton University Press, 1967), 113–50.

14. Kinmonth, *Self-made Man*, 175.

15. Of the roughly 55,000 individuals of student age in Tokyo in 1901, not all gained entry into an educational institution, for 20,000 were not enrolled in any school (*Tōkyō hyakunenshi*, 3:310–14).

16. *Seikō* 6:4 (1 April 1905), 181–83, and 6:5 (1 May 1905), 17–22. Keio and Tokyo Higher Commercial College graduates, however, consistently fed into the Mitsui and Mitsubishi combines and had entrance ratios comparable to that of the First Higher School.

17. A quick search at the National Diet Library in Tokyo shows that of books published between the turn of the century and 1926, close to 250 titles concerning the United States are still extant.

18. *Tobei shimpō*, 6:9 (15 September 1908).

19. Kinmonth, *Self-made Man*, 188.

20. Yanabu tells us that in the early Meiji years, *individual* was translated in various ways *(ichikojin, hitori,* or the complicated *jinminkakko)*. None of the translations encompassed the concept of the individual's relationship with society; all signified a self-centeredness. The educator Fukuzawa Yukichi translated *individual* as *hito* (person), the commonly used Japanese noun, but its very commonness failed to convey the abstract complexities of *individual*. Nevertheless, the use of *hito* helped to promote the use of what Fukuzawa referred to as *odayakanaru* (reasonable, moderate) Japanese in translation as opposed to *shikakubatta* (formal, angular) Japanese. *Ichikojin* was used extensively until the mid-1880s, when *kojin* began to appear, and in 1891, when *individualisme* was translated as *kojinshugi* in a French-Japanese dictionary, *kojin* gradually came to be used more widely. See Yanabu, *Honyakugo seiritsujijō*, 25–42.

21. *Seikō* 4:5 (15 May 1904), 10–14.
22. Ibid., 12.
23. *Seikō* 4:6 (1 June 1904), 43.
24. *Amerika* 12:9 (September 1908), 1–4.
25. Ibid., 2.
26. Ibid., 3.
27. *Seikō* 14:1 (1 June 1908), 7–10. Abe Isō (1865–1949), educated at the first Japanese-administered Christian school, Doshisha Foreign Language School (later University), was a pastor in Japan for four years, then attended Hartford Theological Seminary. He was a key founding member of the short-lived Social Democratic Party in 1901. In the 1920s he became president of a renewed Social Democratic Party and was elected to the Diet in 1928. An advocate of baseball, he admired the utility men for their prowess in playing various positions. "I learned in baseball to obey the captain without question," he wrote, expressing his strong sense of discipline and cooperation. See Cyril H. Powles, "Abe Isoo: The Utility Man," in Nobuya Bamba and John F. Howes, eds., *Pacificism in Japan* (Kyoto: Minerva Press, 1978), 143–67.
28. *Seikō* 19:1 (1 September 1910), 31–34.
29. *Seikō* 24:2 (1 November 1912), 33–35. Educated at MIT, Dan Takuma (1858–1932) taught English until the government hired him to supervise the Miike coal mines in 1881. He retained this important position after the Mitsui Company bought the mines in 1888 and later headed Mitsui's mining enterprises and became chairman of the board.
30. Ibid., 35.
31. Lockwood, *Economic Development*, 249–51. See also the discussions on technology and capital in Lockwood, chapters 4 and 5, and in Nakamura, *Economic Growth*, 60–68.
32. Lockwood, *Economic Development*, 28–32.
33. John W. Dower, "E. H. Norman, Japan and the Uses of History," in Dower, ed., *Origins of the Modern Japanese State: Selected Writings of E. H. Norman* (New York: Pantheon Books, 1975), 31.
34. The Meiji period saw a constant condition of low wages and instability and low morale of the work force (Taira, *Economic Development*, 4). Taira challenged the assumption among some Japanologists that Meiji economic development was rapid and amazing. He interpreted the Meiji Restoration not as a bourgeois revolution but as a revolution in favor of and regulated by the market. Therefore, general economic growth as defined by the appearance of capital-intensive factories was slow. See also Lockwood, *Economic Development*, 138–144, for a discussion of the Japanese standard of living, 1868–1914.
35. The higher one's place on the Tokugawa social scale, the less one handled money, that responsiblity being given to wives, trusted employees, and servants. On the surface, money was handled casually, but in reality money management was done poorly. See Yanagita Kunio, *Japanese Manners and Customs in the Meiji Era*, trans. Charles S. Terry (Tokyo: Obunsha, 1957), 122. On Tokugawa merchants see E. H. Norman, *Japan's Emergence as a Modern State* (1940), in Dower, ed., *Origins*, 156–65.
36. *Seikō* 6:1 (1 January 1905), 20–21.

37. *Seikō* 10:4 (1 December 1906), 18.

38. *Seikō* 15:5 (1 March 1909), 59–65.

39. The early political newspapers assumed a role as voices of newly formed political parties, mainly critical of the new Meiji government. To counter antigovernment criticism, a law restricting freedom of the press was enacted in 1875, then strengthened by revisions in the 1880s, and finally replaced by the Press Law of 1909. Gradually but comprehensively, all publications came under Home Ministry jurisdiction, army and navy censorship, and police enforcement, which weakened and rendered ineffective any liberal opposition voice (Katō and Maeda, *Meiji medeakō*, 136–37; Norman, *Feudal Background*, 444–46; and Mikiso Hane, *Modern Japan*, 119–20). In 1875 sixty journalists were arrested (James L. Huffman, *Politics of the Meiji Press: The Life of Fukuchi Gen'ichirō* [Honolulu: University of Hawaii Press, 1980], 105). Newspaper editors were routinely arrested, to the point that newspapers hired editors whose "chief duty . . . was to serve prison sentences" (Sansom, *Western World*, 352). See also Gluck, *Japan's Modern Myths*, 50–53, for discussion of government suppression and effects on the shaping of political consciousness; and Jay Rubin, *Injurious to Public Morals: Writers and the Meiji State* (Seattle: University of Washington Press, 1984), on the establishment and maintenance of censorship.

40. Huffman, *Meiji Press*, 164.

41. Takagi Takeo, *Shimbun shōsetsushi: Meijihen* (History of newspaper novels of the Meiji period) (Tokyo: Kokusho kankokai, 1974), 105.

42. *Shimbun no ayumi*, 16–17.

43. Yanagita rated the proliferation of translated works as products of "indiscriminate choices," which were like "candy and fruit" but nevertheless broadened readers' world (Yanagita, *Meiji Taishōshi*, 2:215–16).

44. Takagi, *Shimbun shōsetsushi*, 267.

45. Katō and Maeda, *Meiji medeakō*, 57–60. Natsume Sōseki decided to give up his profession as a provincial teacher to become a full-time writer, joining the staff of *Tokyo Asahi* in 1907. The *Yomiuri* then lost its status as the top literary newspaper. *Shimbunhanbai hyakunenshi* (One hundred years of newspaper sales) (Tokyo: Nihon shimbunhanbai kyokai, 1972), 329.

46. *Yomiuri shimbun*, 15 April–1 June 1897. Shunyō was a leading protégé of the popular novelist Ozaki Kōyō and became known as a writer of the moralistic *katei shōsetsu* (family novels), a form that became extremely popular in the late 1890s. These works were easy to read and understand by males and females, young and old. They centered around themes concerning the family, contained "healthy common sense" (usually with women as main characters), and had outcomes in which morality was always the victor (Takagi, *Shimbun shōsetsushi*, 344).

47. In 1887 Disraeli's autobiographical novel, *Contarini Fleming*, Poe's *The Black Cat*, and Dumas' *The Three Musketeers* appeared as serialized newspaper novels (Takagi, *Shimbun shōsetsushi*, 110 and 233).

48. *Yomiuri shimbun*, 15 April 1897. "Smelling of butter" (*batakusai*) connotes that which is intrinsic to the West, whether manners of behavior, attitudes, or material things.

49. Ozaki Kōyō, *Konjikiyasha* (Tokyo: Shinchosha, 1969); originally published in *Yomiuri shimbun*, 1 January 1897–11 May 1902.

50. Takagi, *Shimbun shōsetsushi*, 273. Between 1893 and 1902, six Bertha Clay novels appeared as newspaper series, translated by Kuroiwa Ruikō (1862–1920), the prolific and popular writer of detective and romantic stories and owner of the liberal newspaper *Yorozu chōhō* (Takagi, 242–43). More than forty Clay novels are listed in the *National Union Catalog: Between Two Hearts* (1893); *Another Man's Wife* (1890); *Another Woman's Husband* (1892); *A Dead Heart* (1880); *Her Only Sin* (1900); and so on. These titles give us a sense of the focus in her novels. Although the author's name was a pseudonym of Charlotte Mary Brame, a number of other writers admittedly assumed the same pen name.

51. Takagi, *Shimbun shōsetsushi*, 293. During periods when his creative level was low and he could not keep up with the newspaper's demands, Kōyō coauthored works with his protégés or his name was included as reviewer/reviser of novels by other writers (Takagi, 271).

52. Quoted in ibid., 269.

53. Ibid., 283.

54. Ibid., 276.

55. Ibid., 274–75.

56. Quoted in ibid., 278.

57. The Atami beach scene was so renowned that it became immortalized by a popular song in the 1930s.

58. Kōyō, *Konjikiyasha*, 103–5.

59. Ibid., 8–9.

60. Ibid., 485, note 3.

61. Literary scholar Saigusa Yasutaka placed *Konjikiyasha* in the framework of a new capitalist consciousness that became pronounced after the Sino-Japanese War, when social class differences were becoming more clearly defined. He analyzed the novel as a reaction to and critique of the increasingly prominent attachment to money and materialism. See Saigusa Yasutaka, *Kindai bungaku no risōzō* (The ideal image in modern literature) (Tokyo: Kakushobo, 1961), 123–24.

62. *Seikō* 22:6 (13 April 1912), 165–74. *Kōri* (high interest; usury) is a homonym for *ice* in Japanese. *A-i-su* became the coded term used for usurers.

63. A law was passed to curb usury in 1877, but high interest rates continued to plague Japan, especially the small borrower, whose actual cost of credit could reach 100 percent (Lockwood, *Economic Development*, 289). The usury trade was given a boost after the 1907 panic (*Tōkyō hyakunenshi*, 3:475).

Chapter 6

1. Nevertheless, significant emigration outside of Japan was absent. This meant that urban growth represented "in essence" Japan's natural increase in population between 1872 and 1955 (Wilkinson, *Urbanization of Japanese Labor*, 39–40 and 52). See my chapter 3, note 12, for numerical chart of key areas of Japanese emigration.

2. Shimanuki Hyōdayū, *Shintobeihō* (New passport regulations for crossing to America) (Tokyo: Hakubunkan, 1911), 51–55.

3. Ibid., 38.
4. Ichioka, *The Issei*, 11–12.
5. Various forms of *netsu* (fever; craze) prevailed in the mid-Meiji period, pronouncedly so after the Russo-Japanese War. *Seikō netsu, tokai netsu* (city fever), *Tōkyō netsu, jitsugyō netsu* (business fever), and *kigyō netsu* (enterprise fever), among others, were, in Gluck's interpretation, ideologically motivated descriptions of social upheaval and problems (Gluck, *Japan's Modern Myths*, 157–63). Tōkyō netsu took hold in conjunction with youth migration to Tokyo and the phenomenal increase in the establishment of middle, higher, and vocational schools and colleges during the last decade of the nineteenth century. However, in 1901 more than one-third of the youth who went to Tokyo did not gain entry into an educational institution (*Tōkyō hyakunenshi* 3:310–14).
6. *Amerika* 12:6 (June 1908), 25.
7. *Seikō* 19:1 (1 September 1910), 31–34.
8. Shimanuki, *Shintobeihō*, 76.
9. *Seikō* 5:3 (1 September 1904), 36. See also, Shimanuki Hyōdayū, *Saikin tobeisaku* (Recent notes on crossing to America) (Tokyo: Nippon Rikikokai, 1904), 68–69.
10. In preparing for the immigration authorities' examinations, the Japanese were warned to be physically fit. They should not have trachoma; their eyes should be clear; a venereal disease would prevent their landing; and they had to get rid of pimples and make sure their teeth were in good condition. Finally, Western clothing impressed immigration officials. To avoid becoming an object of ridicule, it was important to practice wearing Western clothes before leaving Japan (Shimanuki, *Shintobeihō*, 85). See also Katayama Sen, *Tobei no hiketsu* (Secrets of crossing to America) (Tokyo: Shuppankyokai, 1906), 8–9.
11. Shimanuki Hyōdayū, *Saikin seikaku tobei annai* (Newest authentic introduction to crossing to America) (Tokyo: Chuyodo, 1901), 118–19.
12. *Amerika* 12:6 (June 1908), 30–31.
13. Shimanuki, *Shintobeihō*, 33.
14. Shimanuki, *Saikin seikaku tobei annai*, 114; *Seikō* 5:3 (1 September 1904), 36.
15. *Amerika* 12:6 (June 1908), 31.
16. After the Russo-Japanese War, Great Britain raised its legation in Japan to the level of embassy, a policy followed by the major European powers and the United States. Diplomatic practice up to World War I prescribed that the exchange of embassies and ambassadors be mutual only between the great powers, a fact not ignored by the Japanese. Oka, "Generational Conflict," 202, n.11.
17. Shimanuki, *Shintobeihō*, 32–34.
18. *Amerika* 12:6 (June 1908), 30.
19. Shimanuki, *Shintobeihō*, 49.
20. *Tobei shimpō* 6:10 (15 October 1908), 9–10.
21. *Seikō* 10:3 (1 November 1906), 16.
22. *Seikō* 5:3 (1 September 1904), 36; *Tobei shimpō* 6:10 (15 October 1908), 11.

23. *Tobei shimpō* 6:9 (15 September 1908), 5 and 25–26.
24. Shimanuki, *Shintobeihō*, 34.
25. Ibid., 35.
26. Shimanuki Hyōdayū, *Rikikōkai towa nanzoya* (What is the Rikikokai?), ed. Aizawa Genshichi (Tokyo: Hobundo, 1980; originally published 1911).
27. In 1904 entering middle-school students numbered 20,000, of which 10 percent would enter universities and 26 percent, junior colleges. See John W. Bennett, Herbert Passin, and Robert McKnight, *In Search of Identity: The Overseas Scholar in America and Japan* (Minneapolis: University of Minnesota Press, 1958), 33.
28. The name was taken from the Chinese phrase meaning "studying under adversity and exerting strenuous effort." *Rikikō* is Romanized as *Rikkō* in some works today, but according to the *kana* reading in Shimanuki's writings, he chose the former.
29. Kinmonth, *Self-made Man*, 245.
30. Shimanuki Hyōdayū, *Seikōno hiketsu* (Sendai: Kogando, 1892); Shimanuki, ed., *Jitchi tobei* (Tokyo: Rikikokai, 1905). Some personal stories of Rikikōkai members are included in Kazuo Ito, *Issei: A History of Japanese Immigrants in North America* (Seattle: Executive Committee for Publication of *Issei*, 1973).
31. Shimanuki, *Shintobeihō*, 6–7.
32. The annual wage in 1904 of a Tokyo municipal employee (including the mayor) was 332 yen, less than one yen per day. *Tōkyōshi tōkei nenpyō* (Annual statistics of the city of Tokyo), 1909. In 1914 the monthly salary of a low-level company employee in Tokyo was twenty-five yen, of which, for a family of three, 53 percent was needed for food (Ishizuka, *Tōkyō no shakaikeizaishi*, 260).
33. Shimanuki, *Shintobeihō*, 6–7.
34. *Kodansha Encyclopedia of Japan* (Tokyo: Kodansha, 1983) 6:95–96, 140; 7:86, 99.
35. Shimanuki informs us that "Dr. Harris," "father to the Japanese in the United States," dedicated his life to "ridding the world of evil" after the Civil War (*Tobei shimpō* 1:1 [May 1907], 3). Merriman Colbert Harris (1846–1921) and his wife were Methodist missionaries in Hokkaido and Tokyo. In 1886 they were transferred to work with the Japanese on the Pacific Coast and Hawaii and organized the Pacific Japanese Mission. They returned to Tokyo in 1905 when Harris was appointed bishop of Japan and Korea; he became bishop emeritus in 1916. He was awarded an imperial decoration and lived in Tokyo until his death. *Dictionary of American Biography* (New York: Charles Scribner's Sons, 1946–58), 4:316–17.
36. *Tobei shimpō* 2:1 (15 September 1907), 41–44.
37. Shimanuki, *Saikin seikaku tobei annai*, 103.
38. *Tobei shimpō* 6:10 (15 October 1908).
39. Shimanuki, *Shintobeihō*, 85ff.
40. *Tobei shimpō* 6:9 (15 September 1908).
41. Shimanuki, *Shintobeihō*, 45.
42. *Tobei shimpō* 6:9 (15 September 1908).

43. *Tobei shimpō* 1:1 (May 1907) and 2:1 (15 September 1907). The Kanda district was fast-developing as Tokyo's secondhand bookstore area and remains so today.

44. *Tobei shimpō* 1:1 (15 May 1907), 23–26. Nitobe Inazō (1862–1933) can be considered an archetypal Japanese Christian of this period. He attended Tokyo Imperial University and Johns Hopkins University and later studied in Germany. Under the influence of the Methodist "Dr. Harris," he became a Christian and married a Philadelphia Quaker. He is noted as the leading Christian educator of the Meiji-Taisho period, founder of Tokyo Woman's Christian College (later University), Japanese representative to international conferences, and the only non-Caucasian to hold the high office of undersecretary at the League of Nations. He was author of a number of works on Japan in English, including his famous book on *bushidō* (*Kodansha Encyclopedia* 6:21–22).

45. *Tobei shimpō* 6:9 (15 September 1908), 5.

46. Shimanuki, *Shintobeihō*, 13–14.

47. Sharon L. Sievers, *Flowers in Salt: The Beginnings of Feminist Consciousness in Modern Japan* (Stanford: Stanford University Press, 1983), 104. A higher girls' school law calling for one institution in each prefecture was passed in 1899 (Passin, *Society and Education*, 98). However, it was not until 1911 that an accredited women's college was established. By 1928 there were only 37 colleges for women, as opposed to 222 for men (Hane, *Modern Japan*, 214).

48. However, Japan was not without demonstrations of opposition. The most notable occurred in February 1891, when the Christian pacifist Uchimura Kanzō (1861–1930), a faculty member at the First Higher School in Tokyo, refused to show appropriate obeisance before the document. For some of Uchimura's writings see Ryusaku Tsunoda, Wm. Theodore de Bary, and Donald Keene, comps., *Sources of Japanese Tradition* (New York: Columbia University Press, 1958), 2:340–50.

49. *Tōkyō hyakunenshi* 3: 358–60; Gluck, *Japan's Modern Myths*, 132–35.

50. Hane, *Modern Japan*, 177.

51. Katayama Sen, *Jiden* (Autobiography) (Tokyo: Kaizosha, 1922), 196–255; Sumiya Mikio, *Katayama Sen* (Tokyo: Tokyo daigaku shuppankai, 1977), 9–19; Hyman Kublin, *Asian Revolutionary: The Life of Katayama Sen* (Princeton: Princeton University Press, 1964), 47–87.

52. Kublin, *Asian Revolutionary*, 51.

53. Katayama, *Jiden*, 232–34; 250–51.

54. From an 1897 article by Katayama, quoted in Sumiya, *Katayama Sen*, 15. Katayama wrote in 1896 that strikes were an important "weapon of the working class" but added that "they did not help workers and inflicted great damage." In 1897 he wrote: "The solution to the labor situation lies in workers' education through organizing"; "progress can then be made gradually, and strikes will no longer be necessary" (Sumiya, 48, 50–51).

55. From an 1897 article in a Christian newspaper, quoted in Sumiya, *Katayama Sen*, 40.

56. Katayama Sen, *Tobei annai*, 7. According to Sumiya Mikio, two editions of *Tobei annai* were published: *Gakusei tobei annai* (Students' introduc-

tion to America) in 1901 and *Tobei annai* in 1903. The difference between the two was that the latter edition included a seven-page chapter on Katayama's student days in the United States. The edition I refer to is the latter, even though the publication date is listed as 1901 in the National Diet Library catalog. The catalog also includes two books by Katayama, one on English conversation and composition and the other on business English, letters, and forms, both published in 1897.

57. Quoted in Sumiya, *Katayama Sen*, 137.
58. Ibid., 137; Katayama, *Tobei no hiketsu*, 1.
59. Katayama Sen, *Zoku tobei annai* (Tokyo: Tobei kyokai, 1902).
60. *Tobei zasshi* eventually became *Amerika*.
61. Sumiya, *Katayama Sen*, 143.
62. Ibid., 211–12. He claimed in 1896 to have taken the name Joseph because the Japanese ideographs *Jo-se-fu* meant "the man who saves the world."
63. When *Rōdōsekai* began publication in 1897, Katayama served as secretary of the newly founded Iron Workers' Union, helping to unionize railroad engineers, firemen, plasterers, printers, cargo boat workers, cooks, and furniture makers, among others. He traveled endlessly throughout Japan giving speeches and attending public meetings and conferences. In 1904 he attended the national convention of the American Socialist Party in Chicago and the Sixth Congress of the Second International, Amsterdam, representing the socialists of Japan. See Katayama Sen, *The Labor Movement in Japan* (Chicago: Charles H. Kerr & Co., 1918), 38–84.
64. For instance, Shimanuki's works; Ishizuka Iozō, *Genkon tobei annai* (Introducing contemporary America) (1903); Yamane Goichi, ed., *Saikin tobei annai* (Introducing America today) (Tokyo: Tobei zasshisha, 1906); Katō Jōshirō, *Zaibeidōbō hattenshi* (The history of our compatriots in America) (Tokyo: Hakubunkan, 1908); Tabata Kisaburō, *Zaibeisha seikōno tomo* (Friend of our successful countrymen in America) (Tokyo: Shimizu shoten, 1908); Watanabe Kanjirō, *Kaigai dekasegi annai* (Guide for workers going abroad) (Tokyo: Tokyo naigai shuppankyokai, 1902); Hirata Eishi, *Tobei annai* (Kobe: n.p., 1916); and Iijima Eitarō, *Beikoku tokō annai* (Guide to crossing to America) (Tokyo, 1902).
65. Katayama, *Zoku tobei annai*, 3–5.
66. Ibid., 4; Katayama, *Tobei annai*, 6–7.
67. Katayama, *Zoku tobei annai*, 5.
68. Katayama, *Tobei annai*, 9.
69. Ibid., 6–7.
70. Ibid., 1.
71. Cited in Sumiya, *Katayama Sen*, 141, from Katayama's article of 1902 on population increase and labor.
72. Katayama, *Tobei annai*, 14. The picture is of a farmer with the hem of his work kimono shoved up into his sash, thus exposing his loincloth without shame.
73. For instance, "Hints for Those Going to America" paved the way for proper behavior: Be back in the hotel before midnight; no noise; don't go out of your room in nightclothes; draw your blinds; no spitting; keep the buttons

on your pants closed; be on time—Americans hate lateness; on visits cut your nails and comb your hair; and so on (Hirata, *Tobei annai*, 49–50).

74. Katayama, *Jiden*, 262.
75. Katayama, *Tobei annai*, 41.
76. Ibid., 21–24.
77. Katayama, *Jiden*, 234–36.
78. Katayama, *Tobei annai*, 24–36.
79. The 33rd Fruit Growers' Convention Proceedings of 1907 described Asians as "well-adapted to that particular form of labor to which so many white men object" (Fisher, *Harvest Labor Market*, 16). Sacramento rice farmer and state senator John P. Irish wrote about the harvest of "low growing field crops" and fruit: "[They] call for reliable labor, resistant to climatic conditions and able to sustain the stopping posture. . . . [T]he short-backed, short-legged Asiatics have proved reliable in all this squat work which must be performed in a temperature of 100 to 110 degrees" (Irish, "Reasons for Encouraging Japanese Immigration," *The Annals* 34 [September 1909]).
80. Katayama, *Tobei no hiketsu*, 5–13.
81. Cited in Sumiya, *Katayama Sen*, 140–41.
82. William Jewitt Tucker (1839–1926) was professor of sacred rhetoric at Andover from 1880. His particular concern was with the social responsibilities of the church, in connection with which he developed courses in sociology and founded Andover House, a settlement that influenced Katayama deeply. Tucker's participation in the publishing of the *Andover Review* attracted the attention of the conservative wing of Congregationalism, and he and four other professors were tried and acquitted before a board of the seminary. In 1893 he became president of Dartmouth College (*Dictionary of American Biography*, 10:41–42).
83. On Katayama's description of Northfield and Moody see *Jiden*, 238–42. Dwight Lyman Moody (1837–1899) began his evangelistic career when he organized a sabbath school over a city market in Chicago. He eventually devoted his life to evangelical and philanthropic work, working with soldiers during the Civil War, then traveled throughout the British Isles, the United States, and Canada, using Northfield, Massachusetts, as his base of operation. His first conference for male college students, in 1886, was so well-attended that he decided to hold it annually. Similar conferences for women occurred beginning in 1893 (*Dictionary of American Biography*, 7:103–6).
84. Sumiya, *Katayama Sen*, 20–23; Kublin, *Asian Revolutionary*, 75–82.
85. Katayama, *Jiden*, 251–72. Katayama described Glasgow, with its razed slums, city-run tenements, city-owned water system, and rent for workers at 20 percent of their wages, as a "supreme model" of city reform.
86. Katayama wrote in his autobiography many years later that Maryville was a "fourth or fifth-rate institution" built for blacks and poor whites. Blacks could be enrolled, although "unenthusiastically," and were not treated equally (*Jiden*, 216).
87. Katayama, *Tobei annai*, 60; *Jiden*, 196.
88. Katayama, *Tobei annai*, 49. Niishima Jō (1843–1890), one of the earliest Christian leaders, left Japan on an American whaling ship before the seclu-

sion laws were lifted. Befriended by the captain, who took him to New England, he attended Amherst College and Andover Theological Seminary. After returning to Japan, he became a Congregational minister and founded Dōshisha English Language School (later University) in Kyoto in 1875, the first Christian institution founded by a Japanese. See Chitoshi Yanaga, *Japan Since Perry* (New York: McGraw-Hill, 1949), 34 and 126.

89. Tabata, *Zaibeisha seikō no tomo*, 30.

90. Kinmonth, *Self-made Man*, 191–92.

91. The Russo-Japanese War and the Japanese government's suppression of the antiwar and social-democratic *Heimin shimbun* (Commoners' newspaper) in 1905 directly influenced Kōtoku's conversion to anarchism. Until then he was a pacifist and believed in socialism through electoral action. In 1910 he was arrested as the leader of a plot to assassinate the emperor, tried secretly, and executed the following year with eleven others, including his lover, Kanno Suga, the first woman to be executed as a political prisoner in Meiji Japan. See Masamichi Asukai, "Kōtoku Shūsui and His Socialism and Pacifism," in Nobuya Bamba and John F. Howes, eds., *Pacifism in Japan* (Tokyo: Minerva Press, 1978), 123–41; and *Tōkyō hyakunenshi*, 3:1194–1202. For a biography of Kōtoku see Fred Notehelfer, *Kotoku Shusui: Portrait of a Japanese Radical* (Cambridge, England: Cambridge University Press, 1971). On Kanno Suga see Sievers, *Flowers in Salt*, chapter 7, and Mikiso Hane, ed. and trans., *Reflections on the Way to the Gallows: Rebel Women in Prewar Japan* (Berkeley: University of California Press, 1988), chapter 3.

92. "At the time propaganda for a pure and simple trade union movement was more and more severely dealt with by the authorities, our labor politics and Socialist agitation had comparative freedom and was rather popular among the people" (Katayama, *The Labor Movement in Japan*, 62–63).

93. Raising rice in Texas interested Katayama as early as 1902. He wrote in *Zoku tobei annai* that production and profits were high and that "because there are many uneducated black wretches ... loathed by whites, Japanese workers would be welcome" (Katayama, *Zoku tobei annai*, 6).

94. Quoted in Sumiya, *Katayama Sen*, 154–55, from Kawakami Kiyoshi, "Japanese on American Farms," *The Independent*, 26 October 1905.

95. *Japanese-American Commercial Weekly*, 26 May 1906. The news item stated that Okazaki Jōkichi, Katayama's partner, raised 200,000 yen with the "wealthy merchant" Iwasaki and planned to establish an agricultural company and promote Texas agriculture for those with 1,000 yen or more as capital. Katayama was not mentioned. On the Texas enterprise, see also Sumiya, *Katayama Sen*, 152–58, and Kublin, *Asian Revolutionary*, 193–94. Sumiya, referring to a San Francisco Japanese newspaperman's account, wrote that the partner appeared in San Francisco with "twenty-some-odd agricultural workers," but the San Francisco immigration officials, suspecting that they were contract laborers, refused to let them proceed to Texas. Kublin, quoting from the same account, wrote that Katayama's partner engaged in a "fraudulent scheme" of promising but not providing Japanese immigrant laborers and ran off with the money. In any case, the venture was fraught with conflict and trouble.

96. Sumiya, *Katayama Sen*, 54, citing Katayama's 1898 article, "To Capitalists."

97. Documents made public in 1963 proved this to be part of an official conspiracy to ban the activities of socialists, anarchists, and social reformers (Asukai, "Kōtoku Shūsui," 123).

98. Watanabe Haruo, *Katayama Sen to tomoni* [ith Katayama Sen] (Tokyo: Wakosha, 1955), 17–84, centers on the writer's friendship with Katayama, socialism, and Japanese socialists in New York City.

99. Kublin, *Asian Revolutionary*, 46.

100. Sumiya, *Katayama Sen*, 224.

101. Ibid., 237.

102. Katayama, *Tobei annai*, 2–3.

103. Ibid., 4–5.

104. Sumiya, *Katayama Sen*, 139.

105. *Tobei shimpō* 1:1 (May 1907), 2.

106. Ishizuka, *Genkon tobei annai*, 5–6.

107. *Nihonteikoku tōkei nenkan* (Annual statistics of the empire of Japan), 1907.

108. *Seikō* 4:6 (1 June 1904), 31.

109. Mark R. Peattie, "Introduction," in Ramon H. Myers and Mark R. Peattie, eds., *The Japanese Colonial Empire, 1895–1945* (Princeton: Princeton University Press, 1984), 13–15.

110. Katō Jūshirō, *Zaibeidōbō hattenshi*, 21–22.

111. Masuji Miyakawa, *Life of Japan* (New York: Baker and Taylor, 1907), 300–1.

112. Miyakawa Setsurō, *Beikoku no uraomote* (America inside and outside) (Tokyo: Kobundo, 1920), 124–27.

113. In its article on Japan's imperialist expansionism, *Seikō* portrayed pre-Sino-Japanese War attitudes toward China and its culture as deference, for it was "our mother country which we followed as our model." However, after the war an ideological turnabout occurred, and "what we had called *Chūkajin* [people of the middle kingdom] became *chanchan bōzu* [an offensive term comparable to "Chinaman"] or went so far as to refer to them as *tonbikan* [pigtail Chinese]." Japan had won victory in the "competition for power." See *Seikō* 4:6 (1 June 1904), 30.

Chapter 7

1. Mr. Sano to Florence Egnus, 27 May 1925, *Honpōjinmibun oyobi seikō-chōsa zakken bessatsu: zaigai honpōjin* (Miscellaneous documents concerning status, character, and conduct of Japanese citizens: citizens abroad), vol. 1 (unbound) 1921–1926, (hereafter cited as *Honpōjinmibun*), RG 3.8.8.22, DFMJ.

2. Japanese Consul General, New York, to Foreign Ministry, Tokyo, 23 April 1925, *Honpōjinmibun*.

3. Japanese law required citizens who came to the United States to register at their local Japanese consular office within seven days of their arrival. This

entitled them to receive a certificate of residency. See chapter 3 herein regarding the establishment of the registration system. Kenzō probably received special treatment, for he had been in the United States since 1920.

4. Itō Kenzō, Statement [1925], *Honpōjinmibun*.

5. Ibid.

6. Frank S. Egnus, Statement, 14 April 1925, *Honpōjinmibun*.

7. Itō Chūzō, Statement, 9 June 1925, *Honpōjinmibun*.

8. Saitō Hiroshi, Japanese Consul General, New York, Statement, 18 November 1925, *Honpōjinmibun*.

9. Japanese Consul General to Foreign Ministry, 23 April 1925; Frank S. Egnus, Statement, 14 April 1925, *Honpōjinmibun*.

10. Saitō Hiroshi, Statement, 18 November 1925, *Honpōjinmibun*.

11. "Egnus gave publicity to the Hearst papers." Japanese Consul General, New York, to Foreign Ministry, 23 April 1925, *Honpōjinmibun*.

12. Saitō Hiroshi, Statement, 18 November 1925, *Honpōjinmibun*.

13. Mr. Sano to Florence Egnus, 27 May 1925, *Honpōjinmibun*.

14. New York Consul General, Statement, 22 September 1926, *Honpōjinmibun*.

15. Contract, 28 September 1926, *Honpōjinmibun*.

16. *Kosekihō ni yori zaigaihonpōjin shotodokesho sono honsekichi kosekiri e sōtatsu no ikken* (Documents concerning notices filed by citizens abroad to be sent to honseki areas according to koseki law), 43 unbound vols., 1909–1921, RG 3.8.7.21, DFMJ. Of the 756 notices, 392 were births and 252 deaths. We can assume that not all the marriages of the Japanese in New York were filed with the consular offices. Nevertheless, in relation to the population, the total was small.

17. In some cases, the wife's full name is recorded, giving us a picture of a wide range of ethnic backgrounds: Ingrid Nelson, Jeanette Stone, Ethel McIntyre, Frieda Olsen, Isabella Orozco, Emily Grey, Hilda Sand, among others. One recorded marriage was between a Japanese woman and a Caucasian male.

18. The ban was issued on 25 February 1921. Katō Bungo, *Saikin no zaibeidōbō* (Tokyo: Nippontosho shuppankyokai, 1921), 322.

19. Two years later in September 1922, Congress passed a law that stripped all female U.S. citizens of their citizenship if they married males ineligible for naturalization—anyone who was not white or African (*Statutes at Large* 42, part 1 [1922]: 1021–22). Kenzō and Florence's marriage occurred in 1923, which indicates that Florence could have been temporarily stateless until the divorce.

20. Glenn, *Issei Nisei*, 31.

21. Katō Bungo, *Saikin no zaibeidōbō* (Recent Japanese citizens residing in America) (1921).

22. *Tobei shimpō* 1:2 (June 1907). For popular accounts of New York see also *Tobei shimpō* 2:1 (15 September 1907); Okamoto, *Nyūyōkushi naigai no jisho;* "Nyūyōku," *Amerika* 11:11 (November 1907), 27–30; "Amerika no tabiji" (Traveling in America), *Amerika* 11:12 (December 1907), 22–25.

23. Mori Ōgai, "Under Reconstruction," trans. and ed. Ivan Morris, *Modern Japanese Stories* (Tokyo: Charles E. Tuttle, 1962), 35–44. Ōgai graduated from the medical department of Tokyo University in 1881, entered the army

as a surgeon, and from 1884 to 1888 was sent to Germany as a medical student. His years in Germany served as the basis for three novels. Considered one of the outstanding Meiji literary figures, he is known not only for his fiction but also as a theater and art critic, innovator, essayist, poet, translator (including works by Goethe, Schiller, Hans Christian Andersen, Washington Irving, Bret Harte, Tolstoy, and Turgenev), and medical practitioner. *Nihon kindaibungaku daijiten* (Encyclopedia of modern Japanese literature) (Tokyo: Kodansha, 1978), 3:364–67.

24. Ōgai, "Under Reconstruction," 43.

25. Ōgai's *Maihime* (Dancing girl), written in 1890, tells the story of a young Japanese student in Germany who falls in love and lives with a German entertainer, Elis. She goes insane after he decides to resume his life in Japan. See Masao Miyoshi's discussion of Ōgai's *Maihime* and the traveling abroad of nascent elites of modern Japan (Miyoshi, *Accomplices of Silence*, 1974, 38–43). Nakamura Mitsuo considered *Maihime* to be Ōgai's "most important" work (*Nihon no kindai shōsetsu*, 65–68).

26. Richard John Bowring, *Mori Ogai and the Modernization of Japanese Culture* (Cambridge: Cambridge University Press, 1979), 47–55.

27. Quoted in ibid., 50–51.

28. Yanagita, *Meiji Taishōshi*, 2:33–60.

29. Anne Walthall stated that marriages tended to "enforce economic divisions and social distinctions": "rich married rich, poor married poor." In China, by contrast, women often married into families of higher position, which could be disadvantageous for the young brides (Walthall, "The Life Cycle of Farm Women in Tokugawa Japan," in Gail Lee Bernstein, ed., *Recreating Japanese Women*, 53–54).

30. Yanagita, *Meiji Taishōshi*, 2:33. Yanagita wrote of pre-Meiji marriage practices in a general way, but differences existed according to locality. The section on love and marriage implies a great deal of individual choice in the selection of a spouse, something that bears careful interpretation. It was true that pre-Meiji courtship practices in some localities accorded more freedom to young people, but the role of the family was primary. This was true particularly in areas where family holdings were small and solidarity and cooperation were necessary for survival. Nevertheless, Yanagita's role as a folk anthropologist and participant during the Meiji transitional period render his observations extremely valuable. See also Walthall, "Farm Women," 50–52; Tadashi Fukutake, *Japanese Rural Society* (Ithaca: Cornell University Press, 1972), 39–41; Ronald P. Dore, *Shinohata: A Portrait of a Japanese Village* (New York: Pantheon, 1978), 166; and, for an examination of marriage customs among rural families in the 1930s, Robert J. Smith and Ella Lury Wiswell, *The Women of Suye Mura* (Chicago: University of Chicago Press, 1982), chapter 7.

31. Yanagita, *Meiji Taishōshi*, 2:36. See also Komobuchi Midori, "Haigūsha no sentaku to kekkon" (Spouse selection and marriage), in Kamiko Takeji and Masuda Kōkichi, eds., *Nihonjin no kazokukankei* (Japanese family relationships) (Tokyo: Yuhikakusensho, 1981), 34. Ezra Vogel stated that with the "possible exception of the European Jews, no other industrialized society" had "marriage-arranging in large segments of the population." See "The Go-Between in a Developing Society: The Case of the Japanese Marriage Ar-

ranger," in George K. Yamamoto and Tsuyoshi Ishida, eds., *Selected Readings on Modern Japanese Society* (Berkeley: McCutchan Publishing, 1971), 12.

32. Eric Hobsbawm, "Introduction: Inventing Traditions," in Eric Hobsbawm and Terence Ranger, eds., *The Invention of Tradition* (Cambridge: Cambridge University Press, 1983; paperback reprint, 1985), 1. Hobsbawm mentioned Japan: "A 'modernization' which maintained the old ordering of social subordination (possibly with some well-judged invention of tradition) was not theoretically inconceivable, but apart from Japan it is difficult to think of an example of practical success." (Hobsbawm, "Mass-Producing Traditions: Europe, 1870-1914," in Hobsbawm and Ranger, 266).

33. Hobsbawm, "Inventing Traditions," 4.

34. Sharon H. Nolte and Sally Ann Hastings, "The Meiji State's Policy Toward Women, 1890-1910," in Bernstein, ed., *Recreating Japanese Women*, 151-54. The authors challenged the heretofore widely held view that Japanese women's inferior role was merely a continuation of the feudal patriarchy of the earlier period in this important examination of the politics of gender construction.

35. Yanagita, *Meiji Taishōshi*, 2:37.

36. Nolte and Hastings, "Policy Toward Women," 151-74. See also Sievers, *Flowers in Salt*, 110-11. On family systems see Seiichi Kitano, "*Dōzoku* and *Ie* in Japan: The Meaning of Family Genealogical Relationships," in Robert J. Smith and Richard K. Beardsley, eds., *Japanese Culture: Its Development and Characteristics* (Chicago: Aldine Publishing Co., 1962, reprint), especially 42-44; and Dore, *City Life*, chapter 8. On transformation of family see Takashi Koyama, "Changing Family Structure in Japan," in Smith and Beardsley, eds.

37. Yanagita, *Meiji Taishōshi*, 2:42.

38. Ibid., 41.

39. Ibid., 42.

40. Baroness Shidzué Ishimoto, *Facing Two Ways: The Story of My Life* (Stanford: Stanford University Press, 1984; first published, 1935), 104-8.

41. Ibid., 107.

42. Ibid., 102. Ishimoto divorced her husband after years of incompatibility. She lived independently and participated in social reform movements that advocated birth control, women's rights, and opposition to Japan's efforts during World War II. In 1944 she remarried a socialist activist with whom she had been working closely. In 1946, using her new name, Katō Shidzué, and running on the Socialist Party ticket, she was elected to the lower house in the first election in Japan in which women cast votes (Barbara Molony, "Afterword," Ishimoto, *Facing Two Ways*, xxiv-xxv).

43. Etsu Inagaki Sugimoto, *A Daughter of the Samurai* (New York: Doubleday & Page, 1925), 53-58.

44. Ibid., 56. The official introductory meeting between prospective couples was not arranged until after extensive investigation by the families through the go-between. Refusal after this meeting meant a serious and major blow to the prestige and status of the rebuffed party. The Inagaki family chose to rectify their son's dishonorable actions by inviting the young woman (who was legally no longer a member of her father's family) to remain in their home until they were able to find a suitable husband for her.

45. Yanagita, *Meiji Taishōshi*, 2:42.

46. Bowring, *Mori Ogai*, 58–59. The average divorce rate in Japan from 1882, when statistics became available, to 1899, the year following the promulgation of the Civil Code, was 2.82 per 1,000 population. Thereafter, the rate steadily decreased. The statistics reflected legal divorces only, however, and not extralegal separations such as expulsion or abandonment of wives or common-law divorces. The divorce rate in Japan was consistently higher than in the United States until 1917. Following that year, the Japanese rate continued to decrease while the American rate rose. Tokuoka Hideo, "Rikon to kodomo" [divorce and children], in Kamiko and Masuda, eds., *Nihonjin no kazokukankei*, 81–82.

47. Bowring, *Mori Ogai*, 107–8. The tensions between mothers and daughters-in-law found their way into fiction in a number of stories, including Ōgai's *Hannichi* (Half a day), published in 1909, and the popular *Hototogisu* (The cricket) by Tokutomi Roka (Tokyo: Iwanami shoten, 1938), first published as a newspaper serial in 1898–99 and subsequently as a book in 1900. It had more than 100 printings.

48. Yanagita, writing in 1930, informed us that couples in some rural areas still followed old customs, such as living apart (the wife may remain at her parents' home in a separate area, with the husband visiting during holidays) or in community lodgings for newlyweds established by the village. These meant that the "bride was not greeted to be positioned under her mother-in-law's knee" (Yanagita, *Meiji Taishōshi*, 2:37–38).

49. Nakamura Masanao, "Creating Good Mothers" (1875), trans. William Reynold Braisted, *Meiroku Zasshi: Journal of the Japanese Enlightenment* (Cambridge: Harvard University Press, 1976), 401–4. Articles in the short-lived *Meiroku zasshi* (1874–75) were written by leading liberals who became active as leaders of Meiji intellectual society after its publication ceased.

50. Nakamura, "Good Mothers," 403.

51. *Seikō* 7:5 (1 October 1905), 31–32.

52. *Seikō*, 18:5 (1 June 1910), 47–53.

53. Ibid., 55–56.

54. Under the Civil Code, married women could not institute independent suits nor manage their own financial affairs. Women were punished for adultery, but men were not (Sievers, *Flowers in Salt*, 111). Sievers's study charted the course of Meiji feminist consciousness, which challenged contemporary policies and acceptance of the ryōsai kenbo formula.

55. Sievers, *Flowers in Salt*, 110.

56. Tōson, *The Family*, 225.

57. Ibid., 178.

58. Yanabu, *Honyakugo seiritsujijō*, chapter 5.

59. Ibid., 91.

60. Ibid., 93.

61. Ibid., 93–94.

62. Ibid., 94.

63. Ibid., 103.

64. Dore, *City Life in Japan*, 158.

65. See Herman R. Lantz, "Romantic Love in the Pre-Modern Period: A Social Commentary," *Journal of Social History* 15:3 (Spring 1982), 349–70. Lantz criticized the modernization theory, which views romantic love as growing out of "value pluralism" and the destruction of the "economic and sustenance functions of the home." Charting love from ancient Rome to seventeenth- and eighteenth-century America, he pointed to its emergence as a reaction to the status quo and denied that romantic love was a modern sociological phenomenon that based family integration on the "affectual [romantic] ties between husband and wife."

66. Yanabu, *Honyakugo seiritsujijō*, 105.

67. Tayama Katai, *Futon* (The quilt) (Tokyo: Iwanami shoten, 1972).

68. Donald Keene wrote that *Futon* changed the course of Japanese literature. It was an early confessional novel, which became an important genre following the Russo-Japanese War. Although it had many "novelistic faults," its "extraordinary success . . . was inescapably bound to the nonliterary fact that it was an undisguised confession by a rather well-known author." See Keene, *Dawn to the West: Japanese Literature of the Modern Era: Fiction* (New York: Holt, Rinehart & Winston, 1984), 246–47. James Fujii, in *Complicit Fictions*, took issue with orthodox views of Japan's modern novels as essentially privatized "confessionals" born of the Western "ideal of individualism." He challenged "a solidly entrenched genealogy of Western Japanology" and read the novels as products that writers shared with their literary colleagues, "born of their disjunction from society," a "result of the social pressures of everyday Japanese life." See especially "Introduction." See also Miyoshi, *Accomplices of Silence*, chapter 1, "The New Language."

69. Katai, *Futon*, 12. See chapter 5 herein for discussion of *Konjikiyasha*.

70. Katai, *Futon*, 13.

71. Ibid., 13–14.

72. Murakami Nobuhiko writes that themes of "agony" in Meiji literature never condemned the family system. See *Meiji joseishi* (History of Meiji women), (Tokyo: Rironsha, 1972), 3:146–54.

73. Masuji Miyakawa, *Powers of the American People*, rev. (New York: Baker & Taylor, 1908), 36.

74. Miyakawa, *Life of Japan*, 70. In this book also, Miyakawa presented an accepting, uncritical, and grateful portrayal of the United States, praising its "unselfish philanthropy and conscientious fidelity" toward Japan after Perry. U.S. support of Japan in the Russo-Japanese War signified that the United States was the "foster-mother" of Japan (Ibid., 139–76).

75. Miyakawa, *Powers*, 36.

76. Miyakawa, *Life of Japan*, 69.

77. Sugimoto, *Daughter*, 120.

78. Ibid., 139.

79. Ibid., 226.

80. Ibid., 189.

81. Although there are no dates that would inform the reader of the precise chronology of Sugimoto's life, she was born "not so long after" the Meiji Restoration in 1868. Her marriage probably occurred around 1890 or

1891, so her second trip to the United States was sometime around 1905–10.

82. Tōson, *Family*, 62.

83. For instance, Mizutani Tomotsune, *Beikoku tsūkan* (A survey of America) (Tokyo: Yuhikaku shobo, 1900); Matsui Hakken, *Beikoku manyūzakki* (A notebook from an American tour) (Tokyo: Hakubunkan, 1901); Abe Isō, *Fujin no risō* (The ideal woman) (Tokyo: Hakubunkan, 1910); Harada Tōichirō, *Nyūyōku* (New York) (1912); Uemura Tsutomu[?], *Beikoku jijō: tobeisha hikkei* (The situation in America: A handbook for people crossing to America) (Tokyo: Naigai shuppankai, 1912); Masaoka Yūichi, *Beikoku oyobi beikokujin* (America and Americans) (1913); Kawaguchi Yoshihisa, *Amerika seikatsu*, (Life in America) (Tokyo: Tada shoboten, 1920); Sasaki Shigetsu, *Beikokuo hōrōshite* (Wandering in America) (1921); Nakane Sōkai, *Seiyō no onna* (Women of the West) (Tokyo: Chobunsha, 1924).

84. Nakane, *Seiyō no onna*, 12.

85. Kawaguchi, *Amerika seikatsu*, 403.

86. Matsui, *Beikoku manyūzakki*, 86.

87. Ibid., 90.

88. Harada, *Nyūyōku*, 282–86.

89. Uemura, *Beikoku jijō: tobeisha hikkei*, 86.

90. Ibid., 95.

91. Donald Keene quoted Kafū's description of his father's routine after returning home from work. He relaxed by changing into a maroon smoking jacket and smoking an English pipe: "I frequently had occasion to reflect ... on what a large number of peculiar objects my father owned" (*Dawn to the West*, 388). The observation is similar to the instructions given to male readers by an 1898 article quoted in Chapter 4 herein.

92. Keene, *Dawn to the West*, 388.

93. Ibid., 390–91.

94. In 1902 and 1903 Kafū published essays on and translations of Zola's novels (which he first read in English translation) as well as a summary translation of *Nana* (Ōkubo Takaki, *Yume to seijuku: bungakuteki seiyōzō no henbō* [From dreams to maturity: the transformation of the Western image in literature] [Tokyo: Kodansha, 1979], 75). Edward G. Seidensticker has introduced a number of Kafū's later works, results of his eventual retreat from both kindai Japan and the West and immersion into the culture of old Edo, the subject matter for his most noted writings.

95. Ōkubo, *Yume to seijuku*, 80–81.

96. Ibid., 77–79.

97. Kafū, *Amerika monogatari*, vol. 3: *Nagai Kafū zenshū* (Complete works of Nagai Kafū) (Tokyo: Chuokoronsha, 1949). After he returned to Japan Kafū also wrote *Furansu monotagari* (Stories from France) based on his eleven months in France.

98. Ōkubo, *Yume to seijuku*, 76.

99. Ibid., 67–71.

100. Ibid., 88.

101. Keene, *Dawn to the West*, 399.

102. Ibid., 400 and Ōkubo, *Yume to seijuku*, 66.

103. Ōkubo, *Yume to seijuku*, 87. The initiation of the Russo-Japanese War peace talks "stirred activity" in the Japanese embassy, necessitating the hiring of "one clerk of honest character." See Nagai Kafū, *Seiyō nisshi shō* (Diary of my trip to the west, abridged), vol. 3: *Nagai Kafū zenshū*, 386.

104. In his diary Kafū tells us about hearing *Carmen* "for the fourth time," his excitement over hearing Wagner, Verdi, Saint Saens, Debussy, and seeing Sarah Bernhardt. At one point he was warned by a friend about rumors of his dismissal from the bank because of his "inappropriate" and "unworldly behavior" (Kafū, *Seiyō nisshi*, 413).

105. Kafū, *Amerika monogatari*, 117–18.

106. "Rokugatsu no yoru no yume" (A dream one night in June), *Amerika Monogatari*, 343–69.

107. Ibid., 354.

108. Ibid., 355.

109. Ibid., 356.

110. Kafū, *Seiyō nisshi*, 410.

111. Kafū, "Rokugatsu no yoru," 357.

112. Kafū writes about his affair with Edith in his diary but not in *Amerika monogatari*. Likewise, Rosalind only appears in the short story in *Amerika monogatari* and not in his diary.

113. Kafū, *Amerika monogatari*, 262–63.

114. Ibid.

Chapter 8

1. *New York Times*, 20 February 1994.

2. See Mary Yoko Brannen, " 'Bwana Mickey': Constructing Cultural Consumption at Tokyo Disneyland," in Amy Kaplan and Donald E. Pease, eds., *Cultures of United States Imperialism* (Durham, NC: Duke University Press, 1993), 617–34. This essay interprets Tokyo's Disneyland, an "exact replica" of Disneyland in California, and looks at how American symbols have been adapted to a Japanese cultural context.

3. The concept of "Occidentalism" is discussed by Sadik Jalal al-'Azm in "Orientalism and Orientalism in Reverse," *Khamsim* 8 (1981), 5–26, and in Deborah Gewertz and Frederick Errington, "We Think Therefore They Are? On Occidentalizing the World," *Anthropological Quarterly* 64:2 (April 1991), 80–91. I am indebted to Ali Mirsepassi for bringing these articles to my attention.

4. Edward W. Said, *Orientalism* (New York: Vintage, 1979).

5. See John W. Dower, *War Without Mercy: Race and Power in the Pacific War* (New York: Pantheon, 1986).

6. See Benedict Anderson, *Imagined Communities*, rev. (New York: Verso, 1991).

7. Renato Rosaldo, *Culture and Truth: The Remaking of Social Analysis* (New York: Beacon, 1993), 102–3.

8. Roland Robertson, "Mapping the Global Condition: Globalization as the Central Concept," in Mike Featherstone, ed., *Global Culture: Nationalism, Globalization and Modernity* (London: Sage Publications, 1990), 21. Robertson's analysis was based on the premise that the agents of the "structuration of the world" are participant societies ("relevant collective actors").

9. Ibid., 28 (ital. in original).

10. Mike Featherstone, "Global Culture: An Introduction," in Featherstone, ed., *Global Culture*, 1-2.

11. Ibid., 12.

12. Masao Miyoshi and H. D. Harootunian, "Introduction," in Miyoshi and Harootunian, eds., *Postmodernism and Japan, South Atlantic Quarterly* 87:3 (Summer 1988), 390. The essay discussed postmodernism's relation (or avowed nonrelation) to politics and how Japan is positioned in the analysis.

13. See Rosaldo, "Imperialist Nostalgia," in *Culture and Truth*, 68-87. Japan escaped political and territorial colonization by the West (although the post–World War II period can be interpreted as such a time), but the longing for "authentic" and "traditional" forms of culture—flower arrangement, tea ceremony, reticence and hesitation in social behavior, and the like—remain as part of the nostalgic Occidental gaze.

14. *Hearts and Minds*, 1974; Karel van Wolferen, *The Enigma of Japanese Power* (New York: Alfred A. Knopf, 1989), 1.

Appendix

1. Of the 154,802 Japanese in California in 1908 who cultivated land, 94,008 came from the southern and western prefectures of Hiroshima, Wakayama, Fukuoka, and Kumamoto. Yosaburo Yoshida, "Sources and Causes of Japanese Emigration," *The Annals* 34:2 (September 1909): 161.

2. The honseki system was originally codified in the seventh century with a Kosekihō (household registry law) as a comprehensive means to assess and tax the population. The practice continued with various alterations and modifications, depending on who was in power. In 1872, the Meiji government established the system designating the family as the legal unit, then in 1898 passed the Kosekihō as a supplement to the Civil Code. Family members were listed in the koseki (household registry) with their relationship to the head of the family. When a son married, his wife's name was added to his koseki and deleted from the koseki of her family of birth. Each family's koseki, which contained information about honseki, was placed with the ken or fu administrative office. The system was a means of identification and gave state sanction to the family as the unit of management, unity, and control.

3. Legally, under the 1872 koseki law, if an individual lived away from his or her honseki for ninety days or more, a notice of temporary residence had to be filed with the government offices in the new area. Three types of temporary residence notices were supposed to take care of every conceivable contingency. However, this system could not work unless all persons moving from their

honseki filed notices each time they moved. Individual neglect rendered it a less-than-foolproof system. Census-taking was based on honseki counts and was tabulated from the records in government administrative offices until 1920, when the National Census Act was passed. As late as 1914, the government used the temporary residence notices to readjust population figures. Itō Shigeru, "Senzen nihon no toshi seichō" (Japan's prewar urban growth), *Nippon rōdōkyōkai zasshi* 24:7 and 8 (July and August 1982), 26–34, 23–37.

4. *Tōkyōshi tōkei nenpyō*, 1924.
5. Gluck, *Japan's Modern Myths*, 33 and 159.
6. *Ryokenkafu shutsugan ni yōsuru zaigaikōkan hakkyū kakushu shōmeishokōfu jinmeihyō* (List of persons issued official certificates by overseas consular offices for passport applications), *Nyūyōku no bu* (New York section), 2 vols., 1912–1924, RG 3.8.2.283, DFMJ.
7. Although the "miscellaneous" category included merchants and dealers as well as laborers and farmers, merchants and dealers made up only 2.5 percent. Kessner, *The Golden Door*, 33–34.
8. Wakatsuki, "Japanese Emigration," 489.
9. Ichihashi, *The Japanese*, 73.
10. *Kosekihō ni yori zaigaihonpōjin shotodokesho sono honsekichi kosekiri e sōtatsu no ikken* (Documents concerning notices filed by citizens abroad to be sent to household registry officials in registered family domicile areas according to honseki registry law), *Nyūyōku sōryōjikan toriatsukai no bu* (New York Consulate General Section), 43 vols., 1909–1921, RG 3.8.7.21, DFMJ. The New York Consul General recorded 756 births, deaths, marriages, or divorces of 533 citizens. The reports listed each citizen's name, honseki, type of notice (birth, death, etc.), name of new entry, and in the case of some births, name, gender, and ranking of child (first, second, etc.).
11. *Ryokenkafu shutsugan ni yōsuru zaigaikōkan hakkyū kakushu shōmeishokōfu jinmeihyō* (List of persons issued official certificates by overseas consular offices for passport applications), *Nyūyōku no bu* (New York section), 1912–1924, 2 vols., RG 3.8.2.283, DFMJ. Information sent to the Foreign Ministry included name, honseki, date of certificate, imin/hi-imin category, reason for certificate (travel, readmission, bringing relatives or employees), and the name of the person being brought to the U.S.
12. Mizutani, *Nyūyōku nihonjin hattenshi*.

Sources Consulted

Primary.

1. JAPAN. GOVERNMENT DOCUMENTS.

A. *Diplomatic Record Center, Foreign Ministry of Japan, Tokyo.*

Beikoku ni okeru hainichimondai zakken. Nyōyōkushū hainichi kankei (Miscellaneous documents concerning anti-Japanese problem in the United States: New York state). 1915. Record Group (hereafter, RG) 3.8.2.288.

Gaikoku zairyū teikoku shinmin tōroku kankei zakken (Miscellaneous documents regarding the registration of imperial citizens residing abroad). 1910. RG 3.8.2.268.

Gaikoku zairyū teikoku shinmin tōroku kisokuseitei narabini kaiseijisshi ikken (Documents regarding the enactment and revised enforcement of the registration regulation of imperial citizens residing abroad). 1908–1910. RG 3.8.7.20.

Hi-imin kankei zakken (Miscellaneous documents regarding hi-imin). 1924–1925. RG 3.8.3.1.

Hokubeigasshūkoku ni okeru honpōjin tokōseigen oyobi haiseki ikken (Records concerning travel restriction and exclusion of Japanese citizens in the United States). 19 unbound vols. 1891–1912. RG 3.8.2.21.

Honpōjinmibun oyobi seikōchōsa zakken bessatsu: zaigai honpōjin (Miscellaneous documents concerning status, character, and conduct of Japanese citizens: citizens abroad). Vol. 1 (unbound). 1921–1926. RG 3.8.8.22.

Kaigai ryokenkafu hennōhyō shintatsu (Passports issued and returned for travel abroad). 204 unbound vols. 1879–1921. RG 3.8.5.8.

Kaigai ryokenkisoku ihan zakken (Miscellaneous documents on overseas passport regulation violations). 4 unbound vols. 1900–1915. RG 3.8.5.21.

Kosekihō ni yori zaigaihonpōjin shotodokesho sono honsekichi kosekiri e sōtatsu no ikken (Documents concerning notices filed by citizens abroad to be sent to household registry officials in registered family domicile areas according to household registry law). 43 unbound vols. 1909–1921. RG 3.8.7.21.

Nihonjin kika ishi todoke ni kanshi zainyūyōku ryōji yori gujō ikken (Report from New York consul concerning notices of intentions of naturalization). 1905. RG 3.8.7.15.

Nyūyōku ryōjikan hōkokusho (Reports of the New York consul general). Vol. 4 (Unbound). *Shisatsuhōkoku* (Investigative report). 1902. RG 6.1.6.6.

Ryokenhōki oyobi dōhōki toriatsukai tetsuzuki ni kansuru kunrei shireizai ryoken kafu torishimari zakken (Miscellaneous documents supervising instructions and orders concerning passport regulations and procedures for adherence to said regulations). 1911–1912. RG 3.8.5.11.

Ryokenkafu shutsugan ni yōsuru zaigaikōkan hakkyū kakushu shōmeishokōfu jinmeihyō (List of persons issued official certificates by overseas consular offices for passport applications). *Nyūyōku no bu* (New York section). 2 vols. 1912–1924. RG 3.8.2.283.

Teikoku kokuseki kankei zakken (Documents regarding imperial citizenship). 1924–1926. RG 3.8.7.28.

Zaibei nihonjinkai seigansho shintatsu no ken (Regarding submission of written petition by the Japanese Association of America). 4 December 1911. *Kaigai tokō kankei zakken* (Miscellaneous documents concerning travel abroad). Vol. 6 (unbound).

Zaigai honpōjin mibun kankei zakken (Miscellaneous documents regarding identity of citizens abroad). Vols. 1–3. 1922–1924. RG 3.8.7.23–9.

Zaigai kakuchi nihonjinkai kankei zakken (Miscellaneous documents concerning Japanese Associations in various areas abroad). 2 vols. 1905–1921. RG 3.8.2.213.

B. Other Japanese Government Publications

Commerce Section, Foreign Ministry. *Imin toriatsukainin ni yoru imin no enkaku* (History of emigrants using emigrant agents). 1909.

Documents Section, Cabinet Secretariat. *Gaikoku ryokenkisoku* (Passport regulations for travel to foreign countries). 1897, 1900, 1907. *Hōrei zensho* (Compendia of laws). Vol. 4 (1897), Vol. 5 (1900), Vol. 2 (1907).

———. *Gaikoku zairyū teikoku shinmin tōroku kisoku* (Regulations regarding the registration of imperial citizens abroad). 7 May 1909. *Genkō hōreishūran* (Existing laws). Vol. 1 (1925).

———. *Imin hogohō* (Immigration protection law). 7 April 1896. *Hōrei zensho* (Compendia of laws). Vol. 2 (1896).

———. *Imin hogokisoku* (Emigrant protection ordinance). 12 April 1894. *Hōrei zensho* (Compendia of laws). Vol. 2 (1894).

———. *Imin hogohō shisoku* (Rules regarding the execution of the emigrant protection law). 1 June 1896. *Genkō hōrei shūran* (Existing laws). Vol. 1 (1925).

———. *Kaigai ryokenkisoku* (Passport regulations for travel abroad). *Hōrei zensho* (Compendia of laws). (1878).

Nihon gaikō monjo (Records of the Foreign Ministry of Japan). Vol. 40. Tokyo: Nihon kokusai rengokyokai, 1961.
Nihonteikoku tōkei nenkan (Annual statistics of the empire of Japan). 1891–1925.
Tokyōshi tōkei nenpyō (Annual statistics of the city of Tokyo). 1901–1924.

2. UNITED STATES. GOVERNMENT DOCUMENTS.

Contract Labor Act. Amendment. Statutes at Large. Vol. 26 (1891).
Contract Labor Act. Statutes at Large. Vol. 23 (1885).
Diplomatic Relations Between the United States and Japan, 1908–1924. Documents for the Year 1925. International Conciliation, no. 211 (June 1925).
U.S. Bureau of Immigration. Commissioner-General of Immigration. *Annual Report.* 1900 and 1901.
U.S. Congress. House of Representatives. *Immigration of Japanese.* House Doc. 686, 56th Congress, 1st sess., 15 May 1900.
———. House of Representatives. Select Committee Investigating National Defense Migration. *Fourth Interim Report.* House Rept. 2124, 77th Congress, 2d sess., May 1942.
U.S. Congress. Senate. *Report of the U.S. Immigration Commission.* Vol. 3. *Statistical Review of Immigration, 1820–1910.* 61st Congress, 3d sess., 1910.
———. Senate. *Response to resolution by Commissioner General of Immigration, report relative to importation of Japanese.* S. Doc. 380, 56th Congress, 1st sess., 18 May 1900.
U.S. Department of Commerce. Bureau of the Census. *Abstracts of the Censuses of the United States.* Twelfth to Fourteenth Censuses. 1900–1920.
———. *Historical Statistics of the United States. Colonial Times to 1957.* Washington, D.C.: Government Printing Office, 1960.
U.S. Department of Justice. Federal Bureau of Investigation. *Reports: Japanese Association of New York, Inc.* 1942.
———. Bureau of Intelligence. *Investigative Reports. 1920–1922.* Microfilm. Record Group 65. National Archives, Washington, D.C.
U.S. Department of State. *Japanese Emigration and Immigration to American Territory. Correspondence from 1892 to January 29, 1908.* 1908–1909.
———. *Papers Relating to Foreign Relations of the United States.* 1891–1924.
U.S. Department of War. Military Intelligence Division. *Memoranda and Reports.* 1918–1930. Record Group 165. National Archives, Washington, D.C.

3. CONTEMPORARY SOURCES.

Abe Isō. *Fujin no risō* (The ideal woman). Tokyo: Hakubunkan, 1910.
Amerika. Monthly. Tokyo. 1907–1909.
Arai Kisaburō. *Dainippon Tōkyōzenzu* (Complete map of Tokyo). 48 × 70 cm. 1894.
Futabatei Shimei. *Ukigumo* (Floating clouds). In *Japan's First Modern Novel: "Ukigumo" of Futabatei Shimei,* trans. and ed. Marleigh Grayer Ryan. New York: Columbia University Press, 1965.

Harada Tōichirō. *Nyūyōku* (New York). Tokyo: Seikosha, 1914.
Hirata Eishi. *Tobei annai* (Introducing America). Kobe: n.p., 1916.
Holt, Hamilton, ed. *The Life Stories of Undistinguished Americans as Told by Themselves.* 2d ed. Young People's Missionary Movement. New York: Routledge, Chapman and Hall, 1990; first published, New York: J. Pott and Co., 1906.
Iijima Eitarō. *Beikoku tokō annai* (Guide to crossing to America). Tokyo: Hakubunkan, 1902.
Irish, John P. "Reasons for Encouraging Japanese Immigration." *The Annals* 34 (September 1909).
Ishimoto, Baroness Shidzué. *Facing Two Ways: The Story of My Life.* Stanford: Stanford University Press, 1935.
Ishizuka Iozō. *Gendai tobei annai* (Introducing contemporary America). Osaka: Ishizuka shoten, 1903.
Japanese-American Commercial Weekly (in Japanese). New York. 1905–1908.
Kamide Masataka. *Kuwayama Senzō-ō monogatari* (The story of the venerable Kuwayama Senzō). Kyoto: Tanko shinsha, 1963.
Katayama Sen. *Jiden* (Autobiography). Tokyo: Kaizosha, 1922.
———. *The Labor Movement in Japan.* Chicago: Charles H. Kerr, 1918.
———. *Tobei annai* (Introduction to America). Tokyo: Rodoshimbunsha, [1901?].
———. *Tobei no hiketsu* (Secrets of crossing to America). Tokyo: Shuppankyokai, 1906.
———. *Zoku tobei annai* (Introduction to America, vol. 2). Tokyo: Tobei kyokai, 1902.
Katō Bungo. *Saikin no zaibeidōbō* (Recent Japanese citizens residing in America). Tokyo: Nihon zushoshuppan, 1921.
Katō Jūshirō. *Zaibeidōbō hattenshi* (The history of our compatriots in America). Tokyo: Hakubunkan, 1908.
Kawaguchi Yoshihisa. *Amerika seikatsu* (Life in America). Tokyo: Tada shoboten, 1920.
Kawamura Tetsutarō. *Saikin katsudō hokubei jigyō annai* (Introduction to recent activities of North American businesses). 1906. Microfilm. National Diet Library, Tokyo.
Kishi Haru. Interviews by author, 21 November 1981, and 7 August 1985, New York City.
Kuriyagawa Hakuson. *Inshōki* (Impressions). Tokyo: Sekizenkan, 1918.
Map of the Enlarged City of Brooklyn. New York: J. B. Beers & Co., 1894.
Markino Yoshio. *When I Was a Child.* London: Constable and Co., 1913.
Matsui Hakken. *Beikoku manyūzakki* (A notebook from an American tour). Tokyo: Hakubunkan, 1900.
Miyakawa, Masuji. *Life of Japan.* New York: Baker and Taylor, 1907.
———. *Powers of the American People.* 2d ed. New York: Baker and Taylor, 1908.
Miyakawa Setsurō. *Beikoku no uraomote* (America inside and outside). Tokyo: Kobundo, 1920.
Mizutani, Shōzō. *Nyūyōku nihonjin hattenshi* (History of the Japanese in New

York). 2 vols. Tokyo: PMC Publishing Co., 1984; first published, New York: Japanese Association of New York, 1921.
Mizutani Tomotsune. *Beikoki tsūkan* (A survey of America). Tokyo: Yuhikaku shobo, 1900.
Mori Ōgai. "Under Reconstruction." In *Modern Japanese Stories*, trans. and ed. Ivan Morris. Tokyo: Charles E. Tuttle, 1962.
Nagai Kafū. *Amerika monogatari* (Stories from America). Vol. 3, *Nagai Kafū zenshū* (Complete works of Nagai Kafū). Tokyo: Chuokoronsha, 1949; first published, 1908.
———. *Seiyū nisshi sho* (Diary of my trip to the West, abridged). *Nagai Kafū zenshū* (Complete works of Nagai Kafū), vol. 3. Tokyo: Chuokoronsha, 1949.
Nakamura Masanao. "Creating Good Mothers" (1875). In *Meiroku Zasshi: Journal of Japanese Enlightenment*, trans. and ed. William Reynold Braisted. Cambridge: Harvard University Press, 1976.
Nakane Sōkai. *Seiyō no onna* (Women of the West). Tokyo: Chobunsha, 1924.
Natsume Sōseki. *Botchan*. Trans. Alan Turney. Tokyo: Kodansha, 1972.
New York Nichibei (in Japanese). Weekly. March–July 1985.
Nyūyōku shimpō (New York news). Semiweekly. 1940–41.
Ōhashi Sahei to Hakubunkan (Ōhashi Sahei and Hakubunkan). Tokyo: Privately printed, n.d.
Ōhori, E. A. *Hopes and Achievements*. New York: Women's Board of Domestic Missions of the Reformed Church in America, n.d.
———. *How and Why I Came to America*. N.p., 1903.
Okamoto Yonezō. *Nyūyōkushi naigai no jisho* (Property in the New York City area). Tokyo: Hakubunkan, 1912.
Ozaki Kōyō. *Konjikiyasha* (The usurer). Tokyo: Shinchosha, 1969; first published, *Yomiuri shimbun* (Tokyo). 1 January 1897—11 May 1902.
Plans of the U.S. Navy Yard, New York, Showing Improvements up to July 1, 1894. N.d., n.p.
Pooley, A. M., ed. *The Secret Memoirs of Count Tadasu Hayashi*. London, 1915; reprint, New York: AMS Press, 1969.
Reformed Church in America, Board of Domestic Missions, Women's Executive Committee. *Annual Reports*, 1909–19. New York: Reformed Church in America.
Sasaki Shigetsu. *Beikoku o hōrōshite* (Wandering in America). Tokyo: Nihon hyoronsha, 1921.
Seikō. Monthly. Tokyo. 1904–1912.
Shibuta Ichiro. "Nyūyōku ni okeru nihonjin no shokugyō" (Employment for Japanese in New York). In *Saikin tobei annai* (Introducing contemporary America), ed. Yamane Goichi. Tokyo: Tobei zasshisha, 1906.
Shimanuki Hyōdayū. *Rikikōkai towa nanzoya* (What Is the Rikikōkai?). Ed. Aizawa Genshichi. Tokyo: Hobundo, 1980; originally published 1911.
———. *Saikin seikaku tobei annai* (Newest authentic introduction to crossing to America). Tokyo: Chuyodo, 1901.
———. *Saikin tobeisaku* (Recent notes on crossing to America). Tokyo: Nippon rikikokai, 1904.

———. *Seikōno hiketsu* (Secrets of Success). Sendai: Kogando, 1892.
———. *Shintobeihō* (New passport regulations for crossing to America). Tokyo: Hakubunkan, 1911.
———, ed. *Jitchi tobei* (Personal stories of crossing to America). Tokyo: Rikikokai, 1905.
Shimazaki Tōson. *The Family.* Trans. Cecilia Segawa Seigle. Tokyo: University of Tokyo Press, 1976.
Sugimoto, Etsu Inagaki. *A Daughter of the Samurai.* New York: Doubleday, Page and Co., 1925.
Swayze, Mrs. Francis. *Finding the Way in a New Land.* New York: Reformed Church in America, Women's Board of Domestic Missions, n.d.
Tabata Kisaburō. *Zaibeisha seikōno tomo* (Friend of our successful countrymen in America). Tokyo: Shimizu shoten, 1908.
Takami, Toyohiko Campbell. *The Shining Stars: The Autobiography of Dr. Toyohiko Campbell Takami.* Ed. Masahiko Ralph Takami. Cold Spring Harbor, NY: n.p., 1945.
Tayama Katai. *Futon* (The quilt). Tokyo: Iwanami shoten, 1972; first published, 1907.
Tobei shimpō (News on crossing to America). Monthly. Tokyo. 1907–1909.
Tōkyō kōtō shōgyōgakkō dōsōkai kaiinroku (Alumni list of Tokyo Higher Commercial College). 1911.
Ueda Ryōzō. *Kaigaitokō hōsoku* (Laws regarding travel abroad). Kishiki-gun: n.p., 1902.
Uemura Tsutomu[?]. *Beikoku jijō: tobeisha hikkei* (The situation in America: a handbook for people crossing to America). Tokyo: Naigai shuppankai, 1912.
Watanabe Kanjirō. *Kaigai dekasegi annai* (Guide for workers going abroad). Tokyo: Tokyo naigai shuppankyokai, 1902.
Yamane Goichi, ed. *Saikin tobei annai* (Introducing contemporary America). Tokyo: Tobei zasshisha, 1906.
Yanagawa Shunyō. *Seiyōmusume katagi* (Characteristics of Western maidens). *Yomiuri shimbun* (Tokyo). 15 April–1 June 1897.
Yanagita Kunio. *Japanese Manners and Customs in the Meiji Era.* Trans. Charles S. Terry. Tokyo: Obunsha, 1957.
———. *Meiji Taishōshi sesōhen* (History of the Meiji-Taisho era: social conditions). 2 vols. Tokyo: Kodansha, 1976; first published, 1930.
———. *Toshi to nōson* (The city and the rural village). Vol. 16, *Teihon Yanagita Kunioshū* (Authentic collection of works by Yanagita Kunio). Tokyo: Chikuma shobo, 1962; first published, Tokyo: Asahi shimbunsha, 1929.

Secondary.

Akamatsu, Alfred Saburo. "The Function and Type of Program of a Japanese Minority Church in New York City: A Proposal for the Establishment of the Japanese American United Church of Christ in New York." Ed.D. dissertation, Teachers College, Columbia University, 1948.

Albert, Michael David. "Japanese American Communities in Chicago and the Twin Cities." Ph.D. dissertation, University of Minnesota, 1980.

Allen, G. C. *A Short Economic History of Modern Japan*. New York: Frederick A. Praeger, 1963.

Anderson, Benedict. *Imagined Communities*. 2d ed. New York: Verso, 1991.

Asō Makoto. "Nihon no kyōiku to kigyōseichō" (Education and the growth of business in Japan). In Hazama Hiroshi, ed., *Nihon no kigyō to shakai* (Japanese business and society). Tokyo: Nihonkeizai shimbunsha, 1977.

Asukai Masamichi. "Kōtoku Shūsei and His Socialism and Pacifism." In Nobuya Bamba and John F. Howes, ed., *Pacifism in Japan*. Kyoto: Minerva Press, 1978.

al-'Azm, Sadik Jalal. "Orientalism and Orientalism in Reverse." *Khamsin* 8 (1981):5–26.

Bailey, Thomas. *Theodore Roosevelt and the Japanese-American Crisis*. Stanford: Stanford University Press, 1934.

Bamba, Nobuya, and John F. Howes, eds. *Pacifism in Japan: The Christian and Socialist Traditions*. Kyoto: Minerva Press, 1978.

Barton, Josef J. *Peasants and Strangers: Italians, Rumanians and Slovaks in an American City 1880–1950*. Cambridge: Harvard University Press, 1977.

Beale, Howard K. *Theodore Roosevelt and the Rise of America to World Power*. Baltimore: Johns Hopkins Press, 1956; New York: Collier Books, 1973.

Befu, Harumi. "A Critique of the Group Model of Japanese Society." *Social Analysis* 5/6 (December 1980).

Bennett, John W., Herbert Passin, and Robert K. McKnight. *In Search of Identity: The Japanese Overseas Scholar in America and Japan*. Minneapolis: University of Minnesota Press, 1958.

Bodnar, John. *Immigration and Industrialization: Ethnicity in an American Mill Town, 1870–1940*. Pittsburgh: University of Pittsburgh Press, 1977.

Bowring, Richard John. *Mori Ogai and the Modernization of Japanese Culture*. Cambridge: Cambridge University Press, 1979.

Brannen, Mary Yoko. " 'Bwana Mickey': Constructing Cultural Consumption at Tokyo Disneyland." In Amy Kaplan and Donald E. Pease, eds., *Cultures of United States Imperialism*. Durham, NC: Duke University Press, 1993.

Briggs, John W. *An Italian Passage: Immigrants to Three American Cities, 1890–1930*. New Haven: Yale University Press, 1978.

Burks, Ardath W. *Japan: A Postindustrial Power*. 2d ed. Boulder, CO: Westview Press, 1984.

Caughey, John L. *Imaginary Social Worlds: A Cultural Approach*. Lincoln: University of Nebraska Press, 1984.

Chan, Sucheng. *Asian Americans: An Interpretive History*. Boston: Twayne Publishers, 1991.

———. "European and Asian Immigration into the United States in Comparative Perspective, 1820s to 1920s." In Virginia Yans-McLaughlin, ed., *Immigration Reconsidered: History, Sociology, and Politics*. New York: Oxford University Press, 1990.

Cheng, Lucie, and Edna Bonacich, eds. *Labor Immigration Under Capitalism:*

Asian Workers in the United States Before World War II. Berkeley: University of California Press, 1984.

Chow, Rey. *Writing Diaspora.* Bloomington, IN: Indiana University Press, 1993.

Chuman, Frank F. *The Bamboo People: The Law and Japanese-Americans.* Del Mar, CA: Publishers Inc., 1976.

Cinel, Dino. *From Italy to San Francisco: The Immigrant Experience.* Stanford: Stanford University Press, 1982.

Connor, John W. *Tradition and Change in Three Generations of Japanese Americans.* Chicago: Nelson-Hall, 1977.

Conroy, Hilary. *The Japanese Frontier in Hawaii.* Berkeley: University of California Press, 1953.

Conroy, Hilary, and T. Scott Miyakawa, eds. *East Across the Pacific: Historical and Sociological Studies of Japanese Immigration and Assimilation.* Santa Barbara, CA: ABC-CLIO Press, 1972.

Conzen, Kathleen Neils. *Immigrant Milwaukee, 1836–1860: Accommodation and Community in a Frontier City.* Cambridge: Harvard University Press, 1979.

Daniels, Roger, ed. *The Asian Experience in North America: Chinese and Japanese.* 47 vols. New York: Arno Press, 1979.

———. "The Japanese." In John Higham, ed., *Ethnic Leadership in America.* Baltimore: Johns Hopkins University Press, 1978.

———. "Japanese Immigrants on a Western Frontier: The Issei in California, 1890–1940." In Hilary Conroy and T. Scott Miyakawa, eds., *East Across the Pacific,* Santa Barbara: ABC-CLIO Press, 1972.

———. *The Politics of Prejudice: The Anti-Japanese Movement in California and the Struggle for Japanese Exclusion.* Berkeley: University of California Press, 1962; reprint, Gloucester, MA: Peter Smith, 1966.

Davis, Kingsley. "The Origin and Growth of Urbanization in the World." In Herbert Moller, ed., *Population Movements in Modern European History.* New York: Macmillan, 1964.

Dictionary of American Biography. New York: Charles Scribner's Sons, 1946–58.

Dinnerstein, Leonard, and David M. Reimers. *Ethnic Americans.* New York: Harper and Row, 1975.

Dore, R[onald] P. *City Life in Japan: A Study of a Tokyo Ward.* Berkeley: University of California Press, 1958.

———. "Mobility, Equality, and Individuation in Meiji Japan." In Dore, *Aspects of Social Change in Modern Japan.* Princeton: Princeton University Press, 1967.

———. *Shinohata: A Portrait of a Japanese Village.* New York: Pantheon, 1978.

Dower, John W. "E. H. Norman, Japan and the Uses of History." In *Origins of the Modern Japanese State: Selected Writings of E. H. Norman.* New York: Pantheon Books, 1975.

———. *War Without Mercy: Race and Power in the Pacific War.* New York: Pantheon, 1986.

Esthus, Raymond A. *Theodore Roosevelt and Japan*. Seattle: University of Washington Press, 1966.
Featherstone, Mike, ed. *Global Culture: Nationalism, Globalization and Modernity.* London: Sage Publications, 1990.
Fisher, Lloyd. *The Harvest Labor Market in California.* Cambridge: Harvard University Press, 1953.
Fujii, James A. *Complicit Fictions: The Subject in the Modern Japanese Prose Narrative.* Berkeley: University of California Press, 1993.
Fukutake Tadashi. *Japanese Rural Society.* Trans. R. P. Dore. Ithaca: Cornell University Press, 1967.
———. *The Japanese Social Structure.* Trans. R. P. Dore. Tokyo: University of Tokyo Press, 1982.
Gaimushō no hyakunen (One hundred years of the Foreign Ministry). 2 vols. Tokyo: Foreign Ministry, 1969.
Gee, Emma, ed. *Counterpoint: Perspectives on Asian America.* Los Angeles: Asian American Studies Center, UCLA, 1976.
Gewertz, Deborah, and Frederick Errington. "We Think Therefore They Are? On Occidentalizing the World." *Anthropological Quarterly* 64:2 (April 1991):80–91.
Gjerde, Jon. *From Peasants to Farmers: The Migration from Balestrand, Norway, to the Upper Middle West.* New York: Cambridge University Press, 1985.
Glenn, Evelyn Nakano. "The Dialectics of Wage Work: Japanese-American Women and Domestic Service, 1905–1940." *Feminist Studies* 6:3 (Fall 1980):432–71.
———. *Issei, Nisei, War Bride.* Philadelphia: Temple University Press, 1986.
Gluck, Carol. *Japan's Modern Myths: Ideology in the Late Meiji Period.* Princeton: Princeton University Press, 1985.
Gordon, Andrew. *The Evolution of Labor Relations in Japan.* Cambridge, MA: Harvard University Press, 1988.
Gutman, Herbert G. *Work, Culture and Society in Industrializing America.* New York: Alfred A. Knopf, 1966.
Halliday, Jon. *A Political History of Japanese Capitalism.* New York: Pantheon, 1975.
Hammack, David C. *Power and Society: Greater New York at the Turn of the Century.* New York: Russell Sage Foundation, 1982.
Hane, Mikiso. *Modern Japan: A Historical Survey.* Boulder, CO: Westview Press, 1986.
———. *Peasants, Rebels, and Outcasts: The Underside of Modern Japan.* New York: Pantheon, 1982.
———, ed. and trans. *Reflections on the Way to the Gallows: Rebel Women in Prewar Japan.* Berkeley: University of California Press, 1988.
Hansen, Marcus Lee. *The Atlantic Migration, 1607–1860.* Cambridge: Harvard University Press, 1940.
Hata, Donald R. *"Undesireables": Early Immigrants and the Anti-Japanese Movement in San Francisco, 1892–93.* New York: Arno Press, 1978.

Hatayama Kikuji. *Zaibei nihonjinshi* (History of the Japanese in America). San Francisco: Japanese Association of America, 1940.

Hazama Hiroshi. "Historical Changes in the Life Style of Industrial Workers." In Hugh Patrick, ed., *Japanese Industrialization and Its Social Consequences*. Berkeley: University of California Press, 1976.

Higham, John. *Strangers in the Land: Patterns of American Nativism, 1860–1925*, 2d ed. New Brunswick, NJ: Rutgers University Press, 1963.

Hobsbawm, E. J. *The Age of Capital, 1848–1875*. New York: Charles Scribner's Sons, 1975.

———. "Introduction: Inventing Traditions." In Eric Hobsbawm and Terence Ranger, eds., *The Invention of Tradition*. Cambridge: Cambridge University Press, 1983.

———. "Mass-Producing Traditions: Europe, 1870–1914." In Eric Hobsbawm and Terence Ranger, eds., *The Invention of Tradition*. Cambridge: Cambridge University Press, 1983.

Huffman, James L. *Politics of the Meiji Press: The Life of Fukuchi Gen'ichirō*. Honolulu: University of Hawaii Press, 1980.

Hunt, Michael H. *The Making of a Special Relationship: The United States and China to 1914*. New York: Columbia University Press, 1983.

Ichihashi Yamato. "Anti-Japanese Agitation." In Roger Daniels and Spencer C. Olin, eds., *Racism in California*. New York: Macmillan, 1972.

———. *The Japanese in the United States*. Stanford: Stanford University Press, 1932; reprint, New York: Arno Press, 1969.

Ichioka, Yuji. "Amerika Nadeshiko: Japanese Immigrant Women in the United States, 1900–1921." *Pacific Historical Review* 49:2 (May 1980).

———. *The Issei*. New York: The Free Press, 1988.

———. "Japanese Associations and the Japanese Government: A Special Relationship, 1909–1926." *Pacific Historical Review* 46:3 (August 1977).

Ichioka, Yuji, Yasuo Sakata, Nobuya Tsuchida, and Eri Yasuhara, comps. *A Buried Past: An Annotated Bibliography of the Japanese American Research Project Collection*. Berkeley: University of California Press, 1974.

Ike, Nobutaka. *Japanese Politics*. New York: Alfred A. Knopf, 1957.

Inoma Kiichi. "Senzen rokujūhachinen no waga imintōkei no gaikan" (Overview of Japanese emigration statistics for 68-year period prior to World War II). *Keishō ronsan* 60 (February 1955).

Iriye, Akira. *Across the Pacific: An Inner History of American-East Asian Relations*. New York: Harcourt, Brace and World, Inc., 1967.

———. *Pacific Estrangement: Japanese and American Expansion, 1897–1911*. Cambridge: Harvard University Press, 1972.

Ishii, Ryōichi. *Population Pressure and Economic Life in Japan*. London: P. S. King and Son, 1937.

Ishizuka Hiromichi. *Tōkyō no shakaikeizaishi* (Social and economic history of Tokyo). Tokyo: Kinokuniya, 1977.

Itō, Kazuo. *Issei: A History of Japanese Immigrants in North America*. Seattle: Executive Committee for Publication of Issei, 1973.

Itō Shigeru. "Senzenki nihon no toshi seichō" (Japan's prewar urban growth). *Nippon rōdō kyōkai zasshi* 280 and 281 (July and August 1982).

Iwata, Masakazu. "The Japanese Immigrant in California Agriculture." *Agricultural History* 36 (January 1962).
Jacobs, Paul, and Saul Landau with Eve Pell. *To Serve the Devil: A Documentary Analysis*. New York: Vintage Books, 1972.
Japan's Modern Educational System: A History of the First Hundred Years. Tokyo: Research and Statistics Division, Minister's Secretariat, Ministry of Education, Science and Culture, 1980.
Jones, Gareth Stedman. *Outcast London*. New York: Pantheon, 1984.
Kageyama Kiichi. "Howaitokarā no suii" (The transition to white-collar work). In Hazama Hiroshi, ed., *Nihon no kigyō to shakai* (Japanese business and society). Tokyo: Nihonkeizai shimbunsha, 1977.
Kasson, John F. *Amusing the Millions*. New York: Hill & Wang, 1978.
Katō, Hidetoshi. "Development of Nineteenth-Century Style: Some Historical Parallels Between the United States and Japan." In Herbert Gans et al., eds., *On the Making of Americans: Essays in Honor of David Riesman*. Philadelphia: University of Pennsylvania Press, 1979.
Katō Hidetoshi and Maeda Ai. *Meiji medeakō* (Thoughts on media during the Meiji period). Tokyo: Chuokoronsha, 1980.
Katzman, David M. *Seven Days a Week: Women and Domestic Service in Industrializing America*. New York: Oxford University Press, 1978.
Kawakami, K. K. *Jokichi Takamine: A Record of His American Achievements*. New York: William Edwin Rudge, 1928.
Keene, Donald. *Dawn to the West: Japanese Literature of the Modern Era*. New York: Holt, Rinehart and Winston, 1984.
Kessner, Thomas. *The Golden Door: Italian and Jewish Immigrant Mobility in New York City, 1880–1915*. New York: Oxford University Press, 1977.
Kindaichi Haruhiko. *Nihongo* (The Japanese language). Tokyo: Iwanami shoten, 1957.
Kinmonth, Earl H. *The Self-made Man in Meiji Japanese Thought: From Samurai to Salary Man*. Berkeley: University of California Press, 1981.
Kitano, Harry H.L. *Japanese Americans: The Evolution of a Subculture*. 2d ed. Englewood Cliffs, NJ: Prentice- Hall, 1976.
Kitano, Seiichi. " 'Dōzoku' and 'Ie' in Japan: The Meaning of Family Genealogical Relationships." In Robert J. Smith and Richard K. Beardsley, eds., *Japanese Culture: Its Development and Characteristics*. Chicago: Aldine Publishing Co., 1962.
Kodansha Encyclopedia of Japan. Tokyo: Kodansha, 1983.
Kollmann, Wolfgang. "The Population of Germany in the Age of Industrialism." In Herbert Moller, ed., *Population Movements in Modern European History*. New York: Macmillan, 1964.
Komobuchi Midori. "Haigūsha no sentaku to kekkon" (Spouse selection and marriage). In Kamiko Takeji and Masuda Kōkichi, eds., *Nihonjin no kazokukankei* (Family relationships of the Japanese). Tokyo: Yuhikaku sensho, 1981.
Kondo, Dorinne. *Crafting Selves: Power, Gender and Discourses in a Japanese Workplace*. Chicago: University of Chicago Press, 1990.
Koyama Takashi. "Changing Family Structure in Japan." In Robert J. Smith

and Richard K. Beardsley, eds., *Japanese Culture: Its Development and Characteristics*. Chicago: Aldine Publishing Co., 1962.

Kublin, Hyman. *Asian Revolutionary: The Life of Sen Katayama*. Princeton: Princeton University Press, 1964.

Kurosawa, Kiyoko T. "Seito Saibara's Diary of Planting a Japanese Colony in Texas." *Hitotsubashi Journal of Social Studies* 2 (August 1964).

LaFeber, Walter. *The New Empire*. Ithaca: Cornell University Press, 1963.

Lantz, Herman R. "Romantic Love in the Pre-Modern Period: A Social Commentary." *Social History* 15:3 (Spring 1982).

Lippit, Noriko Mizuta. *Reality and Fiction in Modern Japanese Literature*. White Plains, NY: M.E. Sharpe, 1980.

Livingston, Jon, Joe Moore, and Felicia Oldfather, eds. *Imperial Japan*. New York: Pantheon Books, 1973.

Lockwood, William W. *The Economic Development of Japan*, expanded ed. Princeton: Princeton University Press, 1968.

McKee, Delbert L. *Chinese Exclusion versus the Open Door Policy, 1900–1906: Clashes over China Policy in the Roosevelt Era*. Detroit: Wayne State University Press, 1977.

Miller, Kerby A. *Emigrants and Exiles: Ireland and the Irish Exodus to North America*. New York: Oxford University Press, 1985.

Miller, Roy Andrew. *Japan's Modern Myth*. New York: Weatherhill, 1982.

Miyakawa, T. Scott. "Early New York Issei: Founders of Japanese American Trade." In Hilary Conroy and T. Scott Miyakawa, eds., *East Across the Pacific*. Santa Barbara: ABC-CLIO, 1972.

Miyamoto, S. Frank. *Social Solidarity Among the Japanese in Seattle*. Seattle: University of Washington Press, 1984; first published 1939.

Miyoshi, Masao. *Accomplices of Silence: The Modern Japanese Novel*. Berkeley: University of California Press, 1974.

———. *As We Saw Them: The First Japanese Embassy to the United States (1860)*. Berkeley: University of California Press, 1979.

———. *Off Center: Power and Culture Relations Between Japan and the United States*. Cambridge, MA: Harvard University Press, 1991.

Miyoshi, Masao, and H. D. Harootunian, eds. "Postmodernism and Japan." *The South Atlantic Quarterly* 87:3 (Summer 1988).

Modell, John. *The Economics and Politics of Racial Accommodation: The Japanese of Los Angeles, 1900–1942*. Urbana: University of Illinois Press, 1977.

Morawska, Ewa. *For Bread With Butter: The Life-Worlds of East Central Europeans in Johnstown, Pennsylvania*. New York: Cambridge University Press, 1985.

Moriyama, Alan Takeo. *Imingaisha: Japanese Emigration Companies and Hawaii, 1894–1908*. Honolulu: University of Hawaii Press, 1985.

Murakami Nobuhiko. *Meiji joseishi*. (History of Meiji women). Vol. 3. Tokyo: Rironsha, 1972.

Myers, Ramon H., and Mark. R. Peattie, eds. *The Japanese Colonial Empire, 1895–1945*. Princeton: Princeton University Press, 1984.

Najita, Tetsuo, and Victor J. Koschmann, eds. *Conflict in Modern Japanese*

History: The Neglected Tradition. Princeton: Princeton University Press, 1982.
Nakamura Mitsuo. *Nihon no kindai shōsetsu* (Japan's modern novels). Tokyo: Iwanami shoten, 1954.
Nakamura Takafusa. *Economic Growth in Prewar Japan*. Trans. Robert A. Feldman. New Haven: Yale University Press, 1983.
Natsume Sōseki. *Botchan*. Trans. Alan Turney. Tokyo: Kodansha, 1972.
Neu, Charles. *An Uncertain Friendship: Theodore Roosevelt and Japan, 1906–1909*. Cambridge: Harvard University Press, 1967.
Neumann, William L. *America Encounters Japan*. Baltimore: Johns Hopkins University Press, 1963.
Nihon kindaibungaku daijiten (Encyclopedia of modern Japanese literature). 5 vols. Tokyo: Kodansha, 1978.
Nolte, Sharon H., and Sally Ann Hastings. "The Meiji State's Policy Toward Women, 1890–1910." In Gail Lee Bernstein, ed., *Recreating Japanese Women, 1600–1945*. Berkeley: University of California Press, 1991.
Norman, E. Herbert. *Feudal Backgrounds in Japanese Politics* (1945). In *Origins of the Modern Japanese State: Selected Writings of E.H. Norman*, ed. John W. Dower. New York: Pantheon Books, 1975.
——. *Japan's Emergence as a Modern State* (1940). In *Origins of the Modern Japanese State: Selected Writings of E.H. Norman*, ed. John W. Dower. New York: Pantheon Books, 1975.
——. *Soldier and Peasant in Japan*. New York: Institute of Pacific Relations, 1943.
Notehelfer, Fred. *Kotoku Shusei: Portrait of a Japanese Radical*. Cambridge: Cambridge University Press, 1971.
Ōhashi Ryūken. *Nippon no kaikyūkōsei* (Japan's class formation). Tokyo: Iwanami shoten, 1971.
Ohbuchi, Hiroshi. "Demographic Transition in the Process of Japanese Industrialization." In Hugh Patrick, ed., *Japanese Industrialization and Its Social Consequences*. Berkeley: University of California Press, 1976.
Oka, Yoshitake. "Generational Conflict after the Russo-Japanese War." In Tetsuo Najita and Victor Koschmann, eds., *Conflict in Modern Japanese History: The Neglected Tradition*. Princeton: Princeton University Press, 1982.
Ōkubo Takaki. *Yume to seijuku: bungakuteki seiyōzō no henbō* (From dreams to maturity: the transformation of the Western image in literature). Tokyo: Kodansha, 1977.
Orii, Kazuhiko, and Hilary Conroy. "Japanese Socialist in Texas: Sen Katayama." *Amerasia Journal* 8 (Fall/Winter 1981):163–70.
Passin, Herbert. *Society and Education in Japan*. Tokyo: Kodansha, 1982; New York: Columbia University Press, 1965.
Peattie, Mark. "Introduction." In Ramon H. Myers and Mark R. Peattie, ed., *The Japanese Colonial Empire, 1895–1945*. Princeton: Princeton University Press, 1984.
Peiss, Kathy. *Cheap Amusements*. Philadelphia: Temple University Press, 1986.

Pilat, Oliver, and Jo Ransom. *Sodom by the Sea*. Garden City, NY: Doubleday, Doran & Co., 1941.
Powles, Cyril H. "Abe Isoo: The Utility Man." In Nobuya Bamba and John F. Howes, eds., *Pacificism in Japan*. Kyoto: Minerva Press, 1978.
Reischauer, Haru. *Samurai and Silk*. Cambridge: Harvard University Press, 1986.
Reubens, Edwin P. "Foreign Capital and Domestic Development in Japan." In Simon Kuznets, Wilbert E. Moore, and Joseph J. Spengler, eds., *Economic Growth: Brazil, India, Japan*. Durham, NC: Duke University Press, 1955.
Riis, Jacob. *How the Other Half Lives* (1890). New York: Dover Publications, 1971.
Roberts, John G. *Mitsui: Three Centuries of Business*. New York: Weatherhill, 1973.
Robertson, Roland. "Mapping the Global Condition: Globalization as the Central Concept." In Mike Featherstone, ed., *Global Culture*. London: Sage Publications, 1990.
Rohlen, Thomas P. *Japan's High Schools*. Berkeley: University of California Press, 1983.
Rosaldo, Renato. *Culture and Truth: The Remaking of Social Analysis, with a New Introduction*. New York: Beacon, 1993.
Rose, Barbara. *Tsuda Umeko and Women's Education in Japan*. New Haven: Yale University Press, 1992.
Rubin, Jay. *Injurious to Public Morals: Writers and the Meiji State*. Seattle: University of Washington Press, 1984.
Said, Edward W. *Orientalism*. New York: Vintage, 1979.
Saigusa Yasutaka. *Kindai bungaku no risōzō* (The ideal image in modern literature). Tokyo: Kakushobo, 1961.
Sakata, Yasuo, comp. *Fading Footsteps of the Issei: An Annotated Bibliography of the Manuscript Holdings of the Japanese American Research Project Collection*. Los Angeles: UCLA Asian American Studies Center, UCLA Center for Japanese Studies and Japanese American National Museum, 1992.
Sansom, G. B. *The Western World and Japan*. New York: Alfred A. Knopf, 1950.
Sawada, Mitziko. "Culprits and Gentlemen: Meiji Japan's Restrictions of Emigrants to the United States, 1891–1909." *Pacific Historical Review* 60:3 (August 1991):339–59.
Seidensticker, Edward. *Low City, High City: Tokyo from Edo to the Earthquake*. New York: Alfred A. Knopf, 1983.
Sheldon, Charles David. *The Rise of the Merchant Class in Tokugawa Japan, 1600–1868*. New York: Russell and Russell, 1958.
Shimbun hanbai hyakunenshi (One hundred years of newspaper sales). Tokyo: Nihon shimbun hanbai kyokai, 1972.
Shimbun no ayumi. (Development of newspapers). Tokyo: National Diet Library, 1972.
Sievers, Sharon L. *Flowers in Salt: The Beginnings of Feminist Consciousness in Japan*. Stanford: Stanford University Press, 1983.

Silverberg, Miriam. *Changing Song*. Princeton: Princeton University Press, 1990.
———. "Constructing a New Cultural History of Prewar Japan." *boundary 2* 18:3 (1991): 63–89.
———. "Constructing the Japanese Ethnography of Modernity." *Journal of Asian Studies* 51:1 (February 1992):30–54.
———. "The Modern Girl as Militant." In Gail Lee Bernstein, ed., *Recreating Japanese Women, 1600–1945*. Berkeley: University of California Press, 1991.
———. "Remembering Pearl Harbor, Forgetting Charlie Chaplin, and the Case of the Disappearing Western Woman: A Picture Story." *Positions: East Asia Cultures Critique* 1:1 (Spring 1993).
Smith, Robert J. "Pre-Industrial Urbanism in Japan: A Consideration of Multiple Traditions in a Feudal Society." In Research Center in Economic Development and Cultural Change, University of Chicago, *Economic Development and Cultural Change* 9:1 part 2 (October 1960).
Smith, Robert J., and Ella Lury Wiswell. *The Women of Suye Mura*. Chicago: University of Chicago Press, 1982.
Smith, Thomas C. *The Agrarian Origins of Modern Japan*. Stanford: Stanford University Press, 1959.
———. "Japan's Aristocratic Revolution." In Smith, *Native Sources of Japanese Industrialization*. Berkeley: University of California Press, 1988.
Still, Bayrd. *Mirror for Gotham: New York as Seen by Contemporaries from Dutch Days to the Present*. New York: New York University Press, 1956.
Sumiya Mikio. *Katayama Sen*. Tokyo: Tokyo daigaku shuppankai, 1977.
———. *Social Impact of Industrialization in Japan*. Tokyo: Japanese National Commission for UNESCO, 1963.
Taeuber, Irene B. "Population and Labor Force in the Industrialization of Japan, 1850–1950." In Simon Kuznets, Wilbert E. Moore, and Joseph J. Spengler, eds., *Economic Growth: Brazil, India, Japan*. Durham, NC: Duke University Press, 1955.
Taira, Koji. *Economic Development and the Labor Market in Japan*. New York: Columbia University Press, 1970.
Takagi Takeo. *Shimbun shōsetsushi: Meijihen*. (History of newspaper novels of the Meiji period). Tokyo: Kokusho kankokai, 1974.
Takaki, Ronald. *Strangers From a Different Shore: A History of Asian Americans*. Boston: Little, Brown and Co., 1989.
Tanaka, Stefan. *Japan's Orient: Rendering Pasts into History*. Berkeley: University of California Press, 1993.
Thomas, Brinley. *Migration and Urban Development*. London: Methuen & Co., 1972.
Thomas, William I. and Florian Znaniecki. *The Polish Peasant in Europe and America*. 5 vols, ed. and abr. Eli Zaretsky. Urbana: University of Illinois Press, 1984.
Thompson, E. P. *The Making of the English Working Class*. New York: Vintage, 1963.
Tokuoka Hideo. "Rikon to kodomo" (Divorce and children). In Kamiko

Takeji and Masuda Kokichi, eds., *Nihon no kazoku kankei* (Japanese family relationships). Tokyo: Yuhikaku, 1981.

Tōkyō hyakunenshi (One hundred years of Tokyo). Vol. 3, *Tōkyōjin no keisei* (The making of the people of Tokyo). Vol. 4, *Taishōki* (The Taisho period). Tokyo: Tokyo Metropolitan Government, 1972.

Tōyama Shigeki. *Kindai nihonshi* (History of modern Japan). Tokyo: Iwanami Shoten, 1975.

Tsunoda, Ryusaku, William Theodore de Bary, and Donald Keene, comps. *Sources of Japanese Tradition*. New York: Columbia University Press, 1958.

Van Alstyne, Richard W. *The Rising American Empire*. Oxford, England: Blackwell and Mott, 1960; New York: W. W. Norton & Co., Inc., 1974.

van Wolferen, Karel. *The Enigma of Japanese Power*. New York: Alfred A. Knopf, 1989.

Vogel, Ezra. "The Go-Between in a Developing Society: The Case of the Japanese Marriage Arranger." In George K. Yamamoto and Tsuyoshi Ishida, eds., *Selected Readings on Modern Japanese Society*, Berkeley: McCutchan Publishing, 1971.

Wakatsuki, Yasuo. "Japanese Emigration to the United States, 1866–1924: A Monograph." *Perspectives in American History* 12 (1979).

Walthall, Anne, "The Life Cycle of Farm Women in Tokugawa Japan." In Gail Lee Bernstein, ed., *Recreating Japanese Women, 1600–1945*. Berkeley: University of California Press, 1991.

Watanabe Haruo. *Katayama Sen to tomoni* (With Katayama Sen). Tokyo: Wakosha, 1955.

White, James W. "Internal Migration in Prewar Japan." *Journal of Japanese Studies* 4:1 (Winter 1978).

Wilkinson, Thomas O. *The Urbanization of Japanese Labor, 1868–1955*. Amherst, MA: University of Massachusetts Press, 1965.

Wray, William D. *Mitsubishi and the N.Y.K., 1870–1914*. Cambridge: Harvard University Press, 1984.

Yamanaka, Tokutarō. *The History and Structure of Japan's Small and Medium Industries*. Tokyo: Science Council of Japan, 1957.

Yanabu Akira. *Honyaku seiritsujijō* (On the development of translation). Tokyo: Iwanami shoten, 1982.

Yanaga, Chitoshi. *Japan Since Perry*. New York: McGraw-Hill, 1949.

Yanagisako, Sylvia Junko. *Transforming the Past: Tradition and Kinship Among Japanese Americans*. Stanford: Stanford University Press, 1985.

Yans-McLaughlin, Virginia. *Family and Community: Italian Immigration in Buffalo, 1880–1930*. Ithaca: Cornell University Press, 1977.

———, ed. *Immigration Reconsidered: History, Sociology, and Politics*. New York: Oxford University Press, 1990.

Yazaki Genkurō. *Nihon no gairaigo* (Japanese words of foreign origin). Tokyo: Iwanami shoten, 1964.

Yazaki Takeo. *Social Change and the City in Japan*. Trans. David L. Swain. Tokyo: Japan Publications, 1968.

Yoneda, Karl G. *The Heritage of Sen Katayama*. *Political Affairs* reprint, 1975.

Yoshida, Yosaburo. "Sources and Causes of Japanese Emigration." *The Annals* 34:2 (September 1909).

Yui Tsunehiko, ed. *Kōgyōka to kigyōsha katsudō* (Industrialization and the role of the businessman). Tokyo: Nihonkeizai shimbunsha, 1976.

Zaibeinihonjinshi (History of the Japanese in America). San Francisco: Japanese Association of America, 1940.

Index

Abe Isō: about, 225n27; on Japanese in West Coast, 100; on leisure activity, 99–100; and racism, 99, 101, 143
abirete (ability): introduction of term, 103
Amerika (magazine), 92, 95, 118, 231n60. *See also* tobei publications
Amerika monogatari (Stories from America), 1, 167. *See also* Nagai Kafū
authority: ambiguities of, 85; attitudinal changes regarding, 74; in *Botchan*, 77; challenges to, 80, 221n90; shifting roles of, in *Ie*, 84–85; concept of, 79; and education, 79; and Meiji government, 77; political elements of, 79–80; redefinition of, 67–68; in small business, 83–84; in *Ukigumo*, 75–76; women and, in *Ie*, 84–85

Botchan (Natsume Sōseki): on authority in civil service, 77–80; definition of term, 221n83; on *Tokyōjin*, 78
Brooklyn Navy Yard: description, 21; Japanese workers at, 21–22

capital: investments, 63; foreign, 216n37
Caughey, John, 6
Chan, Sucheng, 4–5, 207n8
child-raising: comparison, Japan and U.S., 98; in U.S., 97–98
Chinda Sutemi (foreign affairs vice-minister): correspondence on banning *imin*, 48–49; defines *hi-imin*, 48

Christians, 124–26; as challengers of state, 125, 230n48; in Meiji state, 229n35, 230n44. *See also* Katayama Sen; Shimanuki Hyōdayū
chūryūkaikyū (middle class): and contradictions in society, 85–86; defined, 66, 216n41; formation of, 71; identity, 66; multidimensional aspect of, 66; residences, 66–67; residences in Meiji compared to Edo, 216–17n42; as unifying element, 58
Civil Code of 1898, 153
civil servants. See *Botchan;* Japanese government; *Ukigumo*
Coney Island: Japanese amusement concessions, 31–35; Nagai Kafū on, 32–34; rolling-ball game, 203n67; workers at, 33–34. *See also* Kishi, Haru
consumer culture: and consciousness, 62, 215n28; and department stores, 62
cross-racial relations: in *Amerika monogatari*, 169–71; in *Fushinchū*, 150; marriage law in U.S., 235n19; Mori Ōgai and, 150, 236n25; in New York, 36–37, 149, 235n17; and social class, 151. *See also* Itō Kenzō case
cultural knowledge, 3; defined, 6; Japanese, of U.S., 12, 39

domestic workers, Japanese: as butlers, 25; as cooks, 24–25; and education, 23; and isolation, 24; and "manliness," domestic workers, Japanese (*continued*) 26–27; number of, 28; reactions of community leaders, 24, 25–27; and upward mobility, 23–24. *See also* Brooklyn Navy Yard; Takami, Toyohiko Campbell; Japanese immigrants in New York City

Dore, R[onald] P.: on moral conduct, 220n80

family system: effect on men, 155, 158–59, 164; in *Ie,* 158; ideology and reality, 158–59; and laws, 153; and love, 160; and women, 157–58, 238n54

Featherstone, Mike, 179

Foreign Ministry of Japan: correspondence with consular offices in U.S., 41–42, 51, 52; on registration of Japanese citizens in U.S., 49–50, 51, 52, 53–55. *See also* Japanese government

Fujii, James, 8, 198n25, 239n68

Fushinchū (Mori Ōgai), 150–51

Futon (Tayama Katai), 161–62, 239n68

gender relations, 11, 84, 145–73; class positions and, 146, 147, 148; in *Ie,* 84–85; Japanese males and, 148. *See also* cross-racial relations

Gluck, Carol, 8

Hakubunkan (publishing house), 90–91, 223n7

Harootunian, H. D., 179

Hatoyama Haruko: on *ryōsai kenbo,* 157–58

Hayashi Tadasu (foreign affairs minister): on registration of Japanese citizens in U.S., 49–51; on U.S. treaty responsibility, 50

hi-imin (non-migrant): in China, 44; defined, 44–45, 48; and convention, 150; decision to emigrate, 116; introduction of term, 53; number of, in New York City, 184–85, 189 table 4; warnings regarding misuse of category, 9–10, 54–55, 207n9. *See also imin*

Hobsbawm, Eric, 152

honseki (registered family domicile), 14, 46, 242n2; of Japanese in New York, 183, 187 table 1, 188 table 2

Ichioka, Yuji, 2

identity: construction of, 57–58, 59–60, 85, 90; and gender relations, 158–59, 160, 164, 166; and global mentality, 178, 179; and ideology, 8, 95; multidimensional aspect of, 79, 95; and *seikō,* 114; and U.S., 90; and West, 90. *See also chūryūkaikyū;* cultural knowledge; *kindai; seikō; Tōkyōjin; wayō*

Ie (Shimazaki Tōson), 80–82; on American women, 165; on changes in Meiji, 80; on family system, 158; on male role, 158; small businesses and failures, 81–82

imin (migrant): 41, 44, 207n9; identification of, by Japanese government, 49, 51, 53–54; number of, in New York City, 189 table 4; in *tobei* publications, 119–20. *See also hi-imin*

immigration history: Asian American, 2, 4–5; general, 4–5

Ishimoto Shidzué: about, 237n42; on arranged marriages, 154–55

Itō Kenzō case: about, 145–48; Japanese government intervention, 145, 146; parental obstruction, 145, 146; settlement, 147. *See also* cross-racial relations

Iwamoto, Kinichi, 37

Japan: colonialism in Asia, 141–42; colonialist ideology, 143–44; cooperation with U.S., 141, 142–43; map of, 15; and racism, 234n113; on racism in U.S., 142; suffrage, 70, 218n53; urban population, 58, 213n6, 214n22. *See also* Meiji Japan

Japan-U.S. relations, 43, 51–52, 207n8, 210n50; and immigrants to U.S., 42–43, 49–50, 51, 53, 56, 142–43; scholarship on, 42

Japanese Association of America, 53; in New York City, 18, 201n24

Japanese companies, 47, 60, 62, 72, 215n27; in New York City, 26, 30, 200nn16,22

Japanese emigration statistics, 207–8n12; to New York City, 190 table 5; to U.S., 44, 192 table 8; to Asia, 141

Japanese government: ban on *imin* to U.S., 47; ban on "picture brides," 14, 149; civil servants, 71–72, 214n14, 218n56; communal lands and, 217–18n51; correspondence on *imin,* 42, 48; on control of emigrants to U.S.,

INDEX   265

41–42, 45; depiction in fiction, 74–76; domestic policy on emigration, 41–56; goals on relations with U.S., 44–45, 48; on *hi-imin* and *imin*, 48–49, 51, 53–54, 54–55; and Japanese Association of America, 53, 211n56; laws on emigration, 45–46, 47; on passports, 44, 47, 55; personnel and status, 77; redistricting of land, 70, 198n1, 217n50; on registration of Japanese citizens, 49–53; Tokugawa samurai class and, 71, 218n55. *See also* laws, Japan

Japanese immigrant businesses (New York City): amusement concessions, 31–36; boardinghouse, 29–30, 201n33; description of, 28–29; grocery, 28; hiring practices, 27; newspaper, 28–29. *See also* Kishi, Haru

Japanese immigrants in New York City: age of, 185, 191 tables 6,7; class biases regarding, 27, 30–31, 39; community leadership, 18, 20; compared to West Coast, 13–16, 19; cross-racial marriages, 36, 37, 149, 235n17; cultural knowledge about U.S., 12, 39–40; description, 9; and domestic work, 19, 21–22, 22–25, 201–2n35; exodus from Brooklyn to Manhattan, 22; and gambling, 30; gender ratio, 148; Japanese Christian churches, 29; as *kindai* Japanese, 69; and marriages, 36–38, 148, 205n80; points of entry in U.S., 13, 193 table 9; profile of, 3, 13–16, 183–86; and prostitutes, 38–39; and racism, 16, 21–22, 25; segregation in employment, 19, 25, 27, 40; statistics about, 183–86, 187–88 tables 1–3, 190 table 5, 243n10; Tokyo origins of, 68–69; working class and business class, 30. *See also* Iwamoto, Kinichi; Kishi, Haru; Kuwayama, Senzō; *Nyūyōku nihonjin hattenshi;* Takami, Toyohiko Campbell

Japanese immigrants in U.S., 42, 46–47; gender ratio, 204n79; general knowledge of, 2; registration in U.S., 52; scholarship on, 2; statistics, 192 table 8, 204n79; statistics compared to European immigrants, 206n7; in Texas, 211n61; in *tobei* publications, 45, 100, 119–20, 123–24, 132, 133; transmigration from Hawaii, 209n28; and transportation companies, 46, 47; warnings by U.S. government on, 41–42

Japanese writings on U.S.: general description, 6–8. *See also tobei* publications

Katayama Sen: about, 126–40; advice to emigrants, 134–35; and Christianity, 126–27, 128, 136; criticizes Japanese government, 128–29; exile from Japan, 139; and expansionism, 140; on Grinnell College, 134; on *imin* behavior, 130–31; on *hi-imin*, 134; on Japanese in U.S. agriculture, 134; and *kindai*, 140; on labor in U.S., 127, 230n54; and labor-organizing, 231n63, 233n92; and life in U.S., 135–36; marriages, 140; and patriotism, 140; and publications, 127–28, 230–31n56; and racism, 136–37; on reform and *tobei*, 137; and reform Christians in U.S., 136; and socialism, 126, 128; and Texas rice plantation, 137–39, 233n95; as *tobei* advocate, 127; travels in U.S. and Europe, 138; on value of migration, 129–30; on working class and *tobei*, 129, 143

Keene, Donald, 239n68, 240n91

kindai (modern, modernity): attitudes, 104; and behavior, 101; defined, 212n2; and identity, 114; and *Tōkyōjin*, 58–59; transforming of lifestyles, 57, 62, 67, 113

Kinmonth, Earl H., 220nn78,79, 220–21n81, 224n9

Kishi, Haru, 34–36; birth of child, 35–36; in Coney Island, 35; life in Japan, 34; marriage, 34; small business, 35

Konjikiyasha (Ozaki Kōyō): based on American novel, 110; author's aim, 111; on bourgeois materialism, 113; and literary style, 111; on usury business, 112; on wealth, 112, 113

Kuwayama, Senzō, 29–31; on gambling, 30; on operating boardinghouse, 30; on working-class immigrants, 30

labor: attitudes toward, 104; on attitudes in U.S., 98, 115; manual work, 101–2; sanctity of, 102

language, Japanese: changes, 70, 221n85; foreign language skills, 88; and introduction of new terms to Japanese, 89,

language, Japanese (*continued*)
93, 159, 223n2, 224n20; standardized speech, 70, 77
laws, Japan: ban on *imin*, 47; banning of "picture brides," 149; Civil Code, 153; education, 72, 219n61; *Imin hogokisoku* (Emigration protection law), 45–46; *koseki* law, 153, 242nn2,3; on passports, 45; on redistricting land, 198n1; on registration of Japanese in U.S., 52–54
laws, U.S.: Alien Land Laws, 204n79; on contract labor, 41; on marriage and citizenship/naturalization, 235n19; on New York public construction workers, 201n34
leisure activity: and cultural superiority, 99–100; and English women, 100; gendered definition of, in Japan, 100; and sports, 99; in West, 99–100

marriage: failures of, 155, 238n46; and family system, 153; and go-betweens, 153–54; and ideal mates in England, 100; and invention of tradition, 152; and passport laws, 149; practices, Meiji, 152, 236–37n31, 237–38n44; practices, pre-Meiji, 152, 236nn29,30; and *ryōsai kenbo*, 156; Yanagita on, 151–52, 153
Meiji Japan: attitudinal changes, 74; changes in society, 5, 70–71; economic development, 103, 225n34; economic fluctuations, 73–74; effects on youth, 5; small businesses, 82–84, 222nn101,102,107; textile industry, 103; unemployment, 73, 219–20n70; vote in, 70, 218n53; worldview, 6
Meiji-Taisho media: on gender relations in U.S., 9; and ideology, 8; and self-advancement publications, 90–91, 224n9; on success, 10, 90–91; on U.S., 6–8, 9, 87–88. See also newspapers; *Seikō* magazine; *tobei* publications
migration: complexities of, 177
Miyakawa, Masuji: on women in U.S., 163–64; on U.S., 239n74; on U.S.-Japan cooperation, 142–43
Miyakawa Setsurō, 142–43
Miyoshi, Masao, 179, 197–98n17
Mizutani, Shōzō, 16. See also *Nyūyōku nihonjin hattenshi*

money: attitudes in Meiji, 104–5; attitudes in Tokugawa, 225n35; justifications of making, 105. See also *Konjikiyasha; Seiyōmusume katagi; tobei* publications

Nagai Kafū: background, 166–69; class bias of, 38, 39; on Coney Island, 32–34; on knowledge of West, 166–67; life in U.S., 169; in New York, 1, 241n104; on prostitutes in Chinatown, 38; and racism, 39; on women, Japanese and American, 170–72; works, 240nn94,97. See also *Amerika monogatari*
Natsume Sōseki: *Botchan*, 60, 77–80
New York City. See *Amerika monogatari; Nyūyōku nihonjin hattenshi; tobei* publications
newspaper novels: American novels as basis, 105, 110, 227n50; and audience, 106, 110–11; as basis of circulation, 105–6; and Ozaki Kōyō, 110, 227n51; Western novels and, 107, 226n47
newspapers: and censorship, 226n39; mass circulation dailies, 105
Niishima Jō, 20, 137, 232–33n88
Nitobe Inazō, 124, 143, 230n44
Nippon Club (New York City), 30
Nyūyōku nihonjin hattenshi (Mizutani Shōzō): about, 18, 186; on domestic work, 25, 26; focus, 18–19; on racism in New York City, 16–17; on race in U.S., 25; on reception of Japanese in New York City, 16–17; sponsors, 18

O'Brien, Thomas J. (U.S. ambassador to Japan): on *hi-imin* and *imin*, 53; on registration of Japanese in U.S., 49
Occidentalism: evolution in Japan, 175–76; and Orientalism, 175
Ōkubo Takaki, 167

passports, 44, 46, 51, 210n38; administrative responsibilities, 54–55; laws, 45, 208n18; offenses against laws, 46, 209n23; and statistics, 49, 52, 209n26
Peattie, Mark, 141–42
population, Japan: intramigration of, 58, 212nn4,6; voting, 70, 218n53. See also Tokyo

renai (love): definition, 159–60; effect on family system, 160; as form of subversion, 160; Japanese perception of, in U.S., 172; and social freedom, 166
Rikikōkai (club), 122
Robertson, Roland, 178, 242n8
Rosaldo, Renato, 180
ryōsai kenbo (good wife, exemplary mother), 156–58

Saikin tobeisaku (Shimanuki Hyōdayū), 122
Seikō magazine, 118, 119; establishment of, 91–92, 224n13; on success, 87, 88; on U.S., 87
seikō (success): attitudes, 94; attributes of, 87; barriers to, 93; and child-raising, 97–99; and emigration, 93; and failure, 115; and identity, 114; means to achieve, 93; and motives, 93; and negativism, 93–94; and *sekkyokuteki* spirit, 93–95, 104; in U.S., 118; and youth publications, 90, 224n9
Seiyōmusume katagi (Yanagawa Shunyō), 106–10; as reconstruction of Western form, 107, 108; wealth and happiness in, 109–10
Shimanuki Hyōdayū: about, 117, 120; advice to women, 124; and Christianity, 124–25; establishes Rikikō girls' school, 123; establishes Rikikōkai, 121; establishes youth clubs, 120; on family, 124; journey to U.S., 120–21; on passport regulations, 116; publications, 121; as *tobei* advocate, 116, 117; on women, 123
Shitamachi (low district): defined, 215n24; diseases in, 62, 215n32; in Edo period, 61; factories in, 63, 216n36; industrial section, 62; map of, 65; as marketplace, 61–62; merchants in, 68; multidimensional character of, 68; population, 61; as retaining Edo character, 61–62; Shitamachi speech, 78; slums in, 62
Silverberg, Miriam, 6, 197n16, 217n44
small business: capital and interest rates, 83, 222n105; dependence on large industry, 83, 222n102; employer/employee relations, 85; in *Ie*, 79; insecurities of, 83; in Meiji period, 82–84, 222n102

socialists: and Kōtoku Shūsui, 233n91; and social democratic party, 138; state persecution of, 139, 234n97. *See also* Katayama Sen
sports: in Japan and West, 99–100
Sugimoto Etsu: about, 163–64; on American women, 163–65; on arranged marriage, 155; on Japanese men, 164

Takami, Toyohiko Campbell: about, 19–21; arrival in New York City, 20; as domestic worker, 21; on domestic work, 27; education in U.S., 21, 201n28; as Japanese community leader, 201n24; and sponsor Nancy Campbell, 21, 201n29
Takamine, Jokichi, 18, 199n14
Texas rice plantations, 138–39, 211n61, 233n95
tobei advocates, 11, 92, 117, 122–23; and internationalism, 142, 144; and land in U.S., 143; and patriotism, 144; on racism in U.S., 142; on U.S.-Japan cooperation, 142, 143. *See also* Katayama Sen; Shimanuki Hyōdayū; *tobei* publications
tobei netsu (tobei fever), 11, 117; on *netsu*, 228n5
tobei publications, 17–18, 92–93, 117; advice on behavior in U.S., 130–31, 231–32n73; on American qualities, 101; on American women, 165–66; East Coast, 149; and hierarchy of national groups, 101; on *hi-imin*, 119–20; on *imin* to U.S., 45, 119; on *imin* to Hawaii, 45; instructions to *imin*, 118–19, 228n10; on leisure activity, 99–101; on New York City, 17–18, 149; on permanent settlement in U.S., 120; on racism in U.S., 136–37, 142; racist attitudes in, 38, 39, 99, 101, 143, 234n113; on reasons for emigration, 119; on *seikō*, 95–98. See also *Amerika*; Katayama Sen; Shimanuki Hyōdayū; *Tobei shimpō*
Tobei shimpō (magazine), 92, 122–23
Tokugawa merchant culture, 213n11
Tokyo, 10, 57–58; compared to Edo, 61; compared to other cities, 60; description, 60–61; disease in, 62, 215n32; labor/production methods in, 62–63, 215n33; local government, 61, 214n21; manufacturing in, 62; maps, 64, 65; population makeup, 58, 61,

Tokyo (*continued*)
212n4, 213n6, 214–15n23; rebuilding of, 60–61, 214n18; slums in, 62, 215n31; urban mentality, 57–58; wages in, 122, 229n32. *See also* Shitamachi; Yamanote

Tōkyōjin: defined, 58, 59; in *Botchan*, 60, 77–78; compared to *Edokko*, 59, 214n13; and *kindai*, 60; reasons for emigration, 69–71; reason for existence, 59

Ukigumo (Futabatei Shimei), 74–76

unemployment, 73, 219n70; advice on, 101–2, 104

United States: contract labor laws, 41; imperial policy, 40; on Japanese immigrants, 49; Pacific fleet in Asia, 51; on registration of Japanese in U.S., 49. *See also* Japan-U.S. relations; O'Brien, Thomas J.

urban mentality: formation of, 57–58. *See also* identity; *kindai*; *Tōkyōjin*

usury business: in *Konjikiyasha*, 112; rationale for, 113–14; term for usurer, 113, 227n62; interest rates, 227n63

wayō (Japanese-Western): and American mentality, 179; defined, 67; and Japanese global mentality, 178; and material culture, 67; and Nagai Kafū, 169; in *Seiyōmusume katagi*, 107–8; shifting meanings of, 179; and "Western," 67; and women, 162

wealth: accumulation of, 105; justifications for, 105; in *Konjikiyasha*, 112, 113; in *Seiyōmusume katagi*, 110

Western novels: in mass-circulation newspapers, 107

women, 11; and emigration from Japan, 48, 185, 189 table 4, 190 table 5, 191 table 6; and family system, 153; and go-betweens, 154; and ideal mates in England, 100; in Japan, 111, 153, 155, 156, 171–72, 236n29, 237n42; and *kindai*, 162; and passport laws, 149; as *renai* partners, 161–62; in U.S., 162–64, 165–66, 170–71. *See also* crossracial relations; *Fushinchū*; *Futon*; gender relations; Itō Kenzō case; Kishi, Haru; marriage; Nagai Kafū; Japanese immigrants in New York City; Shimanuki Hyōdayū

Yamanote (hill district): described, 63–66, 216n40; as *honseki* of Japanese in New York City, 68–69; map of, 65; residents of, 67, 68; slums in, 68, 217n47; and *Tōkyōjin*, 66; and *wayō* material culture, 67; Yamanote speech, 77, 221n85

Yanabu Akira: on *kindai*, 212n2; on *renai*, 159–60

Yanagisako, Sylvia, 6

Yanagita Kunio, 212n1; on communal land, 70; concept of city, 58–59; on dialects, 70, 221n85; on "folk" and "aristocratic," 59; on foreign commerce, 58, 213n9; on marriage, 151–52, 153–54, 236n30, 238n48

Yans-McLaughlin, Virginia, 4

Yomiuri (newspaper), 105; and Ozaki Kōyō, 110, 111

youth publications, 10, 90–91, 121, 127–28. *See also* Meiji-Taisho media; *Seikō* magazine; *tobei* publications

Designer:	Ina Clausen
Compositor:	Maple-Vail Book Mfg. Group
Text:	10/13 Galliard
Display:	Galliard

www.ingramcontent.com/pod-product-compliance
Lightning Source LLC
Chambersburg PA
CBHW021656230426
43668CB00008B/643